China's Development and Harmonization

The concept of 'harmonization' has become very popular in China, with the Chinese government increasingly applying the term 'harmonious society' to internal affairs and the term 'harmonious world' to international relationships. Harmonization as both an end and a means of China's development is deeply rooted in China's cultural tradition, which emphasizes moderation, balance and harmony between human beings and nature, between different social groups, and between the Chinese and other nationalities. This book examines the experience of enacting the concept of harmonization in China in recent years. It explores this in terms of developments within Chinese society, economic developments and changes in business practices, environmental challenges and coping strategies, and changing patterns of international relations. Throughout, it discusses the gaps between rhetoric and reality, policy and practice.

Bin Wu is a Senior Research Fellow at the School of Contemporary Chinese Studies at the University of Nottingham.

Shujie Yao is Professor and Head of the School of Contemporary Chinese Studies at the University of Nottingham.

Jian Chen is an Associate Professor in the School of Contemporary Chinese Studies at the University of Nottingham.

Routledge Studies on the Chinese Economy
Series Editor
Peter Nolan
Sinyi Professor, Judge Business School,
Chair, Development Studies, University of Cambridge

Founding Series Editors
Peter Nolan, University of Cambridge and
Dong Fureng, Beijing University

The aim of this series is to publish original, high-quality, research-level work by both new and established scholars in the West and the East, on all aspects of the Chinese economy, including studies of business and economic history.

Routledge Studies on the Chinese Economy – Chinese Economists on Economic Reform

China's Development and Harmonization

Towards a balance with nature, society and the international community

Edited by
Bin Wu, Shujie Yao and
Jian Chen

Routledge
Taylor & Francis Group

LONDON AND NEW YORK

First published 2013
by Routledge

Published 2014 by Routledge

2 Park Square, Milton Park, Abingdon, Oxfordshire OX14 4RN

Simultaneously published in the USA and Canada
by Routledge
711 Third Avenue, New York, NY 10017

Routledge is an imprint of the Taylor and Francis Group, an informa business

First issued in paperback 2015

British Library Cataloguing in Publication Data
A catalogue record for this book is available from the British Library

Library of Congress Cataloging in Publication Data
A catalogue record for this book has been requested

ISBN 978-0-415-66567-4 (hbk)
ISBN 978-1-138-95638-4 (pbk)
ISBN 978-0-203-55223-0 (ebk)

Typeset in Times New Roman
by Swales & Willis Ltd, Exeter, Devon

Contents

Acknowledgments

Most chapters in this volume were initially presented at annual conferences of the International Forum for Contemporary Chinese Studies (IFCCS) in Nottingham (2009) and Xian (2010) respectively. We gratefully appreciate the financial support from the Office of the Chinese Language Council International (Hanban), The Nature and Envrionmental Research Council (under ESPA programme NE/G008280/1), The British Academy Conference Support Grant (CSG-53711), and The Leverhulme Centre for Research on Globalisation and Economic Policy (GEP), University of Nottingham Integrating Global Society (IGS). We are indebted to our colleagues for their support throughout the compilation process of this book: Dr Zhengxu Wang, Dr Xiaoling Zhang, Dr Hongyi Lai and Dr Andreas Fulda. Special thanks are also due to Ms Hua Geddes, Ms Jenny Hall and other School administrative members for their full support to the IFCCS series in the past, as well as to Mr Samuel Beatson for proofreading and formatting the whole manuscripts. Finally, we thank Mr Peter Sowden and Ms Jillian Morrison at Routledge for their patience and support during the preparation of the book.

Tables

Figures

Editors and contributors

Editors

Dr. Bin Wu is a Senior Research Fellow in the School of Contemporary Chinese Studies at the University of Nottingham. He received his BSc degree in Physics, MA in Philosophy and Ph.D. in Human Geography. He has a range of research experience and interests in the areas of rural development and sustainability; internal and international migration; worker education and empowerment; global citizenship and higher education reform; diasporic Chinese community development and integration. He is co-editor of two new books: *Sustainable Reform and Development in Post Olympic China* (2010)*, Higher Education Reform in China: Beyond the expansion* (2011), both published by Routledge.

Professor Shujie Yao has been head of the School of Contemporary Chinese Studies at the University of Nottingham since January 2007. He has published widely in many top economics and development journals in the world, including *Journal of Political Economy, Economic Development and Cultural Change, Journal of Comparative Economics, The World Economy, China Economic Review*, among many others. He is a founding editor of *Journal of Chinese Economic and Business Studies*, chief economics editor of *Xi'an Jiaotong University Journal* (Social Sciences). He was editorial member of *Journal of Comparative Economics* (2007–10) and *Food Policy* (1995–2011). Professor Yao is also coordinator of the China and the World Economy programme at the Globalization and Economic Policy Centre at the University of Nottingham and special chair professor of economics of Xi'an Jiaotong University in China.

Dr. Jian Chen is Associate Professor at the School of Contemporary Chinese Studies, the University of Nottingham. He received his Ph.D. in Finance from King's College London, his Masters degree in Management from Xi'an Jiaotong University, and Bachelor's degree in Mechanical Engineering from Hefei University of Technology. He publishes papers and books in corporate finance, corporate governance and financial markets. He is Executive Director of the Nottingham Confucius Institute and also a board member of the Chinese Economic Association (Europe).

Contributors

Lucy Badalian holds a Ph.D. in mathematics and has worked in modeling social processes for more than 30 years in different settings, from private business in the US to various academic positions, most recently as a senior visiting fellow at the LSE, a visiting fellow at the University of Pavia, Italy, and the University of London. She is an expert for the Eurasian Economic Union and serves as the convenor of a project on Eurasia, co-funded by the British Academy and the Russian Academy of Sciences.

Jonathan V. Beaverstock is Professor of Economic Geography at the University of Nottingham, UK. He is the author of over 100 journal articles, book chapters, published conference papers and proceedings, including three books (authored and edited), the latest being: *The Globalization of Advertising* (Routledge, 2011). Jonathan is currently one of the leading researchers on the subject of highly-skilled international labor migration.

Chuanglian Chen is a Lecturer from School of Economics and Management, South China Normal University, China and as a post-doctor in China Merchants Group and the Chinese Academy of Social Sciences, China.

Guojin Chen is a Professor from the School of Economics and Wang Yanan Institute for Studies in Economics, Xiamen University, China.

Li Chen is a Ph. D. candidate in the Department of Development and Management, College of Humanities and Development Studies (COHD), at China Agricultural University. Her main research interests focus on rural development in Northwest China, particularly smallholders' economic behavior; their agency in livelihood innovation and adaptation; as well as the impact of the State's policy changes on the causal structure of vulnerability.

Shuzhong Gu is professor and Deputy Director General and professor, in the Institute for Resource and Environmental Policy, part of the Development Research Centre, of the State Council of China.

Victor Krivorotov holds a Ph.D. in mathematics and has had a long and varied career, including holding such posts as an advisor to the vice-minister of foreign affairs of the SU (later the minister) and counselor on economics in the Soviet/Russian Embassy in Washington DC during 'perestroika'. His main expertise is in modeling for development economics.

Claire Seung-eun Lee is a doctoral candidate in the Department of Sociology at the National University of Singapore. She is currently conducting research on soft power, globalization, mobility and social transformation in Asian societies with an emphasis on China.

Chun Kwok Lei is currently an Assistant Professor of Business Economics at the University of Macau, China. His research interests are the Chinese economy, economic integration and income inequality.

Sabrina Ching Yuen Luk is a Ph.D. candidate at the Department of Political Science and International Studies (POLSIS) in the University of Birmingham. Her research interests include e-government and globalization, comparative healthcare reforms, public policy analysis, public administration and China studies.

Dominik Mierzejewski is assistant professor at the Faculty of International and Political Studies, University of Lodz, Poland. He studied Chinese language and culture at the Shanghai International Studies University (1999–2000 and 2003–2004), and gained a Ph.D. from the University of Lodz (2006). His academic interests include Chinese foreign policy and the political system of China.

Tyler Rooker is a postdoctoral researcher at the Institute of Sociology and Anthropology at Peking University and lecturer in Contemporary Chinese Studies, with a specialism in Chinese Business, at the University of Nottingham. He graduated from the University of California (2006) with a Ph.D. in anthropology for his dissertation on Zhongguancun, known as the Silicon Valley of China. His research areas focus on companies and businesses in China, both from an economic and a socio-cultural perspective.

Gubo Qi gained a Ph.D. in agricultural economics in 1996. She is now a professor and rural development researcher at the College of Humanities and Development Studies, China Agricultural University. Her main fields of expertise are community common pool resource management and Institutional and technology innovation in rural development.

Jackie Sheehan has been an Associate Professor in the School of Contemporary Chinese Studies at Nottingham since 2003. With a BA in Chinese Studies from the University of Cambridge and a doctorate in Chinese history from SOAS, she has published on China's Cultural Revolution and democracy movement; employment issues, industrial relations and labor protests in China; Chinese migrant workers in the UK; and human trafficking between China and the UK. In addition to her academic work, she serves as an expert witness in asylum and criminal cases involving Chinese nationals in the UK, particularly those related to human trafficking.

Kala Seetharam Sridhar is a senior research fellow and head of the Public Policy Research Group at the Public Affairs Centre in Bangalore, India. Kala was with the National Institute of Public Finance and Policy, New Delhi, Assistant and Associate Professor at the Indian Institute of Management, Lucknow, visiting Sir Ratan Tata Trust Fellow at the Institute for Social and Economic Change, Bangalore, and visiting scholar to UNU-WIDER, Helsinki a few times. She has written four books on urban/regional issues as they apply to India, several internationally reviewed journal articles and chapters in books.

Pui Sun Tam is currently an Assistant Professor of Business Economics at the University of Macau, Macao, China. Her research interests include econometrics in theory and application, and the economic development of the Asia-Pacific region.

Jun Tian is Director of the Board and Chief Operation Officer of Fortune Oil Ltd., a Hong Kong based oil company with major business in China. He received his Ph.D. in Economics from the School of Oriental and African Studies, and his Bachelor's degree from Beijing University. He was a board member of the Chinese Economic Association in the UK, and President from 1994–1995.

Benjian Wu is a PhD candidate at the School of Agricultural Economics and Rural Development at Renmin University of China. He received his Bachelor degree from China Agricultural University in 2010. His main research interests are rural finance and rural organizations.

Ting Zuo is a professor and deputy dean in the College of Humanities and Development Studies (COHD), at China Agricultural University. His research interests focus on rural public policy, regional economic development, governance, natural resource management and sustainable development.

Haofang Chai is an assistant researcher in Beijing Academy of Social Sciences and received his Ph.D. from China Agricultural University in 2009. His main research focuses on social innovation, public management, and city development strategy.

Tianlai Gou is a lecturer in the College of Urban and Rural Development, Beijing University of Agriculture. He conducted rural development study and received his Ph.D. from China Agricultural University. His main research interests include natural resource management and poverty alleviation, social innovation, natural resource commodity chains and benefit distribution.

Dr Liu Kaiming is a founder and Executive Director of the Institute of Contemporary Observation (ICO) based on Shenzhen, a leading independent NGO and social enterprise in China specialized in human rights, labour issues, worker education and corporate social responsibility.

Fengyang Li is the Vice Director of Ningxia Centre for Environmental Protection and Poverty Alleviation, engaged in rural development practice for ten years. His main research interests include public participation, social innovation, farmer cooperative organization, farmer-centred research network and natural resource management.

Dr Puyang Sun is Associate Professor at the School of Economics, Nankai University, China. He received his Ph.D. in Economics from the University of Birmingham and his Bachelor's degree in Econometrics from the University of Nottingham, UK. He publishes papers and books in economic growth, regional science and energy economics, in particularly for applied econometrics evidences in China.

Ronnie Vernooy is a rural development sociologist with a particular interest in agricultural biodiversity and natural resource management. He has more than 20 years of experience in managing and conducting participatory research in a number of countries, including Nicaragua, Cuba, Honduras, China, Nepal, Vietnam, and Mongolia. He is an independent consultant and was a program officer at the International Development Research Centre (IDRC), Canada, from 1992 until 2010.

Introduction

President Hu Jintao has promoted the idea of developing a harmonious society in China. The word harmony means that people, whether rich or poor, civilians or in power, city-dwellers or those living in the countryside, Han majority or non-Han minority, men or women, will live together in peace and happiness.

After 34 years of economic reforms and fast growth, China has become a great economic power in the world, overtaking Japan as the second largest economic entity, overtaking Germany as the world's largest exporter, and overtaking the US as the world's largest industrial producer. China may become the world's largest economic entity measured by GDP as early as 2018. Its glory and economic miracle is well-known and admired by many. This is particularly true when the rest of the world, especially the US, the EU and Japan are still struggling to recover from the current world financial crisis.

However, below the surface of China's success and glory, there are many challenges and constraints that the country has to face in the coming decades. Such challenges and constraints include environmental degradation, widening income inequality, corruption, state monopoly, the continuing rural–urban divide, sluggish progress in eliminating poverty, over-dependency on the import of key communities, and the low efficiency of energy and materials. All these problems have threatened and will continue to threaten China's ability to sustain high economic growth.

The country's 12th Five-Year Plan acknowledges these problems and the government has started to pay more attention to the following issues.

- Adjusting economic and industrial structures. Structural transformation includes reducing dependency on external trade and investments for economic growth, as well as increasing domestic consumption as a main driver of growth.
- Increasing energy and material efficiency. This aims to reduce environmental pollution and CO_2 emission. The current level of energy and electricity consumption for each unit of GDP should be reduced dramatically to slow down damage to the natural environment and people's health.
- Improving income distribution. Rising income inequality may be responsible for many of China's current social and economic problems, including the

distorted housing market, social discontent and riots, people's unhappiness and the lack of innovation and technological progress. Equality and social justice are two essential elements of a harmonious society.

- Creating an innovative knowledge economy. Over-dependency on export processing and low-tech manufacturing goods renders China's sustainable development fragile. The Chinese government is keen to create an innovative society and a knowledge-based economy.

Among all the challenges and constraints, rising income inequality is the key concern of social and political instability. Without social stability, China's future development could be jeopardized. Moreover, the ultimate objective of economic development is for common prosperity, rather than that for just a small proportion of the population.

Social justice and harmony are closely linked. To know more of contemporary China, one should have an in-depth understanding of why harmony is important for the society. Harmonization is deeply rooted in the Chinese culture and traditions, which is directly translated as Zhongyong (or the Doctrine of Compromise). It emphasises moderation, balance and compromise between human beings and nature, between different social groups, and between Chinese and other people in the world.

In a modern world, harmony may have a new notion, a notion of a central idea or symbolic gesture applied by President Hu Jintao and Premier Wen Jiabao's Leadership for a clear political and social objective, intending to mitigate social tension and discontent arising from all the social and economic challenges mentioned previously.

The leadership wishes to promote the concept of harmony so that people will learn how to accept a certain level of inequality, corruption and environmental pollution without resorting to riots. On the other hand, they also use harmony to remind themselves and the country's political, economic and social elites that they have to care for the disadvantaged groups in society. As a result, a balance between the advantaged and the disadvantaged can be found to maintain social and political stability so that the economy will continue to grow and the existing political system dominated by the Communist Party will continue to survive without any serious threat and challenge.

Social and political comprise means that the rich and political elite should learn how to control greed and corruption so that the level of social injustice will not go beyond the point where the general public find it unbearable.

The '*Wukan Village*' incident that took place in Guangdong in early 2012 was a typical case where local residents considered the behaviour of village and local township leaders unbearable. Villagers made their unhappiness and discontent clear to the regional government through mass protest and demonstration. The provincial government of Guangdong sensed the seriousness of this incident and decided to deal with the problem through removing and punishing village leaders so that villagers would not make further 'trouble'.

The Wukan incident shows that social instability is a reality in China after a few decades of strong growth and prosperity. It is not necessarily poverty that triggers discontent and unrest. Instead, it is relative poverty, social injustice and corruption that cause instability in Chinese society. Social instability not only threatens China's ability to sustain growth and prosperity, but also threatens the legitimacy and ability of the Party and the government to rule the country, as Premier Wen Jiabao rightly pointed out in his speech to the People's Congress in March 2012, 'corruption can destroy people's lives and the political regime'. As a result, harmony is not just a slogan, but a real instrument to achieve balance and compromise, to achieve sustainable growth and to maintain the leadership of the Communist Party in China.

China's sustainable development and harmonisation are a key area of our research interests in the School of Contemporary Chinese Studies (SCCS) at the University of Nottingham. Since its establishment in 2007, SCCS has rapidly grown. As a leading centre of Chinese studies in the UK and Europe, SCCS has organized an annual conference, under the auspices of The International Forum of Contemporary Chinese Studies (IFCCS). The first two conferences were held in Nottingham, and the third in Xi'an Jiaotong University in China. After each of the annual conferences, the conference organization committee select over 10 articles from about 100 papers presented to the conference for publication as an edited volume.

This current volume consists of 14 articles selected from the second and third IFCCS annual conferences held in Nottingham in 2009 and in Xi'an in 2010. The main theme of this volume focuses on the harmonious development of the Chinese economy and society. The 14 articles collected in this volume will discuss different aspects of harmonisation in the Chinese economy and society.

From a global perspective, the experience and issues of China's development in the past are reviewed and analysed through five chapters in Part I.

Chapter 1 by Domini Mierzejewski provides an interesting reference about the evolution of Chinese foreign policies from Mao's 'revolutionary chaos' to the 'pragmatic language' in Deng and Jiang's period and to the current 'Confucian morality' of a harmonious world. The 2008 Beijing Olympics' key slogan for China is 'One World, One Dream', signalling China's desire to have a peaceful and harmonious world, which is conducive for the country's ambition of modernization, industrialization and rising influence. In this chapter, the author identifies key factors behind the fourth generation of China's communist leadership to create a positive image of China as a peaceful rising power.

Chapter 2 by Lucy Badalian and Victor Krivorotov focuses on globalization of information and communication technology (ICT) and its impact on China. The authors suggest that the ICT revolution has brought new opportunities for the newly industrialising economies, particularly China, to develop a new industrial production system different from the conventional Fordism system. The new system can be illustrated from a new production and business model, or the so called Object-Oriented-Design (OOD) model, which has led to evolving synergies of big and small enterprises, including large SOEs (state-owned enterprises), large state-owned banks (SOBs), foreign invested firms (FIEs) and domestic small and medium-sized enterprises (SMEs). The authors use a case study on the production of motorcycles in Chongqing Municipality to demonstrate the feasibility of the model.

Globalisation, however, is not limited to global mobility of capital and products. It also involves the movement of people in an international labour market. Chapter 3 by Bin Wu and Jonathan Beaverstock studies the employment situation of Chinese seafarers in a globalized labour market. They use international contract workers as an example to examine the segmented global labour market and its impact on the supply, mobility and working conditions of Chinese contract seafarers.

In Chapter 4, Jackie Sheehan investigates human trafficking between China and the UK through a sample of 48 recent cases. She finds that trafficking is able to flourish under cover of the larger and more diverse streams of 'new' migration out of China which have developed in recent years. The study locates trafficking within the context of arranged migration out of China as an activity which even legitimate agents sometimes undertake when a suitably vulnerable client presents themselves, and highlights that many Chinese businesses in the UK mix trafficked with voluntary labor in their workforce, making it even more difficult for law enforcement to identify victims of trafficking.

Looking at different aspects of the labour market which is part of the global chain, Liu, et al. in Chapter 5 pay attention to the working conditions in local firms specialising in export-processing in the coastal region of China. Using both official publications and a survey of 210 export-processing companies in the Yangzi and Pearl River Deltas, the authors provide a detailed analysis on the trends of rising income inequality between rural migrant workers and local employees. They suggest that without reducing pay inequality between different groups of workers, it will be difficult to build a harmonious society in China.

Part II consists of five chapters focusing on the economic aspects of the Chinese development.

In Chapter 6, Jian Chen and Jun Tian use a quantitative approach to identify the key determinants of China's economic growth under reforms. The economic reform program in China has been widely acclaimed as a success. It has led to profound changes in both the structure of the economy and the mechanism of resource allocation.

Economic reforms in China may be judged in terms of the success of transition from a centrally planned economy to a market one, or in terms of economic outcomes – which in turn can be measured in many ways, such as the impact on output, productivity, profitability, and so on. As far as the first criterion is concerned, economic reforms may appear to be less successful. After over three decades of reforms, there are still some goods and services allocated by state orders with regulated prices. On the two pillars of creating a market economy, namely price liberalization and privatization, China seems to lag behind the Central and Eastern European and the Former Soviet Union states (CEEFSU), although it started the transition one decade earlier. But when judged in terms of economic performance, China appears to have been more successful than the CEEFSU.

In Chapter 7, Chuanglian Chen, Guojin Chen and Shujie Yao study whether imports crowd out domestic consumption. This is a comparative analysis on China, Japan and Korea. The authors suggest that a decline in the relative price of imported goods compared to that of domestically produced goods may have different effects on domestic consumption. Such effects may not be accurately detected and measured in a classical permanent-income model without considering consumption habit formation.

To resolve this problem, they employ an extended permanent-income model which encompasses consumption habit formation. Both co-integration analysis and GMM are used to estimate the inter-temporal elasticity of substitution between imports and domestic consumption and the parameters of habit formation as well as the intra-temporal elasticity of substitution. They find that import and domestic consumption are complements in China, but substitutes in Japan and Korea. Different per capita incomes and consumer behaviours between China and the other two countries are two possible reasons for different relationships between import and domestic consumption.

Chapter 8 is a comparative study on China and India about land sales as a tool of public finance by Kala Seetharam Sridhar, Shuzhong Gu and Shujie Yao. The authors assess the role of public land leasing and sales as a financing source in a selection of Indian and Chinese cities. China and India share significant similarities in land leasing and sales as an increasingly important source of finance for local governments. However, institutional arrangements for land use are more fragmented in Indian cities than in their Chinese counterparts. Some policy simulations of transfer of revenues from land leasing and sales by the urban development authorities in India to municipal corporations were carried out. It was found that in some cases, revenues from land leases or sale may account for up to 90% of municipal revenues. In China, land sales did not play an important role until recently due to rapid urban development and rising house prices. By 2010, over 60% of local revenues came from land sales in Beijing and Shanghai as well as other large cities in China. Over-dependency on land sales for local revenues may not be sustainable since they have the tendency to push up house prices to the point where they could cause serious economic and social problems in both countries.

In Chapter 9, Chun Kwok Lei and Pui Sun Tam use a panel unit root approach to study the stochastic convergence of the Greater China economy, which includes mainland China, Taiwan, Hong Kong and Macau.

The hypothesis of 'convergence clubs' and the role of external trade as indicated by the openness ratio are included in the study. They adopt the notion of stochastic convergence and panel unit root techniques, providing evidence in favor of income convergence among the Greater China economies in the post-reform period 1982–2007. They also find that income convergence at the aggregate level is driven by stochastic convergence among low, rather than high openness Mainland China's provinces with Hong Kong, Macau and Taiwan. External trade brings about diversified growth potential to high openness provinces, which leads to divergence of them with the other Greater China economies.

In Chapter 10, Puyang Sun studies ownership and bank performance in China. Since China joined the World Trade Organization (WTO) in 2001, Chinese banks have faced challenges from foreign banks in the absence of protection from the Chinese government. Although Chinese banks have undergone a series of reforms since 1979, serious problems still exist, particularly the negative effect of state ownership on bank performance. Through the fixed and random effect models, the negative effect of non-performing loans and liquidity ratio was still significant in determining bank performance. State-owned banks are less profitable than other banks, although their operational costs are lower. Compared with joint-equity banks, the effect of non-performing loans is more significant in state-owned banks, while the negative effect of the liquidity ratio on bank performance is more significant in joint-equity banks.

Part III of the book consists of four chapters on sustainable development and good governance.

Harmonization and sustainable development in China cannot be achieved without innovation in broad definition which refers to a series of changes or adoptions of new elements in production, organization and institutional arrangement. Accordingly, the last four chapters of this volume focus on the new dynamics or driving forces behind social and political changes in China.

Amongst a number of innovative elements driving China's development, opening and social harmonization, perhaps, none is more powerful than the rapid expansion and popularity of internet use in China. Responding to the digital era, Chapter 11 by Sabrina Ching Yuen Luk focuses on the development of E-government and impact on governance in China, including efficiency, transparency, openness, accountability and responsiveness. Having examined the variety of e-government development in all ministries and provinces, they identify the progress and space for China to further strengthen its quality of governance.

The term harmonization in ancient Chinese philosophy contains an environmental dimension referring to balance and harmonization between human beings and the nature. From this angle, Claire Seung-eun Lee in Chapter 12 uses corporate social responsibility (CSR) as a tool to observe the performance of transnational corporations (MNC) in China regarding energy conservation practices, an important contribution to the development of an eco-friendly harmonized society. For this purpose, the author provides a documental analysis on the CSR policies of MNCs like GE, Sony and Samsung during the Beijing Olympics and argues that MNCs should take the initiative and set a positive example for Chinese companies to follow in the future.

Moving from transnational corporations to China's countryside, Chapter 13 by Gubo Qi at el. draws our attention to the phenomenon of farmer professional cooperatives (FPCs) in China with a special attention to farmers' access to resources against the background of strong governmental intervention. Taking two cases from a village in Shandong province, the authors show the importance of accumulating and enhancing social capital (including personal relationships and networks, trust, close communication and cooperation) on the one hand, and constraints from lacking a sense of ownership and endogenous agency on the other.

The need and potential of farmer innovation cannot be fully understood without a close observation and understanding on innovators. Chapter 14 by Li Chen at el. presents a case study based on in-depth interviews with a large number of innovative farmers in Yanchi, an ecologic fragile and resource-poverty area in Ningxia, to illustrate the characteristics of those farmers, their attitudes, potential and contribution to local sustainable rural development and poverty alleviation.

Shujie Yao, Bin Wu and Jian Chen, 2012

Part I

Global perspective on China's development

1 From morality to morality: the rhetoric of Chinese foreign policy over four decades

Dominik Mierzejewski

Since 1949, China has gone through several ups and downs, starting from establishing the New State, the Great Leap Forward, the Cultural Revolution, the four modernizations, opening up and Tiananmen '89 right the way through to sustainable economic growth and building the 'socialist state with Chinese characteristics.' Every period of China's modern history has been characterized by its own language, rhetoric and propaganda. Throughout the last 30 years, China has been building and strengthening its position in international relations. Rhetoric plays an important role in foreign policy. As a passive aspect of diplomacy, it may play a very useful part in introducing intentions, questions or checking the reactions of third parties.

In the first part of this chapter, the author describes the major differences between the Western and Chinese rhetorical traditions and practices. Important focus is placed on explaining rhetoric and the soft-power nexus. Next, the author analyses the revolutionary rhetoric of the Cultural Revolution. China's rhetorical posture presented the Middle Kingdom as the moral and revolutionary centre of the world. In the third part, the morality of Hu Jintao is compared with 'universal values' and the Wilsonian concept of international relations. This kind of analysis is similar to certain strands of constructivist textual analysis that take note of ways in which political and cultural influences on the foreign policy–making process are inherent in the texts of foreign policy: speeches, planning documents and public relations connected with politics. Taking a foreign policy rhetoric as an example, the author argues that not only do material values play an important role in shaping external affairs, but so too do the non-material aspects such as: culture, identity, ideas or even rhetoric. Social constructivism argues that the ideational structure shapes the identity of the agent. Structure, in Wendt's constructivism, is not material but cultural, defined by the distribution of ideas. The essence of international politics, in the view of Wendt, is ideas rather than material capabilities (Qin and Wei, 2008: 121–124).

This chapter aims to present and analyse the rhetoric of Chinese foreign policy during the Cultural Revolution (1966–1976), described as 'revolutionary morality' and during Hu Jintao's 'harmonious era' where it possesses a 'Confucian morality.' To the author, the most important question concerns the purpose in using moral language instead of pragmatic language, like that presented by Deng

Xiaoping. As rhetoricians, we must ask an initial question: do rhetors intend to utilize their power through/within the act of discourse? In the final part of the chapter, the author tries to prove the hypothesis that China aims to portray itself as a moral and just state, capable of playing an important role in international relations, by means of moral rhetoric. The author will also argue that soft power reveals the legitimate priorities of the state as much as it reinforces the strategic agenda. Finally, the chapter will address the issue of how Chinese leaders have presented the notion of soft power in foreign policy discourse.

Rhetoric and soft power

Rhetoric itself has been broadly discussed by scholars from ancient times till the present. In ancient Greece, Aristotle considered rhetoric as a means of persuasion. He described man as a rational animal, and this kind of stance on human nature affected his rhetoric:

> Underlying the classical tradition is the notion that although men are often swayed by passions, their basic and distinguishing characteristic is their ability to reason. . . . [Thus, for classical rhetoricians] logical argument . . . was the heart of persuasive discource.
>
> (Lunsford, et al., 1984: 38)

On the other hand, Plato in *Phaedrus* realized that rhetoric could be used positively or negatively. The third great ancient thinker, Demosthenes, claimed that 'rhetoric is delivery.'

In Ancient China, thinkers also touched upon the problem of rhetoric (*xiuci*). Chinese had their own sense of rhetoric described as: *yan* 言 (language, speech), *ci* 辞 (made of speech, artistic explanation), *jian* 谏 (advising, persuading), *shui* 说 (persuasion), *shuo* 说 (explanation), *ming* 明 (naming) and *bian* 辨 (distinction, argumentation) (Welch, 1990: 90–95). As Burton Watson in his *Early Chinese Literature* states:

> Public address and discussions of rhetoric in China before the third century BCE are almost totally concerned with efforts to restore order to society, to induce rulers to act wisely, justly, and compassionately toward the people, to encourage the public to respond with loyalty to the regime, and to perpetuate ancient traditions in ritual and social relationships.
>
> (Tu, Hejtmanek and Wachman, 1992: 28)

The earliest examples of Chinese rhetoric are the 'instructions,' especially those concerning the ways in which a minister of state should address a ruler, for it is here that the speaker is expected to be honest, sincere, and forthright, to preserve his own dignity, to avoid flattery and, at the same time, to show respect for the ruler and keep from antagonizing him (Kennedy, 1998: 158). The major difference between the Chinese and Western ways of using rhetoric was that what it had to say about speech, persuasion and other aspects of rhetoric was addressed to rulers or to their own philosophical students. It does not consider techniques for addressing a mass audience. Furthermore, contrary to the West, within the hierarchical system, the Chinese failed to use public discussion that would have an impact on the political system. From Confucius' perspective, the rectification of names (*zhengming*) or rhetoric (*xiuci*) should be subordinated and subservient to, as well as based on *cheng* – the spirit of sincerity (*xiuciliqicheng*). Confucius also remarked: '*I transmit but do not create. Being fond of the truth, I am an admirer of antiquity. I venture to be compared with our old Peng.*'

This famous saying lends sufficient credence to the view that Chinese rhetorical practices value custom over innovation and privilege imitation over creation. (Lu Ming Mao, 1995: 128–129) As John Makeham explains, Confucius did not regard names as passive labels, rather as social and, hence, political catalysts. In this sense, *zheng ming* aimed at transforming Chinese society and its people though the advocacy of certain terms or concepts. In the Chinese rhetorical tradition, thinkers were very much aware of the power of symbols in human motivation, in perception of the reality and in control of human action (Xing, 2000: 5–7).

As George A. Kennedy remarked, the closest Western analogy to the 'rectification of names' in Chinese was the concern held by 17th Century philosophers such as Descartes and, especially, John Locke. They desired to create a precise language for philosophy and science, denying its poetical and rhetorical elements such as metaphor (Kennedy, 1998: 159).

In Taoism, according to Vernon Jensen, the rhetorical principles were described as follows: 1. deprecate eloquence and honour silence; 2. deprecate argumentation; 3. look inward for truths; 4. avoid willful critical thinking and instead utilize spontaneous intuition; 5. rest assertions on time-honored authority; and 6. rely on ethos: sincerity, humility, goodness, respectfulness and trustworthiness. The last and most practical piece of advice was provided by Han Fei of the legalist school. In '*The Difficulties of Persuasion,*' his persuasions were as follows:

> On the whole, the difficult thing about persuading others is not that one lacks the knowledge needed to state his case nor the audacity to exercise his abilities to the full. On the whole, the difficult thing about persuasion is to know the mind of the person one is trying to persuade and to be able to fit one's words to it.
>
> (Ibid.: 163–164)

Similarly, Han Fei advocated that the speaker must know the 'soul' of the listener and adapt the message to his understanding. Han Fei had in mind something more sophisticated and manipulative. Rhetoric was conceptualized in ancient China and terminology was created to describe features of invention and style, but speech was not studied as a separate discipline; it was always thought of as a part of political and moral philosophy (ibid.: 165–166).

The legalist school formulated the definition of rhetoric as subordinate to power. In this context, Barry Brummet's definition sounds similar. In his conceptualization of rhetoric privileges, rhetoric is considered an agency of power, an ontological device through which we construct the world of meaning. Economic status, social position, and military power frame the contexts so important to Brummet's epistemological theorizing. Rhetorical power, so conceived, thus possesses persuasive appeal, designed to control or shape or influence the world around the rhetor. As Barbara Biesecker notes: 'the power of persuasive discourse' is 'to constitute audiences out of individuals, to transform singularities into collectivities, to fashion a 'we' out of a plurality of 'I's,' and to move them to collective action' (Rufo, 2003).

For another scholar, Pierre Bourdieu, power is manifested through a structured discourse – an active phenomenon that rests upon accumulated capital (status), and mediated by the body. Language still has the individualized potential to shape the meaning for an individual; rhetoric contains the capacity to advocate a particular, privileged version of the reality. McGee is right to argue that: 'Virtually nothing about rhetoric is innocent of this power. Pick any rhetorical principle, and we'll put it on the table, and I'll show you how it's connected with power' (ibid.).

A conceptualization of rhetoric as the articulation of power bridges the gap between passive materiality and active discourses of power, allowing for a more complete understanding of the constitutive discourses of power.

The link between rhetoric and power leads to the conclusion that rhetoric itself has become an important component of soft-power – a concept introduced by Joseph Nye. With regard to the 'soft-power' notion, a vast discussion has been held by scholars, mainly from Beijing and Shanghai academic circles. Joseph Nye's concept has been both challenged and developed. Nye concentrated on the potential of arguments to move people, and their ability to attract (*xiyin li*) and shape the preferences of others. Moreover, as Joseph Nye argues, the current leadership should be based on institutions, values, culture and politics in order to shape other people's needs (Nye, 2004: 11–14). If that is the case, this, according to Aristotle, is a major task for rhetoric. Moreover, to the author, rhetoric plays an important role in shaping the image of the country. Portraying itself as a moral, good and reliable partner, any country might be able to win the trust of the third party and build its position in international relations. All the values have been articulated via language, and, what goes with it, the rhetoric is considered, as it was mentioned above, an important component of contemporary diplomacy. Foreign policy discourse is rhetorical, in the sense that it attempts to reconstruct a desired, practical, or normative framework from inconsistent and often competing assumptions that underlie the institutional inertia of a nation-state's foreign policy.

For Chinese authorities, soft-power might be a kind of leverage and agency used in order to exercise political objectives, with the additional dimension of it being both derived from and contributing to domestic stability and the internal strength of the state. Wang Huning's thesis on soft power from 1993 identifies the basic elements of the principle, including the historical texts and ideas related to Confucian, Taoist and Buddhist thought. These represent the Chinese conceptions of winning respect through virtue (*yi de fu ren*), benevolent governance (*wang dao*), peace and harmony (*he*), and, finally, harmony without suppressing differences (*he er bu tong*) (Hayden, 2009: 8–10). Leading Chinese scholars: Men Honghua, Yan Xuetong or Kang Xiaoguang, tried to adapt the foreign concept of 'soft-power' to the realities of the Chinese case. The first has submitted that China's definition of 'soft power' should include: culture, concepts, a model of development, the international system and the international image of China (Men, 2007: 18–19). Yan Xuetong, contrary to Yu Xitian and Liu Gang, says that political power (*zhengzhi shili*) is the most powerful element in the 'soft power' concept. Culture has been inseparably associated with politics. Yu Xitian has considered the ideas, international and domestic system, strategy and politics as deeply rooted in culture which is the core of any 'soft actions' in the international arena (Yu, 2004: 18–19). Li Mingjing builds an argument, based on evidence from leaders and media-reports in China, that soft power is perceived as a 'tool for defensive purposes'– an instrument to create a better image for China, to influence perceptions, and also to defend China from Western culture and ideology (Li, 2008: 287–308). According to Pang Zhongying, Nye's concept was rejected in China. Chinese authorities could not differentiate between soft and hard-power. He advocated for comprehensive power (*zonghe de guojia nengli* or *zonghe guojia li*), where soft and hard-power intertwine. The Chinese definition of 'soft-power' should be made up of economy, education, culture, human resources, political system, diplomacy, international political participation and the resolution of international problems (Pang, 2006: 8–9). Differences in the understanding of power usage between the West and China have played an important role in shaping China's 'soft power' definition. For the Chinese, the clear differentiation between hard (*ying*) and soft (*ruan*) has been difficult to render because, as they have argued, sometimes hard becomes soft and soft becomes hard. (Pang, 2006) Zhang Jianjing says:

> The competition among nation-states appears to be a rivalry of hard power, but behind such rivalry is the competition between institutions, civilizations, and strategies, which are essentially the rivalry of soft power.
>
> (Hayden, op.cit.)

Without promoting Chinese culture and history, since little has been known about the country across the rest of the world, China would be unable to convince the world of its positive intentions. This issue has been pointed out by a scholar from Fudan University – Ni Jianping. Instead of great progress, Chinese authorities have been making plenty of errors (*bu shao wuqu*) while building up the Middle Kingdom's image in foreign media. Aware of the reality of the culture, politics and economies of foreign countries, the decision makers should have applied methods suited to local circumstances (*yin di zhi yi*). In other words, if something is controversial for the target audience (*shou zhong*), it should be modified and announced in a way that would limit any controversies and strengthen Chinese persuasive power (*shuofu li*) (Ni, 2005: online).

Moral-revolutionary centre of the world

The major reason for launching a mass campaign such as the Cultural Revolution, instead of purging political enemies, like Liu Shaoqi or Deng Xiaoping, was to build a new political model that would enlighten the rest of the communist world and, as a result, become the 'world system.' The Chinese Communist Party analysed the international situation within the conceptual framework of contradictions. The world was perceived as a set of contradictions between the good–socialist and the bad–imperialist camp. This added up to the greater potential of the revolutionary chance via 'people's war' promoted by Lin Biao (Van Ness, 1970: 25).

The revolutionary actions required revolutionary rhetoric. The easiest way to inform the Third World was to portray the two superpowers as 'paper tigers' (*zhi laohu*). In spite of their economic and technological superiority, the USA and the USSR were treated as trump cards in the internal struggle for power, and were used to authenticate Chairman Mao's concepts and promote the new state model – the Cultural Revolution. In contrast to the superpowers – imperialists and revisionists – China was portrayed as a moral centre that had the power to revise the unjustified world system.

In the *People's Liberation Daily*, on 4 May 1966, the editorial commentary marked the rhetoric of 'never forgetting class struggle.' This enabled the government and public opinion to define the enemy and redefined new criteria for good and evil (Xing, 2004: 54–55). Apart from using revolutionary rhetoric for internal purposes, China described its foreign enemies and shaped China's foreign activities. Justifying the rebels (*zaofan* or *hongweibing*), Chairman Mao Zedong called for a fight against 'moral enemies' both inside and outside China. The two major cold-war superpowers were seriously criticized, and became the main object of Chinese press attacks.

At the beginning of the Cultural Revolution, the Chinese Communist Party declared that the major enemy of the world was 'imperialism headed by the United States.' 'The anti-imperialist revolutionary struggles of the people in Asia, Africa and Latin America are pounding and undermining the foundations of the rule of imperialism, and colonialism, old and new. . .' (Van Ness, 1970). In the same manner, in May 1970, during Mao Zedong's statement entitled, '*People of the world, unite and defeat the U.S. aggressors and all their running dogs,*' he criticized American imperialism for having 'brazenly dispatched their troops to invade Cambodia.' At the same time, the editorial report in the Peking Review identified Frank Coe and Sol Adler as American friends (Peking Review 1970: 18–19; Renmin Ribao 1970: 3). Nevertheless, the most popular American journalist, praised by the Chinese and Chairman Mao, was Edgar Snow who twice visited Mainland China during 1960 and 1970. During his second visit to China, on 1 October 1970, Renmin Ribao published an article which had the headline, '*The whole World including the American people are our friends.*' This positive American campaign originated from theoretical discussions within the Communist Party of China (Wang and Zhang, 2001: 27–28). In spite of its irregular but brutal attacks on the USA, the Chinese press distinguished between the bad government and the good

American nation. This different attitude meant some American citizens gained reports which had a positive outlook in the press (*Meiguo pengyou*) (Mao Zedong, 1998: 437–438). A different, anti-American rhetoric was an outcome of the current Chinese foreign policy. During the visit to Mainland China of the American table-tennis team in 1971, the Chinese also expressed a positive attitude toward the American people. The editorial comment in Renmin Ribao defined the American visit as a 'friendly visit' (*youhao fanwen*) and remarked on the Americans' enthusiasm: *'they always wanted to pay a visit to China, and now after coming to Beijing, they love it with all their heart.'*

During the Cultural Revolution, the major enemy changed from imperialism to revisionism and social-imperialism. Because of internal contradictions between its leadership, the Soviet Union became the major target of attacks. In April 1967, in her speech to the rebels, Jiang Qing denounced Deng Xiaoping as 'Chinese revisionist no. 2 (no. 1 was Liu Shaoqi), who had gained power and was now building a capitalist road' (*dang nei zui da de zou ziben zhuyi daolu*) (Renmin Ribao 1967: 1–3; Peking Review 1967: 22). Shortly after that, on 5 April, Renmin Ribao published its first article: 'Frankly criticizing Chinese Khrushchev' (Dittmer, 1998: 180–191).

An interesting point was that the next set of statements – about the propagation of good and friendly relations (*fazhang youhao guanxi*) with Washington – were just a matter of time (Wang Hongwen, 1966: 6). Some articles were published in English by the Peking Review, for example *The Bankruptcy of China's 'Devotee of Parliamentarianism.'* 'Chinese Khrushchev' was accused of being pro-Western and employing a western style of governing, parliamentarianism and holding up Jiang Jieshi as a statesman model: 'In this time when Chinese Khrushchev dreamt of a parliamentary road, Jiang Jieshi took a sword and started a people's war' (Peking Review, 1967: 9). This criticism reflected the external situation. China tried to show that both powers blackmailed the rest of the world. In this context, inside of China, it was Mao Zedong who possessed the moral power to fight against inside traitors, and it was China that had the power to fight against outside traitors and save the rest of the world.

The important incidents during the Cultural Revolution commented on by Chinese media were to do with 'Soviet frontier provocations' on the Ussuri River. The anti-Soviet attacks were taken very seriously. As a result of this media campaign, the whole of China was besieged with public protest. It is beyond doubt that all the riots were controlled by the leftist faction. In China's largest cities, anti-Soviet manifestations were widespread, most notably in Peking, in front of the Soviet Embassy. Polish diplomats in Shanghai recorded that:

Within a few hours the crowd had put up posters in the whole city calling on the Chinese people to: Bring down the Soviet revisionist clique; Defeat American imperialism; Bring down Brezhnev, Kosygin and Nixon; Defeat the contemporary, huge Russian, imperialistic Tsar and social-imperialist Soviet Union.

(The Polish Ministry of Foreign Affairs Archives [PMFAA], 1969: File no 207/D II/69)

The anti-Soviet pressure was present not only in the Chinese media, but the propaganda was also projected through several movies, for example 'The New Tsar's crime' (ibid: File no 207/D II/69). In April 1969, the Party Congress began and Chairman Mao Zedong was inaugurated the single leader of the CCP and the great communist guard (Renmin Ribao, 1969: 2). All the slogans were in accordance with the directive of 28 August, which urged people to prepare for war using all 'ideological, material and psychological' means. In this campaign, the PLA played a major role in collecting food, controlling war preparations and arresting counter revolutionary elements (National Archives and Records Administration, 1969: NND 969000).

In comparison with the United States, for example in 1969, the Soviet Union has been more aggressive and more frequently attacked in 'Renmin Ribao.' In March 1969, there were ninety six articles published in the People's Daily against the Soviet Union, while there were just three articles criticizing the United States in the same month, and in April there were none.

In February 1970, the Chinese published an anti-revisionist book entitled, '*Is the Soviet Union Still a Socialist State?*' The authors criticized Moscow and the so-called socialist countries for being anti-revolutionary and pro-capitalistic states (PFMAA 1970: File no D II 0-241-13-70). It was also a good opportunity to scold the USSR for not being a revolutionary state, as it was the 100th anniversary of V. I. Lenin's birthday and, in 1970, the Chinese published an article, '*Leninism or Social Imperialism?*' (Ibid: File no D II 0-241-28-70).

In conjunction with the anti-Soviet campaign, commentators promoted Lin Biao's theory that 'the world's peasants would triumph over the world's bourgeoisie':

> Ten million French workers went on strike in state companies, factories and coal mines. (. . .) The people of France continued their fight against capitalism, supported by nations all over the world. There were similar situations in Sweden, Italy and Canada.
>
> (Renmin Ribao, 1970:1)

The signal to strengthen the pro-Third World campaign was Chairman Mao's Statement on 20 May 1970. Soon after, Mao Zedong stated that imperialism was afraid of the Third World. Driven by the historical determinism, Mao mentioned that:

> A weak nation can defeat a strong, a small nation can defeat a big. The people of a small country can certainly defeat aggression by a big country, if only they dare to rise in struggle, dare to take up arms and grasp in their own hands the destiny of their country.
>
> (Mao Zedong, 1998: 446)

The new uprising was *ante portas* and all revolutionary nations were prepared to fight against 'Yankee imperialism.' For Chinese commentators, for example in Latin America, the new revolution was just about to start. During April 1966, in the Dominican Republic the people rose up against 'the military rulers and their Washington masters' (Peking Review, 1966: 15–17). In Africa, guerrilla warfare had started with Chairman Mao Zedong's instructions: 'The great leader Chairman Mao has taught us: "A nation, big or small, can defeat any enemy, however powerful, so long as it fully arouses its people, firmly relies on them and wages a people's war." The Mozambican patriotic fighters understood very well that they were not only confronting Portuguese colonialism, but also vicious U.S. imperialism,' (Peking Review, 1968: 26–27). The whole situation led up to inevitable victory of the revolutionary thoughts of Chairman Mao and to the felling of Imperialism and hegemonism that were described in the Peking Review as 'a sinking ship' (Peking Review, 1975: 6–8).

In June 1966, Renmin Ribao published articles praising Mao's Thought, for example, 'Mao Zedong's Thoughts are a treasure for Latin America or Foreign friends in Yan'an' (Renmin Ribao, 1966: 5). Moreover, the Red Book was translated into many languages. As Chinese media described, 'Recently people of Khang Khan (Laos) received a Red Book. The people welcomed Chairman Mao's works and said to each other: "The truth came, the truth came"' (ibid.). Chairman Mao's Thoughts were used as a shield against imperialism and American aggression. Friendship associations, for example, the China–Japan Friendship Association, where members held meetings on Chairman Mao's Thoughts fulfilled a similar function (ibid.: 11–14, Peking Review 1966: 6–7).

By portraying foreign countries in the way mentioned above, China presented itself as the moral centre of the world that still faced the next war danger and the vanguard of the world revolution:

> Our great leader Mao Zedong started and held the Great Proletarian Cultural Revolution. We achieved the great success. All Chinese revolutionary masses took Mao Zedong's path. All revolutionary nations welcomed the Cultural Revolution. The World is entering a New Mao Zedong era.
>
> (Ibid.)

The moral dimension of the new diplomatic language

At the beginning of 2004, the Chinese leadership started to promote the 'recovery of national morale.' The basis for further campaigns was created in the *2001 Action Plan for the Development of Civic Morality* and five years later in the *2006 Plan for Cultural Development,* that figured in the 2006–2010 five-year plan. In the context of a new harmonious society as well as a harmonious world, the Confucian revival (*rujia fuxing*) was a turning point. The Chinese PDC admitted that:

> Chinese culture, with over five thousand years of brilliance, has contributed immensely to the progress of human civilization. It is the spiritual bond of our national heritage, of our unceasing dynamism, the source of our power of resistance in the face of difficult challenges and a complex world . . .
>
> (Billioud, 2007: 53)

The processes which took place in the 1990s resulted in a transition in the way in which China presented itself, from victim (*shouhaizhe*) to power (*daguo*). The intellectuals rejected the persistent emphasis on China's '150 years of shame and humiliation' as the main lens through which Chinese view their place in the modern international affairs. 'Patriotic education' and 'the great renaissance of the Chinese nation' (*Zhonghua minzu weida fuxing*) were signs of a new era in Chinese foreign relations (Medeiros and Fravel, 2003: 32–33).

This has been the major issue discussed by Chinese scholars. The abovementioned Wang Jisi says that, as a result of a gradual process of de-Marxisation in Chinese society, there is a general tendency towards seeking an explanation of Chinese theory and practice of international relations in traditional culture. Wang Hunning of Fudan thinks that culture is a dimension of national strength but they still took the Marxist approach, that is, only a state economically and politically strong could use culture as a tool in soft power policy (Chen, 1999: 57–58). To the author, the most important remark concerning China's future status was made by Yan Xuetong, who maintained that status depends on international acceptance (Deng, 2005: 160). Seeking the acceptance of the international community, China has made a considerable progress, but this has still not been sufficient for its foreign partners.

In this context, the Chinese authorities decided to invoke China's ancient tradition of peace. As Samuel Kim states:

> While Chinese image of world order cannot be construed as containing either a crusading or a colonial doctrine, it represented a formidable barrier against the thought of external policy in terms of mutually beneficial interactions between or among equal sovereign states.

> (Kim, 1979:46)

The legitimacy of the Sinocentric world order rested more on moral virtue than military power. It is clear that the traditional Chinese world view left no room for egalitarism in international relations. The Confucian, Sino-centric concepts of morality and ethics, which dictated both domestic and international policy, maintained that through good government, resulting in internal peace and prosperity, China would play a leading role in the world and serve to demonstrate a universal paradigm for other nations. Only moral individuals can create a moral order at every level of society and therefore a moral world with China at its centre. As Feng Huiying admits:

> Confucius scholars differed most with their opponents in their view that the universalized order of the Chinese world should be a cultural order and that the only way to accommodate an expansion should be by means of an outward radiation of cultural influence.

> (Feng, 2007: 20)

Harmony might be provided only by a nobleman (*junzi*) that is ready for self-cultivation (*xiuji*). The *he er bu tong* concept arose from the earlier concept of the *tian ren he yi* (unity between the universe and mankind). In Confucian philosophy it was described as *jun he er butong* (unity between nobleman and the universe). This, as put in the context of international relations indicates that there are no equal partners in foreign affairs (Jia and Li, 2009: 169). The second important value is *zhongyong* – the Doctrine of the Mean. As Li Jianchang argues, the Doctrine of the Mean fails to be understood as a compromise, but rather as the ability to find a proper way of dealing with problems in society (ibid.).

In the modern history of China, the first reformist that took *datong* (the great unity) seriously was Kang Youwei, in a book published seven years after his death. In his 'Book of Datong' he argued:

> States should be abolished, so that there would be no more struggle between the strong and the weak. Families should also be done away with, so that there would no longer be inequality of love and affection. And finally, selfishness itself should be banished, so that goods and services would not be used for private ends.
>
> (Hua, 2005: online)

On the other hand, some scholars mentioned the major argumentation of Mencius: 'to seek domination by force will simply turn the world against you' (Feng, 2007: 21).

Likening to Western idealism

Analyzing the Chinese rhetoric of a harmonious world might be an interesting task in the light of Chinese character *xie* – harmonious. This character is made of two parts: the radical *yan* which means to speak and *jie* which means everyone. Lu Hong, in the People's Daily, explains that it means: 'everyone has freedom of speech.' (Renmin Ribao, 2005: 3).

After a negative evaluation of the 'peaceful rise' slogan, the Chinese authorities decided to soften their foreign policy rhetoric. In April 2004, Hu Jintao and Zeng Qinghong replaced the peaceful rise with peaceful development in their public speeches. In April 2005, at the Asia–Africa Summit in Indonesia, Hu Jintao presented a new Chinese foreign policy formula. Soon after, in May, Li Zhaoxing – the Foreign Minister – admitted that China's major goal would be to strengthen multicultural dialogue and exchange (Renmin Ribao, 2005: 1). The final result was that Hu Jintao presented *hexie shijie* concept during the speech in the General Assembly of the United Nations. He made a 4-point Proposal that guaranteed the world's safety and stability. In his opinion, there were four major conditions needed to 'uphold a lasting peace' (*chijiu heping*). The first one was multilateralism (*duobian zhuyi*), which should be upheld to realize common security. In the contemporary world the international community should abandon a 'cold war mentality' and create a collective system of global security based on the UN Charter and basic values. The international community should oppose any interference in the sovereignty of independent states, internal affairs, arbitrary use of military force, and fight together against terrorism, as well as prevent nuclear weapon proliferation. The second point was about common development (*pubian fazhan he gongtong farong*) that should be promoted in cases when the world is not developing simultaneously, and globalization should be a mechanism for common benefits (*pubian shouyi*), especially for developing countries. Still, world peace would be endangered because of the rich–poor polarization and the lack of a fair multilateral world trade system (*duobian maoyi zhidu*). The international community should prepare a common health system, emphasize the importance of equal rights for women, worldwide development and, finally, a reduction of disparities between North and South. The third point mentioned by Hu Jintao was a spirit of tolerance (*baoyi jinsheng*) as a basis for building a harmonious world. In his opinion, diversity is a characteristic point in the history and development of the mankind and the world needs the cultural exchange between people. The different ways of development, diversity and different historical backgrounds should not affect international cooperation in a negative way. The international community should 'make good for deficiency,' as Mencius' proverb *quchuang buduan* indicated, in order to seek the common ground for cooperation, avoid differences (*qiutong cunyi*), eliminate mutual suspicions and promote more peaceful relations (*he mu*) as well as democracy in international relations. The fourth point encouraged the implementation of the UN reform that will ensure the healthy development of international relations and will be beneficial for people all around the world. The UN and the Security Council needed to proceed step by step, gradually introducing reform and should consider allowing small and medium developing countries, mainly African states, to have an influence on the UN's decisions. It is on this matter that the world needs an extensive consensus (*guangfan gongzhi*) (Hu Jintao, 2005).

In April 2006, at Yale University, Hu Jintao referred to the four basic points of China's culture (*Zhonghua wenming*) made up of: moral concept of Chinese politics (*daode zhengzhi lixiang*), being human as a basis (*yi ren wei ben*), self-improvement (*ziqiang buxi*) or discarding the old ways of life in favor of the new (*gegu dingxin*).

Moreover, in his speech on *hexie* in October 2006, Hu Jintao explained the notion of harmony by using a variety of cultural dimensions coming from Confucius' *datong* and *xiaokang*, through Universal Harmony, Marxism, Maoism or Ideology of Deng Xiaoping and Jiang Zemin. Interestingly enough, the internal concept has not been far different from the internal concept of harmonious *xiaokang* society. Hu Jintao promotes six qualities: rule of law; fairness and justice, honesty as well as fraternalism and harmony with nature (Mahoney, 2008: 115).

Furthermore, in the report presented to the Party Congress in 2007, Hu Jintao mentioned that hegemonism and power politics still exist, and the world needs harmony:

> Hegemonism and power politics still exist, local conflicts and hotspot issues keep emerging, imbalances in the world economy are worsening, the North-South gap is widening, and traditional and nontraditional threats to security are intertwined. All this poses difficulties and challenges to world peace and development.
>
> (Hu Jintao, 2007)

As compared to the original concept of Confucius' harmony, the one presented by Hu Jintao seemed to be more Wilsonian than Confucianistic. One could not resist the impression that China presents itself more universalistic than Chinese. Chinese politicians and scholars hardly admit that this hypothesis might be true. The statement could be compared with Lucien Pye's argument that the *ti-yong* essence and utility formula had it the wrong way around in that modernization calls for the acceptance of universalistic values associated with the world culture, though adapted to local conditions. The *ti* has to be universal values and it is the *yong* that should be related to the Chinese realities (Yahuda, 1997: 8–9).

Before 14 points were presented in April 1917, Woodrow Wilson suggested the peaceful resolution of then contemporary world affairs three times. In mid-1914, he proposed that, for example, small nations should have been equal with the great nations and the world should have 'some sort of association of nations wherein all small guarantee the territorial integrity of each.' In 1916, in his address he postulated the establishing of the League to Enforce Peace. Furthermore, on 21 January 1917, further ideas were presented: that all nations should take the Doctrine of President Monroe as the world doctrine and should not interfere with other nations. To sum up, Woodrow Wilson's points were derived out of four major rules: mutual guarantee of political independence, mutual guarantee of territorial integrity, mutual guarantee against economic warfare and limitation of armaments (Link and Davidson, 1979: 74–75). After the First World War, Wilson and his administration prepared a variety of solutions for Europe's future, especially those that were to ensure peace between France and Germany (ibid.: 90–92). Hidden by peaceful rhetoric, the whole team of advisors worked for the future objectives. One might compare the crisis that ended in 1918, with the global economic crisis of 2008. The nature of both is totally different, but the world needs solutions in any case. The question is about the deeper meaning of a 'harmonious world' in the days after economic crisis. On the other hand, the 'harmonious world' might only serve the building of a Chinese positive image in the global arena (Ramo, 2005: online).

All of the abovementioned speeches presented by Hu Jintao might be given a different interpretation. To the author, the interpretation depends on the target audience. If the audience is inside China, the rhetoric of the Chinese leadership seems 'anti-hegemonist.' If the audience is outside of China, as in the United Nations, the rhetoric is more universalistic or even Wilsonian than Marxian.

Conclusion

Political rhetoric creates the arena of political reality within which political thought and action take place (Windt, 1990: 3–4). Rhetoric in foreign affairs might play an important role in shaping future actions. Firstly, diplomacy has used language to persuade and tried to bring other actors round. Secondly, language might be used to threaten others by the persuasive power that allows for a win in the negotiations. Finally, rhetoric might be used as a defense against verbal attacks from the outside.

The Maoist era saw the government emphasizing the images of China as a socialist country and the supporter of the revolution. The revolutionary rhetoric was used to present China as a moral centre of the world. Convinced that China has to play an important role in international relations, the Chinese Communist Party has endorsed the opinion that both superpowers are against the Third World.

In this context China has tried to place itself in a favorable light, rhetorically as well. China was in favor of common people, not governments and this leads to the conclusion that at that time China was a revisionist state which challenged the Westphalia system of 1648. On the one hand, the revolutionary rhetoric might be understood as a sign of power, on the other, as a sign of material weakness that has only warned others against attacking China, and was a tactical move in a diplomatic game that helped Beijing to avoid the conflict with the United States or the Soviet Union. Moreover, during the Cultural Revolution, Chinese authorities employed provocative language regularly to justify the measures against 'the evils' and to mobilize society for greater achievement. China's international enemies were tantamount to the whole world being enemies. The two superpowers had a dual nature, as Peter Van Ness says: 'they are isolated from the people, and their frantic attempts to maintain themselves in power run contrary to the progress of history' (Van Ness, 1970: 41).

To sum up, both revolutionary rhetoric and political actions were a 'waste of time and money'. Close to Kang Youwei, Mao Zedong's concepts of abolishing states and anarchy brought about great disasters for China's national interests. Chinese revolutionary politics failed, and instead of building up and strengthening its position, China lost its credibility and, as Zhou Enlai admitted in 1971, the leftist destroyed China's foreign policy. (Zhou Enlai, 2000: 481–484).

The second example of the moral rhetoric is linked to Hu Jintao and his concept of harmony and harmonious world. Yan Xuetong states that the only choice for China at that time was to support independent, peaceful diplomacy of *heping waijiao*, and keep or protect world morality and justice (*weihu shijie dayi*) (Yan Xuetong 2000: 15). The moral rhetoric of harmony, as some Chinese scholars pointed out, has helped to create a positive image and, thus, it has made good use of cultural diplomacy. However, the language should be the least controversial and it should be both persuasive and attuned to the audience. The international situation, especially the invasion on Iraq and Afganistan carried out by the US-led coalition, could help to put China in a favorable light. The Chinese government should make good use of its ability to use soft diplomatic language to present China in contrast to the 'hegemonic' power of the United States (Hu, 2000: 68).

It might be an interesting general conclusion that China's use of its moral diplomatic language actually means that the country could shape the future of international relations and play an active role in general. Unlike the US, Britain or France, in its history over the last 200 years, China still hasn't offered a set of foreign policy language, concepts and traditions – such as the Jeffersonian, Jacksonian, Hamiltonian and Wilsonian – that would constitute a point of reference for its future action as a great power (Ash, 2009: online).

Whether they are more revolutionary, Wilsonian or Confucianic, 'moral declarations' of this kind should be interpreted, as Shi Yinhong states, as a declaration of rising power. Similarly to Woodrow Wilson's concept of the Nation League or Roosevelt's concept of the Atlantic Charter, Chinese moral, revolutionary or harmonious world rhetoric all express the Chinese aspiration to play a more important role in international relations and to put China forward as a candidate stakeholder in international affairs.

Bibliography

Ash, T. G., (2009), 'China arrives as a world power today – and we should welcome it', *Guardian*, 2 April 2009. Accessed online: 10 May 2009 from www.ingress.com/~astanart.pritzker/pritzker.html

Billioud S., (2007), 'Confucianism, "Cultural Tradition" and official discourse in China at the start of the new century', *Asian Perspective*, 3: 53

Chai, Jia, Li, Jianchang, (2009), 'Rujia sixiang dui goujian hexie shehui de xianshi yiyi' (The Practical Dimensions of Confucianism in Building Harmonious Society), *Liaoning Xingzheng Xueyuan Xuebao*, 1: 168–169

Chen, G., (1999), *Chinese Perspective on International Relations, A Framework for Analysis*, Hampshire, London, New York: MacMillan Press and St. Martin PressDelury J., (2008), '"Harmonious" in China', *Policy Review*, 148: 36

Dittmer, L., (1998), *Liu Shaoqi and the Cultural Revolution*, New York: East Gate

Hayden, C., (2009), 'The Premises of Soft Power: A Comparative Analysis of Public Diplomacy Policy Rhetoric in China and Japan', Paper presented to the International Studies Association Convention, New York. Accessed online: 12 August 2009 from www.allacademic.com//meta/p_mla_apa_research_citation/3/1/1/7/2/pages311728/p311728-10.php

Hu, Angang, (2000), '*Zhongguo zouxiang*' (Prospects of China), Zhejiang Renmin Chubanshe, Hangzhou

Hu, Jintao, (2005), '*Hu Jintao Chuxi bing fabiao zhongyao jianghua*' (Hu Jintao delivered on important speech), Renmin Ribao, 23 April: 1

Hu, Jintao, (2005), '*Nuli jianshe chijiu heping, gongtong farong de hexieshijie*' (To build hardly a lasting peace, for common and prosperous harmonious world). Online. Accessed online: 24 August 2009 from www.southcn.com/news/china/china05/hjtfbm/hbmzx/200509160019.htm

Hu, Jintao, (2006), 'Yelu Daxue jianghua' (Hu Jintao's Speech at the Yale University). Accessed online 24 August 2009 from www.chinaelections.org/NewsInfo.asp?NewsID=47813

Hu, Jintao, (2007), 'Full text of Hu Jintao's Report at 17th Party Congress', Accessed online: 24 August 2009 from http://news.xinhuanet.com/english/2007-10/24/content_6938749.htm

Hu, Rongrong, (2008), '*Huayu quan yu wenhua waijiao*' (The Power of Speech and the Cultural Diplomacy), *Shijie Jingji yu Zhengzhi*, 5: 68

Hua, Shiping, (2005), 'Inside the Chinese Mind', *The Wilson Quarterly*, 29: accessed via The Questia Library on 15 May 2009

Huiying, Feng, (2007), *Chinese Strategic Culture and Foreign Policy Decision-Making, Confucianism, Leadership and War*, London, New York: Routledge

Kennedy, G. A., (1998), *Comparative Rhetoric: An Historical and Cross-Cultural Introduction*, Oxford: Oxford University Press

Kim, S. S., (1979), *China, the United Nations, and World Order*, Princeton: Princeton University Press

Li, Mingjian, (2008), 'China debates soft-power', *Chinese Journal of International Politics*, 2: 287–308

Link, A. S., Davidson, H., (1979), *Woodrow Wilson: Revolution, War, and Peace*, Wheeling: Harlan Davidson

Lu, Hong, (2005), 'Gongjian hexieshehui' (Together Build the Harmonious Society), Renmin Ribao, 11 May: 3

Lu, Ming Mao, (1995), 'Individualism or personhood: A battle of locution or rhetoric?' in: J. F. Reynolds (ed.) *Rhetoric, Cultural Studies, and Literacy: Selected Papers from the 1994 Conference of the Rhetoric Society of America*, Hillsdale: Lawrence Erlbaum Associates

Lunsford, A. A., Ede, L.S., (1984), 'On distinctions between classical and modern rhetoric', in: R. J. Connors, L. S. Ede, A. A. Lunsford (eds.) *Essays on Classical Rhetoric and Modern Discourse*, Carbondale: Southern Illinois University Press

Mahoney, J. G., (2008), 'On the way to harmony: Marxism, Confucianism and Hu Jintao's Hexie Concept', In Sujian Guo, Baogang Guo (eds.) *China in Search of a Harmonious Society*, Lanham, Boulder, New York: Rowman and Littlefield Publishers

Mao, Zedong, (1998), *Mao Zedong On Diplomacy*, Beijing: Foreign Language Press

Medeiros, E., Fravel, M., (2003), 'China's new diplomacy', *Foreign Affairs*, 6: 32–33

Men, Honghua, (2007), 'Zhongguo ruan liliang pingu baogao (shang)' (The Evaluation Report on China's Soft Power), *Guoji Guancha*, 2: 18–19

National Archives and Records Administration, U.S. Department of State, Director of Intelligence and Research, Intelligence Note 665, September 18, 1969. To: The Acting Secretary, Through: S/S, From: INR - George C. Denney, Jr., Subject: Communist China: War Fears and Domestic Politics, Declassified Authority NND 969000, By NDD NARA Date 1.23.97

Ni, Jianping, (2005), "*Dui wai chuanbo yu 'heping jueqi': guojia xingxiang suzao de shijiao*", (The Foreign Media and 'Peaceful-rise': the perspective of the state's image model). Accessed online: 25 August 2009 from http://media.people.com.cn/GB/22114/50600/50604/3529068.html

Nye, J., (2004), *Soft power. The Means to Success in World Politics*, New York: Public Affairs

Pang, Zhongying, (2006), 'Guanyu Zhongguo de ruan liliang wenti' (On China's Soft Power), *Guoji Wenti luntan* , 42

Peking Review, (1966), 'The People Fight Ahead', 5: 15–17; 'Comrade Teng Hsiao-ping's Speech', 20: 16–19; '*Mao Tse-tung's Thought-Beacon of Revolution for the World's People', 23: 6–7;* 'The Brillance of Mao Tse-tung's Thought Illuminates the Whole World', 27: 11–14

Peking Review, (1967), 'The Bankruptcy of China's Devotees of Parliamentarianism', 40: 9

Peking Review, (1968), 'Soviet Revisionist Clique Cannot Escape the Punishment of History', 10: 22; 'Mozambique People's Armed Forces Grow in Strength', 43: 26–27

Peking Review, (1971), 'Premier Chou Meets American Friends', 42: 18–19

Peking Review, (1975), 'Rise of Third World and Decline of Hegemonism', 2: 6–8; 'Vice-Premier Teng Hsiao-ping's Toast', 49: 8–9

Qin, Yaqing, Wei, Ling, (2008), 'Structure, Processes, and the Socialization of Power, East Asia Community-building and the Rise of China', In R. S. Ross, Zhu Feng (eds.), *China's Ascent, Power, Security, and the Future of International Politics*, Ithaca, London: Cornell University Press

Ramo, Joshua Coper, (2004), *The Beijing Concensus*, London, The Foreign Policy Center, http://fpc.org.uk/fsblob/244.pdf

Renmin Ribao, (1966), '*Mao Zedong shi shijie gemingren de gongtong caifu*' (Mao Zedong is a common happiness of all revolutionary people), June 30: 5

Renmin Ribao, (1967), '*Aiguo zhui hai shi duguo zhui?*' (Patriotism or National Betrayal?), April 1: 1–3; '*Chedi pipan dannei zuida de zou ziben zhuyi daolu de dang quanpai*' (We criticize party members that took the capitalist road), April 2: 1; '*Qiedi pipan Zhongguo de Huluxiaofu*' (Complex critics of Chinese Khrushchev), April 5: 2

Renmin Ribao, (1968), '*Faguo gongren, xuesheng yi zhi yu touzhan de geming qigai jixu menglie zhe fuxiu meila de zibenzhuyi*' (French Workers and Student are continuing their strake against capitalism), June 7: 1.

Renmin Ribao, (1969), '*Yong Mao Zedong sixiang tongshuai yiqie*' (Conscientiously Study Chairman Mao's Thoughts), January 1: 2

Rufo, K., (2003), 'Rhetoric and Power: Rethinking and Relinking' *Argumentation and Advocacy*, 40: accessed via the Questia Library 12 August 2009

Smith, A., (1997), *Publishing on the Internet*, London: Routledge Online

The Polish Ministry of Foreign Affairs Archives [PMFAA] (1969), The Anti-Soviet Demonstration, Shanghai, 05.03.1969, Confidential, File no D II Ch 241-15-69; Urgent message, Confidential, Warsaw, 21.04.1969, File no 207/D II/69

The Polish Ministry of Foreign Affairs Archives [PMFAA] (1970), Remarks on book 'Is the SU still a socialist state?', Peking, 23.02.1970, Confidential, File no D II 0-241-13-70; Chinese Propaganda on the SU, Peking, 20.05.1970, Confidential, File no D II 0-241-28-70

Tu, Weiming, Hejtmanek, M., Wachman, A., (1992), *The Confucian World Observed: A Contemporary Discussion of Confucian Humanism in East Asia*, Honolulu: East-West Center

Van Ness, P., (1970), *Revolution and Chinese Foreign Policy, Peking's Support for Wars of National Liberation*, Berkeley, Los Angeles, London: University of California Press

Wang, Hongwen, (1967), '*Tong Meidi jiang youhao jiu shi beipan*' (Approval for Friendly Relations with American Imperialism is a National Betrayal), Renmin Ribao, October 16: 6

Wang, Hongwen, (1967), '*Ba Zhongguo de Huluxiaofu pipan*' (Let's criticize Chinese Khrushchev), Renmin Ribao, April 7: 3

Wang, Xuezhen and Zhang, Zhangong, (2001), '*Suno dui Xin Zhongguo de fanwen yu Zhong Mei Guanxi*' (Snow's visit to the New China and sino-american relations), *Zhongguo Waijiao*, 7: 27–28

Welch, K. E., (1990), *The Contemporary Reception of Classical Rhetoric: Appropriations of Ancient Discourse*, Hillsdale: Lawrence Erlbaum Associates

Windt, T. O. Jr., (1990), *Presidents and Protesters: Political Rhetoric in the 1960s*, Tuscaloosa: University of Alabama Press

Xing, Lu, (1998), *Rhetoric in Ancient China, Fifth to Third century, B.C.E.: A Comparison with Classical Greek Rhetoric*, Carbondale: University of South Carolina Press

Xing, Lu, (2000), 'The influence of classical Chinese rhetoric on contemporary Chinese political communication and social relations', In Heisey, D.R., (ed.) *Chinese Perspectives in Rhetoric and Communication*, New York: Ablex Publishing Co.

Xing Lu, (2004), *Rhetoric of the Chinese Cultural Revolution*: The Impact on Chinese Thought, Culture, and Communication, Univ of South Carolina Press

Yahuda, M., (1997), 'How much has China learned about interdependence?' In D. Goldman, S. G. and Segal, G. (eds.), *China Rising, Nationalism and Interdependence*, London, New York: Routledge

Yan, Xuetong, (2000), *Meiguo baquan yu Zhongguo anquan* (American Hegemony and China's Security), Tianjin: Tianjin Renmin Chubanshe

Yong, Deng, (2005), 'Better than Power: "International Status" in Chinese Foreign Policy', In Deng, Yong and Wang, Fei-Ling (eds.), *China Rising, Power and Motivation in Chinese Foreign Policy*, Lanham, Boulder, New York: Rowman, Littlefield Publishers

Yu, Xitian, (2007), '*Ruan liliang jianshe yu Zhongguo dui wai zhanglue*' (Soft Power Building and China's Foreign Strategy), *Guoji Zhanwang*: 19–20

Yu, Xintian, (2010), 'Wenhua, ruanshi li yu Zhongguo waijiao zhanlue' (Culture, soft-power and China's foreign policy) Shanghai Renmin Chubanshe, Szanghai 2010.

Zhou, Enlai, (2000), Waijao Wenxuan (Zhou Enlai on Diplomacy), Zhongyang Wenxuan Chubanshe, Beijing 2000.

2 Globalization via local participation: implications of Object-Oriented Design (OOD), a new business model in China's rise

Lucy Badalian and Victor Krivorotov[1]

Introduction

On 16 August, 2010, Japan (GDP $1.286 trillion) lost its place as the world's No.2 economy to China (GDP $1.335 trillion). This is a remarkable achievement. Only recently, an extreme multilayered variability of coexistent traditional and modern economic forms, typical for China and other developing countries was perceived as a liability hindering modernization.

In a stark contrast to the uniform mass production of the twentieth century, globalization benefits from customization and local small-series production/consumption, both on the supply and demand-sides. We attribute this shift to the all-permeating radiation of a new and little noticed business-model of modular-design/distributed-production. We call it Object-Oriented-Design, further OOD, to honour its genetic link to the software industry, the first to depend on modularity. OOD was born in the ICT revolution. It shook-off business perceptions and brought in unheard-of efficiencies to the most backward areas, including government services, planning and the fluid formation of supplier value chains 'on-demand,' previously prohibitively expensive (Zysman, et al., 2011).

In China, the affordability and scale of domestic long-term credits, part of the impressive Chinese stimulus along with the lure of its vast markets and the rising value of local expertise has brought in such powerhouses as GM, GE, etc., as eager partners to strategic Chinese SOEs. The supply chains have stretched down to involve local SMEs. This has contributed to the rise of a new beast in the stead of the Fordist vertical, controlled by the West up to the 2008 crisis. The up-and-coming 'distributed' multinational depends on OOD-enabled synchronization of its global partner companies within immense value chains. Sharing funding, markets and expertise, partners' inner workings remain shielded through encapsulation.

OOD may be on par with Fordism in its role for the twenty-first century. Wintelism, an intermediate business/production model,[2] was instrumental in preserving the Fordist vertical by containing its mounting costs under conditions of globalization/outsourcing. This was accomplished through strengthening Western controls over intellectual property and brand-names (Zysman, 2002). In its turn, the principle of modularity challenges Wintelism, opening-up a radically new option of picking and combining functionalities via generic modules at one's own will. The existence of such generic modules makes copyright-style protection extremely difficult.[3]

OOD may further reduce costs as compared to mass production by using nonstandard resources. In the twentieth century, standardization of production methods, resources and mass markets was the backbone of the US economy. In contrast, OOD welcomes diversity, a collection of modules from vast libraries of available options.[4]

By challenging standardization OOD may also lead to a dramatic social restructuring. What was formerly the big and controlling may now be fading in favor of the small and nimble. As a side-effect, this may open a way also to immense geopolitical restructuring. See the unprecedented economic and political growth of a whole lineup of large non-European countries collectively known as BRICS. This is the first instance of non-Western-based economic growth in a half-millennium.

In the twentieth century, the US rose to dominance after developing its unique model of Fordism. OOD holds the potential of becoming the dominant business model of the twenty-first century, with similar geopolitical consequences. In China, OOD seems tailor-made for its centuries-old traditions of cooperative neighbour-enterprises. The higher flexibility, lower starting costs and trends towards resource-sipping efficiency come from synergies between diverse horizontally-integrated forms: SOEs, FDI, local companies, SMEs, down to township/ village-sized and family enterprises.

This chapter addresses the following questions:

- Literature on a new business paradigm, the source of productivity surge in a new dominant economy. We compare the Industrial Revolution, the Second Industrial Revolution and the ICT Revolution.
- The organizational principles of OOD-modular-design/distributed-production, a new production paradigm based on the ICT Revolution with a radical potential for cost-cutting and resource-saving.
- Chongqing – a case-study of Chinese über competitiveness.
- The role of the 2008 crisis in the Chinese economic growth due to the new attractiveness of its local markets for the leading multinationals.
- The emergent strategies of the rising economy of the twenty-first century based on self-synchronization of its diverse parts: big and small, urban and rural, and so on.

We conclude that the great chance China has may be pointing not outward, to export-oriented industries, as it was in the case up to the crisis, but inward, to the creation of vast and diverse domestic markets. Its future success depends on the domestication of the huge inland territory, which lay dormant and under-producing throughout millennia, while preserving its fragile ecosystem and social diversity. For the past dominants, the path to success lay through boosting their food and resource production. The same applies to China.

OOD is currently a hypothesis on a major trend for productivity-gains waiting on future empirical research.

The rise of a new superpower in history: is it China's turn now?

In an entrenched popular opinion, every technological revolution has brought forth its own superpower. Theoretically, things seem clear-cut: a superpower must be rising on the unsurpassed strength of its emergent economy, with extraordinary productivity, which cannot be matched either by the fading dominant power or anyone else. Low labor costs alone cannot provide a lasting economic foundation, thus, the rise must come from an extraordinary prowess in innovation. Among the examples: the British Empire in the nineteenth century and the US in the twentieth century in the aftermath of two technological revolutions, steam-coal and electricity-oil respectively; along with the possibility of China similarly rising to superpower status due to the ICT Revolution.

However, there are many difficulties in proving/disproving this thesis. This chapter joins the growing body of research, including Williamson (1984), Hobsbawm (1999) and Mokyr (1993) on the Industrial Revolution and Schurr, et al. (1960), Rosenberg (1976), Devine (1983), David (1991) and Atkeson and Kehoe (2001) on the Second Industrial Revolution, Zysman, et al. (2011) on the ICT Revolution. Taken together, they relate the productivity surge not to innovations per se, but to a specific business model, appearing decades after the crucial innovations. Among these: the Smithian steam-factory for the nineteenth century; the Fordist vertical corporation for the twentieth century; and a new OOD-entity for the twenty-first century, its exact shape yet unknown. A new business model is seen crucial for gainfully employing new technologies/funding them by creating demand for the most productivity-improving applications. This explains the productivity paradox (David, 1990) of a decades-long delay between the crucial inventions and the productivity rise of the next superpower.[5]

Alfred Chandler (1977) resolved this mismatch by attributing the US success to its new business model rather than innovations. He emphatically separated the 'visible hand' of US-style managerial capitalism from the earlier 'invisible hand' of the Smithian British-style steam-factory. He saw such organizational elements as the Fordist vertical, with headquarters, board of directors, corporate policies, etc., as critical for the US success. While new technologies of oil-electricity were adopted also by any other industrial country of the time, the US had the emergent corporation, amply funded by mass middle classes through the joint-stock-market. Thus, it grew into the superpower of its time, while others lagged. Extending Chandler's findings (1977) to the ICT Revolution, we see OOD as crucial in the economic surge of China, a rising superpower of the twenty-first century.

Obviously, cheap labor doesn't make a superpower. A new business model presents the only working pathway to the future. Analyzing OOD, a potential business model for the ICT Revolution may present a crucial guideline for both Chinese businesses and policy-makers.

Today, the ICT Revolution is a game-changer. It is widely accepted that the complexity of new technologies is forcing/enabling distribution of substantial and growing design costs along the entire value-chain (Porter, 1998). This implies a momentous change in the emergent business strategies. Instead of twentieth-century-style standardization, success in the twenty-first century, both at corporate and country level, depends on the ability to synchronize/harmonize the interaction of many diverse large and small producers in intricate, well-coordinated cross national product networks (CNPNs).

The Chinese economy, which trended to diversity through its history, got its first chance with the movement from Fordism to the modularity of *Wintelism (Windows+Intel)*, an intermediate/hybrid business model of early globalization.

> Fordism was an argument about balancing within a national economy rigid production systems and fluctuating demand. Lean production was about production innovation and the relationship amongst national production systems. Flexible specialization was about community. Wintelism in the end is about the integration of production systems across borders.
>
> (Zysman, 2002)

The business-model of Wintelism is associated with 1990s outsourcing, when credits were plentiful. It was the source of US resurgence after the 1980s competitive loss to Japan. OOD presented the next step in the evolution of the new business model. The Chinese economy received a new boost, in addition to its vital role in Wintelist outsourcing when the 2008 crisis revealed the shortage of 'long' investment funds for Wintelist value-chains. In the new climate of credit scarcity OOD reduces costs by distributing innovation/entry costs along horizontal value-chains. Chinese companies gain substantially due to their access to domestic funding and their local diverse expertise. This helps to avoid substantial expenses of Fordist verticality.

Wintelism, basically a proto-OOD system, brought the ICT Revolution to China in the 1990s, through consumer-led PC customization of standardized DIY (Do It Yourself) assembly of store-bought components. China surged (Dutton, 2005) on the off-shelf assembly-principle radiating the fruits of the PC revolution to as far as remote villages. The principles of modular-design/distributed-production from off-shelf parts and components spread to other areas, including automotive parts, enabling outsourcing and globalization.

This also helped the US, whose industry regained its global competitiveness during the 'miraculous 130 months of U.S. economic booming in the 1990s' (Weiping and Zhu, 2004). Zysman (2002) explains that this was achieved in 'a struggle over setting and evolving de facto product-market standards, with market power lodged anywhere in the value-chain, including product architectures, components, and software.'

The emerging world in general and China in particular may have gained the most from the ICT Revolution. Radiation of advanced technologies led to a new modular business model, as local clustered enterprises were incorporated in global CNPNs.

The concept of CNPN(Zysman, 2002) explains the Chinese surge after its 2001 entry to the World Trade Organization (WTO). Resembling Britain in the late eighteenth and early nineteenth centuries, China became the main outsourcer and the 'global workshop.' The emergent 'lean-and-mean' distributed multinational exited national value-chains in favor of CNPNs/global outsourcing. Nevertheless, the Fordist-vertical was alive-and-well. Gaining remarkable CNPN fluidity, it preserved controls through fully owned standards/intellectual property. In the globalizing economy:

> CNPNs compromise a clever division of labor in which different value-chain functions are carried on across national boundaries by different firms under the coordination either of a lead MNC for its own production or of a Production Service Company (PSC) who manages the production value-chain for clients.
>
> (Zysman, 2002)

In the earlier, vertically integrated Chandlerian corporation, suppliers were controlled through direct ownership. Now, in an increasingly modular Wintelist corporation, any link in the value-chain could become central by owning the crucial piece of intellectual property, which dictated standards across the board. It became unnecessary to own one's suppliers – see the current success of Apple. In the 1990s, the leading automotive companies, from GM to Ford and Toyota, spun away their parts-suppliers, respectively Visteon, Delphi and Denso.

The emergent MNC (Multi-National Corporation) easily moved its production across national borders, tightly controlling its fluid supplier value-chains, many of these Chinese, by owning brand names, patents, property rights, etc. The exclusivity of intellectual knowhow was thus at the core of the 'new' economy of the 1990s–2000s. Value was created through services, while production was easily outsourced: its margins were lower, since profits went to owners of know-how. Financials surged ahead, outpacing grease-covered manufacturers.

Starting from the Clinton administration, the 'new' economy of globalization and outsourcing was based on Wintelism. The 2008 crisis showed the limits of the Western services-based control of the core enterprise over its faraway suppliers. With credits tighter, firms were looking for 'improved quality, lower cost and utilising the suppliers' knowledge & expertise,' even if this meant suppliers' involvement in innovation and product development (Lodhi and Khan, 2010).

Today, in the aftermath of the 2008 crisis, shifting rules of the game open a new chance for China. With Western funding scarce, China gains by investing abroad and through the new attractiveness of its local markets. Leading multinationals rush-in carrying much-needed technologies/expertise.

Supply-side globalization: Chinese participation in CNPNS

Jeffrey Immelt, the CEO of G.E., expects better long-term margins from advanced manufacturing as compared to services, including financials.[6] However, investment-wise, manufacturing is costly – a good-sized solar-panel plant, about $70 million, is 'more than twice the total investment in Google' before it went public in 2004 (Lohr, 2010).

The tectonic shift of the ICT revolution may offer a new chance to newcomers, part of rapidly radiating CNPNs (Zysman 2002). Functionally, a CNPN is a 'distributed' multinational, a composite, logistically-complex structure of encapsulated modular entities. They range in size, location, functionality and expertise: West to East, public and private, big and small, each possessing crucial resources and knowledge. As ICT Revolution radiates globally OOD gradually replaces Fordist-vertical and mass-production with customization within a diverse loosely-connected network of FDI, SOE, SMEs, etc.

Within this evolving paradigm change, the product design, the most expensive part of lineup (Porter, 1998), is made affordable via modularity, turning manufacturing into a CNPN-based assembly of modular 'off-shelf'/made-to-order parts/components. In OOD, design is used for quality control, a necessity within global value-chains where buyers are located far away from suppliers and cannot control them directly. The software business found this solution first, in the 1980s, in OOD-modularity, encapsulation and cooperation between large distributed teams of programmers/testers (Booch, 2007). Old-fashioned linear code-writing was replaced with an assembly of functional reusable modules picked-out at will from extensive Dynamic-Link-Libraries (DLLs). In PC-manufacturing the modular principle was extended to tangible production. The related rise of Wintelism led to the resurgence of US-based dominance on the PC market, based on outsourcing,[7] which put China on the map. The related computerization of inventories and parts specifications worked DLL style and paved the way to other spheres of production enabling B2B, B2C, etc., markets down to C2C,[8] where China participated actively.

Modularity also helps in distributing the costs of design/production of the end-product along the entire value-chain: each supplier is fully responsible for its components. Distributed schemes oftentimes present a 'hubs-and-spokes' configuration, potentially, with several centres, whose functionalities and responsibilities must be encapsulated, both to preserve commercial secrets and avoid complications.

Thus, modularity enables diversity through encapsulation, ensuring the coexistence of diverse and quite possibly incompatible forms within a single CNPN. OOD grew into a global trend, by attracting/involving peripheral producers/consumers, via customization for new vast and diverse markets. Fordism was in retreat from the 1980s, due to scarcity of uniform inexpensive resources for its assembly lines. China grew on the emergent trend of diversification and outsourcing, as basically the only country able to provide small-series on-demand (Economist, 2011). The intermingling of modern and traditional forms of neighbourhood cooperation, advantageous for OOD, turned China into an economic power.

OOD was a valuable, though underappreciated and underused tool of the Chinese economic growth. Local and latent sources of supply/demand could now be externalized, creating novel opportunities. The costly vertical production 'in-house' could now be replaced by OOD-style 'off-shelf' outsourcing/cooperation, which, up to this time, was often hindered by corporate/cultural incompatibility. The spread of CNPNs made China into a global workshop by creating a worldwide demand for a large assortment of standard off-shelf parts/components. Cross-brand interchangeability greatly sped-up the time to market lowering development costs. This led to the rise of motley collaborating structures, both through mergers and part-time ownerships/partnerships (Renault-Nissan, GM-Wuling etc).[9] Replacing Fordist mass-production, parts/components are now mass-designed to be used cross-brand/cross-platform.[10] Thus, OOD-based materialization of latent corporate demand boosts the supply-side. This is multiplied many times over by a similar boost from the demand-side, since off-shelf parts and components can now be used cross-platform.

The 2008 crisis made it clear that the main growth potential is in the growing markets of the developing world. While the Western economies stall and the related demand shrinks, the developing world as a whole grows at 4.2–4.3% in 2011–12, providing the bulk of corporate profits. The leading Western corporations, including GE and GM, are shifting their priorities and forming new OOD-style Chinese-based CNPN-partnerships.

Achieving a balance between several strong and disparate partners, i.e. G.E. and AVIC (Aviation Industry Corporation) of China, was formerly a 'mission impossible.' Modularity makes it doable via encapsulation, through well-defined protocols of mutual interactions based on the division of areas of expertise and the related functionality. Project-centred multi-layered structures replace factory-based Fordist verticals, providing an answer to the complexity of modern technologies. By reducing costs of design/implementation formerly done 'in-house,' OOD and its precursors grew widespread. Market-segmentation becomes widespread in the consumer society; virtual communities author complex products via crowd-sourcing/cloud-computing (open-source code, Wikis etc). This newly awakened intellectual power exceeds the capacity even of the largest firms, including Microsoft.

OOD, as a new business/production model, focuses the energy of a large horizontally-structured CNPN (Zysman 2002). Challenging projects are handled at minimal costs, by avoiding costly institutional solutions and involving outside expertise. OOD appears, by any other name, in a wide range of applications, from faraway McDonalds' franchises to Boeing's Dreamliner and Chinese stimulus/infrastructure projects. Below, we document its gradual rise through diversity of post-Fordist forms/models.

Chongqing: a case-study of Chinese über-competitiveness

In China, the Chongqing motorcycle factory was at the forefront of OOD production-style (Badalian and Krivorotov, 2009). An underappreciated technological innovation helped to significantly lower the bike's price, to $400, as compared to Honda's $4,000. This was due to a manufacturing paradigm shift.[11] As mass-production matured, manufacturing became relatively easy and inexpensive as compared to growing design costs. For any serious modification, not only do parts have to be redesigned to precise specifications, but also the production line, with all its parts. Thus, asset inertia limits technological change to incremental steps, as firms strive to avoid major redesigns (Ehrlenspiel, et al., 2007).

The Chongqing motorcycle factory radically reduced design costs of the Fordist-style mass-production by accepting OOD-like modularity of design. Similar to the software industry (Booch, et al., 2007), modules with a well-defined functionality, such as the wheel, engine, etc., were encapsulated and made accessible only through standard sockets on a frame/chassis (a tangible version of software module's header). Obviously, modules can be reused in diverse configurations as long as they fitted a socket.

In Chongqing, the reigning capital of affordable motorcycles, any wheel, engine, frame, and so on, could be used at one's will if it fitted the most basic specifications: size, weight, input-output sockets etc. Chongqing was hardly alone in pursuing this principle of cross-platform interchangeability through encapsulation. First, it appeared in the virtual world, shifting code-writing from operational to object-oriented and functional (open-source community, Linux, Wikis, eBay etc). The paradigm radiated globally, reducing the costs of designing/building hardware, from cellphones/gadgets, to Boeing's Dreamliner, to handle design cost/complexity exceeding the budget of any single corporation.

China is well-equipped to benefit from OOD-methods of designing and making things due to its traditionally cooperating neighbour-businesses, turned into economical and efficient suppliers, a major productivity booster of modernity.

The 2008 crisis as a watershed for China: OOD in CNPNs of the emergent 'distributed' multinational

Up to the 2008 crisis, modularity of OOD helped to preserve the Fordist-vertical by boosting its productivity/reducing costs. Suppliers remained subordinated by the uniformity of Wintelist standards, patents and intellectual property. The ultimate means of control came from major Western financials, running the global system of dollar-denominated credits.

This system suffered a major blow in 2008, when easy credit lines, the lifeblood of globalization, were suddenly frozen. In the post-crisis reality producers faced contracting demand and mounting cost pressures, due to the jump in joblessness. Credit became scarce, as higher risks/uncertainties depleted bank reserves.

In this environment, the Chinese stimulus provided an irresistible source of long-term credit, attracting a bevy of Western hi-tech companies. The crisis opened opportunities for strategic hi-tech purchases in the West (Chesapeake Energy Corporation). Even majors, on the scale of G.E./GM, announced strategic partnerships with Chinese SOEs: contraction in demand pushed to cost-reduction and search for credits/new markets.[12]

It is hardly yet another wrinkle of outsourcing. Cost pressures and credit scarcity are levelling the field for Western and Chinese counterparts, increasing the value of partnerships. Each partner brings crucial expertise, as part of a horizontally-built CNPN. Two or more large hubs could never coexist before: harmonization of a CNPN through protocols/interfaces has thus become a production necessity. Members of a CNPN have had to accept industry-wide 'off-shelf' interfaces/protocols or risk incompatibility. The rise of common interfaces/protocols in the ICT Revolution has formed the core of OOD: diverse entities, shielded through encapsulation, could now be conjoined fluidly within CNPNs.

The loose parts of the Chandlerian corporation are being reconfigured by adding also suppliers as part of a CNPC value chain, on principles of modular-design/distributed-production. In its time, the cheap off-shelf PC-production has caused a rapid price drop and a forest-fire radiation of the digital revolution. Today, post-crisis institutionalization of OOD may lead to a similarly dramatic cost-cutting for hi-tech design, currently the most expensive aspect, by commoditizing modular affordable 'off-shelf' systems/components.

Following the example of Boeing's Dreamliner, which was built in close cooperation with suppliers,[13] China pioneers in the assembly of planes from 'off-shelf' parts, such as Pratt-Whitney/GE engines etc. Aviation Industry Corporation of China (AVIC) is in a strategic cooperation with G.E., with both of them aspiring to become a civilian plane-maker, despite rather limited expertise in the field. Thus, OOD, a trend, first started for PCs and in the virtual world, is increasingly showing its power in the physical world of tangible nuts-and-bolts manufacturing.

The newfound fluidity of product, industry, etc, blurs the lines between diverse companies and their markets, with head-on competition of all against all. Google bumps heads with Apple as a phone-producer and also with Amazon, but now as a knowledge-distributor. Phone and cable companies become indistinguishable. Cameras and music-players are pushed out by phones. A Chinese battery-maker envisions itself as an electric car-producer, while G.E. aspires to become a civilian plane-maker. This trend creates new opportunities for China, through strategic purchases/alliances. In the brave new world of all against all, the rise of OOD creates new opportunities for CNPN suppliers of crucial systems/components, up to creating their own brand-names, from phones to planes. HTC makes a Facebook-cobranded Android phone, while Apple still controls suppliers vertically.

The introduction of Fordism in the twentieth century led to immense productivity gains. The OOD-business model holds the same promise of higher productivity and cost-efficiency. Fordism replaced hand-fitted car parts with mass-produced standard parts, interchangeable within a model. This greatly reduced production costs, and not only for Detroit, as the entire industry followed its lead. Now, on a higher plane of standardized design of the twenty first century, parts/components become interchangeable across models/brands.

Salomon Fabricant (1941) attributed the rise of the US economy in the twentieth century to its ability to lower its production costs about tenfold, with a similar increase in production volumes. This paid for the higher salaries of American workers. By assembling costly custom-made designs from cheap 'off-shelf' systems/components, OOD might repeat this feat in China, with higher output/lower costs compensating for higher labor/investment costs of complex modern technologies. In IT, large customized software systems are now routinely assembled from 'off-shelf' encapsulated modules due to standard *usb* plugs for peripherals: printers, headphones etc. Standardization of interfaces/protocols is the next step up, surpassing standardized mass-produced parts of Fordism. China has advanced well along this promising road.

Demand-side globalization: the value of local markets

During the *first stage* of globalization, from the 1980s and up to the 2008 crisis, Chinese exports expanded benefiting from Wintelism and other early versions of OOD, part of the ICT Revolution (Zysman, et al. 2011). The Western markets became the initial training grounds for turning diversity from a liability into an advantage. After the 2008 crisis, the Western markets shrunk and their purchasing power fell. Globalization was now ready to expand to new, potentially huge and incredibly diverse developing markets.

The *second stage* of globalization after the 2008 crisis might completely reshape global societies and their lifestyles/economies. With Western markets depressed, the rising demand of the developing world fueled the handsome 4.2–4.3% annual global economic growth and brought-in sizable corporate profits.[14] BRICS countries, in general, and China in particular, strengthened by its economic stimulus, became the engine of the global economy. The business climate shifted, with more growth opportunities in these countries as compared to the maturing Western economies.

Among new challenges was the lack of mass-demand/mass-markets in the developing world, which was more used to bazaars. Mass demand is a late-twentieth-century phenomenon from the US, with decades of publicly-funded mass-education and TV movies/ads culminating in patterns of mass consumption. In contrast, the developing world presents a smorgasbord of diverse forms, summarily an economy of scope rather than a mass economy of scale.[15]

Today, the growing scarcity of mass resources leads to readjustment of old patterns and priorities. In China, widespread SMEs help in accommodating diversity as part of a larger corporate lineup. Similar diversity is also present in the German Mittelstand (Small Medium Enterprises), which are considered the backbone of the German economy. Despite this, within the mass-production economy, the SMEs were often ignored by economists as backward and less-efficient. Meanwhile, their ability to operate on small local markets, serving many lower-income customers, often, as part of a much larger corporate lineup, becomes crucial for the ICT Revolution and is being gradually acknowledged (Berghoff, 2006; Herrigel, 2000).

Below, to demonstrate the full OOD-potential, we complement the supply-side story told above, with the description of simultaneous shifts in the consumer society, demand-side. In a nutshell, supply-side development mostly took place in China, which grew to become the global consumer-goods manufacturer par excellence. The related demand was supplied by the US mass society from the 1980s and up to the 2008 crisis. Even now, the US market remains central for the success of any global brand due to the reserve role of the dollar, which remains the main currency of international transactions. For example, to buy Middle-Eastern oil, any country or firm have to first sell their goods for dollars.

Today, the worldwide markets are being reshaped. In the long-term perspective, the depressed markets of Southern Europe,[16] repopulated by migrants, including those coming from China, present an important growth resource, instead of a liability as part of an economically depressed region, as they are currently seen. From the 1980s, Southern Europe served as an entrepôt to developing markets, on the fringes of Europe, close to Africa. It is burdened with debts, which make its people more flexible. The importance of long-term economic ties is duly acknowledged by the Chinese government, which buys EU bonds and businesses, providing a welcome lifeline.

The 1980s South-European textile boom presents a good case-study of the global spread of OOD-like forms during the supply-side development of the first stage of globalization. This boom ended in with a bust in 2001, after the Chinese entry to the WTO.[17] Today, during the second stage of globalization, demand from low-income customers, including the EU, promotes SMEs entering new regions. In the 1980s, the push came from Europe and radiated out: from Italy to Spain, then up to Northern Africa, Tunisia and Morocco. Now, it has returned through the developing world to the EU, with Chinese companies gaining new markets. This highlights the SME-based potential of cross-pollinating Northern Africa and Southern Europe, due to the similarity of their geographical conditions. Among many examples is MediaTek, a Taiwanese chip designer, is an oxymoron, a fabless chipmaker and the focus of our case-study on the evolution from low to hi tech under competitive pressures. It reported that its second quarter profits for 2009 were up an astounding 80% compared with the year before (at $277 m).MediaTek specializes in designing bundles of chips for handsets, digital players, etc, outsourcing its designs to smaller producers, who own actual production fabs (chip factories). The Economist reports that 'a handset firm there [in mainland China – LB] used to need 20m yuan ($2.9 m), 100 engineers and at least nine months to bring a product to market. Now 500,000 yuan, ten engineers and three months will do.[18] As a result, Chinese handset-makers now number in the hundreds.' This is an SME-driven economy of scope at its best.[19]

The innovative 'distributed' multinational runs a novel model of 'mass' production by sophisticated ICT-built and managed value chains. Mass-production coexists with local flows of customized and small-series products. The ongoing shift in advanced industries, from IT to plane-making, diverges from mass uniformity, previously cultivated through mass media and public schools. Instead, there rises a notable trend towards product-personalization and market-segmentation, pronounced from the 1990s – ICT-Revolution empowered communities, including the virtual ones. Their collective muscle enhances their productive/consuming power, turning them into trend-setters.[20]

The new types of market segmentation, which create new types of demand within emerging and incredibly diverse communities can hardly be matched by large corporations, including traditional Fordist multinationals. Among many examples are online communities armed with new technological tools including various wikis, open source software, cloud-computing, crowd-sourcing etc. Such trends are challenging giants, including Microsoft, who are in the pursuit of new markets and opportunities. Today, the PC is fading, while cloud-computing, smartphones and a plethora of business activities on mobile platforms shift to the Internet and its virtual neighbourhoods. Online, everything is up-to-date, with no outdated or unwanted goods which oftentimes clutter the brick-and-mortar stores and cause losses.

Our examples and case-studies testify to the often-doubted (Brynjolfsson, 1993) power of the ICT Revolution showcased in (Zysman, et al., 2011). Far from being confined to the office paperwork, novel opportunities for non-traditional producers servicing diverse emerging markets come from new CNPN logistics, a product of the ICT Revolution, which manages the difficult feat of joining together diverse suppliers within the 'distributed' multinational. This is a remarkable growth resource and, undoubtedly, a factor in the rise of economic giants within the developing world: China, India, Brazil etc.

In the 1980s, the maturity of Fordism and the rise of a new business paradigm pushed towards novel behaviours.[21] Wintelism presented a new adjustment allowing it to thrive under conditions of market segmentation by incorporating Marshallian externalities and outside suppliers within the vertical. However, this opened a Pandora's Box by starting a plethora of novel cooperative behaviors. The Wintelist (Windows + Intel)-duopoly was already much more horizontal. As OOD evolved, the uniformity of the Fordist vertical was gradually pushed out. Instead of a few giants, there were several intensely competing large platforms, forming the core of the related CNPNs. Among examples are Apple-centred and Android-centred phone-makers, service-providers, application developers and code-writers. Their high margins come from cooperation within their own value-chains, while competition and court battles rage between platforms and the related CNPN groups and value chains. China benefits from this shifting landscape by creating its own corporate groups with Western majors: AVIC/GE, Wuling/GM etc. Each of them is surrounded by a 'halo' of related local SMEs/public entities, servicing their group at various levels. It is like the scale of ICT complexity is overwhelming even the largest corporations, which adjust by forming horizontally-organized CNPNs: supplier cooperation comes to the forefront, enabled by OOD-modularity/encapsulation and 'off-shelf' systems/components.

It is not like there were no cooperative corporate groupings before. The Japanese *keiretsu* and the Korean *chaebol* were arranged around a major bank, coordinating mutual actions and sharing investments. However, after a short and lush bloom, where concerted efforts helped, the old-time *keiretsu* suffered from the rigidity of its grouping. Its members were also startlingly shielded from market demands and could easily lose their touch with reality. This rigidity was loosened only recently. Now, OOD-modularity-style, the same company may enter several diverse groupings.

As shown above, in the Chongqing motorcycle factory, roles of competition and cooperation were readjusted under new technological paradigm of modularity. The prices were lowered dramatically through better cooperation of neighbour-enterprises. After agreeing on the initial bike's architecture they competed against each other on price/quality of each part: wheels, frame etc, even while adhering to the basic specs. On a larger scale, the Chinese successes of 'open economic zones' and the recent stimulus further showcased the potential of a well-designed mix of competition–cooperation in the spirit of OOD, directing market players towards desired ends. Each participant: the central government, local administration and companies, took care of its own functionalities, with modular Marshallian externalities acting in concert.

Emergent synergies

In this chapter we have documented the rise of a new OOD-model based on modular-design/distributed-production. Its complex logistics are run with the help of

ICT tools and involve encapsulation of diverse players within large cooperating CNPNs (Zysman, 2002). The related horizontally-organized institutional environment presents a drastic shift from the vertical integration of Fordism.

Production on-demand is native for OOD, building on many economically important synergies, oftentimes uniting former antagonists

Within the reshaped OOD-type interrelationship, the highly educated professional labor force exits the tedium of the assembly line and can exercise its strong points by taking care of design, assembly-on-demand and marketing. These are crucial human talents/Marshallian externalities within the ICT-led economy of scope. The machine, meanwhile, excels at uniformity and production, pertaining to the economy of scale. The emerging patterns of man-machine interplay presume new complex cooperative–competitive behaviours, aiming to reduce transaction costs, these costs were wildly elevated by the unwieldiness of the mass-production economy but can now be reduced significantly due to the ICT Revolution.

China excels in production-on-demand, which presents its strongest point, in the need of further enhancement.

OOD-related modularity and encapsulation presume functional integration

Function-based self-organization within a larger group is the next evolutionary frontier after the Smithian labor-division. Labor-division thus advances from operational (factory, conveyor-belt) to market-based self-organization of modular players, experts in diverse areas: from design/component-production/assembly to marketing/legislature/financials. The OOD-potential for self-synchronization was showcased by the recent success of the Chinese stimulus: localities played the leading role in selecting areas of investment and organizing a value-chain. Other examples of cooperative/competitive groups around a project were presented above (Boeing's Dreamliner, Android-Apple, AVIC/GE, Wuling/GM etc).

Hubs-and-spokes: cooperation/harmonization of the big and the small

OOD-encapsulation is also crucial for harmonizing variously-sized players: larger participants serve as hubs, and smaller ones as spokes, voiding the need in costly vertical institutional integration. To avoid conflicts, tasks are encapsulated and separated. The large hub remains responsible for synchronizing the architecture, supporting brand-names, marketing, design etc. Meanwhile, flexibility is preserved as suppliers may remain as small as reasonable. Marshallian externalities create the base for specialist collaboration. This is the most common and established form of OOD-style cooperation/encapsulation, which includes the classical franchise/vendor capitalism; Inditex/Zara, Mango; MediaTek etc. China is successfully using this scheme in various enterprises, including auto and plane manufacturing as described above.

OOD-enabled public–private partnership

Cooperation of private entities with the government may resolve the investment problem, guaranteeing publicly-funded credits, product orders and protection from corporate raids. Private firms are famously loath to invest in projects with unpredictable long-term returns. This especially applies to revolutionary, hard-to-commercialize technologies and infrastructure projects. In China, government participation provides a source of affordable credits, guaranteed orders etc. This helps in surmounting the 'big-moat' mentioned by G.E.'s Immelt as cited above. Reducing the time to commercialization may provide a crucial help to the regional economy by improving its tax base, helping to domesticate a territory and improve its yields.

The OOD-style functionality-based modules may improve national and firm-level security by encapsulating critical technologies during commercialization. Historically, large infrastructure projects used to be paid for from the public purse, the only institution with sufficiently large funds. It is both qualified for forming communally-important goals and able to fund the related super-long investments with unpredictable returns. Among examples: the rural electricity and roads in the US were built during the New Deal; the highway/byway system of the Eisenhower administration etc. Meanwhile, the private firm is free of many shortcomings of public institutions: their rigidity/lack of flexibility, innate tendency to corruption, and disregard to market demand/returns. The starring role of Chinese government/municipalities was showcased by the recent success of the Chinese stimulus.

OOD-based integration of diverse players may enable domestication of underutilised territories through sustainable, long-term development

The OOD-style encapsulation helps in alleviating the transaction costs of coordinating several clashing forms of ownership, with diverse time horizons, differing goals etc. In the context of a locality this enables socialization of property, first introduced in (Badalian and Krivorotov, 2009b, 2009c), which presents a synergy of diverse social forms. Owners at various levels holding crucial functionalities are supported by the entire locality and contribute to an important public good – the domestication of its territory. The reward for the entire *commons* comes from the higher productivity of formerly underperforming territories.[22] This strategy is prominent in China, with its ambitious and successful five-year plans.

Conclusion

Today, the global economic crisis is reshaping the world economic system through emergent development strategies. In the interconnected globalized world, China acquired a new prominence of a global economic powerhouse. Its roles, responsibilities and development choices have become crucial for the international community, reeling from the fall in margins and a rise in indebtedness. By taking the lead in developing a new production style of OOD, China may be steering the international community out of its current dependence on standardized, mass production economy, which has matured, to a more productive economy of knowledge based on producing goods 'on-demand.'

In contrast to mass production, fast becoming obsolete, the new business-model of OOD is based on harmonizing diversity through encapsulation and modularity. This includes synchronization of the public and private; international and local; long-term goals and short-term profits; big enterprises (FDI, SOEs) and SMEs of small neighbourhood producers. In the rising globalizing economy China is already putting its mark on many important issues such as economic growth, climate change and scientific and technological innovation.

To what extent will China succeed in the domestication of its territory? Would this involve new strategies and policies for increasing food production on its sparsely populated inner territories,[23] and, presumably, extending the related innovation to similar areas of the developing world? Answers to those questions may be crucial in shaping the twenty-first century for the entire humanity.

In the course of history, the leading country of its time played an enormous role by pioneering, perfecting and spreading around a brand new style of economy and the related institutions. It was able to open up enormous new territories to new levels of productivity, which would benefit even those far away from it. This greatly increased the global output and made it possible to feed many more people on the level unattainable before. Thus, up to our times we, as a species, managed to escape the Malthusian trap by moving onward and domesticating new places. In this line, the Industrial Revolution was led by Britain, while the mass production economy was born in the US. Both events greatly increased the productive power of the global economy.

In our near future, the vector of change points at the last remaining wastelands. Some of these are deep in the Chinese mainland, but there is also the potential of the Boreal forests, Amazonian jungle, African savannah and Asian deserts, up to the Inner Mongolia etc. These lands are extremely fragile. Ahead lays the enormous challenge of boosting their productivity without causing wholesale damage. Today, we are witnessing the earliest stages of this process enabled by digital technologies.

The vector of development is shifting to the East. This chapter has presented a hypothesis on its future trends, highlighting the need of thorough empirical research in the near future.

Notes

1 The authors would like to use this occasion to extend their gratitude to their many colleagues, instrumental in developing the concept of OOD. Heartfelt thanks go to Bin Wu for his constant support and unwavering patience, Jian Chen, his kind co-editor, Academician Sergey Glazyev of the Russian Academy of Sciences, our dear colleague for many years and the author of a complementary concept of the 'technological way', Prof. Eric Hobsbawm, our friend and mentor for many years, our blind reviewers and Sam Beatson, the diligent proof reader. There are many more left out for the lack of space – thank you. As always, the mistakes are our own.

2 The fading of Fordism after the 1980s was discussed within the Regulation theory (Boyer 1986), raising the fundamental question of what comes after Fordism. While the Regulation theory and other researchers (Atkeson and Kehoe, 2001) never provided a decisive answer, a later group of researchers proved more successful in its discovery of Wintelism (Zysman, 2002).

3 The ongoing court battle between Apple and Samsung challenges the formerly inviolate issue of patents and copyrights. Copyright for a separate module becomes meaningless, since a brand new module can easily recreate the same functionality. It is hardly easy to answer a question: does a given module resemble someone else's product because it is copied or due to the same functionality?

4 A decades-long delay between a technological revolution and a superpower rising on the coattails of its inventions seems persistent across eras. And indeed, as shown by Schurr, et al. (1960), Rosenberg (1976), Devine (1983), and David (1990, 1991) the knowledge needed to use new technologies to their utmost effect was organization-specific and difficult to transfer across organizations and, we must add to that, across business models. Even the Industrial Revolution, obviously the source of the British power during the rise of a new business model based on the self-motivation of small shop owners and artisans (Hobsbawm, 1999), is now questioned, with the current research (Mokyr,1993)failing to find any measurable increases in productivity up to the nineteenth century, while crucial inventions date to the early 18th century. The same is the case with the US which had productivity surging in the 1930s (Bernanke and Parkinson, 1992), (Bordo and Evans, 1993), and became a superpower after WWII, while inventions in electricity, internal combustion engine etc. were made in Europe, about 70 years earlier. A similar situation of the lack of measurable gains in productivity was also widely discussed regarding the ICT Revolution.

5 The conventional argument claimed that just as an agricultural economy gave way to a manufacturing economy, an industrial economy was giving way to a service economy. Hence, their arguments went, industrial production was of 'diminishing importance' (Zysman, 2002)

6 Wintel = Windows + Intel, with software written in object-oriented languages, such as C++, Java etc.

7 This 'alphabet soup' refers to Business to Business, Business to Consumers, etc, which are various computerized markets of parts and products.

8 The amazing spread of CNPN-level interrelationship was disclosed during Japan's recent earthquake/tsunami: a shutdown of a few critical plants brought global production lines to a standstill, raising prices (Economist, March 29, 2011).

9 BMW hybrid Twin-Power-Turbo engine is to be used in Chinese cars; likewise, Wuling platforms are in GM cars; Shanghai's Tongji University researchers work on the future German-Chinese electric car and on the Mini-E (electric Mini), BMW's Active E (fully electric cars) would be built on the chassis of BMW 1 Coupé, new Audis Q3 use the chassis of VW Tiguan and many of its parts/components. The same cross-brand and cross-country interchangeability is practiced by other hulking car-consortia: Renault-Nissan, Ford-Mazda-Volvo, VW-Audi-Skoda-Bentley-Lamborghini-Porsche-Suzuki, Fiat cross-pollinates with Ferrari, Maserati, Alfa Romeo and truck manufacturer Iveco, along with Chrysler, Dodge, Jeep and Ram. Hummer is owned by the Sichuan Tengzhong Heavy Industrial Machinery Co, a Chinese four-year-old manufacturer of cement-mixer trucks and tow-trucks with just 4300 employees. So the pattern is fairly typical, since this crossbreeding greatly speeds-up the time to market and lowers development costs. Daimler owns Mercedes-Benz, Maybach, smart, and the Freightliner and Sterling truck businesses. Renault and Nissan are joined at the hip. Indian conglomerate, Tata, the maker of the world's cheapest car, the two-cylinder Nano, also owns Land Rover and Jaguar – a fact often overlooked in Jaguar's and Land Rover's marketing briefs. Tata bought Jaguar and Land Rover in 2008 from Ford for a song ($1.7 billion Aussie dollars versus $US2.5 billion for Jaguar paid by Ford in 1989 and $US2.75 billion for Land Rover bought from BMW in 2000). Even then, the ongoing operational issues have placed Tata under immense financial pressure. Similarly, Hyundai owns Kia, which explains, for example, why the powertrains of the Santa Fe R 2.2 and the Sorento are so 'apparently . . . identical'. www.caradvice. au/51978/editors-column-who-owns-your-brand/

10 Just as it was presented in p.0 above, not technologies per se, but a paradigm shift opened a pathway to a major productivity surge.

11 i.e., many US-based solar-panel manufacturers abandoned US plants. It turns out that, despite scant support from the US government and uncertain outlook for long-term credits, their advanced technologies still let them lower prices for US-made panels to about $2-per-watt. The Chinese producers, however, could go down to a buck, helped by cheaper capital from local banks and municipal tax incentives. The flight to China became inevitable (Bradsher, 2011).

12 Boeing was unable to match deep-pocketed Airbus and had to lower design costs dramatically. The design/construction of major parts/systems of its Dreamliner were de facto outsourced to several high-end suppliers, while Boeing, as the general contractor, held the specs and controlled the process.

13 Among typical examples, Burberry reported record profits from moving store openings to China. Burberry Reports '30% Rise in Second Half Sales to 860 million GBP' in the Guardian 19 April 2011. www.guardian.co.uk/business/2011/apr/19/burberry-lvmh-sales-increase

14 In 1898 Alfred Marshall (Marshall, 1898) pointed at the theoretical possibility of an economy of scope as a viable alternative for the efficiencies of scale. It can be inferred that Marshall saw the lower overhead costs of the economy of scope as a counterbalance to its inherently higher transaction costs, due to difficulties of lining up suppliers, customers etc in a viable value-chain. For Marshall the economy of scope offered a tantalizing chance for gaining the benefits of the big from the small and the nimble. The scale efficiencies could be thus generated on the cheap, while also utilizing the flexibility of small production series. He believed that cooperation of small neighbour-enterprises provided the means to avoid significant upfront investments and the related costly mistakes. These findings were rediscovered in the 1980s, since they helped in explaining the notable success of family-based small businesses in Southern Europe, from Italian mom-and-pop shops, gradually, spreading further, to Spain, Morocco . . .

15 The Marshallian economy of scope did indeed work in the past, but only intermittently. Occasionally, it produced spectacular results: see the cottage industry preceding the British factory. However its successes were rather transient, tied to extremely low labor remuneration, to compensate for higher transaction costs. As soon as labor costs increased, the economy of scope lost to the economy of scale: i.e., the factory replaced the cottage industry.

16 This dissolved the advantage of cheap labor in textiles and production of other consumer goods in Southern Europe. Among few post-2001 survivors was the so called 'fast apparel' of 'firms without a factory'. This was an ICT-fuelled return to origins: successful companies Mango, Inditex/Zara etc. started by putting-out to local suppliers, while taking care of design/marketing/logistics.

17 This underscores the rising importance and new meaning of the main *Marshallian externalities, namely, specialist knowledge, subsidiary industries and specialized labor force*. They become the embodiment of the local specialized knowledge and the tools for adjustment to local tastes/markets. Localities create demand for rising forms of modular-design/distributed-manufacturing. The new types of value-chains are working within *functional* labor division, which is the next logical step after the *operational* labor division of the Smithian factory of the 19th century. Note that the division of functionalities along value-chain distributes both responsibilities and costs. This advances the Smithian principle of labor division to the next level of complexity/execution, from manufacturing to managing product lifecycle: design/production/sales/maintenance. Costs are equitably distributed and shared along value-chains, with the market as the ultimate optimizer. Theoretically, the gain in flexibility and the speed-to-market of fluidly shifting and harmonized designer-producer hub-and-spokes value-chains might more than compensate for the lost scale, regained within the economy of scope through cooperation of big and small players. This reading of the Marshallian theory might

have been recently corroborated by the reality. In the crisis, the global fashion industry was reeling under loads of unwanted mass-produced apparel. Meanwhile Zara/Inditex thrived, due to its small series, seen as fashionable and better value. The crisis underscored the dangers of mass production, its obsolescence leading to waste/losses, due to technological progress/changes in fashion. It highlighted the benefits of small series designed on-demand cheaply, with end products always up-to-date and matched with demand from buyers.

18 Fabless and fearless. How a Taiwanese firm became one of the world's fastest-growing chipmakers. The Economist. 6 August 2009.

19 The activism of small groups demonstrated the power of a grass roots campaign by re-electing the first black US president.

20 As mass-production matured, the traditional Chandlerian vertical corporation lost competitiveness. Paradoxically, it was simultaneously both too small to fund innovation in-house and too large to change/adapt easily. After reaching a certain size, it grew unwieldy: transaction costs increased, while margins shrunk. The classical economy-of-scale hit its size limits. The same logic worked in the natural evolution: when growth in size became too costly (dinosaurs), development fostered complex behaviours (mammals).

21 Elinor Ostrom (1990) received the 2009 Nobel Prize for her analysis of economic self-governance, focused on the commons, whose efficiency she showed.

22 For example, by introducing new biotechnology, locally efficient mixes of cultures (potatoes, millet etc), aquaculture, husbandry on the new level of productivity, all of them integrated together in synergy-like relationship resembling living ecosystems in the nature. Among other benefits, this presumes integration of local populations within local industries to promote careful husbandry of communal resources.

Bibliography

Atkeson, Andrew, Kehoe, Patrick J., (2001), 'The Transition to a New Economy after the Second Industrial Revolution', *NBER Working Paper* 606

Badalian, Lucy, Krivorotov, Victor, (2007), 'Russia and China: Prospects of interaction in new fuel-and-energy conditions', *Far Eastern Affairs* 2: 52–72

Badalian, Lucy, Krivorotov, Victor, (2009a), 'Technological shift and the rise of a new finance system. The Market-Pendulum Model', *The European Journal of Economic and Social Systems*, 21, 2: 233–266

Badalian, Lucy, Krivorotov, Victor, (2009b), 'Economic development as domestication of a geoclimatic zone: the historic East-West divide and the current trends towards its closure', *Journal of Innovation Economics*, 2009/1: 13–48

Badalian, Lucy, Krivorotov, Victor, (2009c), 'The wealth of the emerging world – the next 15–25 years', *Journal of Development and Agricultural Economics*, 1(4) July, 2009: 83–102

Badalian, Lucy, Krivorotov, Victor, (2009d), 'East and West: 2 approaches to survival and their synthesis under the ecological pressure', *Far Eastern Affairs*, 3

Berghoff, Hartmut, (2006), 'The end of family business? The Mittelstand and German capitalism in transition, 1949–2000', *Business History Review*, 80, 2

Bernanke, B. and Parkinson, M., (1992), 'Procyclical labor productivity and competing theories of the business cycle: Some evidence from interwar U.S. manufacturing industries', *Journal of Political Economy* 99: 439–459

Booch, Grady, et al., (2007), *Object-Oriented Analysis and Design with Applications*, Boston: Addison-Wesley

Bordo, Michael D. and Evans, Charles L., (1993), 'Labor Productivity During the Great Depression', *NBER Working Paper* No. 4415, www.nber.org/papers/w4415.pdf

Borrus, Michael, Zysman, John, (1997), 'Globalism with borders: The rise of Wintelism as the future of industrial competition', *Industry and Innovation*, 4, 2

Boyer, Robert, (1986), *La Théorie de la régulation: une analyse critique*, Paris: La Découverte

Bradsher, Keith, (2011), 'Solar Panel Maker Work to China', *The New York Times*, January 14

Brynjolfsson, Erik, (1993), 'The Productivity Paradox of Information Technology: Review and Assessment', *Communications of the ACM*, December, 1993

Campbell, Jeffrey R., (1998), 'Entry, exit, embodied technology, and business cycles', *Review of Economic Dynamics*, 1: 371–408

Chandler, Alfred, (1977), *The Visible Hand: The Managerial Revolution in American Business*, Cambridge, MA: Belknap Press of Harvard University Press.

Chandler, Alfred D., (1992), 'Organizational capabilities and the economic history of the industrial enterprise', *Journal of Economic Perspectives*, 6: 79–100

Chari, V.V., and Hopenhayn, Hugo, (1991), 'Vintage human capital, growth, and the diffusion of new technology', *Journal of Political Economy*, 99: 1142–65

David, Paul A., (1990), 'The dynamo and the computer: An historical perspective on the modern productivity paradox', *American Economic Review*, 80: 355–61

Davis, Steven J., Haltiwanger, John C., Schuh, Scott, (1996), *Job Creation and Destruction*, Cambridge, Mass.: MIT Press

Devine, Warren D. Jr., (1983), 'From shafts to wires: Historical perspective on electrification', *Journal of Economic History*, 43: 347–72

Dutton, William, (2005), *Transforming Enterprise: The Economic and Social Implications of Information Technology*, Mass.: MIT Press

Economist, (2009), 'Fabless and fearless. How a Taiwanese firm became one of the world's fastest-growing chipmakers', Leader on 6 August

Economist, (2011), 'China's economy Bamboo capitalism. China's success owes more to its entrepreneurs than its bureaucrats. Time to bring them out of the shadows', Leader on 10 March: www.economist.com/node/18332610?story_id=18332610

Ehrlenspiel, K., Kiewert, A., Lindemann, U., (2007), *Cost-Efficient Design*, New York: Springer, jointly published with ASME

Fabricant, Salomon, (1941), 'The Relation between Factory Employment and Output since 1899', UMI, www.nber.org/chapters/c6609.pdf

Herrigel, Gary, (2000), *Industrial Constructions: The Sources of German Industrial Power*, Cambridge: Cambridge University Press

Hobsbawm, E., (1999), *Industry and Empire: The Birth of the Industrial Revolution*, Penguin Books, New York: New Press

Hosaka, Tomoko A., (2010), 'China overtakes Japan in 2Q as No. 2 economy', *AP*, 16 August

Lodhi, Ashhaq, Khan, Aamer, (2010), 'Suppliers' involvement in Innovation & NPD : A study of the wind turbine industry', Linnaeus University, Faculty of Business, Economics and Design, Linnaeus School of Business and Economics

Lohr, Steve, (2010), 'G.E. Goes With What It Knows: Making Stuff', *NY Times*, 4 December

Marshall, A., (1890), [1920] *Principles of Economics*, London: Macmillan

Mokyr, Joel, (1993), *The British Industrial Revolution: An Economic Perspective*, Boulder: Westview

Ostrom, Elinor, (1990), *Governing the Commons: The Evolution of Institutions for Collective Action*, Cambridge: Cambridge University Press

Porter, Michael E., (1998), *On Competition*, A Harvard Business Review Book, Harvard Business School Press.

Prencipe, A., Davies, A., Hobday, M., (2003), *The Business of Systems Integration*, Oxford: Oxford University Press

Rosenberg, Nathan, (1976), 'On technological expectations', *Economic Journal* 86: 523–35

Schurr, Sam H., Netschert, Bruce C., Eliasberg, Vera, Lerner, Joseph, Landsberg, Hans H., (1960), *Energy in the American Economy, 1850–1975: An Economic Study of its History and Prospects*, Baltimore: Johns Hopkins Press

Weiping, Huang, Zhu, Wenhui, (2004), 'Wintelism: America's New Economy and the Micro Basis for World Industrial Restructuring', Institute of American Studies, Chinese Academy of Social Sciences, http://ias.cass.cn/en/show_mgyj.asp?id=46

Williamson, Jeffrey G., (1984), 'Why was British growth so slow during the Industrial Revolution?', *The Journal of Economic History*, 44, 3: 687–712

Zysman, John, (2002), 'Production in a Digital Era: Commodity or Strategic Weapon?', BRIE Working Paper 147, September, http://brie.berkeley.edu/publications/WP147.pdf

Zysman, John, et al., (2011), 'The new challenge to economic governance: the digital transformation of services', In: *Innovation in Public Governance*. Amsterdam, IOS Press

3 Globalization, mobility and the working conditions of contract Chinese seafarers

Bin Wu and Jonathon V. Beaverstock

Introduction

Globalization is intricately linked to labor migration and mobility worldwide. As William Johnston (1991: 115) suggested, '[T]oday we talk about world markets for cars, computers, and capital. Tomorrow we will talk about a world market for labor'. Indeed, labor mobility and migration across national boundaries have become a major issue attracting the attention of the world media, politicians and academic scholars. However, opinions vary with regard to the nature of the global labor market and its relations with other scalar markets. Manuel Castells (1998: 93) has suggested that, 'labor markets are not truly global, except for a small, but growing segment of professionals and scientists'. In contrast, Ronaldo Munck (2002: 4) has identified two dimensions of globalization, namely, 'deterritorialization' and 'brazilianization'. The former refers to the decline of the nation-state, which cuts across political frontiers in order to, 'seek the best return for their investment wherever that may be', whereas the latter is related to the rise of informal labor in the receiving countries, leading to 'diversity, unclarity and insecurity of people's work and life' (Beck, 2000: 1). While the former has contributed to labor mobility across national borders, the latter has caused an emergence of 'immigrant sectors' in host countries, where segmented labor markets have developed to allow foreign workers to undertake a range of employment opportunities, both formal and informal.

In this chapter, we are concerned with the interconnections of different skill segments and their impact on the working conditions of migrant Chinese seafarers. These workers were chosen for the focus of the study for three main reasons. Firstly, international shipping has become a highly-globalized industry, which has established a global labor market (GLM) for seafarers since the 1970s, resulting in two-thirds of the world's seafarers being involved in movement across national boundaries on a daily basis (Alderton, et al., 2004; Seafarers International Research Centre [SIRC], 2003). Secondly, China is now a major player in the international shipping industry in terms of the scale of its seafaring labor pool and the supply to the GLM (Zhao, 2002). Thirdly, a global governance framework has been established to monitor the working conditions and performance of world seafarers, providing a benchmark to observe the varied labor standards in different countries, including China (ILO, 2006). China's continuous economic transformation has inevitably affected the working conditions of Chinese seafarers, which provides a unique opportunity to observe the dynamics and impact of globalization on the mobility and working conditions of these workers.

Following this introduction, the rest of this chapter is divided into seven parts. Part two provides a brief discussion of segmented labor market theory, drawing upon Doeringer and Piore's (1971) 'dualist' labor market approach, in order to contextualize segmentation in the seafarers' division of labor. Part three discusses flags of convenience (FOC) and the making of the GLM for seafarers. Part four posits an analytical framework which discusses the division of seafarers into a two-tier model of those who work on (a) Chinese state-owned enterprise (SOE) and (b) foreign ships, which serves as the framework for the case study of Chinese seafarers. Part five introduces the case study of Chinese seafarers and focuses on the mobility patterns between Chinese SOE and foreign fleets, which is followed in part six by a discussion of the variations of working conditions and wages of Chinese seafarers. Part seven analyses the complexity of the Chinese labor market and highlights the institutional constraints of the market from a seafaring mobility perspective. Finally, in the conclusions, the chapter reports the significant findings of the empirical study and comments on how these results have contributed to a finer understanding of both segmented and GLMs for Chinese seafarers.

But, first, it is important to outline briefly the methodological foundations of the data collection on the working conditions and mobility of Chinese seafarers. The data reported in the chapter were derived from three sources. First, it was derived from the SIRC's (2003) global seafaring labor market database. Second, it was derived through the execution of two questionnaire surveys in Hong Kong (492 respondents) and China (268 crew agencies), respectively in 2003 to 2004.Third, it was derived from ethnography, a three-month period of observation and interviews (with a maximum of 46 interviews) being completed, undertaken on board two foreign ships (26 and 20 on each ship, respectively) in 2006 and 2007. The on-board-ship research was recorded in field notes and offers a unique opportunity and insight into the working and living conditions of Chinese contract seafarers in the GLM.All the primary data collection was undertaken by the first author of this chapter.

Theory of segmented labor markets

Labor market segmentation or 'dualist' approaches recognize that the labor market has different occupational and sector-specific characteristics and qualities, which (re)produce uneven and disproportionate labor queues, performance and rewards in separate segments of the workforce (Storper and Walker, 1989). The key argument of labor market segmentation or 'dualism' is that the functionality of the labor market discriminates between wages and conditions of work, and not necessarily the skill attributes of the individual (Leontaridi, 1998). Doeringer and Piore's (1971) 'dualist' approach argues that the labor market was categorized into two segments: primary; and secondary. The primary segment was characterized by high-wages, career ladders, training, promotion, good working conditions, stability in employment and equity, and jobs were clustered in hierarchically based internal labor markets (ILMs) which 'protected' the workers from the uncertainties of the external labor market. In contrast, the secondary labor market segment was external to the ILM where employment opportunities were characterized by low-wages, little prospect of career advancement, poor working conditions, instability and severe supervision. Doeringer and Piore's dualist labor theory wasn't without its critics, especially in that it didn't focus enough on explaining the intricacies of the secondary segment (Hayter and Barnes, 1992). Doeringer and Piore (1971) and other 'dualist' theories (Edwards, Reich and Gordon, 1975) have come under scrutiny since the 1970s because structural changes in economy, spurred by recession, technological change, and fragmentation in the production, have transformed the functioning of segmented labor markets.

The occupations of seafarers are certificated by the Standards of Training, Certification and Watchkeeping, regulated by the International Maritime Organisation Convention. The demarcation of seafarers' labor roles is segregated by the department worked on board (e.g.deck, engine) and occupation/rank, consisting of: ratings, who are relatively unskilled and perform manual labor tasks; trainee officers or cadets, who take at least three to four years to obtain the most junior officer certification; and officers, who are either classified with the deck or the engineer department, depending on training and certification (Glen, 2008). Data supplied by the Baltic International Maritime Council/International Shipping Federation (BIMCO/ISF) (2005) estimated that there was a global supply of 1.187 million seafarers in 2005, with 446,000 officers and 721,000 ratings compared to a demand for the same period of 1.062 million, 476,000 and 586,000, respectively (Glen, 2008). By drawing together research on seafarers labor market characteristics (Alderton, et al., 2004; Li and Wonham, 1999; Sampson and Schroeder, 2006), it can be argued that the tightly demarcated occupations of ratings, junior officers and senior officers, fits into the conceptualisation of segmented labor markets, with evidence of flexibility through the use of contracted labor via crew recruitment agencies[1]. Ratings can be categorized in the secondary segment of the labor market, depending upon their contractual status to the shipping company or recruitment agency. In the case of officers, those contracted to the shipping company are in the primary segment, but if officers are being contracted onto ships via recruitment agencies, then their position may rest in the secondary or external segment, where the firm can shrink and expand labor depending on market conditions. But, moreover, the degree of primary and secondary segmentation in the seafarers' labor market is just as intricately linked to the registration status of the ship (national flag or FOC) as it is to qualifications, certification and demarcation in the division of labor on board ship.

Globalization and the making of the GLM for seafarers

Globalization in the international shipping sector is characterized by two interconnected phenomena: opening registries (FOC) (Winchester and Alderton, 2003; Sampson, 2003) and a GLM for seafarers (Alderton, et al., 2004). Historically, international merchant ships were governed by the national-flag registered system in which the flag of the ship registered, and the nationalities of the ship owner, manager and crew, were the same. Since the 1970s, the FOC system has dominated the international shipping industry (Lane, 1996). Under the FOC system, for instance, a UK-owned ship may not be registered by its own flag, instead a foreign flag from Panama is used, which allows the ship owner/manager to recruit qualified, but cheaper seafarers from worldwide labor pools, regardless of the constraints of UK regulations (Alderton, et al., 2004). To date, about two-thirds of world merchant fleets have adopted the FOC system (UNCTAD 2004).

The institutional change symbolized by the flag change has resulted in the development of new seafaring-supply countries in emerging markets (e.g. Philippines, India, China, Ukraine, Russia) to compete with those 'expensive' seafarers from traditional maritime countries (e.g. Greece, Japan, Norway, Germany, UK, Italy) (Lane, 1996; Sampson and Bloor, 2008). As a result, a GLM for seafarers has emerged, but the emergence of this GLM has brought about many challenging issues to labor studies, which were usually territory-based and assuming homogeneity of the seafaring labor force. A typical example is the BIMCO/ISF (2000, 2005) world seafarers' surveys, which assumed that there was no difference with regard to the quality of world seafarers who can move freely across the boundaries of companies, fleets and nationalities. However, there are great variations in terms of maritime education, training and qualification systems between nation-states, and in countries like China which has yet to open its labor market for foreign ship owners and managers.

Using the term 'two-tier employment' in the global economy, Donn (2003) distinguishes two types of labor standards in the world maritime industry: 'upper-tier' and 'lower-tier'. The upper-tier sector refers to those fleets flagged with national flags, which provide the crew with a 'western' standard of living, higher wages, better benefits and better treatment while on board. By contrast, the lower-tier sector consists largely of fleets registered as FOC with little unionisation, less collective bargaining, lower wages and longer working hours. However, Donn has ignored the existence and importance of national fleets in developing countries like China, and also, the complexity of the working conditions of world seafarers in the era of globalization.

Furthermore, in examining the international campaign of the International Transport Workers' Federation (ITF, 2005) against the FOC system, Lillie (2004) categorizes the maritime labor market into three segments according to the use of flags:

1. *Industrial country flags* are well-regulated, well-paid, and covered by national collective agreements (Segment 1);
2. *International flags* (FOC) are usually occupied by low- or mid-wage maritime seafarers (Segment 2);
3. *Developing country flags have their* wages determined by national rather than international standards (Segment 3).

According to Lillie, the aim of the ITF is to prevent ships from moving from Segments 1 and 3 to Segment 2. The ITF has been successful in establishing and promoting an international standard for seafaring wages and labor standards for Segment 2, which is significantly higher than the national standards in Segment 3. By 2004, 6811 vessels will have signed agreements with the ITF to implement international standards of working conditions and wages, representing 45.6 percent of the total number of FOC fleets in the world, in contrast to 29 percent in the early 1990s (ITF, 2005; Koch-Baumgarten, 1998).

Whilst much research has focused on the GLM (Segment 2), little is known about the impact of the GLM on the working conditions, wages and labor mobility of seafarers from developing seafaring supplier countries (Segment 3), some of which may have large national fleets like China. Bearing in mind that the ITF has covered nearly half of the seafarers of the FOC vessels, we are concerned about the other half of seafaring workers, including Chinese seafarers, who work in the GLM without equal treatment. To address this issue, it is important to have an understanding of the division and mobility of world seafarers between global (or FOC) and national labor markets like China.

Divisions of labor for world seafarers: a two-tier model

The establishment of the GLM for seafarers does not mean the dissolution of a national (or 'regional' in the case of EU) border. From a supply perspective, seafarers from emerging market countries have the choice of working for national fleets or foreign companies. From a demand perspective, the cost of crewing is one of many factors which influences ship owners/managers' choice of home or foreign seafarers. It results in a 'double structure' on both the demand- and supply-sides. Though not all seafarers would like to have the chance to work for foreign ships, they can be divided into two groups: 'national (or traditional) seafarers' who prefer to stay in national fleets; and, 'global seafarers' who prefer to work in a multi-cultural environment or multinational crewing pattern (Wu, et al., 2006). In order to lower costs, some international shipping companies have to reserve senior positions for 'home' seafarers and leave the rest for 'foreigners'.

The 'two-tier' model is introduced in this study to take into account the complexity of supply and demand related to national (or regional) identity. In a GLM environment, a UK shipping company can recruit non-EU seafarers in order to reduce the crewing cost, whilst an Indian seafarer may look for a better paid job outside the national fleet. The supply and demand conditions can be satisfied when a global network for recruitment agencies is established. Therefore, a two-tier model is used to deal with the relations between national (or regional) and GLMs, and all qualified seafarers world-wide are categorized into national or global seafarers. The former refers to those who are from the source country, the latter refers to those who work on 'foreign' ships (Figure 3. 1).

Accordingly, the 'two-tier' model consists of seven major points:

1. The world seafaring labor force consists of two types of seafarers: national (or regional) and global;

46 *Bin Wu and Jonathon V. Beaverstock*

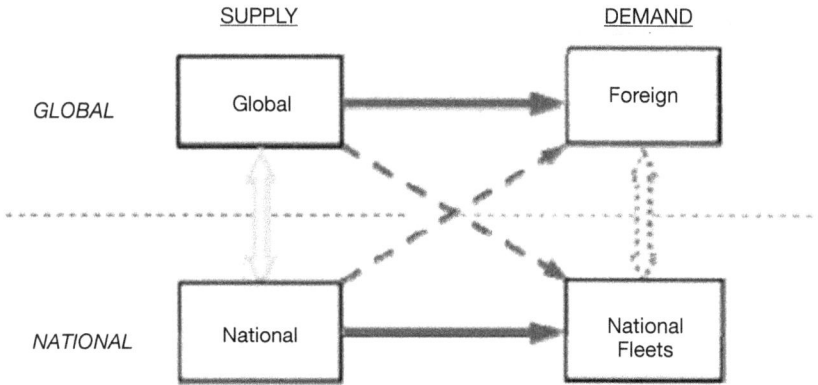

Figure 3.1 The two-tier model: A framework for world seafarer survey

2. A 'national (or regional) border' is recognized by the national identity of a ship defined by the nationality of the ship owner or the country of economic benefit;
3. The distinction between national and global seafarers can be recognized by matching the national identity of the ship;
4. On the supply-side, there are two sources of seafarer employment: nationa-land foreign fleets;
5. On the demand-side, a shipping company can recruit either national or global (foreign) seafarers or both, depending on the regulations and preference of the company;
6. Globalization at seas is related to 'flag change' from national to FOC registra-tion, resulting in the emergence of a new category of seafarers world-wide, 'global seafarers' in the upper-tier, who work on foreign ships;
7. The movement of seafarers between national and global market segments reflects the competition and change in the two labor markets.

The two-tier model is useful in that it provides a conceptual framework: (1) to reflect the seafaring labor market segments in supplier countries like China; (2) to compare the working conditions and wages of seafarers between sectors (national vs. foreign vessels); and (3) to monitor the flow of seafarers across national borders. Applying the two-tier model to SIRC's global seafarer database, Wu (2006) found that 68 percent of the world seafaring labor force work in the GLM and less than one-third (32%) belonged to the national labor market (Table 3. 1)

Furthermore, table 3.1 also shows that the majority of active seafarers in the major supplier countries work in the GLM, with the exceptions of China and Rus-sia whose national fleets have taken over half of the seafaring labor force. This is particularly true for China who accounted for 5.2 percent of the GLM, ranking fourth after the Philippines, India, and Ukraine, in 2003. The participation rate of

Table 3.1 Distribution of seafarers in global and national labor markets (2003)

Rank	Country	% in the GLM	% of seafarers in selected countries
1	Philippines	41.5	98.2
2	India	8.8	89.4
3	Ukraine	7.6	79.0
4	China	5.2	20.5*
5	Russia	4.9	47.1
6	Poland	4.0	91.8
7	Indonesia	3.7	80.4
8	Myanmar	2.7	82.1
9	Romania	2.4	83.1
10	Croatia	2.0	83.3
	Other	17.3	—
—	Total	100.0	68.0

Source: Wu, B. 'Transformation from traditional to global seafarers: an assessment of Chinese seafarers in the global labor market', unpublished speech to the *Shenzhen International Forum for Quality Seafarers*, 19–20 April 2006.

Chinese seafarers in the GLM is 20.5 percent, much lower than the other major emerging market seafaring nations. Many questions arise regarding why China's share in the GLM is so small given its huge population and employment pressure, and its advantages in maritime education and training infrastructure. In Wu and Sampson's (2005) comparison of major seafarer supply countries (China, India, Philippines and Russia), the selected countries can be divided into two groups in terms of participation in the GLM: India and the Philippines have the majority of seafarers (over 85%) participating in the GLM; and, China and Russia, who occupy a smaller proportion (less than 50%) of the total, national seafaring labor force. It is worth noting that Wu and Sampson (2005) also show that Russia has the highest proportion of senior officers (29% compared to China's 14.2%) and the majority of the Filipino seafarers (70%) serve as ratings (compared to China's 58.1%).

Taking into consideration the two-tier labor market and the limited success of the ITF, great variations exist in the working conditions and wages among seafarers from the developing world. This is particularly true for Chinese seafarers who have not joined the ITF, as there exists political tension between the Chinese authorities and the ITF. Consequently, the working conditions and wages of Chinese seafarers are different from their counterparts in other countries. According to the International Shipping Federation (ISF, 2006), Chinese seafarers' working conditions are characterized by long sailing contracts and low wages in the GLM. For example, typical Chinese Chief Officers (C/O) and Able Seamen (AB) earn about half of the median income of the sampled seafarers worldwide, and, undoubtedly, Chinese seafarers earn significantly lower wages than their Indian and Filipino counterparts at either Officer or rating levels (table 3.2).

It is difficult to understand why Chinese seafarers contribute such a small proportion to the GLM when they are so 'low cost' in the GLM, given China's economic development and per capita income are more competitive better than that of India and the Philippines (US$4,300 compared to 4,000 and 2,500 respectively

Table 3.2 Seafarers' wages by nationality and rank (2005, USD/month)

Rank	World average	Indian	Filipinos	Chinese	Chinese/World
Chief Officer	3800	3544	2800	2039	53.7%
Able Seaman	1372	1111	1226	676	49.3%

Source: all data from International Shipping Federation (ISF): *The ISF Year 2005*, except Chinese Able Seaman (from author's survey data).

[Wu and Sampson, 2005]). Such an issue will now be addressed through a discussion of the mobility of Chinese seafarers in the GLM.

The mobility of Chinese seafarers

The emergence of FOC fleets and the 'open policy' in China has made it possible for Chinese seafarers to develop their seafaring careers in the GLM. The number of Chinese seafarers working in the GLM has increased by 331 percent, from 9,733 in 1993 to 42,000 in 2002 (China Coordination for Seamen Employment [COSE], 2005). To understand the growth and constraints of Chinese seafarers in the GLM, it is necessary to take into account the structural change of China's seafaring recruitment and management system. In the 1980s, almost all the ocean seafarers were permanent employees of SOEs. Today, the 'open-policy' has loosened the labor market mechanism in China. On the demand-side, alongside the SOEs (e.g. COSCO, China Shipping), foreign ship owners/managers have become a major source for Chinese seafarer recruitment. However, under the current labor regulations foreign employers cannot directly employ Chinese seafarers. Instead they have to go through a licensed recruitment agency. There are two types of Chinese recruitment agencies involved in seafaring 'labor export' affairs: SOE shipping companies, who send their SOE seafarers to foreign ships; and, independent recruitment agents, who recruit and send 'contract' seafarers to foreign ships. Most Chinese contract seafarers are 'free seamen' who only have short-term contracts (per voyage) with the recruitment agencies to work on foreign ships. A small proportion of them are new graduates from maritime institutes who have to sign a 3 to 5 year contract with the recruitment agents in order to work for foreign shipping companies. The demand for these 'free seamen' has increased, as many private shipping companies have set up in China for international freight business. As a result, a two-segment seafaring labor market which involves national and foreign ships is developing in China. On the supply-side, Chinese seafarers can be categorized by SOEs and contract seafarers. In Wu's (2004) survey of the employment status and working location of Chinese seafarers between national and foreign sectors, it was found that 71 percent (348) of the sample seafarers were SOE employees, of which over one quarter were working for foreign companies. In contrast, only 30 percent (144) were contract seafarers and most of them (over two-thirds) were 'free seamen'.

From this data, we can offer four major insights into China's seafaring labor market. First, Chinese seafarers are increasingly complex and heterogeneous in terms of employment status (SOE employee and contact seafarers) and working locations (on national owned vessels or foreign owned vessels), compared with only one employer (SOE company) and one location (SOE company own fleet) two decades ago. Second, foreign shipping companies provide working opportunities for some SOE employees, and, importantly, new contract seafarers (especially 'free seamen'), which has resulted in a transition from an SOE monopolized system to a two-tiered labor market. Hence, the growth of Chinese exported seafarers to the GLM cannot be separated from the development of contract seafarers in China. Third, the Chinese seafaring labor market is still in its infancy because SOEs are still dominating the Chinese seafaring recruitment and management system, playing a double role of being the ship owners of SOE fleets and recruitment agents for foreign companies. This structure has not only influenced the recruitment and management of Chinese contract seafarers, but also their training and career development in the GLM. Fourth, the two-tiers of labor export are related to each other. The supply of Chinese seafarers is largely determined by the needs and working conditions of SOE fleets, such as China Ocean Shipping Company (COSCO), China Shipping, etc. Under the strong influence of the SOEs, Chinese 'free seamen' are not really free to be employed by foreign companies. This has not only restricted their loyalty to foreign employers, but also impeded the improvement of working conditions and wages in the GLM.

Chinese seafarers are highly mobile between the national and foreign fleet sectors. Taking three voyages as examples, Wu (2004) showed that over two-thirds of SOE seafarers continued working on the national fleet, 15 percent remained in the foreign fleet and 20 percent moved between national and foreign fleets. By contrast, 40 percent of the contract seafarers continued working on the foreign fleets, whilst 46 percent moved between the national and foreign fleets, and for Chinese SOE seafarers, their experience of working on foreign vessels would help their decision to move from SOEs to become 'free seamen'. According to a survey of Chinese freemen registered in the China Maritime Service Centre in 2005 (Wu, 2005), two-thirds of them were previously SOE employees, and 30 percent were fishing workers. Moreover, the mobility of seafarers (leaving SOE companies to become 'free seamen') depends on their educational background and position they hold in that less-educated seafarers tended to leave SOE companies more than highly-educated ones, which confirms that the higher the rank in SOEs, the more difficult for aspiring free seamen to leave the company. The opportunity and need for an GLM has brought about a 525 percent increase in the number of 'free seamen' since 2000, from 4,000 in 2000 to approximately 25,000 in 2007 (Wu, 2005).

Variations in working conditions and wages

The mobility of Chinese seafarers across SOE and foreign labor market segments is closely related to variations in the working conditions and wages between SOE and recruitment agency labor contracts. As Chinese seafarers are not allowed to hold contracts with foreign employers, they must sign a contract with a recruitment agency to gain valid documents to work for a foreign company. The contracts with an agency can be divided into three types:

i. Long-term employment contracts. This type of contract applies to the employees of SOE shipping companies and recruitment agencies as they have long-term contracts with foreign shipping companies to establish a pool of Chinese seafarers for their fleets. They will provide similar wages, welfare and social security benefits as those who work on a national fleet, in accordance with the laws and regulations designated by the government. For example:

> A second officer, has been a seafarer for five years since he graduated from Dalian Maritime University. He entered an SOE shipping company and signed an eight year employment contract and was allocated to the company's labor export sector whose function is to provide seafaring labor services for foreign shipping companies. As a result, he has been working on board a Taiwanese ship and kept his employment as an SOE seafarer. In terms of working conditions, he needs to hand over his seamen book and certificate document to his employer once he completed a sailing contract for the Taiwanese ship. The main difference between the SOE and Taiwanese ship is the workload due to a lower crewing level on the foreign ship, and also more promotion opportunity compared with working on board the SOE company vessel.
>
> (Fieldwork notes).

ii. Long-term tied contracts. This type of contract does not entail any welfare and social security benefits, and restricts the leave of seafarers within the period of contract (3 to 5 years). New university graduates with little bargaining power are usually offered this type of contract. For example:

> On a Norwegian-owned ship, a group of Chinese crew who came from the same crew agency in Shanghai had signed a five year contract with the agency. Unlike an SOE shipping company, however, this agency does neither cover maritime education or training costs, nor provides any welfare and social security whilst aboard the Norwegian vessel
>
> (Fieldwork notes).

iii. Short-term sailing contracts. This type of contract applies to those experienced or high skilled seafarers who do not wish to sign long-term contracts with recruitment agents, as this will limit their mobility in the GLM. It also applies to new or less skilled workers with whom recruitment agencies do not want to sign a long-term contract. All 'free seamen' fall into this category. For example:

> The Chief Engineer has 16 years seafaring experience, with the first seven years as an SOE employee. He decided to leave the company and become a 'free seaman' for two major reasons: to receive a higher wage

and for career development. A seafaring career for a junior professional like himself was limited in the SOE as there was a surplus of seafarers andpriority for promotionwas always given to those who had joined the company earlier. As a 'free seaman', he has served on many foreign ships whose standards of entrance and maintenance for Chinese seafarers are higher than other foreigners. Although he served successfully and was promoted by those companies, he never stayed for more than three sailing contracts. The reason why he was mobile in the GLM was that he had to go through a Chinese crew agency to work for a foreign company every time. If he was satisfied with a foreign company and would like to stay there longer, he needed to sign a contract with the Chinese crew agency every time rather than with a foreign employer directly. To maintain his professional standards and safety records, he prefers to be highly mobile across foreign companies in order to reduce the control and abuse by Chinese crew agencies.

(Fieldwork notes).

In practice, the boundaries for the three types of contract are not always clear. For instance, many SOE employees who have their welfare and social security benefits cut are likely to be Type II contract holders because they are not allowed to take their seamen's book and certificates with them to work for the foreign shipping companies unless their SOE employers send them. In addition, the same recruitment agency may sign different contracts with different crew: some can enjoy welfare and social security benefits (Type I) whilst some cannot (Type II). Many free seamen were asked to sign a long-term service contract with the recruitment agency before they were sent to a foreign ship. At the end of a voyage, however, the signed contract cannot impede their movement, as the agent is unable to detain their personal documents and certificates. In general, 'free seamen' have a higher wage than the agent-tied seafarers, who in turn have a higher wage than the employment contract holders. Moreover, long-term employed contract holders (SOE or agent-owned seafarers) are entitled to other welfare and social security benefits paid by the SOE companies or agencies. This is in contrast to 'free seamen' who cannot enjoy these benefits. The differences among the three types of contract need to be examined carefully because in most cases, welfare and social security can be compensated by higher wages. For the purpose of this chapter, the term contract seafarer refers to both Type II and Type III labor contract holders.

There are great variations in the wages of Chinese seafarers. Seafarers of the same rank in the same recruitment agency may receive different wages due to different pay schemes offered by different shipping companies. Similarly, seafarers employed by different recruitment agencies may receive different wages although they have the same ship owner offering the same pay package. The variations in wages are identified at three levels: (i) income difference in different sectors, but with the same employer (e.g. two SOE seafarers with the same job title and working experience may receive different wages due to working on an SOE vessel and aforeign-owned ship, respectively); (ii) income difference due to different recruitment agencies (e.g. agency-employed seafarers and 'free seamen' working for the same foreign ship); and, (iii) income difference between Chinese and other national crew members working on the same ship with the same job title.

Wu (2007) illustrates the income differences of a sample of Chinese seafarers in different sectors, and between Chinese seafarers and other nationalities in the GLM in table 3.3. For instance, despite the same type, size and freight route, exported seafarers who are SOE employees, but working on foreign ship can earn 35 percent more than their counterparts on company vessels. The difference in pay for employees in the same company reflects the labor market situation and also the difference in the skills required. Officers for foreign ships are required to have better English writing and communication skills than their counterparts on company owned fleet. Table 3.3 also shows that 'free seamen' can earn more than SOE exported seafarers, as the former do not have any welfare and social security benefits. The wage difference between Chinese and other nationalities (world average) in the GLM can be explained by the low-cost strategy of Chinese recruitment agencies and in some cases the discriminatory attitudes of international ship owners and managers towards Chinese seafarers.

There is a significant gap between the actual wage a Chinese seafarer receives and the expenditure a foreign ship owner allocates in preparing contract documentation. It is stipulated by Chinese labor regulations that pensions, medical and other social security benefits should be included. In order to comply with the current national regulations, it is lawful for Chinese recruitment agencies to reserve a proportion, up to 25 percent of a Chinese seafarer's wage for this purpose. Most recruitment agents take fees from the seafarer wage every month on top of the fees charged to the foreign ship company, but it is not clear how these sums are used. Some of them may use this money to pay seafarers' pensions and insurance, and also, the expenses incurred in preparing documents, medical examinations, training and onshore break wages. Taking an SOE company as an example, the onshore break wage ranges from 1,200 Yuan (US$150)/month for Captain to 800 Yuan (US$100)/month for a rating, in 2006. All contract seafarers, however, do not receive any benefits from the recruitment agents, and, therefore, need to pay all expenses themselves (pension, insurance for example). In this case, all sums deducted become part of the profit of the recruitment agencies. Compared with the small administrative fees charged to the recruitment agency (normally less than

Table 3.3 Wages by labor market segmentations (US$/month)

Rank	National	Exported	Freemen	World average
Captain	2505	3400	4072	6135
C/O	1544	1861	2607	4495
2/O	1068	1230	1701	2473
3/O	846	1037	1416	2108

Source: A combination of two tables from author's survey data.

US$ 100/month), the sum extracted from a contract seafarer's wage may be three times or more, a major source of seafaring recruitment income.

Our research findings illustrate the scale of sums taken from the Chinese crew (table 3.4). Five significant observations can be made from this data. First, the agent's sum provides an important source of income for the agency as each crew member contributes US$300 on average each month, which exceeds the need for social security contributions. In fact, most, if not all, crew members are 'free sea-men', and the agent is not expected to make this contribution to their welfare and social security benefits. Second, the allotment system has a significant impact on seafarers' actual income, as these fees account for nearly one quarter of a seafar-er's wage, and nearly 40 percent in some ranks. Third, as a lesser amount is taken from higher-rank crew members, this is leading to an increased wage gap between the Captain and AB (able seamen) from 3.53 times to 5.36 times. Furthermore, many senior officers expressed their concern in the interview about the negative impact of the income gap between senior officers and ratings. In addition, recent research into Chinese consumers' perception of income and reward suggests that as the wealth gap grows between 'the haves' and 'the have nots', the wealthy become even more expectant and even selfish in their attitude towards ever-higher income and reward (Yu, et al., 2009).

Fourth, the wage scheme and agent allotment policy are not made transparent to crew members. Thus, most Chinese seafarers are unaware of the wage package the foreign ship owner offers and how much the agents take from them. Fifth, quite often more than one recruitment agency is involved in the recruitment process, resulting in a long-chain between the ship owner and seafarers, and the longer the supply-chain, the lower the seafarers' wages.

The complexity of opening up the Chinese labor market

Due to the continuous expansion of international merchant fleets and the shortage of a world seafaring labor force, Chinese seafarer wages have continued to rise in recent years. The growth rate, however, varies greatly with company and rank. Our research shows the contrast of Chinese crew-wage growth in two foreign-owned ships visited, belonging to two foreign shipping companies (table 3.5). For

Table 3.4 Extraction of agent allotment from seafaring wages (2006)

Rank	Total wage	Agent allotment	Actual income	Agent taking (%)
Captain	3158	208	2950	6.6
C/O	2039	89	1950	4.4
2/O	1632	382	1250	23.4
3/O	1574	574	1000	36.5
Bosun	1000	300	700	30.0
AB	895	345	550	38.5
Total	*27414*	*6464*	*20950*	*23.6*
AB: captain	*3.53*	—	*5.36*	—

Source: First author's fieldwork on board survey in 2007. There are a total of 22 crew members.

Ship A, only senior officers (including Captain, Chief Officer, Chief Engineer and 2nd Engineer) and some junior officers (2nd Officer and 3rd Engineer) enjoyed income growth of 19 percent to 24 percent compared with the previous year. There was a decrease of actual income earned for other ranks and, in particular, all ratings due to a drop in the foreign currency exchange rate. As a result, the income gap between AB and Captain was further widened from 4.14 times in 2006 to 5.1 times in 2007. By contrast, Ship B adopted a totally different structure to deal with Chinese crew wages. Instead of focusing on the welfare of the senior officers, all ranks received a wage increase of about 30 percent. After the wage adjustment, the Chinese crew of Ship B enjoyed the highest seafaring wage amongst Chinese contract seafarers, whilst the wage gap between AB and Captain was kept constant at 3.7 times (table 3.5).

Interestingly, our findings represent two different approaches to Chinese seafarers in the GLM (table 3.5). Ship B's structure is closer to the working conditions of the regulated GLM, in which senior officers and ratings are treated equally as international counterparts. This is in contrast to Ship A which remunerates on the shortage of officers in general, and the welfare of senior officers in particular. Compared with Ship B, Ship A represents the mainstream of the Chinese seafaring labor market, characterized by different segmentations, unregulated operations and inequality between officers and ratings in wage and welfare.

The inequality between senior officers and ratings on foreign ships was more serious than the data revealed (table 3.5). In Ship A, for instance, an ordinary seaman (OS) got only $600/month for the first contract instead of getting $735/month for his rank, then $650 for the second contract, and subsequently $700 for the third and fourth contracts. The OS cannot receive the full wage of $735 until the fifth contract. In addition, the OS earned only $300 out of the total $600 monthly wage for the first three months being a new seafarer joining this agency. In contrast, the senior officers were treated favorably. They were awarded 'seniority bonus' (to Captain, Chief Engineer, Chief Officer and 2nd Engineer), amounting to US$100

Table 3.5 A comparison of seafarers' wage and growth pattern

Rank	Ship A			Ship B		
	2006	*2007*	*%*	*2006*	*2007*	*%*
Captain	3703	4604	24.3	4002	5200	29.9
C/O	2500	3101	24.0	2707	3510	29.7
2/O	1600	1900	18.8	1905	2470	29.7
3/O	1471	1471	0	1609	2080	29.3
Bosun	1040	1051	1.1	1192	1547	29.8
AB	895	902	0.8	1072	1383	29.0
AB: Capt.	*4.14*	*5.1*	—	*3.73*	*3.76*	—

Source: First author's fieldwork onboard survey in 2007.

Notes: in this table, national and exported seafarers are SOE employees but working on different ships: national ones on company owned vessel while exported seafarers work on the foreign ship.

in the first year, $200 in the second year and $500 in the fifth year accordingly. Differing from Ship B, furthermore, 20 percent of the crew wage of Ship A was kept by the agency as a deposit until they completed the voyage satisfactorily. This is in quite common amongst Chinese recruitment agencies. Interestingly, all crew members of Ship A had signed Type II contracts with the recruitment agency. That means they do not have any welfare and social security benefits. In contrast, the majority of crew members on Ship B were 'free seamen' who were recruited by three different recruitment agencies.

These differences are rooted in the different mechanisms of interaction between the foreign ship owner, recruitment agents and Chinese seafarers. For Ship A, there is almost no direct communication between the employer and the crew. The crew of Ship A were unaware of how much the foreign employer had actually paid to them. In addition, a senior officer complained that he had never received any commendation even when his team had performed very well. In contrast, Ship B encouraged all ranks of the crew to commit to the company. They were offered an enhanced pay scheme, bonus and benefits and, importantly, their efforts and achievements in ship management and maintenance were acknowledged.

Ships A and B represent two types of employment relationship. For Ship A, there was a lack of commitment and trust between the company and the crew as the recruitment agency played an overwhelmingly dominant role. In contrast, the role of the recruitment agent for Ship B was reduced to a minimum. The company had set up an office in China to deal with all recruitment matters before submitting the final documents to the agent. Therefore, the agent in this case can only charge the administrative fees. Undoubtedly, most Chinese seafarers would welcome this form of system because they can gain benefits from the ship company directly. Such an employment structure in Ship B is better labelled 'semi-direct employment' compared with the indirect employment pattern of Ship A. Due to the current labor market regulations in China, foreign employers have to pay their Chinese business partners for the loyalty of the Chinese crew to the shipping company. This empirical study indicates clearly the economic benefits of the new structure adopted by Ship B. In the future, it is expected that Chinese seafarers will be employed more by foreign employers directly, which has become a common practice of the GLM for other nationalities.

The semi-direct employment structure adopted by Ship B is not unique as many foreign shipping companies have set up their offices in China, representing a new phase in the Chinese seafaring labor market, in which Chinese seafarers have more opportunity to communicate with the representatives of foreign employers. As the Chinese contract seafarers are obtaining more benefits from such opportunities there may be strong resistance from the Chinese recruitment agents, who will try to block direct interaction between the Chinese seafarers and foreign employers. For example, COSE has criticized a Singaporean company for contacting and recruiting Chinese seafarers through a semi-employment pattern similar to that of Ship B. The high profile of the Chinese authority suggests that there is still a long way for China to further open its labor market, which has significant impact on the working conditions and wages of Chinese seafarers in the GLM.

Conclusion

This chapter has revealed the impact of the GLM for seafarers on the mobility and working conditions of Chinese contract seafarers. By couching the study in segmented labor markets and bringing original empirical evidence from different sources, the study has shown a complicated and evolutionary picture of Chinese seafarers in work with both national, SOE, and foreign ships. To address the research issues posited at the outset of this chapter, five major conclusions are drawn from this unique empirical study.

First, globalization at sea, which is symbolized by the popularity of the FOC system and the GLM for seafarers, has had, and continues to have, a profound impact not only on Chinese seafarers' perspectives towards employment, working conditions and career development, but also on the national seafaring resource and management system. The most salient change is the emergence of a two-tier labor market structure in China in relation to the supply and demand of Chinese seafarers. Whilst SOE and foreign ship owners/managers are competing to recruit a high-quality labor force, Chinese seafarers are no longer homogenous but increasingly heterogeneous in terms of employment relations, professional perspectives and preferences, etc. As it has been discussed, Chinese seafarers can be broadly divided into two types according to the nature of their contracts: SOE employees; and, 'free seamen'. The former, including those agent-owned seafarers, have a long-term contract with the SOE shipping company or recruitment agent, and they are entitled to all welfare and social security benefits stipulated under the national regulations. The latter, representing the majority of contract seafarers, have only short-term contracts with recruitment agents in order to access and work for foreign shipping companies. Compared with the former, the latter are likely to obtain a higher wage with little welfare and social security benefits. Between the above two categories, there are many contract seafarers who are tied by recruitment agents without any welfare and social security benefits.

Second, the emergence of a two-tier labor market structure in China has resulted in two types of mobility amongst Chinese seafarers: A) movement across the boundaries between national and foreign fleets without any change of their employment status; B) moving from SOE employees to 'free seamen'. Evidence has shown that these two types of mobility are interwoven. On the one hand, the successful experience of many SOE employees working on foreign ships provides a sound basis for the later decision to become 'free seamen'. On the other hand, many SOE seafarers try to find opportunities boarding foreign vessels before making any decision about changing employment status to be a 'free seaman'. As working for foreign companies is getting more popular amongst Chinese seafarers, the labor market has witnessed a significant expansion of 'free seamen' since 2000.

Third, the shift from being an SOE employee to a 'free seaman' is driven by a higher wage and low welfare system in the GLM. This conflicts with the current labor regulations, which require all SOE companies and recruitment agencies to take responsibility for the welfare of Chinese contract seafarers, at least the same as those working on a national fleet. Whilst some recruitment agencies do comply with the national regulations, most may not and this results in competition between recruitment agencies and great variations in seafaring wages amongst Chinese seafarers.

Fourth, the two-tier labor market structure has challenged the national seafaring resource and management system in which SOE shipping companies are still dominant. Furthermore, SOE companies are playing a double role, as ship owners of national fleets and recruitment agencies for foreign shipping companies, which have impeded the development of an effective regulation system targeted at contract seafarers for the GLM. As a result, unsurprisingly, Chinese seafarers are vulnerable to various labor exploitations, including long-term tied contracts, various deposits and a double charge to both foreign companies and Chinese seafarers, taking part of a seafarer's income which then becomes part of an agent's profits rather than social security inputs.

Fifth, in relation to the progress of economic and social reforms in China, there is still a long way for China to go in terms of opening its seafaring labor market to foreign shipping companies. The lack of communication between Chinese seafarers and foreign companies is a major barrier for their career development in the GLM. Nonetheless, it is encouraging to see that more and more foreign companies are based in China. Given the fact that a global labor governance framework has been established for the international shipping industry, the mobility of Chinese seafarers in employment, coupled with the development of independent trade union, can certainly help to raise their working conditions to international standards.

Returning to the broader labor market segmentation frameworks, the research findings illustrate very clearly the precarious nature of Chinese seafarers in the secondary and, or external segments of the GLM (using Doeringer and Piore's term, 1971), particularly those 'exported' SOE employees and 'free seamen' on foreign ships. Of greater significance, however, are the two factors which manipulate the Chinese seafarers' labor market, which are not discussed at great length in conventional dualist approaches: the role of the state; and labor market intermediaries, like recruitment agencies. In China, the state still has a strong hand in the functioning of the planned economy, and our evidence of SOE employees exemplifies how the state can still control and regulate Chinese seafarers on national fleets, which, depending on rank and seniority, can place them in both primary and secondary segments of the labor market. In contrast, the 'gate-keeping' effect of recruitment agencies, with their precarious employment practices, categorize Chinese 'free seamen' into a secondary (and external) labor market segment, where all contracted labor has minimal terms and conditions of work, and are penalized (through allotments to agencies) for employment outside of the SOE system. As China continues to have tight regulations concerning the business activities of foreign firms in the country, particularly in contractual relationships with Chinese labor, Chinese recruitment agencies will continue to play an active intermediating role in the structure and articulation of segmented labor markets for Chinese seafarers, whether SOE employees on national or foreign fleets, or contracted 'free seamen' on foreign ships.

Note

1 It is quite normal in the international shipping industry that a ship owner or management company who control or manage a fleet (number of ships) may not have their own contracted seafarers. Instead, they may sign a contract with one or many recruitment agencies in different countries to secure the supply of seafarers to meet specific labor market shortages at any particular time. This has resulted in many recruitment agencies emerging in major seafarer supply countries like the Philippines, India and East Europe.

Bibliography

Alderton, T., Blood, M., Kahveci, E., Lane, T., Sampson, H., Thomas, M., Winchester, N., Wu, B., Zhao, M., (2004), *The Global Seafarers: Living and Working Conditions in a Globalized Industry*, Geneva: International Labor Office

Baltic and International Maritime Council with International Shipping Federation (BIMCO/ISF), (2000; 2005), *Manpower Updates: The Worldwide Demand for and Supply of Seafarers*, published by BIMCO/ISF every five years

Beck, U., (2000), *The Brave New World of Work*, Cambridge: Polity

Castells, M., (1998), *The Information Age Volume III: End of Millennium*, Oxford: Blackwell

China Coordination for Seamen Employment (COSE, 2005), 'A letter to ASP Shipping Group about the regulations of Chinese exported seafarers', September 6, http://chinca. mofcom. gov. cn/aarticle/xuehuidongtai/200509/20050900358820.html

Doeringer, P., Piore, M., (1971), *Internal Labor Markets and Manpower Analysis*, Lexington, Mass.: D C Heath.

Donn, C. B., (2003), 'Two-tiered employment in the global economy: The world maritime industry', *Institute of Industrial Relations Research Paper*, No 24, http://www. lemoyne. edu/library/mgmt_wp/wp2002-002.pdf

Edwards, R. C., Reich, M., Gordon, D. M., (1975), *Labor Market Segmentation*. Lexington Mass.: D C Heath

Glen, D., (2008), 'What do we know about the labor market for seafarers? A view from the UK', *Marine Policy*, 32, 12: 845–855

Hayter, P., Barnes, T., (1992) 'Labor market segmentation, flexibility, and recession: a British Columbian case study', *Environment and Planning C*, 10, 3: 333–353

International Organisation (ILO), (2006), *Maritime Labor Convention*, Geneva: ILO

International Shipping Federation (ISF), (2006), *The ISF Year 2005*, London: ISF

International Transport Workers Federation (ITF, 2005) 'The 2004 Annual Report of the ITF's campaign against flags of convenience and substandard shipping', London: ITF, http://www. itfglobal.org/infocentre/pubs.cfm/detail/1324

Johnston, W. B., (1991), 'Global work force 2000: the new world labor market', *Harvard Business Review*, March–April Issue: 115–127

Koch-Baumgarten, S., (1998), 'Trade union regime formation under the conditions of globalization in the transport sector: attempts at transnational trade union regulation of flag-of-convenience shipping', *International Review of Social History*, 42, 3: 369–402

Lane, T., (1996), 'The social order of the ship in a globalized labor market for seafarers', in Crompton, R., Gallie, D, Purcell, K. (eds) *Changing Forms of Employment*, London: Routledge, 83–106

Leontaridi, M. R., (1998), Segmented labor markets: Theory and evidence', *Journal of Economic Surveys*, 12, 1: 63–100

Li, K., Wonham, J., (1999), 'Who mans the world fleet?' *Maritime Policy and Management*, 26, 3: 295–303

Lillie, N., (2004), 'Global collective bargaining on flag of convenience shipping', *British Journal of Industrial Relations*, 42, 1: 47–67

Munck, R., (2002), *Globalization and Labor: the New 'Great Transformation*, London, New York: Zed Books.

Sampson, H., (2003), 'Transnational drifters or hyperspace dwellers: an exploration of the lives of Filipino seafarers aboard and ashore', *Ethnic and Racial Studies*, 26, 2: 253–277

Sampson, H., Bloor, M., (2008), 'When Jack gets out of the box: The problems of regulating a global industry', *Sociology*, 41, 3: 551–569

Sampson, H., Schroder, T., (2006), 'In the wake of the wave: globalization, networks, and the experiences of transmigrant seafarers in northern Germany', *Global Networks*, 6 (1): 61–80

Seafarers International Research Centre (SIRC), (2003), *Global Labor Market Database*, Cardiff: Cardiff University,

Storper, M., Walker, R., (1989), *The Capital Imperative*, Oxford: Blackwell

Winchester, N, Alderton, T., (2003), *Flag State Audit*, Cardiff: Cardiff University, SIRC

Wu, B., (2004), 'Participation in the global labor market: experience and responses of Chinese seafarers', *Maritime Policy and Management*, 31,1: 69–72

Wu, B. 2005. 'Chinese seafarers in transition: trends and evidence', the Seafarers International Research Centre's Fourth International Symposium. Cardiff University, 7th July, online: www.sirc.cf.ac.uk/symp.html

Wu, B., (2006), 'Transformation from traditional to global seafarers: an assessment of Chinese seafarers in the global labor market', unpublished speech to the Shenzhen International Forum for Quality Seafarers, 19–20 April (available from the author)

Wu, B., (2007), 'Vulnerability of Chinese contract workers abroad: A case of the working conditions and wages of Chinese seafarers', an unpublished paper presented to ICAS 5 Conference, 3 August, 2007, Kuala Lumpur (available from the author)

Wu, B., and Sampson, H., (2005), 'Reconsidering the cargo sector and seafarer labor market: a 21st century profile of global seafarers', *Ocean Yearbook*, No. 19, Chicago: University of Chicago Press, 357–380

Wu, B., Lai, K. H., Cheng, T. C., (2006), "Emergence of 'new professionalism' amongst Chinese seafarers: empirical evidences and policy implications", *Maritime Policy & Management*, 33, 1: 35–48

United Nations Conference on Trade and Development (UNCTAD, 2004), *Review of Maritime Transport, 2004,* New York and Geneva: United Nations

Yu, Z., Bastin, M., Wang, D. (2009), 'Perhaps Moliere was right? To be richer is to be more miserly', *Journal of Social Behaviour and Personality*, 37, 6

Zhao, M., (2002), 'The consequences of China's socialist market economy for seafarers', *Work, Employment and Society*, 16, 1: 171–183

4   Hidden in plain sight: Chinese victims of transnational trafficking to the UK[1]

Jackie Sheehan

Introduction

This chapter explores the experiences of Chinese victims of transnational trafficking to the UK. The general increase in out-migration from China over the past 30 years and especially since the late 1990s, the emergence of new 'sending' areas beyond the traditional ones (Skeldon, 2007), and the expansion of Chinese business and Chinese communities into new parts of the world, have created larger and more diverse streams of Chinese migration that can now truly be termed global. It is under cover of these streams of willing and informed migrants, documented and undocumented, that trafficking takes place of individuals who have been deceived about the terms and destination of their migration. UK government statistics show that Chinese citizens form one of the largest groups of transnational trafficking victims by nationality (UKHTC, 2011), and offer some support for the view of the stereotypical Chinese victim as a young woman trafficked into the sex industry. However, using a sample of 48 victims (43 women and 5 men) from 2007 to 2011,[2] my research shows that there is a wider range of Chinese victims ending up in the UK in terms of age, gender, employment destination, and even immigration status, than is often supposed. Four brief case studies are presented here in order to illustrate this range of experience. Drawing on the experiences of the whole sample of victims, I argue that trafficking should be located within the context of arranged migration out of China, and that rather than there being clearly identifiable individuals who are exclusively traffickers, it is often more a case of identifying exploitative and controlling relationships between agents and willing but deceived migrants that can be defined as trafficking.

Much academic writing on trafficking into the UK seeks to downplay both the total number of victims and the proportion of migrants who can be classed as having been trafficked, and this is especially true when it comes to research on migrants working in the sex industry in the UK. Unfounded and sensationalized media reports of upsurges in trafficking for sexual exploitation around major international events, such as the 2006 World Cup in Germany, have been shown to have little basis in fact (Hsu, 2011), and scholarly research has emphasized the small proportion of migrant sex workers in London who regard themselves as having been exploited, deceived and/or coerced into that work (Mai, 2011).

I certainly do not regard all of those who end up working in the sex industry as victims of deception, coercion or exploitation, rather than as migrants making rational choices among the limited employment options open to them in the UK. I have no personal or political agenda with reference to the sex industry per se, but in my sample, there are clear-cut cases of women who were deceived and coerced into sex work in the UK, as well as number of cases of minors who by definition did not consent to performing the sex work they ended up doing in the UK, although I have not ventured an estimate of the relative percentages of those willingly engaged in sex work and those coerced into it, as I simply do not have the data with which to do this. What I can prove from my sample is that in addition to the 'typical' cases of the trafficking of women and girls into the sex industry, of which there are plenty, there are also cases of trafficking for domestic servitude and forced labour, with victims ending up in any form of employment in the UK where Chinese migrants are to be found; cases of the trafficking of teenage boys and men; and even one case where a Chinese migrant who had a valid work visa for the UK ended up being trafficked and re-trafficked into unpaid work in coercive conditions.

An overview of human trafficking from China to the UK

The performance of every country in the world in combating human trafficking is monitored in the annual US State Department Trafficking in Persons (TIP) Report (USSD, 2011). The efforts being made against trafficking by the Chinese government have been recognized in successive TIP Reports, and China has implemented a National Action Plan to Combat Trafficking (NAPCT) for 2008–2012 (State Council of China, 2007) which has improved procedures for the identification and support of domestic trafficking victims. The Chinese police estimate there to be about 20,000 of these per year, while other agencies involved with victims put it at around 50,000 per year. But there are also weaknesses in the PRC's anti-trafficking programmes: Chinese law does not recognize men or boys aged over 14 as victims of trafficking; China's claims of thousands of trafficking prosecutions include offences, such as child abduction for adoption, which do not fall within the international definition of trafficking (broadly, the use of force, fraud, or coercion to exploit a person for profit); and China has been unable to prove that much headway is being made against official complicity in trafficking. Louise Shelley points out that moving individuals across national borders without the correct documentation is intrinsically difficult to do, and cannot be accomplished without a degree of complicity at some stage of the process (Shelley, 2010: 6), while the general problem of police and government complicity in the activities of organized crime in China is well documented (Zhang and Chin, 2008; Chin and Godson, 2006).

The final weakness of the first NAPCT is that it has offered almost nothing for Chinese citizens who were transnationally trafficked. Apart from some dedicated facilities serving China's borders with Burma, Thailand and Vietnam, transnational trafficking victims never gain access even to the few shelters in the PRC which cater specifically for victims of trafficking. These shelters provide no counselling or psychological support and only permit domestic victims to stay for a short period of time, after which they are supposed to rely on their families, and will be returned home even if family members were implicated in their trafficking. Compared to the likely total of about 50,000 domestic victims of trafficking per year, it is impossible to make a useful estimate of the scale of transnational trafficking. All we can tell from the available evidence is that it seems to be increasing and to be reaching new parts of the world, such as Africa (*Modern Ghana News*, 2009), as an inevitable corollary of the global reach and growing scale of international Chinese business activity and migration. Shelley (2010: 7, 37) points out that the combination of rising demand for cheap, flexible (some would say disposable) migrant labour in developed economies along with ever-tighter restrictions on legal migration is inherently criminogenic, as undocumented migrants will fill labour demand which cannot be met legally, and this constant stream of undocumented migrants is the perfect cover for trafficking into EU countries, including the UK.

One of the drawbacks of victim-centred research on trafficking is that victims can only give information on those parts of the operation with which they have come into contact. They may know how much their immediate employer is earning from forcing them to work for little or no money, but they will probably not know for how much money they have been bought and sold within the UK, or to what extent someone higher up is profiting from their exploitation. Louise Shelley (2003) found that trafficking out of China was 'conducted not only by small networks but is often part of a highly organized trade that delivers individuals across continents. A recent analysis by Interpol of the different telephone logs connected with Chinese smugglers in different cities in Europe revealed a very different business structure than that observed by local European law enforcement. While the police in each city thought they were observing a small smuggling organization, in fact all these groups were merely cells of a larger network that all reported back to a single major human smuggler in China. Using data provided by the U.S. law enforcement, Interpol discovered that the same crime boss ran the smuggling rings on different continents.' (Shelley, 2003: 121)

A more recent ILO publication also cautions against assuming no links between the small groups or networks discovered by police and much more extensive organizations, pointing out that the trade is deliberately organized so that discovered groups cannot implicate those higher up the chain, even though it is possible for local recruiters to have links to those who ultimately profit most from people-smuggling and trafficking (Li 2010: 25–26; Gao and Poisson, 2010: 45–46). The UK police's Child Exploitation and Online Protection (CEOP) Centre in successive reports (CEOP 2009; CEOP 2010) found Chinese transnational trafficking networks to be the best organized and most sophisticated ones in operation. Other work on the structure of trafficking organizations, without necessarily contradicting Shelley, places more emphasis on the fluidity and flexibility of the typical network, rather than the existence of a top leadership, and on its fitness for purpose with regard to transnational trafficking. Analysts of Chinese organized crime identify different organizational forms of ethnic Chinese criminal groups in different markets, noting that for inherently transnational activities such as human trafficking, money laundering, and drug smuggling, networks which are 'horizontally structured, fluid, and opportunistic' (Chin, 2009: 232), or 'cellular' rather than hierarchical (Wong, 2007: 133), are the dominant form, resembling legitimate Chinese business networks more than they do the traditional, hierarchical Hong Kong or Taiwanese Triads. This supports my finding that 'traffickers' may actually be legitimate migration agents some of the time, but ready to traffick suitably vulnerable people when the opportunity arises, and with the connections to, for example, suppliers of fake passports that enable them to do it. It should be noted, therefore, that 'opportunistic' trafficking out of China is not necessarily small-scale, ad hoc, or unconnected with emerging organized-crime networks, although, as Chin (2009: 231–2) found with much drug trafficking involving ethnic Chinese businesspeople, it is not Triad activity as that would be traditionally understood.

The accounts of the individuals in my sample of their migration journeys tally closely with other research on how undocumented migrants are moved from China to the EU, describing networks of facilitators with different roles ('recruiters, gang leaders, harbourers, and guides' (Gao and Poisson, 2010: 45), access to safe houses (Gao and Poisson, 2010: 45–6; Pieke, 2010: 150–52) across a number of countries, and able to procure multiple false travel documents for numbers of victims on different routes to the UK. Generally speaking, the longer a migration journey from China to the EU takes, the more dangerous it is, with a high risk of women in particular suffering physical and sexual violence, and sometimes sexual exploitation, over a period of months or even years. Ceccagno, et al. confirm that instances of rape of Chinese women are common (Ceccagno, et al., 2010: 103), while Gao and Poisson (2010, 46–50) report that migrants travelling overland are typically robbed of their few possessions by successive people escorting or guarding them in a process of repeated 'assault and humiliation in transit', as well as risking death through accident or illness because of the harsh conditions of their journey. A Chinese migrant who eventually reached Italy reported that two who attempted to escape from an Istanbul safe house were badly beaten by their smugglers in front of the other migrants, and that they were shown a gun to dissuade them from further resistance (Ceccagno, et al., 2010: 103), and migrants to the UK also report sexual abuse of women, as well as violence (Pieke, 2010: 150–152).

Rape en route to the UK or on arrival is not only a way of preparing female victims for work in the sex industry (it was the very first sexual experience of a number of the young women in my sample), but also a way of isolating and controlling female victims generally. An agent knows that a Chinese woman who has been raped will feel desperately ashamed of the experience and will above all not want anyone else to know about it (Chan, 2009; Gil and Anderson, 1999). Thus rape makes a victim even less likely to try to seek help, reinforcing her dependence on her traffickers. Often a trafficker will maintain a benign appearance and treat victims well over the first stages of a journey, before dropping the pretence once they are too far from China to be able to return on their own, especially as they have no money, only have their travel documents or tickets in their hands when passing through border controls, and may not even know which country they are in. The shock of this sudden change in demeanour, with a formerly benevo-lent 'uncle' turning cold, cruel, and often physically abusive, seems to knock any remaining confidence in their own judgement and ability to affect events out of many victims. The way in which traffickers inculcate dependency and obedience in their victims, virtually brainwashing them into fearing authority figures and even social workers in transit and destination countries, is reminiscent of the kind of control exercised by perpetrators over victims of long-term domestic abuse. The more obvious means of guards, locked doors, violence and withholding of food and drink are not always needed to ensure that trafficking victims remain under their exploiters' control.

As already noted, a trafficker will sometimes assume the 'benevolent uncle' pose to 'groom' a victim, especially a young, female one, presenting himself as a benefactor making arrangements for her to work abroad with no thought of per-sonal reward. With orphaned or left-behind children in China, a trafficker may pose as an old friend of deceased or absent parents in order to assert quasi-familial authority over the victim and to convince them that he/she is acting in their best interests. There is some evidence from among my sample of cases that Chinese government campaigns warning about the dangers of being trafficked have had some effect, as several victims, or their parents, reported being wary at first of an agent who eventually trafficked them, and trying to be careful in choosing a migration agent, not accepting the first offer they received. But traffickers have a nose for vulnerability in all its forms, as my sample of cases shows: former street children, orphans, abandoned and left-behind children, many of whom experi-enced physical and/or sexual abuse in the informal foster-care arrangements in which their absent parents left them; victims of domestic violence; teenagers orphaned and made homeless simultaneously by the 2008 Sichuan earthquake; and individuals who were desperate to leave China after a family member got into trouble with the authorities. One trafficker even reassured an orphaned 16-year-old victim by joking 'Don't worry, I'm not going to sell you!' before selling her to a massage parlour as soon as they arrived in London.

All Chinese who migrate abroad use an agent. There are legitimate migration agents who will only move clients who qualify for a work, business or study visa; there are also agents ('snakeheads') who smuggle undocumented migrants with fake papers, for a higher fee than qualified migrants need to pay (from ¥80,000 to ¥400,000, depending on the circumstances (Pieke and Xiang, 2007: 10; Li, 2010: 28)); and there are traffickers, who ask for little or no money up front, making vague assurances that their victims can pay them back once earning abroad, when in fact they intend to exploit the victim at the destination, sometimes en route as well, to earn a sum in the same range as that charged by snakeheads. Some agents offer only one of these three kinds of migration, but others are engaged in two or all three of them. This means that there are apparently legitimate agents in China, with per-manent offices, telephone land lines, and glossy advertising handed out in public, who will smuggle clients who do not qualify for legal migration, and who are also prepared to deceive and exploit through trafficking vulnerable clients who cannot obtain a valid visa and cannot pay the kind of fees required to be smuggled abroad.

This significantly undermines the effectiveness of campaigns to scare potential victims away from the 'bad' agents, as some of those involved in trafficking run legitimate businesses as well. We can tell that it is not simply a case of individuals within a legitimate agency tipping off traffickers about vulnerable clients; to obtain a valid UK work visa for a Chinese migrant, an agent must specify the UK employer of that migrant, so if a woman with a valid work visa ends up being trafficked into domestic servitude in the UK, the only possible conclusion is that a legitimate agency was complicit in trafficking. The intermingling of legally facilitated, smuggled, and trafficked migrants under the control of the same people and along the same routes makes it even more difficult to detect victims of trafficking. It might be the case that an agent puts together a group of seven or eight migrants to leave China for a third country before travelling on to the EU, often providing them with new clothes, luggage, and even hair-cuts so that they can pass for Korean, Japanese, or Hong Kongers, and for one or two in the group to be trafficked, as they are not able to pay any fee for the agent's services, while the others are willing clients of the same agent and, once the final instalment of their fee is paid on their arrival in the UK, need have no further dealings with him. With victims of trafficking, however, the agent has received little or no money up front, and intends to earn it back through exploitation. To earn the equivalent of what snakeheads charge takes several years here, even in the sex industry, but a greater danger emerges if a trafficking victim is discovered and sent back to China before a trafficker or buyer has had his money's worth, as it would take literally more than a lifetime to earn the same amount there (Gao and Poisson, 2010: 53–4).

Case study 1: Nina,[3] Sichuan Province

Nina's case is one of a number in my sample which fit the image of a 'typical' Chinese trafficking victim, the teenager sold into sex work in the UK. She was recruited at 18 from a poor family in Sichuan. Initially the family planned for her father to migrate, but the agent who recruited her convinced them that it was easier for young people to find work, and that Nina would be safe as part of a group of people going abroad for factory work. Her family paid ¥200,000, their entire savings plus loans, but they understood that money was still owed to the agent and would have to be paid later. The recruiter put her on a train to Beijing, and she was collected at the airport by another agent who travelled with her on several flights, ending up in the UK.

In the UK, she was denied permission to phone her parents and tell them she had arrived safely (usually the point at which a final payment to the agent is made and the client is released). Instead, she was driven to a private house, tied up and locked in a room with other young Chinese women, all tearful and distressed, and deprived of food and water. She recounts that, from time to time, one of the women would be taken out of the room, and would not come back. She believes she was sold to a brothel owner; she did not hear a sum of money mentioned, but she was brought out of the room and presented to a man who indicated approval and took her with him, still tied up, blindfolded, and concealed on the back seat of a car, to another house some distance away. Here he raped her twice and showed her pornographic films in preparation for sex work. She was horrified that this was what she was expected to do, and begged to be allowed to earn money any other way, but she was persuaded to obey through a combination of food deprivation, false promises of imminent release if she co-operated, and occasional physical violence. She saw up to ten clients a day, and was locked into the house except when she was escorted to a hotel to see clients there. After more than a year (she remembers two periods when clients, who were mostly not Chinese, wished her a happy Christmas) of completely unpaid sex work, a regular client helped her to escape after seeing injuries caused by her pimp.

Typical features of Nina's experience include deception about whether enough money had been paid up front for her to be transported to the UK and then allowed to go free and find her own work; being traded within the UK; working in a small establishment where two other women, apparently not trafficked, were able to come and go freely, while Nina was always locked in and guarded; and her eventual escape with the help of a client. Other features common to many Chinese trafficking victims in the UK are that Nina was detained as an illegal immigrant, which did not help the mental-health problems already brought about by her traumatic experiences. Only when she confided some of her story to a 'befriender' at the detention centre was she identified as a victim of trafficking.

Case study 2: Linda, Shandong Province

Linda, in her mid-30s, became the family breadwinner after her husband became too ill to work, although he still managed to subject her to severe domestic violence. She sought work abroad partly to earn more to support her children (she gave up hope of divorcing her abusive husband when he threatened she would never see the children again), and partly for respite from her husband's violence, and it was probably her evident vulnerability as a victim of domestic abuse which led to her being trafficked. Linda stresses how careful she was to find a reputable, legal agency, although she did have to borrow ¥170,000 from loan sharks to pay the fees. The agency arranged a visa for her and she completed a short training course in Western cookery (to cater for foreign visitors to the Beijing Olympics) in the UK before returning to China for a short time and then going back to the UK for a work placement.

But when she arrived in the UK for the second time, she was taken to a private house and locked in a bathroom with no food and water only from the toilet cistern, and then forced to work as an unpaid child-minder for a Chinese family. After a month the house was raided by police, but she was allowed to go, and, crucially, was not asked anything about her time in the UK or identified as a victim of trafficking, because her work visa was still valid, thanks to the 'reputable' agency. She then worked freely for just over a year and was able to pay back about ¥90,000 of her debt, before her luck ran out again. Between jobs, she met a Chinese woman on a train who offered her work child-minding in Belfast, and within three days, this woman was able to procure a passport to get Linda to Northern Ireland, where she once again found herself in domestic servitude. Her captors were not merely exploitative employers; the man of the house was involved in organized crime and ran a number of cannabis farms around Belfast. Linda was forced to work as 'gardener' in one, and was raped twice by the boss when he visited the house. She was freed after a few weeks when the drug squad raided the property and was identified as a victim of trafficking, but was too afraid to press charges against her rapist, given his organized-crime background.

One of the eye-opening features of this case is that a migrant worker with a valid visa, who has met all the conditions to work legally in the UK, could still be trafficked by an apparently reputable agency in China. If Linda had been discovered in a raid on a brothel or massage parlour, she would very likely have been questioned to see if she might be a victim of trafficking. But these questions are not asked of migrant workers with valid visas, or of undocumented migrants found in a takeaway or on a construction site, even though there are cases of trafficked labour from China anywhere in the UK where Chinese migrant workers can be found. If more trafficking victims are to be identified and receive support and protection, a wider view needs to be taken of who might be a victim of trafficking, including not only sex workers, not only undocumented migrants, and, as the next two cases show, not only women.

Case study 3: Mark, Hebei Province

Mark was seventeen when his mother, his only close relative, was detained by the police. With the money a friend passed to him from her, he paid an agent to get him out of China as quickly as possible, as far as Singapore. While he was living rough around a railway station in Singapore, he was spotted by an agent who offered him factory work in France. The main danger signal (apart from the obvious vulnerability of a homeless, depressed teenager effectively without family) is that he only paid about ¥10,000, all the money he had left, for his papers and a flight to France, which can barely have covered his travel costs, and certainly not an agent's fees and expected profit. On arrival, he was told he would have to work to pay off an unspecified debt for an unspecified period of time. He worked for a total of two years for contacts of the agent, first in a French factory, and then labouring in the Czech Republic. When he tried to escape from his captors (all the workers were kept locked in a cellar when not working), part of his finger was chopped off as a punishment, and he was told next time it would be his hand. Worse was to come when his traffickers killed another worker and forced him to help dispose of the body in the woods. He eventually got away from his captors and came to the UK, where he was detained as an illegal immigrant.

Key features of Mark's case include the simple point that Chinese men do get trafficked to the EU for forced labour. China does not recognize men or boys aged over 14 as victims of trafficking, which together with the much higher profile of female victims trafficked into the sex industry, makes them a doubly neglected group, excluded from any available support if returned to China, and mostly remaining under the radar in the countries where they are exploited. The other striking factor in his account was that he showed symptoms of the same kind of trauma as do female trafficking victims who have been raped. He reported that even in the UK, he thought he saw his traffickers' faces in the crowds, and had to avoid areas where Chinese people congregated because of his overwhelming fear of running into them again. My last case study shows that this fear was not as far-fetched as might be imagined.

Case study 4: Tony, Fujian Province

Tony was seventeen and living in rural Fujian with his elderly grandmother when he was offered the chance to work abroad by agents who said he could pay back the fee once he was earning in UK. They greatly exaggerated how easy it would be for him to earn enough to pay them within a short period of time, all danger signals of intent to traffick a would-be migrant. His traffickers were confident they could get away with abusing and exploiting him, as his grandmother, an impoverished elderly woman with low status in the community, would not be able to call on any powerful contacts to cause them trouble in return; this, too, is a form of vulnerability to trafficking. Tony endured a long journey through multiple countries including Croatia, where in a safe house under armed guard, he and the other migrants were taught basic Korean phrases to help them get through Customs on false South Korean passports. But in London, the agents demanded ¥200,000 from him, and when his grandmother couldn't raise the money, he was severely beaten in front of the other migrants as an example of what happened to defaulters; two years later, he still bore some of the scars. As soon as he could get up, he managed to escape through an unsecured window and find refuge in a Chinese-owned business some distance away.

After that, he changed his name and avoided London completely for a year, but the day he went to Chinatown for a friend's wedding, he ran into his former captors in a pub. One of them recognized him instantly, and was even still carrying his photograph. They put him back to work as a housekeeper and then a gardener in their cannabis farms in northern England, and then, when they felt they had him under sufficient control, he was used to collect doctored passports from the gang's forger and deliver them around London. He was arrested in a raid on the forger's premises, but was acquitted on all charges when he was found to have acted under duress as a victim of trafficking.

In some respects, Tony's is a typical case: he was deliberately deceived about the terms on which he was being taken to the UK and made a brutal example of when the unexpected demand for payment came; and he was made to work in cannabis farms, an increasingly common use of both undocumented and trafficked Chinese labour in the UK. For former trafficking victims to end up working in the trafficking network is also not unheard of; in China, there have been instances of adolescent girls trafficked as brides who later, numbed by the trauma of their own early experiences, helped traffick children from their extended family (*China Daily*, 2010). What is more unusual is for it to be recognized that a victim can still be under traffickers' control and in constant fear of them without being held under lock and key, and that after years of conditioning against it, they cannot be expected to go to the UK police to seek help.

Conclusions

There are some Chinese-run businesses in the UK that only use trafficked labour (mostly small-scale brothels, but also, in my sample, a street-selling ring and some cannabis farms), which indicates, among other things, that a ready supply of victims is available. More troubling, however, and much more difficult for police and other agencies to deal with, is the fact that much trafficked labour here is employed alongside non-coerced workers, anywhere that Chinese migrant labour is found – in catering, construction, decorating and shop-fitting, child-minding, street selling, food processing and agriculture, as well as in the sex industry. Although they may not depend on trafficked labour, these businesses are clearly prepared to use it when it is on offer from their network of contacts. The still-growing, global streams of Chinese migrants are the perfect hiding place for trafficked labour, and assuming that the category of 'trafficker' can always be separated from 'people-smuggler' or 'legitimate migration agent' will continue to hinder efforts to identify and assist Chinese victims of transnational trafficking.

Notes

1 This research has benefited from consultation with a number of individuals who, because they work in law enforcement or in close collaboration with Chinese government agencies, have requested not to be identified by name or organizational affiliation. I nevertheless extend my thanks to them all for the valuable insights they have shared. Any non-attributed facts here come either from these sources, or from my case data. I am also grateful to those who commented on an early version of this chapter at Nottingham University's Institute for the Study of Slavery Seminar on 8 March 2012. It goes without saying that any remaining errors of understanding or interpretation here are mine alone.
2 I have obtained details of these cases through serving as an expert witness in asylum tribunals or (less often) the criminal courts. As all cases went to appeal, sometimes to several appeals, and the individuals' accounts were accepted as reliable by top barristers specializing in trafficking cases, experienced psychiatrists, staff from specialist NGOs such as the Poppy Project and the Helen Bamber Foundation, and in most cases by an Immigration Judge, I am confident that their veracity has been established.
3 I have randomly assigned English names to the victims featured here to protect their real identity.

Bibliography

Ceccagno, A., Rastrelli, R., Salvati, A., (2010), 'Exploitation of Chinese immigrants in Italy', in Gao Yun (ed.), *Concealed Chains: Labour Exploitation and Chinese Migrants in Europe*, Geneva: ILO, 89–137

CEOP (2009), *Strategic Threat Assessment Child Trafficking in the UK*, www.ceop.police. uk/Documents/child_trafficking_report0409.pdf.

CEOP (2010), *Strategic Threat Assessment Child Trafficking in the UK,* www.ceop.police. uk/Documents/ceopdocs/Child_Trafficking_Strategic_Threat_Assessment_2010_ NPM_Final.pdf.

Chan, K. L., (2009), 'Sexual violence against women and children in Chinese societies', *Trauma, Violence and Abuse* 10, 1 (January 2009): 69–86.

Chin, K., (2009), *The Golden Triangle: Inside Southeast Asia's Drug Trade*, Ithaca New York: Cornell University Press).

Chin, K., Godson, R., (2006), 'Organized crime and the political-criminal nexus in China', *Trends in Organized Crime* 9, 3: 177–195

China Daily (2010), 'Traffickers "did not know it was wrong"', 5 March 2010, www.chi-nadaily.com.cn/cndy/2010-03/05/content_9540217.htm.

Gao, Yun, Poisson, V., (2010), 'Exploitation of Chinese migrants' vulnerabilities in France', in Gao Yun (ed.), *Concealed Chains: Labour exploitation and Chinese Migrants in Europe*, Geneva: ILO: 33–88.

Gil, V., Anderson, A. F., (1999), 'Case study of rape in contemporary China: a cultural-historical analysis of gender and power differentials', *Journal of Interpersonal Violence*, 14, 11: 1151–1171

Hsu., A., (2011), '"40,000" victims: sex trafficking, the 2006 World Cup, and the 2012 Olympics', *Migration Pulse*, 12 September 2011, www.migrantsrights.org.uk/migra-tion-pulse/2011/40000-victims-sex-trafficking-2006-world-cup-and-2012-olympics.

Li, M., (2010), 'An overview of the migration mechanism between China and Europe', in Gao Yun (ed.), *Concealed Chains: Labour Exploitation and Chinese Migrants in Europe*, Geneva: ILO: 19–32

Mai, N., (2011), 'Migrant workers in the UK sex industry: Final policy-relevant report', Institute for the Study of European Transformations, London Metropolitan University, www.londonmet.ac.uk/fms/MRSite/Research/iset/Nick%20Mai/Migrant%20Workers %20in%20the%20UK%20Sex%20Industry%20Project%20Final%20Policy%20Releva nt%20Report.pdf.

Modern Ghana News (2009), 'Chinese traffickers in tears over jail sentence', 26 June 2009, www.modernghana.com/news/2204063/1/chinese-traffickers-in-tears-over-jail-sentence.html.

Pieke, F. N., (2010), 'Migration journeys and working conditions of Chinese irregular migrants in the united Kingdom', in Gao Yun (ed.), *Concealed Chains: Labour Exploi-tation and Chinese Migrants in Europe*, Geneva: ILO, 139–168.

Pieke, F. N., Biao, Xiang, (2007), 'Chinese migration, Neoliberalism, and the state in the UK and China', University of Oxford BICC Working Paper Series no.5, October 2007

Skeldon, R., (2007), 'The Chinese overseas: the end of exceptionalism?', in Mette Thuno (ed.) *Beyond Chinatown: New Chinese Migration and the Global Expansion of China*, Copenhagen: Nordic Institute of Asian Studies Press, 35–48.

Shelley, L., (2003), 'Trafficking in women: the business model approach', *Brown Journal of International Affairs* 10, 1 (Summer/Fall 2003), 121, http://policy-traccc.gmu.edu/ resources/publications/shelle58.pdf.

Shelley, L., (2010), *Human Trafficking: A Global Perspective*, Cambridge: Cambridge University Press

State Council of China (2007), *China National Plan of Action on Combating Trafficking in Women and Children (2008–2012)*, 13 December 2007, translated at www.hsph.harvard. edu/population/trafficking/china.traf.08.pdf.

UKHTC (2011), 'National Referral Mechanism Data', accessible from the Serious and Organized Crime Agency website at www.soca.gov.uk/about-soca/about-the-ukhtc/statistical-data.

United States State Department (USSD) (2011), *Trafficking in Persons Report*, 27 June 2011, www.state.gov/g/tip/rls/tiprpt/2011/164231.htm.

Wong, A., (2007), 'Chinese crime organizations as transnational enterprises', in K L Thachuk (ed.), *Transnational Threats: Smuggling and Trafficking in Arms, Drugs, and Human Life*, Westport, Connecticut: Praeger Security International, 113–142

Zhang, S., X., Chin, K., (2008), 'Snakeheads, mules, and protective umbrellas: a review of current research on Chinese organized crime', *Crime, Law and Social Change*, 50, 3: 177–195

5 Inequality between migrants and locals: evidence from export-processing factories in the Yangzi and Pearl River Deltas

Liu Kaiming, Tyler Rooker, and Bin Wu[1]

Introduction

China's economy has grown rapidly over the past thirty years, beginning with the reform and opening of China by Deng Xiaoping. Yet, curiously, the reduction in income inequality as seen in other East Asian economies through growth brought about by market reforms has not occurred; in fact, income inequality has been exacerbated. This phenomenon is most apparent in the income inequality existing between rural and urban China, but increasingly this spatial gap is realized within cities, between migrant and local urban workers. Why does rapid economic development in China fail to reduce income inequality? And what are the factors that determine it?

The above questions are addressed through an investigation of the export-processing industry in the Yangzi and Pearl River Deltas (YRD and PRD, respectively). These regions are of special importance, not only for the high numbers of migrants and length of time engaged in reformed economic activities, but because they are regions with a high concentration of export-processing companies. Hence, examining income and development in these regions yields strong evidence of the factors generating the continuing wage inequality suffered by China's migrant workers.

Data in this chapter comes from two main sources: official statistical data and a recent survey carried out by the Institute of Contemporary Observation (ICO), a non-governmental organization dedicated to understanding globalization, corporate social responsibility, and migrant labor rights in China. The later survey examined 210 export-processing factories in the YRD and the PRD, through surveys, interviews, and observations from 2008 to 2009.

The remainder of this chapter is structured in the following way. The next section gives a brief introduction to the phenomenon of urban–rural migration and the existing inequality in China since its reform and opening in 1978. Following this section, the key policies that made the export-processing industry a generator of economic growth and the subsequent rise in demand for cheap labor are examined, particularly with respect to the YRD and PRD. In this context, the next section examines income inequality between migrant workers and local workers in urban areas, showing emergent trends. This official data is compared with data from the research on migrant-worker working conditions that was carried out in 210 facto-ries. Finally, the factors determining inequality are discussed before conclusions are drawn in the final two sections.

Origins of the new working class

The rapid, sustained growth in China's economy since 1978 is by now an old story. Over the past thirty years, China's GDP averaged annual growth of 9.8 percent, outpacing the rest of the world by 6.8 percent (Hu, 2011). In the process, China's economy and society underwent a phenomenal transformation there has been a rise in its own political-economic power and it is increasingly integrated with the global economy.

Yet despite this economic miracle, the fruits of economic development are not shared equally by different social groups in China. For example, the rural population in China benefits only marginally from economic reform and growth. According to the World Bank (2009), the portion of the population that subsists on less than $1.25 per day (in purchasing power parity, PPP, terms) numbered 254 million in 2005. Clear geographical inequality is observed in terms of the poverty population, since almost all (97.5 %) of the poor live in rural areas, while the vast majority (81.9 %) are concentrated in central and western China, far from the affluent coastal cities. In other words, the number of rural people in China fitting the World Bank definition of poverty in purchasing parity terms is 247.7 million, making up one-third of the total rural population. If the minimum subsistence rate is increased to $2 per day in PPP, China would have a poor population numbering 472 million, consisting of 63 percent of the rural population (Ibid:15).

There can be no denying that China has made great strides in reducing absolute poverty over the past two decades. Yet in terms of relative poverty, rural China continues to suffer, and one clear process that results is the massive population movement from rural areas to urban ones, with the goal of finding employment opportunities. This shift, which includes the single greatest population migration in world history, amounts to more than 400 million people changing from agri-cultural to non-agricultural activities. As this 'non-agriculturation' process has been constant over the past thirty years, the population engaging in these shifts are termed 'peasant-worker' (*nongmingong*) or 'floating population' (*liudong renkou*), depending primarily on whether they are local residents or not.[2]

The term 'peasant-worker', an amalgamation of the terms agricultural 'peas-ant' and industrial 'worker', as a single term of reference refers simultaneously to social status and occupation: a 'peasant' status in an urban area, doing manual labor as a 'worker'. This type of worker population emerges at the end of the Cul-tural Revolution in the mid-1970s, though it solidifies with the emergence of town-ship and village enterprises (TVEs) in the late 1970s and early 1980s. The reform of the rural economy, allowing individual families to contract their land from the government, gives some townships and villages surplus capital, as well as surplus labor from more efficient individual farming of the land. As a result, industrial and commercial enterprises emerge in some townships and villages, especially in Jiangsu province, Zhejiang province, and other fringe areas encircling urban areas. Farmers from rural areas then allocate part of their labor to engaging in non-agricultural activities, earning high wages as, at this time, TVEs are much more efficient, profitable, and nimble than state-owned enterprises that ignore market signals or allocate output according to government plans only. In 1984, there were 52 million rural workers in non-agricultural enterprises, and that number has more than doubled, to 106 million, by 1992 (Yu, 2003). While they did not necessarily leave their homes as migrants, 'peasant workers' emerged early on in the reform era as a population that leave their farms to engage in industrial and commercial, non-agricultural, work.

The second shift over the past thirty years is movement, or migration, by former rural farmers away from townships and villages in which they were born. Hence there is the emergence of a 'floating population' as a term that reflects the existence of this group. These farmers not only leave their homes to do commercial and industrial (i.e. non-agricultural) work, they travel across county boundaries to do so, travelling to urban areas such as towns, county-level cities, and cities proper. Hence migrant workers are a group that engages in non-agricultural work, but has non-local origins.

While reform of China's economy allows for farmers to contract their land and allocate their own labor outputs and for townships and villages to form enterprises, it also coincides with China's opening to the outside world, especially in terms of investment by foreign companies (FDI) first in special economic zones, and later in specified coastal open cities. When FDI poured into the PRD following policy loosening, foreign and private enterprises generated demand for cheap migrant labor in their factories, employing over 5 million migrant workers by 1986. The sudden emergence of these 'floaters', whose origins were non-local and work was heavily industrial, give rise to the characterization of a social disaster – a 'peasant workers flood' (*mingongchao*) – inundating the area.

According to National Bureau of Statistics (2009), the number of inter-provincial workers is 120 million in 2000, 140 million in 2008, and 151 million in late 2009 (with 2008 numbers of total peasant workers being 225 million). Further, the majority of workers (70.4%) come from central and western China, and their destinations (66.7%) are the eastern coastal areas.[3] They are spread across multiple industries, though concentrated in manufacturing and construction (37.9% and 18.3%, respectively; Ibid.).

As indicated by naming their movement with the pejorative 'flood', China's migrant workers face social exclusion in the destinations to which they migrate. This is caused in part by the *hukou*, or origin and occupation registration, system that was implemented in the early 1950s (Cheng and Seldon 1994). The *hukou* system divides the population into rural and urban, based on place of birth, and agricultural and non-agricultural, based on occupation. Given the geographical inequality in China, rights, statuses, and opportunities are divided according to different categories of *hukou*. Hence migrant workers, despite the fact that they engage in non-agricultural work, are unable to enjoy the privileges and resources enjoyed by those with origins in urban areas where migrants work, the local urban employees.

Rights to the city in China undergo their most important transformation following the liberation of China in 1949. Following the Soviet model of internal passports, the *propiska*, China implemented the *hukou* to control population movements, most especially to prevent the rural population from overloading the city with demands, since China's industrial policy is to invest heavily in cities with surplus from the countryside (Fan 2008; Rooker 2011; Naughton 2008). In reality, however, the *hukou* is a social governance tool, equating the social origin of an individual with his/her mother's birthplace and work status. Hence it bears a similarity to hereditary systems of social origin, where individuals obtain different rights of policy, economic development, citizenship, and social welfare based solely on birth.

The reform and opening of China in 1978 fundamentally changed both China's industrial policy and its economic development process. Moving, or growing, out of the planned economic system, reformed China provided opportunities for many forms of economic organizations to spawn and grow, including rural business units, private enterprises, and foreign companies. As a result, despite the continued strength and dominance of state-owned enterprises in terms of economic output and employment, demand for labor increased dramatically. Desire for economic opportunities by farmers, too, adds to the pressure on the rigidity and exclusion of the *hukou* system keeping non-locals and agricultural workers out of urban employment. The central government acknowledges this pressure by authorizing the establishment of a Temporary Residence Permit, allowing peasants to engage in business, trade, or work outside the countryside as long as they did not rely on the state for grain, housing, or other benefits that state enterprise employees enjoyed (Yu, 2002).

In 1992, following a national resumption of economic reform policies personified in Deng Xiaoping's visit to and support of the Shenzhen special economic zone during his Tour of the South, the economic climate became even more welcoming to newly-emergent business entities. In this climate, as the lowest-cost laborers, migrants are even more in demand. With growing numbers of migrants in cities and urban areas, national and local governments made concerted efforts both to police migrant movements and activities, and to protect the interests of local (urban) residents. The Ministry of Labor and Social Security, the Ministry of Public Security, and other government bodies promulgated policies to restrict, fine, and control the new 'rural' population that had appeared in cities. In particular, the 'Method of Detention and Repatriation', in force from 1982 to 2003, enables local police in urban areas to detain and transport back home anyone without proper identification, work papers, and a temporary residence permit.[4]

In the 2000s, restriction and control policies of both central and local governments led to increasing criticism and demonstrations. In 2003, the State Council published a circular to improve social services and management for migrant workers (State Council, 2003). It seeks to improve the discriminatory policy environment for those peasant workers who enter the city to do work, preventing collection of duties and protecting their rights. Yet the lack of a national social security system, including no national education, hygiene, sanitation, or housing systems, combined with the restriction on free movement around the country and cities, means that each provincial and local urban government creates its own systems for labor management and regulation. Hence, discrimination and social exclusion continue on a massive scale across China.

This type of *social exclusion*, then, is a phenomenon that extends throughout China, but is also recognized in countries throughout the globe. The United Nations Development Program defines social exclusion as insufficient civil or social rights and includes inability to access political and legal systems with which to exercise rights. When the majority of the social population controls resources, rights, commodities, and services, and prevents minority populations from accessing these, or refuses to allow participation by minority populations in formal social relations and activity, this is social exclusion. As a result of exclusion, social inequality consists of unequal quality of life, non-enforcement of social justice, and unfair access to economies of scale. The result of social exclusion is thus long-term poverty, since individuals in minority populations have no way to increase their opportunities, or those of their children, in the local society (Levitas, et al., 2007).

Despite their being the majority of the population, peasants in China are socially excluded from local populations in urban areas to which they migrate and work, including both migrants and peasant workers. While peasant-workers are excluded based on *hukou* as well, since non-agricultural *hukou* status gives local urban employees access to resources, rights commodities and services that local peasant workers lack, they are not the core subject of the discussion in this chapter. The *hukou* system prevents floating migrants from participating in social security schemes and public services, due to their rural (non-local) status. There are no political resources or legal channels for migrants to pursue, ensuring that they have no protection of rights otherwise allocated to them as workers in the city. Thus while economic growth and China's success in general, and export-processing success in particular, have been building on the backs of migrant workers, they do not share in the benefits that result from economic development.

Engine of thirty-year growth: export-processing in the PRD and YRD

The story of China's rise as an export producer as a result of reform and open policies of 1978 is widely told so only a general outline is given here. The end result, that China is now well-established as the 'world's factory' (see, e.g., Zhang, 2006), processing goods for export to the world, is well-known. In 2008, China's foreign trade reached $2.56 trillion and its current account surplus was $426 billion (NBS, 2009).

In becoming the 'world's factory', China has a quite specific development plan that focuses on stimulating exports to lead the economy. This process begins with policies in the early 1980s, when a comprehensive series of laws and regulations came into effect to support the development of export-led industrialization. Hence the mind-boggling numbers: in 1981, the value of exported manufacturing goods from China is only $2.64 billion (6% of total GDP); in 2008, exported manufacturing goods sky-rocketed to $135.27 billion (31.2% of total GDP) (NBS, 2009).

The origin of this massive growth in manufactured exports is in Shenzhen, set-up as a special economic zone adjacent to Hong Kong. In the 1980s, export-led manufacturing quickly spreads throughout the Pearl River Delta and up to other coastal areas. The model is based on 'three imports and one compensation' (*sanlai-yibu*), meaning that three types of inputs are imported to China and then are processed for re-export, namely raw materials, unassembled components, and prototype models. The 'one compensation' is provision of equipment, technology, and management in return for labor and land, with the eventual turning over of the factory to the local Chinese partner after a specified time. In the early twenty-first century, the PRD and YRD are two giants in the industrial manufacturing bases for the export-processing industry – two massive engines of China's economic growth.

The Pearl River Delta is an alluvial delta where the Pearl River empties into the sea. Technically, it includes Hong Kong and Macau, though generally it references the riverbanks and coastal areas in the Guangdong province of China, some 11,000 square kilometres. In economic terms, the PRD encompasses the Guangdong cities of Guangzhou, Shenzhen, Foshan, Zhuhai, Dongguan, Zhongshan, Huizhou, Jiangmen, and Zhaoqing – a total administrative area of over 24,000 square metres and a 2008 *hukou*-registered population of close to 43 million people, accounting for 14 percent and 61 percent of these totals for all of Guangdong province, respectively. Through the *sanlai-yibu* and other preferential policies, China encourages entrepreneurs from Hong Kong, Macao and Taiwan to set up factories in the area, most notably starting with Shenzhen and Dongguan (Yang, 2006). Owing to the successes, these policies are spread throughout other cities and regions in the Delta. Over a 28-year period from 1980 to 2008, the PRD averaged an annual growth rate of 20.9 percent,[5] constituting a true 'economic miracle'. Starting as a poor, rural area buffering mainland China from Hong Kong, the area has grown into one of the richest urban regions in China.

The Yangzi River Delta is another alluvial delta situated at the mouth of the Yangzi (*Changjiang*) River. It overlaps Shanghai as well as the provinces of Southern Jiangsu and Western and Northern Zhejiang, including the cities of Shanghai, Suzhou, Wuxi, Changzhou, Zhenjiang, Yangzhou, Taizhou (Jiangsu), Nantong, Hangzhou, Ningbo, Shaoxing, Huzhou, Jiaxing, and Taizhou (Zhejiang), covering an area of just under 100,000 square kilometres, and with a registered *hukou* population of 75 million in 2008 (see Baidu, 2011). As a strategically important region for the heavy-industry plan prior to the reform, the YRD did not open up to outside investment or participate in export activities as early as the PRD. Hence its economic growth was stagnant for a longer period. However, since the mid-1990s, rates of FDI growth have accelerated significantly, and large numbers of factories have moved from the PRD to the YRD. In the early twenty-first century, the YRD has overtaken the PRD as the region with the largest amount of FDI in China, with a concentration in export activities. Beginning in 2001, the YRD has had higher growth rates in exports than the PRD, and the rate is accelerating. By 2004, the YRD was the largest export processing base in China.

The stellar performances of the PRD and YRD over the past thirty years cannot be understood without addressing the role of migrants as a form of cheap labor: the *sanlai-yibu* process highlights imported materials and exporting to markets, but it is the migrants as intermediary processors that add crucial value, allowing profit to be accrued by factory owners both in China and through FDI. In the PRD and YRD there are a total of 85 million migrants, of whom 59 million are inter-provincial and 25 million are intra-provincial, a number that accounts for 60 percent of the total number of migrants nationally.[6] The backs of migrants have shouldered the PRD from a sleepy rural area into an industrial powerhouse; migrants painstakingly labor to lift the YRD onto the world stage as a global export centre.

Focusing on particularly large and successful cities in the PRD and YRD makes the relationship between social exclusion and wage inequality more clear. Further, the divergence between migrant and local workers' wages is a significant area in which to investigate the existence, persistence, or narrowing of inequality between different segments of worker in the export-processing sector, one of the core engines of China's growth as argued above. Given the length of time export-processing has developed in China, and its overwhelming employment of the working class and particularly migrants, this industry is especially important for understanding inequality in China.

For this purpose, an investigation of working conditions in the export-processing sector was conducted in the PRD and YRD from February 2008 to August 2009. It involved four provinces (Guangzhou, Shanghai, Jiangsu, Zhejiang), twenty one cities/counties, and a total of two hundred and ten factories. Among them, seventy nine or 37.6 percent are from the PRD and one hundred and thirty one or 62.4 percent are from the YRD (see Annex 5.1). Based upon a long-term collaboration and trust between the Institute of Contemporary Observation (ICO), international trading companies and global supply chain firms, we had access to and conducted the survey across the sampled factories. To ensure accurate information, a standardized and strictly implemented procedure was established to guide collection of information in the field. With a guideline of national regulations in relevant areas such as labor contract, occupational health and safety, welfare and social security, the process of the investigation used a combination of workplace observation, document review, and interviews with a number of owner/managers and workers.

The empirical data collected from our survey in PRD and YRD allows us to compare the treatment of migrants in export-processing factories to that of local urban employees, and to local minimum wage standards,[7] which can be gained from official data. As a result, this data analysis is used to examine one component of the central question of this chapter concerning economic growth in China and local employee-migrant social inequality. In particular, we examine whether growth translates to increases in wages earned by migrant workers, and the trends/gaps between migrant and local workers in terms of income growth. Since official (NBS) data provide a clear picture of official working standards, the next section begins the comparison by examining the policy and legal concept and content of 'minimum wage'.

'Minimum wages': what do we learn from official data?

With respect to income inequality in urban China in the last two decades, the term 'minimum wage' used by local governments has provided a useful but not necessarily accurate picture of reality. Based upon official data, this section intends to draw a picture about income gaps between migrant and local workers in relevant cities involved in our survey before we show the details of working conditions in sampled factories.

The introduction of a 'minimum wage' itself resulted from concerns about the increasing labor disputes in coastal regions. In 1992, after several labor disputes and cases where workers' employment rights were egregiously violated, the Shenzhen city government, a vanguard of China's economic reform and opening, instituted a minimum standard for wages. Following this, in 1993, the central government Ministry of Labor issued *Provisions Regarding Minimum Wages of Enterprises*. This was updated in 2003 with the *Provisions on Minimum Wages*, issued by the Ministry of Labor and Social Security (MOLSS 2006). These regulations stipulated that local government had to consider five factors when assessing the minimum wage: 1) the minimum living costs of urban residents; 2) individual social security and housing fund contributions; 3) average wage level, usually in the province but can be more local; 4) unemployment rate; and 5) the local economic development situation, compared to the national level. The minimum wage is set to be from 40 to 60 percent of the average monthly wage earned in the area.

Table 5.1 is a comparison between the minimum wage and the average monthly wage of local urban employees in important PRD and YRD cities. The annual growth rate of local urban employees' wages over the sixteen years from 1992 to 2008 averages 15.7 percent in these cities. Minimum wages in these areas do not grow at the same speed – precipitating a *decline* in the minimum wage standard as a proportion of local urban employees' average wage, with minimum wages in these cities making up less than 30 percent of urbanites' wages in the past ten

Table 5.1 Minimum wage (MW) and its proportion of urban employee average salary (UEAS) in selected cities and years, RMB/month

City	Item	1993	1995	1998	2001	2005	2008
Shenzhen	MW	286	300	330	440	580	900
	% of UEAS	42.24%	29.32%	21.54%	20.35%	21.43%	27.61%
Dongguan	MW		350	350	450	547	770
	% of UEAS		43.37%	36.76%	33.36%	23.24%	23.28%
Guangzhou	MW		320	380	450	574	770
	% of UEAS		37.78%	31.83%	24.39%	20.32%	22.71%
Shanghai	MW	210	270	325	490	690	960
	% of UEAS	44.59%	34.93%	32.34%	33.11%	30.87%	29.16%
Nanjing	MW		210	280	430	620	850
	% of UEAS		34.48%	35.58%	31.14%	25.36%	23.38%
Hangzhou	MW		230	270	410	610	850
	% of UEAS		38.59%	31.76%	27.02%	23.56%	28.67%

Source: The above six cities' bureaus of statistics and bureaus of labor from 1993 to 2008.

years. In terms of measurable income, the national average for local urban workers in 2008 is a monthly income of 2,436 yuan, with an unadjusted annual growth rate of 15.3 percent (adjusted for inflation, the growth rate is 9.4%; NBS 2009). Also in 2008, the average for local urban workers in PRD and YRD is 2,776 yuan, 14 percent higher than the national average.

The income gaps between migrant and local workers can be illustrated from the case of Dongguan, a new city specialising in the export-processing industry located in the heart of the PRD. Like Shenzhen, it is an agricultural county in southern Guangdong province prior to the reform and opening of China in 1978. At that time there were only 1,290 small state- and collectively-owned factories; by 2008, the number of foreign-invested enterprises alone sky-rocketed to over 14,700 (DGBS, 2009). Utilizing $37 billion in FDI, the export-processing industry focuses on electronics, machinery, clothing, food, plastics, and chemicals, becoming a pillar industry[8] for the local economy. With explicit intervention by the local government with favorable policies, Dongguan becomes the locus for an agglomeration of labor-intensive, export-processing factories. The combination of foreign investment and cheap labor has generated massive wealth, and local urban employees and residents enjoy prosperity from this rapid economic growth. One index of this is local urban employees' average monthly wage, which shot up to 3,293 yuan in 2008 from only 395 yuan in 1992, while the annual income of urban residents rose to 30,272 yuan in 2008 from only 372 yuan in 1979 (ibid). Even Dongguan's local peasants benefit from economic growth: their net income of 12,328 yuan in 2008 is 82 times the level of 1978, an average annual growth in income of 16 percent (ibid.).

Yet migrant workers in Dongguan, despite making up 90 percent of the workforce, did not benefit in the same way from economic growth. This has not always been the case. In the early 1980s and, in particular, at collectively-owned and foreign-invested enterprises, migrant workers had equivalent or even larger incomes than local urban employees in state-owned enterprises. Even in the period from 1988 to 1992, there is no significant difference between the wages of these groups. But with the implementation of the minimum wage policy in 1994, divergence between wage levels begins to appear. The 1994 minimum wage is set at 50 percent of the average wage of local urban employees, or 350 yuan (ibid). However, this standard has remained frozen for five years, and once adjusted upward, grew quite slowly relative to wages and costs of living in Dongguan. Figure 5.1 shows the wage gap that emerged over the period from 1994 to 2008, with the average of the city including a higher proportion of migrant workers, and local urban employees enjoying a high rate of wage growth. What Figure 5.1 clearly shows is that the gap between city average wages and those for local urban employees expanded from a little less than half in 2000, to approximately two-thirds less in 2008.

The real situation: working conditions in sampled factories

The factories surveyed present a picture of the contemporary situation in the heavily migrant worker-dominated export-processing industry in China. This section uses data collected from 210 sampled factories to show real wages and work-

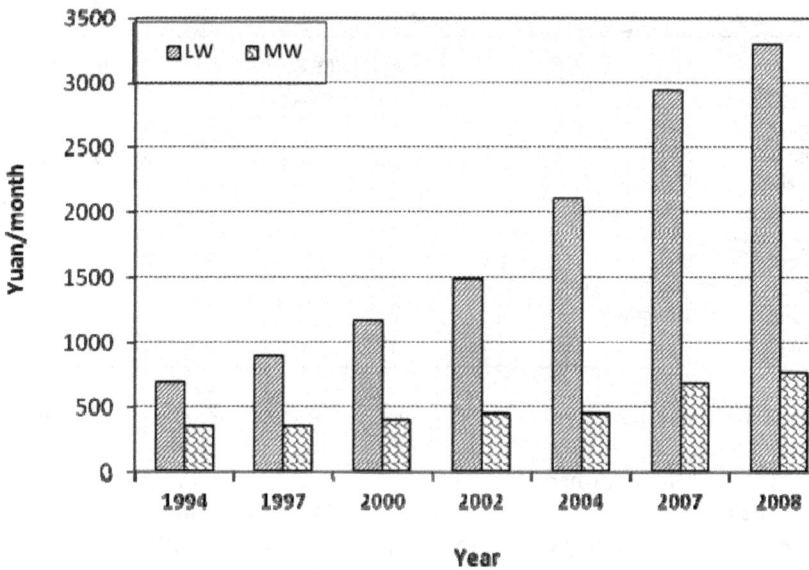

Figure 5.1 Average wage for local urban employees (LW) and minimum wage for migrant
workers (MW) in Dongguan

Source: DGSB 2009.

ing hours of migrant workers, which reveals the gaps from minimum wages and
demands of relevant laws and regulations.

The sampled factories produce a variety of goods for exports, with the majority, numbering 133 or 63 percent, being in the textile and garment sector. The
capital invested in these factories also varies: 128 (61%) are China-invested enterprises, either local state-owned or private; 47 (22%) are Hong Kong-owned; 15
are Taiwan-owned; 10 are joint ventures; and 5 are Japanese-owned. In terms of
the number of employees, the majority (133) have between 100 and 500 employees; more than one-quarter (55) have over 500 employees, and the rest have less
than 100 employees. The total number of employees in all the factories surveyed
was 87,269, with two-thirds of the total being female, and one-third male. Finally,
81 percent of these employees are migrant workers, 15 percent are local peasant
workers, and 4 percent are local urban residents.

The survey data reveals that the average wage of migrant workers in the factories is 1,146 yuan per month. The averages for the YRD and PRD are 1,196 yuan
and 1,095 yuan per month, respectively. More than 23 percent of all workers
have monthly wages *below* the required minimum wage set by the local government. For the majority of workers whose wages were above the minimum, this
includes overtime pay (See Table 5.2). Workers average 10.7 hours of work
per day, 66.4 hours over 6.6 days per week, and over 120 hours of overtime
per month, having an average of only 2.2 days off per month. In addition, only
28 factories pay overtime in accordance with China's Labor Law[9] regulations;

Table 5.2 Working house and pay in sample factories (2008) [/CAP]

City	Minimum wage	Real wages	Overtime (hours/month)	Overtime in total working hours
Shanghai	960	1235	101	36.7%
Nanjing	850	1065	88	33.6%
Suzhou	850	1120	113	39.4%
Wuxi	850	1179	122	41.2%
Hangzhou	960	1147	108	38.3%
Ningbo	960	1208	119	40.6%
Guangzhou	860	1160	138	44.2%
Shenzhen	1000/900	1247	115	39.8%
Dongguan	770	971	103	37.2%

some 172 factories pay only ordinary wages for overtime or pay less than the premium required in law.

Taking Shenzhen, where the highest wage in our survey is found, as an example, the average wage of migrant workers is 1,247 yuan/month, 247 yuan, about one quarter (24.7%) higher than the local minimum wage of 1000 Yuan/month. Such income, however, is based upon a total of 289 hour labor inputs per month, of which 174 hours (21.75 days × 8 hours), or 60 percent, are normal working hours while 115 hours, or 40 percent, are overtime work. Should workers wish to, and be allowed to, work only normal working hours, they would receive only 742 yuan/month, or 26 percent lower than the local minimum wage (according to current pay rate). Should owners follow Labor Law regulations, workers in the surveyed factories would receive 2,020 yuan per month (at the rate of 1.5 times minimum wage for overtime, not counting weekend and holiday pay rates), 62 percent higher than their current average income level.

As distinct from migrant workers, local urban employees in these factories are concentrated in management, office work, and skilled labor. Generally, they are paid higher salaries in better jobs with social insurance payments paid on their behalf. Also in contrast with migrant workers, local peasant workers are employed mostly on the edges of the YRD and PRD regions. They have more work experience and higher wages, with 80 percent participating in either local rural social insurance or urban social insurance.

Higher prices and costs of living in these cities compared to medium- and small-sized cities exacerbate the existing wage inequality. Migrant workers in large cities can barely meet their subsistence needs, and so the income inequality between migrant workers and other working groups in the same cities generates social polarization.

Piece-rate system: an interpretation of migrant workers' poor working conditions

The significant gap between real wages in sampled factories and local minimum wages raises a question about why relevant labor regulations are not realized in practice. On the basis of our investigation, of all the factors responsible for the poor working conditions, the piece-rate system and its ubiquity are clearly influential in this regard.

All of the two hundred and ten factories surveyed employ a piece-rate system or quota-based system, built on the Taylorist ideas of time management and motivation. Piece-rate systems calculate wage on a per item basis, thus remunerating employees based on the total number of products produced, a target set in advance. Thus, the system does not pay employees based on the number of hours they work, but based on the number of outputs within a certain period of time. This method of calculating wages has been used in China's manufacturing industry since the 1980s as an incentive mechanism, and has become widely adopted in export-processing production lines.

While an effective mechanism for motivation, the piece-rate system does not increase the income of workers, operating instead as a means for factory management to reduce workers' salaries and avoid paying statutory benefits. Workers' output is directly linked to the unit price of products. But without collective bargaining and participation in factory management, workers do not participate in the setting of piece-rate prices and item quotas. Hence, management often manipulates the unit price and quota to reduce effective income. Export-processing factory workers in interviews reveal that increases in working time and productivity do not increase wage levels. Instead of increasing motivation for more income, the piece-rate system simply increases psychological pressure to reach pre-set quotas.

Inability of unskilled or semi-skilled workers to meet specific production quotas also enables factory management to justify paying wages below the minimum wage standard. Piece-rate systems cause confusion in terms of overtime and its payment since both workers and managers see only unit prices of products. Market demand is passed directly onto workers vis-à-vis unit prices in the piece-rate system.

For employers, using the piece-rate system to determine daily wages links working time with output. Irrespective of the time required to produce a specific output, wages are paid only according to the amount produced. Manipulating piece-rate unit prices and daily quotas allows employers to adjust workers wages up or down without any oversight. From a practical point of view, labor productivity is increased since hours spent working overtime to meet quotas or increase the number of units does not count towards wages. In this way, unit prices are more competitive and workers more unlikely to complain about hourly wages fluctuating.

Yet for workers, this system of reimbursement simply links work with money, so they feel no sense of corporate identity or attachment to the company, increasing employee turnover. This, in turn, creates staffing problems and a permanently unskilled nature to the workers at export-processing factories. Workers, too, are permanently earning low wages and have no security in their jobs.

With the piece-rate system in place, wages are paid only for output; hence workers cannot take any form of leave from work without losing wages. China's labor law requires that employers provide special protection to female workers who become pregnant, give birth, or are breastfeeding. Further, workers are entitled to a minimum of three months maternity leave, during which workers should receive wages equal to their wages while at work. The authors find that the vast majority of companies in the survey do not provide these special protections for pregnant workers. With one exception, where 30 percent of ordinary wages are paid, all the factories in the survey (2009) do not pay any wages for maternity leave. Further, given the strict monitoring of family planning authorities, high costs of childbirth in urban areas, and lack of maternity and medical insurance, pregnant workers choose to resign and return to their homes in rural areas to give birth and breastfeed.

Chinese law also requires that employees who work more than one year in a company be entitled to annual leave of a minimum of five days or even more depending on the length of service to the company. But with the piece-rate system and implementation of short-term (no more than one year) contracts, factories avoid providing these days off.

Discussion and conclusion

China owes much of its economic success and development over the past thirty years to the export-processing and export-oriented industries. Foreign investment and processing of imported materials for re-export has allowed China to leverage its abundance of cheap labor to accumulate capital, transfer technology, open markets, and exploit natural resources. In this sense, labor – and especially migrant labor in the export industry – is the source of China's economic miracle.

However, increasing and intensifying inequality from the 1980s, in spite of economic development and overall prosperity, leads to questions about the origins and social exclusion involved in China's cheap labor. In fact, it is the monopolization of power by the state that maintains and supports social inequality, suppressing equitable overall economic gains in favor of local actors. Monopolizing power means that workers have no opportunity to organize as independent stakeholders to strike or bargain with management. As long-term temporary workers who are not welcome in urban centres, migrant workers depress wages and earn no benefits from state programmes such as social insurance and public works. Meanwhile, corporations purchase labor from unbalanced markets with no concern for workers' welfare, needs, or social responsibility.

China has experienced over sixty years of peace, averaging 6 percent economic growth over that period – more than twice the rate of the world. Yet in terms of the human development index (HDR, 2009), China has been stagnant; in terms of the minimum standard of living, in 2009 more than 60 percent of its population lives below it, 80 percent of which are those with an agricultural *hukou*, living far from urban centres.

Looking at the 'four Asian tigers' (South Korea, Singapore, Taiwan, and Hong Kong) and their economic development, export-oriented strategies for development allow countries to industrialize and urbanize through technology transfer and division of labor. Therefore, the problem of inequality in China is not an inherent characteristic of the export-processing industry in a developing country, but rather a broader problem that allows economic growth and development to accelerate, rather than even out, the divisions between local urban economy and the interests of migrant workers. The goal of resolving wage inequality and elimination of poverty requires that workers be empowered and welcomed as a social, political, and economic power in China's urban areas.

From the data presented in this chapter, the growth in social inequality over the past thirty years, despite China's phenomenal growth, is a glaring social fact that demands both policy and corporate changes. The extreme localism of China's social insurance system and policy implementation is no doubt a contributor to the problem. Highly mobile migrants, even those who return year after year to the same factories, do not gain advantages or benefits from urban areas, depriving them of rights to the city at the same time as the city refuses to accommodate their lifestyles and needs. Aside from more regional or national policy implementation, the situation requires more institutions and local organizations that will address migrant needs and lobby on their behalf.

The emergence of peasant-worker and floating population migrants in China, during a time of 'miraculous' growth, points to the emergence of a new social class. This chapter has used a survey or floating population workers in 210 factories of the YRD and PRD, where export-processing is concentrated, to examine a specific aspect of social inequality, i.e. wage inequality. The growing disparity is cause for great concern. As China emerges as the second-largest GDP in the world, and upgrades its export processing, the need for sustainable and capable labor is even more apparent. In this context, this chapter points to a key problem in social-economic organization and institution building that must be addressed for China to continue its growth as a world economic power.

Notes

1 This chapter is an outcome of a project funded by the Centre for Advanced Studies, University of Nottingham under its Research Development Funds with the theme of empowerment of Chinese migrant workers in the UK and China.
2 Data from the Sixth National Population Census conducted by the National Bureau of Statistics shows that China's rural population fell to 674 million in 2010 from 816 million in 2000; and its urban population rose to 666 million in 2010 from 460 million in 2000. Also, while the data show that, in the past 10 years, there have been approximately 120 to 150 million per annum moving from the rural areas to the cities, a large number of these migrants will leave work subsequently, to be replaced by other rural residents entering the city. Hence, the authors estimate that in the past 10 years there has been a total movement of peasants into the city for work of 400 million people. See NBS (2011).
3 According to provincial statistics, top exporters of migrant labor were Henan (21 million), Sichuan (20 million), Jiangsu (17 million), Hunan (12 million), Anhui (11 million), Hubei (10 million), Jiangxi (10 million), Guangxi (8 million), Chongqing (7 million), Shanxi (6 million), and Guizhou (6 million). See Ministry of Human Resources (2009) and Rooker (2011).
4 Author's calculation based upon PRD's urban economic development data from Guangdong Statistical Yearbook 2009

5 Author's calculation based upon population statistics from Guangdong, Zhejiang, Jiangsu, and Shanghai provinces.
6 The current statistical counting procedure used by the China National Bureau of Statistics (NBS) counts urban local employees as those with local, non-agricultural hukou – though their place of employment must be classified as a state-owned, collective, joint-stock, or foreign business. Hence those local employees of small private and individual businesses are excluded from national statistics. Peasant workers – those local individuals, who have a rural or agricultural hukou, are also excluded by NBS figures.
7 On 24 November, 1993, the Ministry of Labor issued 'Provisions on Enterprise Minimum Wage', and on 30 December, 2003, the Ministry of Labor and Social Security passed 'Provisions on Minimum Wages' effective 1 March, 2004. See MoLSS 2006.
8 A 'pillar industry' is defined as an economic sector deemed strategic in terms of defence, job creation, technology, or competitiveness.
9 According to China's Labor Law, overtime should be paid at 150% ordinary pay for ordinary days, 200% for off-days, and 300% for statutory holidays. Article 27 of 'Law of the People's Republic of China on the Protection of Women's Rights and Interests' and article 62 of 'Labor Law of the People's Republic of China'

Bibliography

Asian Development Bank, (2007), 'Key Indicators 2007: Inequality in Asia', accessed online: from http://www.adb.org/Documents/Books/Key_Indicators/2007/default.asp

Ari-Kokko, (2001), 'Export-led Growth in East Asia; Lessons for Europe's Transition Economies', *European Institute of Japanese Studies Working Paper* (Stockholm School of Economics) October 2001

Baidu, (2011), 'Yangzi River Delta' [*Changjiang sanjiaozhou*], Access online: accessed on 15 December, 2011 from http://baike.baidu.com/view/181899.htm

Cai, Fang, (2000), *China's Floating Population,* Zhengzhou: Henan People's Publishing House

Camps, Enriqueta, Camou, Maria, Maubrigades, Silvina, Mora-Sitja, Natalia, (2006), 'Globalization and Wage Inequality in South and East Asia, and Latin America; A Gender Approach', Accessed online: from http://ehsanz.econ.usyd.edu.au/papers/Camps.pdf

Chang, Hong, Zhang Haiyan, Gao, Xing, (2009), 'Workers Work More But Earning Less, The CPPCC Members Called For Raising The Proportion Of Income In GDP', *Xinhuanet*, August 27, Accessed Online: from http://news.xinhuanet.com/politics/ 2009-08/27/content_11950306.htm

Cheng, Hukou T., Selden, M., (1994), 'The origins and social consequences of China's hukou system', *The China Quarterly*, 139, 644–688

Dongguan Statistics Bureau (DGSB), (2009), 'Sixty Years of Wind and Rain, Leading to Brilliance: The Success of Dongguan's Development 60 Years After the Establishment of New China' [*Fengyu liushinian, pinbo zhu huihuang: xinzhongguo chengli 60 nian lai dongguan jingji shehui fazhan chengjiu*], Dongguan Party History Net. Accessed online: from http://dgds.sun0769.com/dgds/shownews.asp?id=182&page=1

Fan, Cindy, (2008), *China on the Move: Migration, the State, and the Household.* London: Routledge

Gosling, Matilda, (2008), 'A Better Balance between the Supply and Demand of Skills: Addressing Income Inequality in China and India', *Centre for Skills Development Working Papers Series*, March 2008

Gu Shengzu, (2007), 'Solve the problem of migrant workers' need to coordinate the development of industrialization and urbanization', *China Economic Times*, April 24

Guangdong Bureau of Statistics, (2002–2008), 'Economic and Social Development Statistical Bulletin', Accessed online: from www.gd.gov.cn/govpub/tjsj/tjkx/200802/t20080229_43340.htm

Guangdong Social Security Administration Bureau Small Group, (2008), 'Research on Problems of Transferring Basic Retirement Insurance' [*jiben yanglao baoxian guanxi zhuanyi jiexu wenti yanjiu*], China-EU International Research Conference on Social Security Insurance and Transference of Retirement Insurance, 25–26 February, Guangzhou

Guo, Shutian, (1990), *Imbalance of China,* Shijiazhuang: Hebei People's Publishing House

Hertel, T.W., Fang, F. Zhai, (2006), 'Labor market distortion, rural–urban inequality and the opening of China's economy', *Economic Modeling*, 23

Hu, Jianlan, (2011), 'Improvement of living standards in China since its economic reform: progresses and policy implications', [gaigekaifang yilai zhongguo minsheng fazhan zhuangkuang ji gaijin duice], *Modern World and Socialism* [Dangdai shijie yu shehuizhuyi]. Online at http://theory.gmw.cn/2011-07/15/content_2286055_3.htm

Hu, Liang, (2008), 'China's Per Capita Income Out of Poverty into the Mid-Stream', *Xinhua News Agency*, October 28

Human Development Report (HDR), (2009), Overcoming barriers: Human mobility and development, New York: UNDP, online at:
http://hdr.undp.org/en/reports/global/hdr2009/

Jiangsu Bureau of Statistics, (2002–08), 'Economic and Social Development Statistical Bulletin' Accessed online: at http://www.jssb.gov.cn/jstj/djgb/qsndtjgb/200902/t20090216_108678.htm

Lee, Lulu, (1991), 'The process of modernization and reform of the social structure – analysis of contemporary Chinese institutional structure', *Sociology*, 1

Levitas, Ruth, Pantazis, Christina, Fahmy, Eldin, Gordon, David, Lloyd, Eva, Patsios, Demi, (2007), 'The Multi-dimensional Analysis of Social Exclusion', A Research Report for the Social Exclusion Task Force, British Cabinet Office, University of Bristol, online at www.bris.ac.uk/poverty/downloads/socialexclusion/multidimensional.pdf

Liu, Kaiming, (2003), *Migrant Labor in South China*, Beijing: Xinhua Publication House

Ministry of Human Resources and Social Security and National Bureau of Statistics. 2008. 'Human Resources and Social Security Statistics Bulletin 2008'. Accessed online: 5 August, 2011 from www.gov.cn/gzdt/2009-05/19/content_1319291.htm

Ministry of Labor and Social Security (MOLSS), (2006), 'Provisions on Minimum Wage' [*Zuidi gongzi guiding*], accessed online: from www.molss.gov.cn/gb/ywzn/2006-02/15/content_106799.htm

National Bureau of Statistics (NBS), (various years), *China Statistical Yearbook*, accessed online: from www.stats.gov.cn/tjsj/ndsj/

National Bureau of Statistics and the Ministry of Human Resources and Social Security, (2009), 'Survey of Employment and Social Security for Migrant Workers', National Statistical Information Net, September 21, *in Chinese* www.stats.gov.cn/was40/gjtjj_detail.jsp?channelid=33728&record=22

National Bureau of Statistics (NBS), (2001), *China Development Report 2001*, Beijing: China Statistics Press

National Bureau of Statistics (NBS), (2009), *China Statistical Yearbook 2008*, Beijing: China Statistics Press

National Bureau of Statistics. 'Notice of Important Data from the 2010 Sixth National Population Census (Document No. 1)' [2010 *nian diliuci quanguo renkou puji zhuyao*

shuju gongbao (di 1 hao)], accessed online: 22 November, 2011 from www.stats.gov.
cn/tjgb/rkpcgb/qgrkpcgb/t20110428_402722232.htm

Naughton, Barry, (2008), *The Chinese Economy*, Cambridge: MIT Press

Qin, Hui, (2007), 'Low human rights advantage of China's development', *China Report
Weekly*, December 06, 2007, www.chinaweek.com/ html/3267.htm

Rooker, Tyler, (2011), 'Migrants making technology markets' in Bridge, Gary, Watson,
Sophie (eds.), *The New Blackwell Companion to the City*, 193–209. West Sussex:
Blackwell

Shanghai Bureau of Statistics, (2002–2008), 'Economic and Social Development Statistical Bulletin'. Access online: from www.drcnet.com.cn/drcnet.common.web/DocView-
Summary.aspx?docid=1890043&chnid=3650&leafid=3406&gourl=/drcnet.common.
web/Doc

Shanghai Human Resource and Social Security Bureau and Shanghai Statistical Bureau,
(2009), 'Notice on the Publication of Average Level and Growth Rate of Wages in
Shanghai, 2008' [*Gongbu shanghai shi 2008 niandu zhigong pingjun gongzi ji zeng-
zhanglv de tongzhi*]. Accessed online: from www.12333sh.gov.cn/07zcfg/gfxwj/200903/
t20090327_1063115.shtml

State Council General Office, (2003), 'State Council General Office Notice Concerning
Improvement of Services and Management of Migrant Workers' [*Guowuyuan ban-
gongting guanyu zuohao nongmin jincheng wugong jiuye guanli he fuwu gongzuo de
tongzhi*]. Access online: from http://www.gov.cn/zwgk/200508/12/ content_21839.htm

Suzhou Labor and Social Security Bureau, (2009), 'Issuance of Enterprise Wages Guid-
ance Level of Suzhou, 2008' [*Suzhou shi 2008 nian qiye gongzi zhidao jiawei chulu*].
Online at www.suzhou.gov.cn/asite/show.asp?ID=48606

Tang, Jianguang, (2004), 'The truth of Sun Zhigang's death' [*Sun zhigang siwang zhenx-
iang*], *China News Weekly* [*Zhongguo xinwen zhoukan*], 2 October

World Bank, (2009), 'China – From Poor Areas to Poor People: China's Evolving Poverty
Reduction Agenda – An Assessment of Poverty and Inequality in China', New York: the
World Bank. online at: https://openknowledge.worldbank.org/handle/10986/3031.

Yang, Chun, (2006), 'Overseas Chinese investments in transition: The case of Dongguan',
Eurasian Geography and Economics 47, 5: 604–622

Yang Junxiong, (2009), 'Migrant workers' monthly wage was 1,205 yuan in 2008', *China
Economic Daily*, March 17

Yu, Depeng, (2002), *Urban-Rural Society – From Isolation to Open: Research on China's
Huji and Hukou Systems* [Chengxiang shehui – cong geli zouxiang kaifang: zhongguo
huji zhidu yu hujifa yanjiu], Jinan: Shandong People's Press

Yu, Li, (2003), 'The empirical analysis for Chinese township enterprises absorbing labor
force' ['Zhongguo xiangzhen qiye xina laodong jiuye de shizheng fenxi'], *Management
World* [Guanli shijie] (3), accessed online: 12 July, 2011, from wenku.baidu.com/view/
cc83b3b81a37f111f1855bf4.html

Zhang, Kevin H. (ed.), (2006), *China as the World Factory*, London: Routledge

Zhejiang Bureau of Statistics, (2002–2008), 'Economic and Social Development
Statistical Bulletin', accessed online: from www.zj.stats.gov.cn/art/2009/2/27/art_164_
141.html

Zhou, Xiwu, (2008), *Personal Experience: The Rise the Shenzhen's Industrial Economy*
[*Qinli: Shenzhen gongye jingji de jueqi*], Shenzhen: Haitian Press.

Zhong, Xiao-Han, (2005), 'China's regional wage evolution in the period of reform', *Journal of Tsinghua University (Social Science Edition)*, 03

Annex 5.1 Geographical locations of sampled export-processing factories

Province	Location	Factory
Guangdong	Guangzhou	10
	Shenzhen	17
	Dongguan	28
	Foshan	7
	Huizhou	6
	Zhaoqing	2
Shanghai	Shanghai	15
Jiangsu	Nanjing	5
	Suzhou	15
	Wuxi	14
	Changzhou	7
	Zhenjiang	2
	Yangzhou	8
	Nantong	6
Zhejiang	Taizhou	2
	Hangzhou	19
	Ningbo	9
	Taizhou	3
	Jiaxing	18
	Huzhou	2
	Shaoxing	6

Part II

Understanding Chinese economic development

6 Chinese economic growth, reform and key factors behind these: a quantitative analysis

Jian Chen and Jun Tian

Introduction

The economic reform programme in China has been widely acclaimed as a success (Naughton, 1995, 1997; Lardy, 1998). It has led to profound and massive changes in both the structure of the economy and the mechanism of resource allocation, which has coincided with rapid economic growth. But has economic reform been an unambiguous success in China?

To answer this question we must first specify the criteria for judgement, as the adoption of different criteria may lead to different conclusions. Economic reforms in China may be judged in terms of the success of the transition from the centrally planned economy to a market economy, or in terms of economic outcomes – which in turn can be measured in many ways, such as the impact on output, productivity, profitability, and so on. As far as the first criterion is concerned, Chinese economic reforms may appear to be less successful. After over two decades of reforms, there are still some goods and services allocated by state orders with regulated prices, and furthermore, there has been no large-scale privatisation programme. On the two pillars of creating a market economy, namely price liberalisation and privatisation, China seems to be behind the Central & Eastern Europe and the Former Soviet Union states (CEEFSU), although it started the transition one decade earlier (Pomfret, 1997). But when judged in terms of economic performance over the course of the reform period, China appears to have been more successful than the CEEFSU.

In this chapter we take the improvement of economic performance in terms of productivity as the primary criterion. While economic reforms in CEEFSU were undertaken to change their economic systems, economic reforms in China were undertaken to promote economic growth and to improve economic efficiency. Chinese economic reforms have been implemented as a means of achieving *economic goals*. Economic liberalisation proceeds only when it can create and maintain the growth momentum. In the choice between transition and growth, the Chinese leaders' priority has been the latter.

This chapter seeks to assess the extent to which the phenomenal buoyant economic performance of China can be attributed to its reform strategies. Sachs and Woo (1994) argued that China's outstanding economic performance has little to do with gradualism, but much to do with its unique economic structure. One question to be addressed in this chapter relates to the major sources of growth in the Chinese economy and their connection with structural changes arising from economic reform.

In contrast to the pessimistic view of the Chinese reform experience, there is also an optimistic view. Recent literature on China is full of references to 'lessons from China' for other transition economies, to the institutionalisation of 'a virtuous reform circle' that will allow China to grow out of its problems, and to the emergence of a 'new, superior economic mechanism'. In particular, McMillan and Naughton (1992) argued that state-owned enterprises are preferable and privatisation is not crucial. The truth of this claim is the second issue to be addressed in this chapter. We shall examine whether gradual reforms in the state industrial sector have achieved their intended objectives.

This chapter contains econometric analyses using a large data set to identify sources of economic growth. We estimate an expanded aggregate production function using data from 30 Chinese provinces from 1978 to 2005. As is shown below, the analysis of the provincial data reveals that China's spectacular performance is attributable to the expansion of the non-state sector, and the degree of openness and investment in both physical and human capital. In addition, regional economies with a larger state industrial sector are found to be associated with lower productivity and slower economic growth, which contradicts the optimistic view of partial reforms in the state industrial sector. In particular having shareholdings concentrated in the hands of large institutional investors and less equity held by the state appears to be desirable. However, the impact of an ownership mix on economic performance is not always strong.

Growth of the Chinese economy over the reform period

Ever since economic reform began in 1978, rapid economic growth has followed. Table 6.1 shows the growth record of China in the reform period from various data sources. From 1978 to 2009 real output in terms of GDP grew at 9.92 percent per year, or at 8.72 percent on a per capita basis. Annual growth was particularly rapid between 1982 and 1988, averaging 11.3 percent or 9.7 percent per capita over the six- year-period, before slowing down sharply from 1988 to 1990 with the political crisis in Tiananmen Square. Vigorous growth, however, resumed in 1991. The growth of real GDP reached 12.8 percent in 1992, 13.4 percent in 1993 and 11.6 percent in 1994. Since then, the economy of China entered a modestly high and stable growth period with a band of 7 to 9 percent. The years from 2005 to 2007 saw the third wave of rapid growth of over 10 percent, making China now the second largest economy in the world.

Not all economists took this impressive official data at face value. Lund (1995), and Goodhart and Xu (1996) believed that in a country which at times of inflationary stress still relies on price controls for certain key commodities and raw materials, inflation may be underestimated and output overestimated. Sachs and Woo (1997), and Rawski (2001), argued that there is reason to believe that official output (GDP in particular) growth rates are exaggerated. First, the nominal output value may be reported as real output value by production units such as collectively

Table 6.1 Output growth of China since 1978

	1978	1980	1985	1990	1995	2000	2005	2009
GDP (*Yuan* bn) in 1990 price	650	763	1275	1855	3269	4863	5218	8061
Annual growth of GDP (over the previous year)	11.7%	7.8%	13.5%	3.8%	10.5%	8.0%	7.3%	9.3%
Population: (Million)	963	987	1159	1143	1211	1267	1276	1335
GDP per capita: (*Yuan*)	675	773	1100	1623	2699	3838	4089	6161
Annual growth of GDP per capita (over the previous year)	10.2%	6.5%	11.9%	2.3%	9.3%	7.1%	6.6%	8.5%
International Trade (USD bn)								
Export	9.7	18.1	27.4	62.1	148.8	249.2	762.0	1201.6
Import	11	20.0	42.3	53.5	132.1	225.1	659.9	1005.9
Capital Markets								
Capitalisation (*yuan* bn) current price	N/A	N/A	N/A	N/A	347.4	4809.1	4352.2	24394
No of listed companies	N/A	N/A	N/A	10	323	1088	1154	1718
Capital raised (*yuan* bn) Current price	N/A	N/A	N/A	0.5	15.0	210.3	125.2	496.8

Sources: China Statistical Yearbook 1985, 2010.

owned enterprises. Second, officials at local industrial bureaux have an incentive to exaggerate output growth in order to enhance their career advancement. Third, the procedure for reporting the base-year values of new production lines exaggerates their importance. Fourth, base-year prices are inconsistently used. As a result of these tendencies to exaggerate the growth of real output, the implicit deflators for the industrial output of SOEs and COEs rose consistently less than the factory-gate price index of industrial output, which is based on surveys of the prices (plan and market prices) received by a sample of industrial SOEs, mostly large and medium, for their products.

However, the revaluation of industrial output on the basis of what is believed to be the appropriate price index does not lead to results that are substantially different from the official ones (Sachs and Woo, 1997). For instance, the annual growth rate of GDP from the official source is 8.9 percent during 1979 to 1984 and 9.7 percent during 1985 to1993; the corresponding figures using the consistent base year are 8.8 percent and 9.4 percent; when the factory-gate price index is used, the annual growth rate of GDP over these two sub-periods are 8.9 percent and 7.5 percent. Furthermore, economic growth in China over the last three decades is so visible that no one can seriously believe that it is merely a statistical illusion.

Despite the dismay, the apparent progress that has been made in China, in terms of the consumption of food and consumers' goods, is real. Economic efficiency improvement, coupled with the reduction in the aggregate savings ratio has led to a surge in living standards (see Annex 6.1, Tables A1–A4). The level and quality of food intake has improved dramatically. The quantity of consumer durable goods consumed in both urban and rural households has also increased considerably and hedonic shopping, an integral part of life in the developed West, has also become commonplace in many Chinese cities (Yu and Bastin, 2010). The living space per person has more than tripled. Measured by a comprehensive welfare indicator, the Human Development Index, which is a weighted average of life expectancy, adult literacy, years of schooling and income (PPP$), China in 2010 had a value of 0.663 as compared with Norway, 0.94 at the top and Sierra Leone, 0.275 at the bottom of the league table.[1] In CEEFSU, rapid transition has led to an increase in age-specific mortality rates, especially for middle-aged men (see Eberstadt, 1994 for East Germany; Ellman, 1994 and Flemming and Matthews, 1994, for Russia). In contrast, age-specific mortality and life expectancy beyond childhood have remained static, while infant mortality has been reduced and life expectancy at birth has increased in China.

It is also useful to place China's growth record in an international context.[2] From 1980 to 2009 China outperformed the most relevant comparator country, India by a margin of 4 percent in terms of the annual growth rate of GDP (See Table 6.2). Chinese growth performance during the period is also considerably better than that of average low and middle-income countries.

China's performance is even more outstanding when compared with countries in the CEEFSU (see Table 6.3), most of which have experienced negative economic growth at some stage since 1990 and during and after the recent finan-

Table 6.2 China and other developing economies: annual growth of GDP, 1980–2009

	China	India	Low Income Countries	Middle Income Countries
Total	10	6.3	3.5	4.6
Agriculture	4.6	3.4	2.9	3.0
Industry	11.6	6.5	4.3	4.8
Services	11.7	7.6	3.8	5.5

Sources: World Bank, WDR, 2010.

Notes: Figures for low and middle-income countries exclude China and India.

Table 6.3 China and other transition economies: annual growth of GDP, 1985–2009

	1985–90	*1990*	*1995*	*2000*	*2005*	*2009*
China	7.8	8.4	9.0	8.4	11.3	9.2
Russia	1.3	−13.1	−4.1	10.0	6.4	−7.8
Bulgaria	2.6	−13.5	−1.8	5.4	6.4	−5.5
Czech	1.8	−14.2	5.9	3.3	6.3	−4.1
Slovakia	1.5	−16.2	6.5	2.2	4.5	−7.8
Hungary	0.6	−12.0	1.5	5.2	3.9	−6.7
Poland	0.3	−7.6	6.8	4.0	3.6	1.7
Romania	−2.1	−13.4	8	2.1	4.2	−8.5

Sources: World Development Indicator 2009.

cial crisis. We note that such a comparison demands qualification. Observers did expect that rapid transition would follow a 'J' curve, meaning that output must fall before a long-term growth path can be established.[3] According to this J-curve view, liberalisation must first largely destroy old economic structures before economic resources can be efficiently re-deployed.

An encouraging feature of economic growth in the reform period is that total productivity growth has become a more important source of China's economic growth (Hu and Khan, 1997). In China, physical investment played a dominant role in output growth in the pre-reform period. Capital accumulation contributed to over 65 percent of the output growth, while labor and productivity growth contributed 16.9 percent and 18.0 percent of the output growth respectively, in the central planning era of 1952 to 1978. In the 1979 to 1994 period, productivity growth accounted for about 42 percent of the aggregate growth, while the contributions of capital and labor growth are 46 percent and 13 percent, respectively (Hu and Khan, 1997). The Chinese growth process is in sharp contrast to the post-war growth of Hong Kong, Singapore, South Korea and Taiwan. While the growth of output and manufacturing exports in the newly industrialized countries of East Asia is unprecedented, the growth of total factor productivity in these economies is not (Young, 1995). In contrast to the belief held by most economists that productivity growth in these economies is extraordinarily high, a careful data analysis by Young (1995) showed that the output growth in these economies has been mainly driven by factor accumulation.

Sources of economic growth

At face value, the above statistics would suggest that China's economic reform has been extremely successful. However, China underwent numerous structural changes in the reform period. It is not clear whether China's performance is due to such structural changes or to the country's unique style of economic reform. To what extent is economic growth in China attributable to economic reforms, and how have these reforms led to growth? To answer these questions, it is necessary to explore closely the major sources of economic growth. In this chapter, we specify and estimate an expanded production function using provincial data from 1978 to 2005 to identify determinants of economic growth. We begin by looking at hypotheses arising from the relevant literature on the causes of economic growth in China.

Suggested sources of economic growth

A variety of market-oriented reforms and increased integration into the global economy are generally acceptable explanations for the rapid economic growth observed in China. The first reform accomplished was the adoption of the Household Responsibility System (HRS) in agriculture, which liberalized agriculture from the inefficient commune system in the early 1980s. The HRS does not involve privatisation of land, but it has nonetheless generated significant productivity gains.[4] Under the new regime, private farm households are the primary production units, paying a fixed amount of rent for use of the land in the form of an output quota; after fulfilling the output quota, the farm household is permitted to keep the remaining output for its own consumption or for sale at the market. The agricultural reform coupled with price increases for agricultural products has greatly improved the peasant incentives, which have in turn translated into substantial productivity gains. As shown in Table 6.4, agriculture was a leading growth sector during the period of agricultural reform, and the agricultural contribution was as high as that of any industry.

Table 6.4 Sectoral contribution to GDP growth percentage

Sector	Growth in 1979–1993	Growth in 1979–84	Growth in 1985–1993
Primary sector	16.5	31.8	11.6
Manufacturing sector	51.6	34.1	48.3
Industrial SOEs	13.8	20.3	11.7
Industrial COEs	25.0	12.8	28.9
Individual-owned Industrial enterprises	5.9	0.2	7.7
Other ownership forms of industrial enterprises	6.9	0.8	8.9
Construction sector	5.7	5.2	5.9
Tertiary sector	26.2	28.9	25.3
Total	100.0	100.0	100.0

Source: Sachs and Woo, 1997.

The second factor which is believed to be a driving force of economic growth in China is the expansion of the non-state sector, broadly defined to include the urban collective sector, township and village enterprises (TVEs), and private and foreign businesses (see Table 6.5). As we can see from the table, the importance of SOEs in the industrial sector has steadily declined since 1978. The role of the state sector is being replaced by the non-state sector during the period, but by different forms of firms with different ownership systems. The early stage of economic trans-formation (1978–1995) was characterized by the important role played by rural-based collective and individual enterprises, namely TVEs. The share of TVEs in China's GDP rose from 9 percent in 1978 to 36.6 percent in 1995. However, since 1995, we have witnessed the swift increase in importance of the firms under the category of 'Others', which is a mixture of all non-state or non-state ownership dominated firms, including TVEs, private enterprises, foreign firms with different ownership structures, and joint-stock companies.[5]

As a result of the economic system restructuring, the role of SOEs has been declining. SOEs produced only 26.7 percent of industrial output and employed only 20 percent of workers, down from 77.6 and 47.5 in 1978, respectively (see Table 6.5).

The third factor is the expansion of the foreign trade sector and the inflow of foreign capital. China retreated from a protectionist position on trade in the late

Table 6.5 Shares of output and employment by state-owned enterprises in the industrial sector

Year	State sector		
	% of gross industrial output	*% of fixed capital investment*	*% of total industrial employment*
1980	76	82	—
1985	65	66	—
1990	55	66	—
1995	34	54	67
1996	36	53	66
1997	32	52	65
1998	50	54	60
1999	49	53	58
2000	47	50	54
2001	44	47	49
2002	41	43	44
2003	38	39	38
2004	35	36	30
2005	33	33	27
2006	31	30	25
2007	30	28	22
2008	28	28	20
2009	27	31	20

Sources: Lin and Zhu (2000) and *China Statistical Yearbook* 2002–2010.

Note: From 1998 on, the data are for the SOEs and the firms controlled by the State.

1970s. Under the open-door policy, restrictions on imports were reduced and local government units as well as collective and private firms were given autonomy to promote exports. The official exchange rate of the Chinese currency continuously declined until it increasingly approximated to the market rate. In consequence, the ratio of foreign trade – both exports and imports – to GDP increased from 13.2 percent in 1978 to 44.24 percent in 2009 (see Table 6.6). China has risen from 13th place in 1978 to now the largest trading economy in the world.

In the realm of international trade, China enjoys two advantages over other transition economies (Pomfret, 1997). First, China has a clear comparative advantage in labor- intensive manufacturing. Labor costs are low, literacy rates high, and the pool of unskilled workers huge. Second, China's international transactions were repressed rather than distorted by central planning. Although China missed the opportunity for export-led growth during the period of isolation, China also avoided the consequences of Common Mutual Economic Agreement (CMEA) planning, which distorted the export of many other centrally planned economies by enforcing a planned pattern of specialisation.

Meanwhile, foreign investment rose rapidly, from a negligible amount in 1978 to US$90 billion of foreign funds utilized in 2009, with a total amount of US$942.6 billions during the period of 1978 to 2009 (NBS, 2010, Table 6-13). To a large extent, this was initially attributable to special economic zones, which were established to encourage foreign investment by giving foreign investors favorable tax concessions and a suitable infrastructure for their businesses, then spread over all regions of China. In essence, foreign trade and investment are believed to have facilitated economic development in China via three channels (Chow, 1993, 2002; Lardy, 1994, 2002). First, foreign trade and investment have a knowledge spill-over effect brought about by the inflow of advanced technology and management practice. Second, foreign investment fills the gap left by domestic investment in the process of capital accumulation, and foreign

Table 6.6 Exports and imports as a percentage of GDP: 1960–2009

	International trade/GDP (%)	*Foreign Direct Investment ($Bn)*
1960	8.96	
1965	7.24	
1970	5.00	
1975	9.58	
1976	9.28	
1978	9.80	
1980	12.62	3.1 (1979–1984)
1985	23.05	1.7
1990	29.98	3.5
1995	40.19	37.5
2000	43.91	40.7
2005	63.22	60.3
2009	44.24	90.0

Sources: *Chinese Statistical Yearbook,* 1985, 2002, 2010.

trade expands China's production possibility frontier inclusive of trade. Third, exclusively foreign-owned enterprises and joint ventures created competition in the market place and forced state-owned and collectively-owned enterprises to be more efficient (Lardy, 2003).

The fourth factor is reform of the state industrial sector. Although SOE reforms fall short of privatisation, they have nevertheless produced respectable productivity gains (McMillan and Naughton, 1992). Although industrial output by SOEs only accounts for around 8.1 percent of the total output in 2009, the state-controlled joint-stock companies contributed an additional 26.4 percent (NBS, 2010). SOE's incentives are arguably enhanced as they are commercialized. SOEs are allowed to keep some fraction of their profits, in contrast to the past when all profits had to be remitted; SOEs workers and managers' pay are now related to performance, also a change from the past; SOEs now sell and purchase in free markets, while everything was bought and sold at state-controlled prices in the past; SOEs are now given an increasing degree of freedom to make operational decisions, while they were merely plan executors in the past. In addition to these changes in the internal management system, another possible channel through which SOEs' incentives were sharpened is increased product-market competition as a result of the entry of non-state firms. As state protection contracted, SOEs were increasingly exposed to market discipline. It is thus increasingly necessary for them to produce at a high enough quality and low enough price to persuade consumers to buy from them rather than their competitors.

Saving behaviour is argued to be the fifth factor behind China's favorable performance (Woo, 1994; Kraay, 1998; Loayza, et al. 2000). Figures 6.1 and 6.2 show that China's savings rate, which is household savings as a percentage of disposable income, is extremely high when compared with other countries in both East Asia and the West.

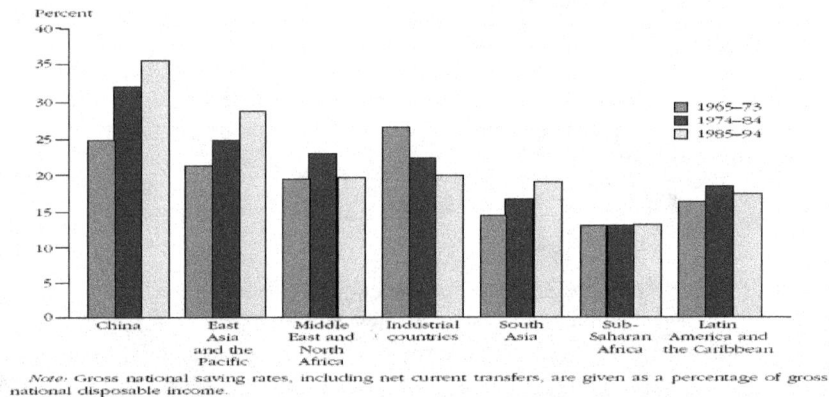

Note: Gross national saving rates, including net current transfers, are given as a percentage of gross national disposable income.

Figure 6.1 Median gross national saving rates by region, 1965–1994

Source: Loayza, et al., 2000, Figure 1.

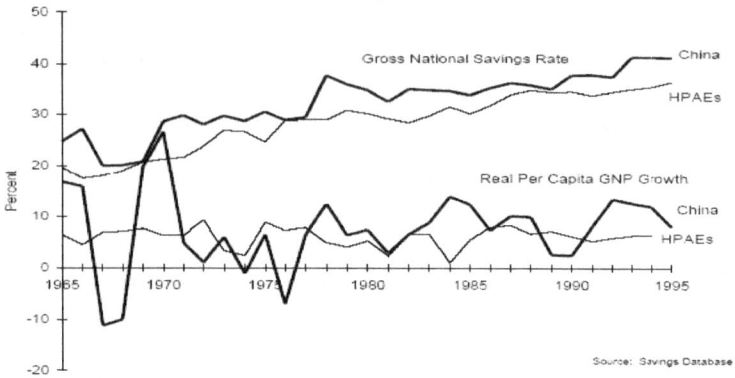

Gross national saving is expressed as a percentage of gross national disposable income (GNP plus net transfers), both at current prices.

Figure 6.2 Saving and growth in China: 1965–1995

Source: Kraay (1998), Figure 1.

Note: HPAEs – High Performing Asian Economies

The high household saving is a precondition for Rostow-type economic growth. Moreover, it played an important role in stabilising the Chinese economy by reducing the need for the government to meet the excessive resource demand of the SOE sector by money supply expansion. We will cover the fifth point in more detail in the following sections.

Empirical analysis

China is a country of substantial regional variations and offers a wide range of growth experiences, which enables us to test for various explanatory reasons for the growth process in the country. In this section, we estimate aggregate production using data from 30 Chinese provinces from 1978 to 2005 to identify the relative importance of various growth and efficiency determinants in the light of our discussions in the previous section. The aggregate production function is written as

$$Y_{it} = f(t, L_{it}, K_{it}, Z_{it}) + \varepsilon_{it} \tag{6-1}$$

where $i (= 1, 2, ..., n)$ represents a regional economy (province), $t (=1, 2, ..., T)$ time period, Y aggregate output, L raw labor, K physical capital, Z a vector of efficiency and growth determinants and ε is the error term. With the inclusion of Z, equation (6-1) is an expanded production function. The specification is justified by the fact that labor and capital are not the only inputs to the aggregate production process. A normal production function corresponds to the production possibility frontier, but we assume that some of the regional economies are located inside the frontier at the outset of economic reforms. The relative efficiency level of these regional economies, as measured by their distance from the frontier, depends on regional characteristics denoted by Z. As economic reforms proceeded, the variables of the Z vector evolved in terms of their values leading to changes in the relative efficiency of regional economies. In view of our discussion in the previous section, it is hypothesized that Z includes the following elements:

$$Z = (\text{TVE, TRADE, SAVE, SOE, HUMAN, t*TVE, t*TRADE,} \\ \text{t*SAVE, t*SOE, t*HUMAN})$$ (6-2)

where TVE denotes the importance of TVEs in the regional economy, TRADE the degree of openness towards the rest of the world, SAVE the saving behaviour of households, SOE the importance of the state industrial sector in the regional economy. Note that these variables have both a level and a growth effect. The level effect of a Z variable is measured by its coefficient, and the growth effect is measured by the coefficient of the interaction term between the variable and time t.

Our data consists of a panel of observations on output, labor, capital and other variables for 30 provinces during 1978 and 2005. The original sources of data are the Chinese Statistical Yearbook (NBS, 1995–2006) and China's Provincial Statistics (Hsueh, et al., 1993). Output, Y, is measured by GDP at 1978 constant price. The price deflator is the general price index at the provincial level. The price index for Tibet is not available, and the national general price index is therefore used for the province.

Labor is measured by total employment. An ideal measure for this variable is actual working time and takes into account quality heterogeneity. But at the provincial level, there is no information available for us to construct a better measure than the current one.

Capital is constructed using the standard perpetual method:

$$K_t = I_t + (1-\xi)K_{t-1}$$ (6-3)

where we represents investment in fixed assets at 1978 constant, and the national rate of depreciation. The investment series was found in Huseh, et al. (1993) including investment in residential and non-residential construction, investment and renovate investment in fixed capital by the state, collective and private sectors. The investment series excludes business inventories which are usually treated as a component of investment in the literature. Although inventories become increasingly significant in China as it is transformed from a command economy to a market economy, information on inventories was mixed with working capital in the production process ('circulating funds'), which does not conform to the definition of inventories in the literature.

For the initial value of capital stock, we used the value in 1958 (= 235.2 billion *yuan*) as estimated by Hu and Khan (1997). This involves a questionable assumption that the initial values of all provinces are identical. Nevertheless, since a lengthy historical investment series is used, which is traced back as early as 1958, the impact of an inaccurate initial value is therefore unimportant.

The national rate of depreciation is derived from Hu and Khan (1997). There are two problems here. First, the official rate is low, which is only 3.6 percent on average, and bears little relation with the true vintage price functions that characterize the relative efficiency profile of capital assets (Hu and Khan, 1997). Second, the national rate of depreciation fails to reflect substantial variation in capital consumption across provinces. In the absence of relevant information, we have added the annual growth rate of GDP to the national rate of depreciation in an attempt to approximate the regional rates of depreciation. This treatment is based on the assumption that rates of physical depreciation of capital assets are proportional to the growth rates of regional economies.

The measurement of the Z variables is relatively straightforward. TVE is measured by TVE labor as a percentage in the total labor force. TRADE is measured by the ratio of total imports and exports to GDP. SOE is the proportion of SOE labor in the total labor force. HUMAN is measured as university students as a percentage of total population. SAVE is total investment in fixed capital assets as a percentage of GDP.

Table 6.7 shows estimated results of the expanded production function. The Cobb-Douglas formulation is assumed to approximate the underlying production technology. Three estimators are employed to estimate the model: ordinary least squares (OLS), dummy variable least squares (DVLS) and generalised least squares (GLS).

We first consider the OLS results. As indicated by adjusted R-sq, 96 percent of regional variation in output can be explained by the expanded production function. Output elasticity with respect to labor and capital is plausible in magnitude and highly significant. Their sum is equal to 0.78, suggesting decreasing returns to scale. The hypothesis of constant returns to scale is rejected even at the 0.1 percent level of significance. Remarkably, all the Z variables are highly significant.

The effect of TRADE on the output level is given by:

$$\partial Y / \partial TRADE = 0.11 + 0.00 * t = 0.11 \tag{6-4}$$

which means that other things being equal a province produces more output if the volume of its international trade relative to GDP is larger. Since labor and capital are controlled for, the implication is that regional economies with more trade with the rest of the world tend to be more efficient. Regional economies that fall into this category are mainly coastal provinces such as Guangdong and their development has largely been driven by foreign trade. The level effect of trade appears to be constant, as the coefficient associated with the interaction term between TRADE and t is zero. The effect of TRADE on output growth is given by:

$$\partial Y / \partial t = 0.00 * TRADE \tag{6-5}$$

Table 6.7 The production function for regional economies

	OLS	DVLS	GLS
Constant	1.13***		
	(3.56)		
t	−0.02	−0.01	−0.01
	(−0.58)	(−0.51)	(−0.55)
Labor	0.59***	0.42	0.78
	(14.91)	(3.65)	(20.47)
Capital	0.29***	0.51	0.14
	(10.17)	(4.49)	(6.17)
TRADE	0.11***	0.09	−0.04
	(3.93)	(−2.92)	(−2.65)
t*TRADE	0.00	0.01	0.00
	(0.89)	(1.95)	(1.08)
SAVE	−0.42***	−0.23	−0.28
	(−6.90)	(−7.09)	(−8.63)
t*SAVE	0.03***	0.03	−0.03
	(8.03)	(14.50)	(15.22)
SOE	0.01	−0.26	−0.17
	(0.13)	(−6.00)	(−4.14)
t*SOE	−0.01	−0.01	−0.01
	(−0.73)	(−3.22)	(−2.75)
TVE	0.11***	0.10	0.09
	(4.42)	(3.16)	(3.13)
t*TVE	0.00	0.09	0.02
	(1.69)	(5.58)	(5.77)
HUMAN	0.40	0.24	0.36
	(7.82)	(6.80)	(11.34)
t*HUMAN	−0.01	−0.01	−0.02
	(−2.14)	(6.36)	(−4.95)
R^2	0.96	0.99	0.91
Adjusted R^2	0.96	0.99	

Notes: figures in parentheses beneath the estimated coefficients are t-ratios.

which is not significantly different from zero. Thus, while internal trade has a positive level effect, its growth effect is negligible.

The level effect of SAVE is given by:

$$\partial Y / \partial SAVE = -0.42 + 0.03 * t \tag{6-6}$$

which suggests that the effect of physical investment initially appears to be negative and becomes increasingly positive along with time. This result is not implausible. In an economy where the investment policy is still largely dictated by the government capital may flow to regional economies with lower efficiency. The injection of investment does not produce an instantaneous effect. Rather, the efficiency effect will only materialise after some periods. However, the effect of investment on output growth given by:

$$\partial Y / \partial t = 0.03 * SAVE \tag{6-7}$$

is significantly positive, which means that regional economies with more physical investment grow faster.

Both the presence of the SOE sector has neither a level nor growth effect as the coefficients of SOE and t*SOE are not significantly different zero as the coefficients. In contrast, the level effect of TVEs given by:

$$\partial TY / \partial TVE = 0.11 + 0.02 * t \tag{6-8}$$

and the growth effect given by:

$$\partial Y / \partial T = 0.02 * TVE \tag{6-9}$$

are both significantly positive.

Among the growth determinants we identified that HUMAN has the largest level effect which is:

$$\partial Y / \partial HUMAN = 0.40 - 0.01 * t \tag{6-10}$$

but the level effect appears to decline over time. The growth effect of HUMAN given by:

$$\partial Y / \partial t = -0.001 * HUMAN \tag{6-11}$$

is significantly negative.

Since we used panel data, the OLS estimator is arguably not wholly appropriate as it simply pools the data. In other words, the OLS treats time series and cross-section data as cross-section data, ignoring the fact that the coefficients may change over time as a result of structural changes. Another problem associated with the OLS is that it may suffer from omitted variable bias. The Z variables included in our model may not be exhaustive, and there may well be other growth determinants ignored by our specification. An example of such omitted variables is the condition of infrastructure such as transportation and telecommunication. Since the condition of infrastructure is likely to be conducive to the level and growth rate of output and correlated to some of the included variables (e.g. TRADE, SAVE and HUMAN), the omission of the infrastructure variable might lead to biases in the estimated coefficients of the included variables. This is just one example. There are other possible omitted variables such as central government policies which favor some areas (special economic zones), quality of labor force and so on.

Estimators suitable for panel data are dummy variable least squares (DVLS) and generalised least squares (GLS). The basic framework for DVLS and GLS allows the intercept to be constant over time and specific to the individual cross-sectional unit (which is the province concerned in our case). The individual effect captures otherwise unmeasured variables which are time-invariant and specific to each province (e.g. infrastructure, quality of labor force, and special economic zone). The estimators for panel data can mitigate the omitted variable bias if any.

The choice between DVLS and GLS can be made on the basis of a Hausman test. Under the null hypothesis that the included variables are uncorrected with the time-invariant error components, both the DVLS and GLS are unbiased and consistent, but the GLS is more efficient. Under the alternative hypothesis that the included variables are correlated with the errors, the DVLS is unbiased and consistent, whereas the GLS is not. The Hausman test yields a statistic of 30.67 with degrees of freedom equal to 13. The hypothesis that the individual effects are uncorrected with the included variables should be rejected and the DVLS is therefore preferred.

Consistent with the Hausman test, the DVLS and GLS results are substantially different. There are also differences in the results between the DVLS and the OLS. In view of the Hansman test result, we believe that the OLS estimator is biased due to the correlation between the included variables and time-invariant individual effects. As we see shortly, the DVLS results appear to be more plausible than the OLS in terms of the sign of the coefficients.

While OLS estimator suggests that international trade has no significant effect on economic growth, the DVLS indicates that regional economies with a greater degree of openness of a regional economy towards overseas markets tend to grow faster. The growth effect of SAVE remains the same as before, although the level effect is less negative than before.

Recall that the SOE sector has little efficiency and growth effect according to the OLS results. The DVLS yields negative coefficients for the SOE variable and the interaction term between SOE and t, which imply that regional economies with a larger SOE sector tend to be less efficient and that the inefficiency effect of SOEs increases with time. It is easy to conjecture that this is because reforms in the state industrial sector lagged behind reforms in other sectors.

While the OLS results show that TVEs have a level but not growth effect, the DVLS estimator suggests that regional economies with a larger TVE sector tend to be not only more efficient, but also to grow faster. The results regarding the HUMAN remain the same, although the DVLS suggests a smaller level effect.

To summarise, our data analysis confirms that international trade, TVEs, investment in physical and human capital are positive sources of China's remarkable economic performance. The results do not, however, support the view that SOE reforms have been successful.

Conclusion

This chapter seeks to evaluate the performance and influences of economic reforms in China in the past 25 years. Judged by economic performance, we conclude that economic reforms in China have been extremely successful. Such success has manifested itself not only in rapid output growth, but also in improved economic efficiency. Furthermore, the success of China's economic reform may also be reflected in the deepening transition of the economic system.

There are five factors that have contributed to superior economic performance in China. The first is the Household Responsibility System adopted in the rural sector as a replacement of the inefficient commune system. The second has been the dramatic development of the non-state sector (including collectives, township and village enterprises, private and foreign-owned businesses and their mixtures – shareholding companies), which has now replaced the state sector as the engine of economic growth. The third factor is foreign trade and the inflow of foreign capital, which have brought to China the capital and knowledge it has so much needed, as well as the competitive force which made the domestic sector more efficient. Fourthly are the reforms of state-owned enterprises, which include the enhancement of material incentives and increases in decision-making powers – in particular, the right of residual claims. A high savings rate in China has provided redundant and stable capital for all sectors in China and is the fifth factor that explains the rapid growth of the Chinese economy.

These factors were econometrically tested by OLS and DVLS methods. The results confirm that all factors were significant in explaining the sources of growth, although the results from OLS and DVLS were not consistent in all tests. The results are not supportive of the view that SOE reforms have been successful. This conclusion reminds us that reforming the state-sector is difficult and complex, and that the full transition to a market economy will be an enduring task.

Notes

1 World Bank, *World Development Reports* 2010.
2 We note that due to differences in consumption baskets and the difficulties in making purchasing power and exchange rate adjustments, inter-country comparisons are suspect.
3 Gomulka, Stanislaw, (1991), 'The causes of recession following stabilisation.' *Comparative Economic Studies*, 33, 2: 71–89; Murrell, Peter, (1990), 'Big bang versus evolution: eastern European reforms in the light of recent economic history,' *Plan Econ Report*, June 29.
4 It can be argued that there is allocative efficiency under the HRS, as land allocated to households cannot be freely reallocated even when land is not in use.
5 The Ministry of Agriculture estimated that, by the end of 1998, about 80 percent of China's TVEs had been converted into shareholding cooperatives, shareholding companies, partnerships, or proprietorships, or had been reformed through merger, leasing, collateral contracting, or bankruptcy (Dong, et al., 2002: 815).

Bibliography

Chow, Gregory, (1993), 'How and Why China Succeeded in Her Economic Reform,' *The International Symposium on the Theoretical and Practical Issues of the Transition towards the Market Economy in China*, Haikou, 1–3 July

Chow, Gregory, (2002), *China's Economic Transformation*, London: Blackwell

Eberstadt, Nicholas, (1994), 'Demographic shocks after Communism: Eastern Germany, 1989–93,' *Population and Development Review* 20: 137–152

Ellman, Michael, (1994), 'The increase in death and disease under "katastroika"', *Cambridge Journal of Economics,* 18: 329–355

Flemming, John and Robin Matthews (1994), 'Reform in Russia,' *National Institute Economic Review* 149, 65–82

Gomulka, Stanislaw, (1991), 'The causes of recession following stabilization,' *Comparative Economic Studies* 32: 71–89

Goodhart, Charles, Chenggang, Xu, (1996), 'The rise of China as an economic power,' *National Institute of Economic Review,* 55: 56–80

Hsueh, Tien-tung, Li Qiang, Liu, Shucheng, (1993), *China's Provincial Statistics: 1949–1989*, Boulder: Westview Press

Hu, Zuliu F., Mohsin, S. Khan, (1997), 'Why is China growing so fast,' *IMF Staff Papers*, 44, 1: 103–131

Kraay, Avart, (1998), *Household Saving in China*, A Report for World Bank research project: 'Saving Across the World: Puzzles and Policies,' Washington D.C.: World Bank

Lardy, Nicholas, (1994), *China in the World Economy*, Washington D.C.: Institute for International Economics

Lardy, Nicholas, (1998), *China's Unfinished Economic Revolution*, Washington D.C: The Brookings Institution

Lardy, Nicholas, (2002), *Integrating China into the Global Economy,* Washington, D.C.: Brookings Institution Press.

Lardy, Nicholas, (2003), *Trade Liberalization and Its Role in Chinese Economic Growth*, Prepared for an International Monetary Fund and National Council of Applied Economic Research Conference 'A Tale of Two Giants: India's and China's Experience with Reform and Growth,' New Delhi, November 14–16

Lin, Y. M. and Zhu, T., (2000), 'Ownership Reform and Corporate Governance: The Case of China's State-owned Enterprises', *Working paper for the SJE International Conference on Corporate Governance and Restructuring in East Asia*, Hong Kong University of Science and Technology

Loayza, Norman, Schmidt-Hebbel, Klaus, Servén, Luis, (2000), 'Saving in developing countries: An overview,' *The World Bank Economic Review,* 14: 393–414

Lund, Jakob, (1995), 'China: Statistical haze hides growth path,' *Asian Monetary Monitor*, 19, 3, (May–June), 13–23

McMillan, John, Naughton, Barry, (1992), 'How to reform a planned economy: Lessons from China,' *Oxford Review of Economic Policy* 8, 130–43

Murrell, Peter, (1990), 'Big bang versus evolution: eastern European reforms in the light of recent economic history,' *Plan Econ Report*, June 29

National Bureau of Statistics of China, (various years), *Chinese Statistical Yearbook,* Beijing

Naughton, Barry, (1995), *Growing Out of the Plan: Chinese Economic Reform, 1978–1993*, New York, N.Y.: Cambridge University Press

Naughton, Barry, (1997), *The China Circle: Economics and Technology in the PRC, Taiwan, and Hong Kong*, Washington: Brookings Institution Press

Pomfret, Richard, (1997), 'Growth and Transition: Why Has China's Performance Been So Different?' *Journal of Comparative Economics* 25: 422–440.

Rawski, Thomas, (2001), 'What's Happening to China's GDP Statistics?' *China Economic Review* 12, 347–354.

Sachs, Jeffery, Woo, Wing Thye, (1994), 'Structural factors in the economic reforms of China, Eastern Europe, and the former Soviet Union,' *Economic Policy* 18: 102–145

Sachs, Jeffrey, Woo, Wing Thye, (1997), 'Chinese economic growth: Explanations and the tasks ahead,' in Joint Economic Committee of the United States Congress, *China's Economic Future: Challenges to U.S. Policy*, U.S. Government Printing Office, Washington

D.C., 1996; reprinted in A.M. Babkina (ed.), (1997), *Domestic Economic Modernization in China*, Nova Science Publishers

Woo, Wing Thye, (1994), 'The art of reforming centrally planned economies: Comparing China, Poland, and Russia', *Journal of Comparative Economics*, 18: 276–308

World Bank, (2010), *World Development Reports 2010*, Washington DC

Young, A., (1995), 'The tyranny of numbers: Confronting the statistical realities of the East Asia growth experience,' *Quarterly Journal of Economics*, 100: 644–680

Yu, Chunling, Bastin, M., (2010), 'Hedonic shopping value and impulse buying behaviour in transitional economies: A symbiosis in the Chinese Mainland Market,' *Journal of Brand Management*, 18, 2

Annex 6.1

Table A 1 Annual consumption per capita in urban areas (kilograms)

	Grain	Edible Vegetable Oil	Pork	Poultry	Eggs	Seafood
1978	195.5	1.6	7.7	0.4	2.0	3.50
1980	214.0	2.3	11.2	N/a	2.3	N/a
1985	134.8	5.8	16.7	3.2	6.8	7.1
1990	130.7	6.4	18.5	3.4	7.3	7.7
1995	97.0	7.1	17.2	4.0	9.7	9.2
2000	82.3	8.2	16.7	5.4	11.2	9.9
2005	76.98	9.25	20.2	9.0	10.4	12.5
2009	81.33	9.67	20.5	10.5	10.6	n/a

Table A 2 Annual consumption per capita in rural areas (kilograms)

	Grain	Edible Vegetable Oil	Pork	Poultry	Eggs	Seafood
1978	248.0	2.0	5.8	0.3	0.8	0.8
1980	257.0	2.5	7.7	0.7	1.2	1.1
1985	257.0	4.0	11.0	1.0	2.1	1.6
1990	262.0	5.2	11.3	1.3	2.4	2.1
1995	258.9	5.8	10.6	1.8	3.2	3.4
2000	249.5	7.1	13.4	2.9	5.0	3.9
2005	208.9	6.0	15.6	3.7	4.7	4.9
2009	189.3	6.3	14.0	4.7	5.3	5.3

Table A 3 Living space per capita (square meters)

	Urban	Rural
1978	4.2	8.1
1980	5.0	9.4
1985	6.7	14.7
1990	9.9	17.8
1995	11.8	21.0
2000	20.3	24.8
2009	n/a	33.6

Table A 4 Consumer durables in urban and rural areas (per 100 household sets)

	Color TV		Computer		Washing Machine		Refrigerator	
	Urban	Rural	Urban	Rural	Urban	Rural	Urban	Rural
1978	0.3[1]	0	0	0	0			
1980	0	0			0	0	0	0
1985	17.2	0.8			48.3	1.9	6.6	0.1
1990	59.0	4.7			78.4	9.1	42.3	1.2
1995	89.8	16.9			88.9	16.9	66.2	5.2
2000	116.6	48.7	9.7	0.47	90.5	28.6	80.1	12.3
2005	135.6	84.0	41.5	2.1	95.5	40.2	90.7	20.1
2010	136.0	108.9	65.7	7.6	96.0	53.1	95.3	37.1

Sources: *China Statistical Yearbook*, 1981, 1984, 2002, 2010.

Notes: TV sets per 100 persons.

7 Do imports crowd out domestic consumption? A comparative study of China, Japan and Korea

Chuanglian Chen, Guojin Chen and Shujie Yao[1]

Introduction

A decline in the prices of imported goods (imports) has two counteractive effects on the current demand for domestically produced goods (domestic consumption). First, it raises demand for imported goods and crowds out domestic consumption. This is the so-called intra-temporal substitution effect. Second, as imported goods become cheaper, real current income rises, leading to higher domestic consumption in the current period at the expense of future consumption. This is the so-called inter-temporal substitution, or income, effect.

Whether the intra-temporal and inter-temporal effects will lead to a net crowding out of domestic consumption will depend on the relative sizes of the intra-temporal elasticity of substitution (AES, hereafter for convenience) and the inter-temporal elasticity of substitution (IES, hereafter for convenience) of domestic consumption.[2]

If AES is larger than IES, a decline in the prices of imported goods will reduce domestic consumption, or *vice versa*. It is worth noting that a decline in the relative prices of imported goods *vis-à-vis* domestically produced goods can be caused by domestic currency appreciation. As a result, the empirical results from this study will have some useful implications on foreign exchange policy or other price reforms.

Some empirical studies have investigated IES of both imports and domestic consumption in a rational framework based on a Life Cycle / Permanent Income Model (LCPIM). Ceglowski (1991), for example, investigates the role of inter-temporal substitution in US import demand using a model of import consumption based on LCPIM, and estimates the inter-temporal elasticity for imports to be about 0.8, while the implied relative price elasticity of import consumption to be about 1. These results indicate that import consumption may respond to changes in their inter-temporal prices, as well as changes in their price relative to that of domestic substitutes.

Clarida (1994) employs a simple rational-expectation permanent-income model to derive a structural econometric specification of demand for imported consumer goods. He estimates the average long-run price elasticity of import demand to be −0.95 using a co-integrating approach. The average elasticity of import demand with respect to a permanent increase in real spending was 2.15. Amano and

Wirjanto (1996) examine the importance of inter-temporal substitution in US import consumption using a model of permanent income that allows for random preference shocks and additive separateness of a utility function. Using a co-integration approach, they show that IES for domestic and import consumption were 0.6 and 0.9, respectively. Using the GMM approach, the estimated IES were 1.4 and 4.3, respectively. However, the J-test tends to reject the model which indicates that IES estimated from GMM appears implausible. The empirical results show that IES estimated from intra-temporal optimality condition and from Euler equations are hardly equal.

Nishiyama (2005) argues that, the existence of heterogeneous agents, the rich and the poor, and habit formation in the economy seem to explain this empirical dilemma. On the other hand, Muellbauer (1988), Eichenbaum, Hansen and Singleton (1988), Ferson and Constantinides (1991), Ogaki and Park (1997) and Croix and Urbain (1998) all find that habit formation helps to account for consumption dynamics and explains why empirical data frequently reject the life cycle hypothesis.

Habit formation is one form of time-inseparability, which means that the level of consumption is easily adjusted upward, but difficult to adjust downward. Just like the ancient Chinese proverb 'it's easier to go from rags to riches than riches to rags'. The idea of introducing habit formation into the utility function can date back to Duesenberry (1949). He assumes that utility in each period not only depends on current consumption, but also on past consumption. Therefore, habit formation can measure the change of consumption on the utility, and describe the irreversibleness of consumption.

Croix and Urbain (1998) extend previous work done by Clarida (1994) and Ceglowski (1991) by considering a two-good version of the lifecycle model introducing time-inseparability in household's preferences, and then use quarterly data for USA and France to test the model. With the information contained in the observed stochastic and deterministic trends, they derive a co-integration restriction to estimate curvature parameters of the instantaneous utility function. The remaining parameters are estimated in a second step by GMM. The constancy of different parameters is investigated both in the long run and the short run. Habit formation turns out to be an important factor of import demand, and negligence of habit formation may lead to frequent rejection of the lifecycle hypothesis.

In order to deal with inconsistent IES estimated from intra-temporal optimality condition and from Euler equations, Nishiyama (2005) proposes the cross-Euler equation approach as a prescription for this empirical dilemma, and finds that the Euler equation for domestic non-durable goods is specified incorrectly, while the Euler equation for imported non-durable goods is somehow correctly specified. Croix and Urbain (1998) and Nishiyama (2005) introduce habit formation into the permanent income hypothesis model and find that habit formation turns out to be an important factor for both import and domestic demand.

In this chapter, we first extend the classical permanent-income model by introducing habit formation. Our theoretical model will be more realistic and robust to avoid the empirical dilemma described by Nishiyama (2005). If the parameters of habit formation are set to zero, the model degenerates to the classical model employed by Ceglowski (1991), Clarida (1994), Amano and Wirjanto (1996) and Xu (2002).

We then investigate whether import demand crowds out domestic demand in China, Japan and Korea. Following Cooley and Ogaki (1991), a two-step procedure is used. In the first step, a co-integration approach is used to estimate the co-integrating estimators of IES of import and domestic demands. In the second step, the estimated parameters derived from the first step are plugged into an Euler equation, and use GMM to estimate the parameters of habit formation of import and domestic demands.

The empirical results show that import and domestic consumptions are complements in China, but substitutes in Japan and Korea. It suggests that lower per capita incomes and different consumption behaviour of Chinese consumers from their Japanese and Korean counterparts may explain this difference.

The rest of this chapter is organised as follows. Section 2 describes the theoretical model incorporating habit formation into a classical two-good permanent income model. Section 3 presents the structural econometric methodology, and methods to calculate Marshallian price elasticity, expenditure elasticity, modified IES and modified AES, and then discusses their implications on the relationship between import and domestic demands. Section 4 provides the empirical data used in this chapter. Section 5 reports the empirical results and analyzes whether imports crowd out domestic consumption in China, Japan and Korea. Section 6 concludes.

Theoretical model

Ceglowski (1991), Clarida (1994), Amano & Wirjanto (1996) and Xu (2002) employ a two-good permanent income model with additively separable preferences to derive a structural econometric equation and then take full advantage of the well-developed theory of co-integration to investigate the relationship between imported and domestically-produced goods. However, there would be an empirical dilemma, as IES parameters estimated from the intra-temporal optimality condition and from Euler equations are inconsistent. Nishiyama (2005) argues that the existence of heterogeneous agents, the rich and the poor, and habit formation in the economy seem to explain this puzzle.

In order to overcome this problem, we introduce habit formation into the additively separable instantaneous utility function of the representative household. Consumer utility in each period depends on both present and past domestic and import consumption. Our two-good permanent income model is based on Muellbauer (1988) and Croix and Urban (1998), where the instantaneous utility function of the representative household is defined as follows:

$$u(D_t^*, F_t^*) = \begin{cases} \dfrac{D_t^{*1-\rho}}{1-\rho} + \dfrac{F_t^{*1-\upsilon}}{1-\upsilon} & \text{if } \rho \neq \upsilon \neq 1 \\[2ex] \ln D_t^* + \ln F_t^* & \text{if } \rho = \upsilon = 1 \end{cases} \tag{7-1}$$

Where $D_t^* = (1-\gamma)^{-1} (D_t - \gamma D_{t-1})$ and $F_t^* = (1-\delta)^{-1} (F_t - \delta F_{t-1})$ are the total flows of domestic and import consumptions, respectively. $\delta (\in [-1,1))$ and $\gamma (\in [-1,1))$ index the importance of habit formation of domestic and import consumption. If they are positive, the larger the values are, the greater the impact does previous consumption have on current utility. In order to maximize his or her expected lifetime utility under a lifetime budget constraint, a representative agent would choose to smooth consumption over the whole lifetime. If they are negative, indicating that the goods present some durability (Ferson and Constantinides, 1991), in which case previous consumption still contributes to current utility. Note that, we only consider the impact of one-period lagged consumption on current utility. The dynamic optimization problem of a representative household is formulated as follows:

$$\underset{\{D_t^*, F_t^*\}}{Max} \; E_0 \left\{ \sum_{t=0}^{\infty} \beta^t u(D_t^*, F_t^*) \right\} \tag{7-2}$$

Where E_0 is an expectation operator based on period zero information, β a subjective discount factor, P_t^F and P_t^D respectively denote prices of imported and domestically-produced goods. Assuming $P_t = P_t^F/P_t^D$, we can derive the lifetime budget constraint of the agent as follows:

$$A_{t+1} + D_t + P_t F_t \leq Y_t + (1+r_t)A_t \tag{7-3}$$

Where A_t is the real assets held by the household at time t, Y_t is the stochastic labor income at time t, r_t stands for real interest rate from period t to $t + 1$. Using the Lagrangian approach to solve the above optimal problem, we can obtain an intra-temporal or static first-order condition and Euler equations:

$$P_t \left(\frac{1}{1-\gamma} \right) \left(\frac{D_t - \gamma D_{t-1}}{1-\gamma} \right)^{-\rho} \left[1 - \beta\gamma E_t \left(\frac{D_{t+1} - \gamma D_t}{D_t - \gamma D_{t-1}} \right)^{-\rho} \right]$$
$$= \left(\frac{1}{1-\delta} \right) \left(\frac{F_t - \delta F_{t-1}}{1-\delta} \right)^{-\upsilon} \left[1 - \beta\delta E_t \left(\frac{F_{t+1} - \delta F_t}{F_t - \delta F_{t-1}} \right)^{-\upsilon} \right] \tag{7-4}$$

$$E_t \left[\beta(1+r_{t+1}) \frac{(D_{t+1} - \gamma D_t)^{-\hat{\rho}} - \beta\gamma (D_{t+2} - \gamma D_{t+1})^{-\hat{\rho}}}{(D_t - \gamma D_{t-1})^{-\hat{\rho}} - \beta\gamma (D_{t+1} - \gamma D_t)^{-\hat{\rho}}} - 1 \right] = 0$$

$$E_t \left[\beta(1+r_{t+1}) \frac{(F_{t+1} - \delta F_t)^{-\hat{\upsilon}} - \beta\delta (F_{t+2} - \delta F_{t+1})^{-\hat{\upsilon}}}{(F_t - \delta F_{t-1})^{-\hat{\upsilon}} - \beta\delta (F_{t+1} - \delta F_t)^{-\hat{\upsilon}}} \left(\frac{P_t}{P_{t+1}} \right) - 1 \right] = 0 \tag{7-5}$$

The above model has two advantages. First, it generalises the classical model of consumer behaviour used in Ceglowski (1991) and others to allow for richer dynamics. In particular, under this scheme, as to the existence of habit formation, current import consumption can be substituted for current domestic consumption (intra-temporal substitution) or future import consumption (inter-temporal substitution). In fact, if the parameters of habit formation are set to zero, the model degenerates to a classical model in Ceglowski (1991).

Secondly, the model is more realistic by introducing habit formation, as it is one form of time non-separable preferences which are found to be important factors considered by socio-psychologists. In our framework, current utility in each period not only depends on current consumption, but also on past consumption. Furthermore, the static first-order condition and Euler equations derived from this model would be more robust to avoid the empirical dilemma described by Nishiyama (2005).

Structural econometric equation and methodology

Taking logarithms on both sides of equation (7–4) and adopting the linear approximation of one-order Taylor's expansion proposed by Muellbauer (1988), we have,

$$\rho \ln D_t - \ln P_t - \upsilon \ln F_t + c = \frac{\upsilon}{f + (1-\delta)/\delta} \Delta \ln F_t - \frac{\rho}{g + (1-\gamma)/\gamma} \Delta \ln D_t$$

$$+ \ln\left[1 - \beta\gamma E_t \left(\frac{D_{t+1} - \gamma D_t}{D_t - \gamma D_{t-1}}\right)^{-\rho}\right] - \ln\left[1 - \beta\delta E_t \left(\frac{F_{t+1} - \delta F_t}{F_t - \delta F_{t-1}}\right)^{-\upsilon}\right] \quad (7\text{-}6)$$

$$+ o(\ln D_t) + o(\ln F_t)$$

Where $c = \ln[(1-\gamma)/(1-\delta)]$, $o(\ln D_t)$ and $o(\ln F_t)$ denote high-level order terms of ln D_t and ln F_t, respectively. g and f respectively stand for the average $\Delta\ln D_t$ and $\Delta\ln F_t$. ln P_t, ln F_t and ln D_t are co-integrated in equation (7.6), as long as these variables are $I(1)$.[3] In that case, $\Delta\ln D_t$ and $\Delta\ln F_t$ are $I(0)$ and the right hand side variables in (7.6) are covariance stationary or ingredients of stochastic disturbance.

Based on Engle and Granger's (1987) two-step method, the asymptotic distribution of GMM estimators in the second step are independent of the first-step estimators since the estimated $\hat{\rho}$ and $\hat{\upsilon}$ converge faster than the GMM estimators.[4] In analogy to Cooley and Ogaki (1991), our first step takes the right-hand side of (7.6) as disturbance term ε_t with a co-integrating approach to estimate the co-integrating estimators of IES of import and domestic consumptions. Our second step plugs in the estimated values from the first step into an Euler equation (7–5), and uses GMM to estimate the parameters of habit formation for import and domestic consumptions.

The first step co-integrating relationship is given by:

$$\ln D_t = c' + \frac{\upsilon}{\rho} \ln F_t + \frac{1}{\rho} \ln P_t + \varepsilon_t \quad (7\text{-}7)$$

Where $c' = -c/\rho$, ε_t is I(0) with mean zero. $1/\rho$ denotes IES between domestic consumption and imports, υ/ρ stands for their intra-temporal elasticity of substitution

(AES). All these parameters are used to calculate the Marshallian price elasticity of imported goods and expenditure elasticity of imported and domestically-produced goods.

The Marshallian price elasticity and expenditure elasticity of imported goods are shown below, respectively.[5]

$$\eta_{F,P} = -\frac{1}{\upsilon}\left[1 - \frac{(1-\upsilon)(1-s)}{(s\upsilon/\rho)+(1-s)}\right] \text{ and } \eta_{F,(D+PF)} = \frac{\rho}{\upsilon}\left[\frac{1}{s+(\rho/\upsilon)(1-s)}\right] \quad (7\text{-}8)$$

In an additively separable utility function, according to Ogaki (1992) and Nishiyama (2005), the Marshallian expenditure elasticity of domestic goods is given by:

$$\eta_{D,(D+PF)} = \left[\frac{\rho}{\upsilon} + s\left(1 - \frac{\rho}{\upsilon}\right)\right]^{-1} \quad (7\text{-}9)$$

Where $s = P_t^D D_t / (P_t^D D_t + P_t^F F_t)$ denotes the share of spending on domestic goods. Thus, the Marshallian expenditure elasticity of domestic goods, in analogy to the Marshallian price elasticity and expenditure elasticity of imported goods, is also time-varying.

In the second step, estimated coefficients obtained from (7–7) are plugged into an Euler equation (7–5). GMM is then used to estimate the parameters of habit formation of import and domestic consumptions.

When habit formation is allowed for, the inter-temporal choice becomes more complex. Now, the agents recognise the impact of current choices on their future tastes as to the existence of habit formation, which will render $1/\rho$ and $1/\upsilon$ invalid to measure IES of domestic and import consumption (Constantinides, 1990). However, Boldrin, Christiano and Fisher (1995) and Croix and Urbain (1998) construct IES in a deterministic framework, which is modified by habit formation, or defined as modified IES. Adapting their derivation to our case, the modified IES of domestic and import consumption, are given in (7–10).

$$\frac{1}{\tilde{\rho}} = \frac{1}{\rho}(1-\gamma)\frac{1-\gamma\beta/(1+g)^\rho}{1+\gamma^2\beta/(1+g)^{\rho+1}} = a\frac{1}{\rho} \text{ and } \frac{1}{\tilde{\upsilon}} = \frac{1}{\upsilon}(1-\delta)\frac{1-\delta\beta/(1+f)^\upsilon}{1+\delta^2\beta/(1+f)^{\upsilon+1}}$$

$$= b\frac{1}{\upsilon} \text{ and } \frac{1}{\tilde{\upsilon}} = \frac{1}{\upsilon}(1-\delta)\frac{1-\delta\beta/(1+f)^\upsilon}{1+\delta^2\beta/(1+f)^{\upsilon+1}} = b\frac{1}{\upsilon} \quad (7\text{-}10)$$

Where β is a subjective discount factor, a and b are modified factors, γ and δ denote habit formation of domestic and import consumptions, respectively. g and f respectively stand for the average $\Delta\ln D_t$ and $\Delta\ln F_t$. Note that $\tilde{\upsilon}/\tilde{\rho}$ is the modified AES between import and domestic consumptions.

According to Amano, Ho and Wirjanto (1998) and Nieh and Ho (2006), there are three testable implications on the relationship between import and domestic consumptions.

(a) If $1/\tilde{\rho} > \tilde{\upsilon}/\tilde{\rho}$, import consumption and domestic consumption are complements, under which, the modified IES of domestic consumption is larger than
the corresponding modified AES.

(b) If $1/\tilde{\rho} < \tilde{\upsilon}/\tilde{\rho}$, import consumption and domestic consumption are substitutes,
under which, the modified IES of domestic consumption is less than the cor-
responding modified AES.

(c) If $1/\tilde{\rho} = \tilde{\upsilon}/\tilde{\rho}$, import consumption and domestic consumption are independent,
or unrelated.

Data

This chapter uses data from 1994M01 to 2010M04 (196 observations) for China
and Japan. Due to missing observations, Korean data only covers the period
1995M01–2010M04 (184 observations). Monthly data are seasonally adjusted.

Monthly data are constructed in constant US dollars for imports of Food and
Direct Consumer Goods for Japan, and imports of Consumer Goods for Korea. As
direct import consumption goods data for China are unavailable, they are indirectly
obtained using information provided by the United Nations Statistics Division.
According to the correspondence between Standard International Trade Classification (SITC) Revision 3 and Broad Economic Categories (BEC), data are derived
from 19 BEC basic categories. According to the correspondence between BEC
with the basic classes of goods in the System of National Accounts (SNA), data are
derived for consumption goods, intermediate goods and capital goods in SNA.[6]

Per capita nominal or real values are obtained by dividing the respective total
values by total population. All real values are measured in constant 2005 US dollar prices.[7] As data for domestic goods are unavailable, following Clarida (1994),
they are constructed by subtracting per capita import consumption from per capita
total consumption (DN_t), which is obtained from dividing total retail sales by total
population. Thus, per capita real domestic consumption is defined as follows:

$$D_t = \left(DN_t - P_t^F F_t\right)/ P_t^D \qquad (7\text{-}11)$$

Where DN_t is nominal per capita consumption expenditures, F_t per capita import
consumption, P_t^F implicit price index of imported consumer goods and P_t^D producer price index of domestic consumer goods.[8] The relative price P_t is defined
as the ratio P_t^F/P_t^D. Real interest rate is defined as the difference between inflation
rate and Interbank Offered Rate for China or 1-month government bond yield for
Japan and Korea.

All the data are collected from *IMF*, China Custom Statistics, China's Economic Internet Database (CEInet), China's External Trade Indices, The People's
Bank of China, Bank of Japan and CEIC Global Database.

Empirical results

Summary statistics are reported in Table 7.1. The share of spending on domestic
goods in China is larger than that in Korea, but smaller than that in Japan. China's

Table 7.1 Summary statistics of selected variables

Country	V	Average	Std. Dev.	Minimum	Maximum	Obs
China	$\ln D_t$	10.3	0.70	9.1	11.7	196
	$\ln F_t$	8.1	0.24	7.3	8.6	196
	$\ln P_t$	−0.2	0.29	−0.9	0.2	196
	r_t	2.2%	0.05	−16.7%	9.6%	196
	s	92.4%	0.03	84.1%	97.5%	196
Japan	$\ln D_t$	11.2	0.13	10.9	11.6	196
	$\ln F_t$	8.1	0.15	7.8	8.5	196
	$\ln P_t$	−0.1	0.15	−0.4	0.3	196
	r_t	1.7%	0.01	−1.2%	4.1%	196
	s	96.1%	0.01	91.7%	97.4%	196
Korea	$\ln D_t$	12.5	0.23	11.6	12.9	184
	$\ln F_t$	10.6	0.30	9.6	11.1	184
	$\ln P_t$	0.03	0.11	−0.1	0.3	184
	r_t	3.9%	0.03	−0.7%	9.7%	184
	s	85.4%	0.02	77.5%	91.1%	184

Notes: (1) $s = P_t^D D_t / (P_t^D D_t + P_t^F F_t)$ denotes the share of spending on domestic goods.
(2) The unit of import and domestic consumption is US$ million.

import consumption and domestic consumption are all lower than Korea's and Japan's. One noticeable difference among the three countries is that China has the highest volatility in domestic consumption. The negative average value of $\ln P_t$ means the import price index is lower than the producer price index for China and Japan, while for Korea it has an opposite meaning. Among the three countries, Korea has the highest real interest rate and Japan the lowest.

Table 7.2 presents the results of *ADF* and *PP* tests; the critical values for *ADF* and *PP* tests are given by MacKinnon (1996). In both methods, a constant term is included in the level equation but not in the first difference one. Besides, lag order for *ADF* test is selected by the SC criterion, while bandwidth for *PP* test is selected

Table 7.2 Unit root test results

V		Levels				1st difference			
		ADF		PP		ADF		PP	
		Mode	Stat.	Mode	Stat.	Mode	Stat.	Mode	Stat.
China	$\ln D_t$	(C,N,13)	−0.58	(C,N,12)	−0.41	(N,N,12)	−2.95	(N,N,8)	−13.80
	$\ln F_t$	(C,N,13)	0.39	(C,N,5)	0.88	(N,N,12)	−5.67	(N,N,37)	−28.67
	$\ln P_t$	(C,N,3)	−1.60	(C,N,4)	−2.25	(N,N,2)	−12.59	(N,N,12)	−25.62
Japan	$\ln D_t$	(C,N,13)	−1.49	(C,N,8)	0.22	(N,N,12)	−4.13	(N,N,11)	−81.42
	$\ln F_t$	(C,N,11)	-0.18	(C,N,4)	−0.06	(N,N,10)	−9.28	(N,N,37)	−40.08
	$\ln P_t$	(C,N,1)	−1.97	(C,N,0)	−1.30	(N,N,0)	−8.74	(N,N,6)	−8.41
Korea	$\ln D_t$	(C,N,12)	−1.37	(C,N,14)	−2.33	(N,N,11)	−3.14	(N,N,92)	−25.78
	$\ln F_t$	(C,N,2)	−2.72	(C,N,6)	−1.37	(N,N,1)'	−13.71	(N,N,25)	−20.15
	$\ln P_t$	(C,N,1)	−2.20	(C,N,3)	−1.81	(N,N,0)	−9.94	(N,N,11)	−9.52
5% critical values			−2.88		−2.88		−1.94		−1.94

Notes: *ADF* test based on (C, T, K), C = constant, T = trend, K = lag order. *PP* test based on (C, T, B), B = bandwidth.

by Newey and West (1994). The test results suggest that the null hypothesis of a unit root cannot be rejected at the 5% critical level. The results of *ADF* and *PP* tests suggest that $\ln D_t$, $\ln F_t$ and $\ln P_t$ are *I(1)*.

As all the concerned variables are I(1), the full modified ordinary least squares (FMOLS) and dynamic least squares (DOLS) are used to estimate the long-run co-integrating parameters. According to Phillips and Hansen (1990), Hansen (1992, 2002) and Stock and Watson (1993), FMOLS and DOLS estimators possess the same limited distribution as the full information maximum likelihood estimators and hence are asymptotically optimal. Where FMOLS is based on semi-parametric corrections for endogeneity and serial correlation, by increasing leads and lags of the first differences in the regression can also correct endogeneity and serial correlation. Hence, DOLS estimators are super-consistent and the properly rescaled *t* and Wald statistics for hypotheses about estimators have the conventional asymptotic distributions (standard normal and chi squared). The proper rescaling is to multiply the usual *t* value by $(s/\hat{\lambda})$ and the Wald statistics by $(s/\hat{\lambda})^2$.[9]

Engle and Granger (1987) suggest applying the *ADF* t-test to the residuals in order to test for the null hypothesis of no co-integration. The sixth column in Table 7.3 gives the results. No drift is included in the test equation for the level residuals. The test results reject the null hypothesis of no co-integration, meaning that $\ln D_t$, $\ln F_t$ and $\ln P_t$ are co-integrated. The L_c statistics cannot reject the null hypothesis of variables co-integrated at the 1% critical level based on FMOLS.

Overall, the results presented in Table 7.3 are encouraging. They show that the estimated parameters for $\ln P_t$ and $\ln F_t$ from the two approaches are statistically

Table 7.3 Co-integration regression results: DOLS and FMOLS of equation (7–7)

	Method	Cst.	ln P_t	ln F_t	ADF	Lc	SupF	MeanF	Implied IES	
									$1/\hat{\rho}$	$1/\hat{\upsilon}$
China	DOLS	2.869	1.891	0.946					1.891	1.999
		(1.52)	(7.08)	(1.66)	−3.24	—	—	—		
	FMOLS	2.939	1.983	0.930		0.323	2.622	6.205	1.983	2.132
		(2.65)	(8.47)	(2.77)	−4.38	[0.14]	[0.20]	[0.20]		
Japan	DOLS	4.140	0.291	0.878					0.291	0.331
		(4.49)	(3.03)	(7.70)	−1.80	—	—	—		
	FMOLS	4.884	0.252	0.786		0.684	6.610	14.10	0.252	0.321
		(7.84)	(3.19)	(10.21)	−2.28	[0.01]	[0.04]	[0.10]		
Korea	DOLS	6.726	0.343	0.540					0.343	0.635
		(15.43)	(4.34)	(13.17)	−2.53	—	—	—		
	FMOLS	5.981	0.370	0.610		1.035	7.164	13.77	0.370	0.606
		(6.21)	(2.03)	(6.78)	−2.86	[0.01]	[0.03]	[0.11]		
1% critical values of test for parameter instability						1.03	8.50	18.6		

Notes:
(1) Numbers in parentheses are *t*-values, 10%, 5% and 1% critical values are respectively 1.65, 1.96 and 2.58. Numbers in square brackets are *p*-values. Critical values of L_c, *SupF* and *MeanF* see Hansen (1992, 2002).
(2) FMOLS estimates are based on *VAR(1)* prewhitening procedure and Pzrzen kernel. DOLS estimates are based on one lead and one lag of first differences.
(3) $1/\hat{\rho}$ and $1/\hat{\upsilon}$ are respectively implied IES of domestic and import consumption based on equation (7–7).
(4) Null hypothesis of ADF test is no co-integration.

significant with *a priori* expected signs. We also find that the estimators are little different from each other obtained from two different estimation methods. The FMOLS estimates of IES of domestic consumption for China, Japan and Korea are respectively 1.983, 0.252 and 0.370 and the corresponding AES between import and domestic consumption are 0.930, 0.786 and 0.610. The DOLS estimates of IES of domestic consumption are respectively 1.891, 0.291 and 0.343 for China, Japan and Korea and the corresponding AES between import and domestic consumption are 0.946, 0.878 and 0.540.

These estimated co-integration parameters show that China not only has the largest IES, but also the largest AES. The IES of import consumption can be obtained by dividing the IES of domestic consumption by the AES between import and domestic consumption. The results are given in the eleventh column of Table 7.3. Obviously, China has the largest IES of domestic consumption. In the second stage, the estimated parameters ($1/\hat{\rho}$ and $1/\hat{\upsilon}$) from the co-integration analyses are plugged into an Euler equation (5) and GMM is used to estimate the parameters of habit formation for import and domestic consumptions.

The columns *SupF* and *MeanF* are derived to test for the consistency of parameters with asymptotic critical values provided by Hansen (1992, 2002). The test results cannot reject the null hypothesis of parameters consistency at the 1% level in all regression models.

Hansen (1992, 2002) constructs a test for co-integrating parameters instability on the basis of FMOLS estimation. The *SupF* test is in the spirit of traditional Chow tests. The procedure is as follows. It first calculates a standard Chow F-statistics for a fixed break point t/T, and then considers the sequence of statistics by varying the location of the break. The final statistics is the following sequence.[10]

$$SupF = \sup_{t/T \in [0.15, 0.85]} F_{t/T} \tag{7-12}$$

SupF statistics sequence is used to test for co-integrating parameters instability in order to see how a policy shock, for example, exchange rate adjustment, affects estimated results. The test results are given in Figures 7.1 to 7.3 for China, Japan and Korea, respectively.

Figures 7.1 to 7.3 outline the sequences of $F_{t/T}$ in the interval [0.15, 0.85]. The tests do not reject the null hypothesis of co-integrating parameters instability at the 5% level for all three countries, indicating that $\ln D_t$, $\ln F_t$ and $\ln P_t$ have a long-run and stable co-integrating relationship.

Based on the estimated parameters (implied IES $1/\hat{\rho}$ and $1/\hat{\upsilon}$ in Table 7.3), GMM is used to estimate the parameters of habit formation of import and domestic consumptions. The results are given in Table 7.4. In addition, the following vectors are used as instruments: constant, trend, D_t/D_{t-1}, F_t/F_{t-1}, P_{t-1}/P_t and $1 + r_{t-1}$.

Following Amano and Wirjanto (1996), we set $\beta = 0.99$, and the consistent HAC covariance matrix is given by Newey and West (1987), while the weight of the auto-covariance is given by Quadratic Spectral (QS) kernel. $J - test$ is Hansen's (1982) test for over-identifying restrictions, asymptotically chi^2 distributed with n degrees of freedom, where n is the number of over-identifying restrictions and is

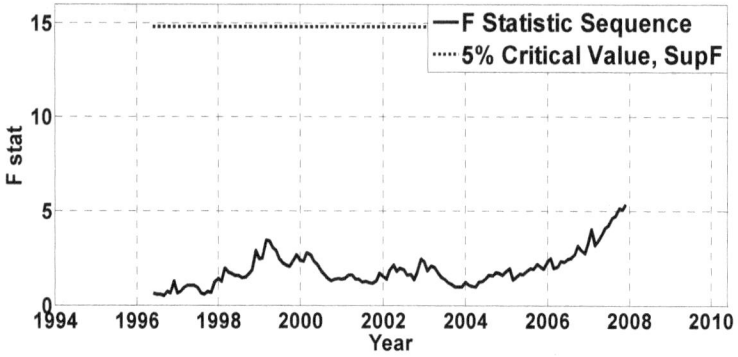

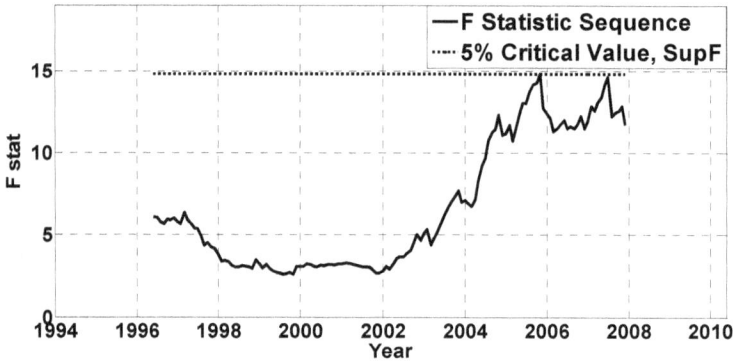

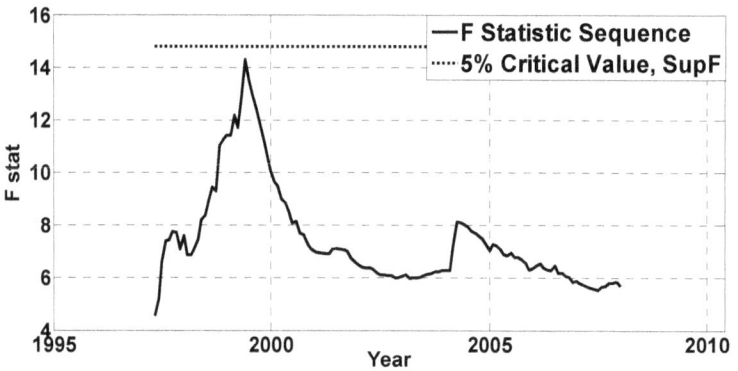

Figure 7.1, *Figure 7.2* and *Figure 7.3* Constancy of co-integration parameters for China, Japan and Korea respectively

equal to ten for all models. *Wald*$_{\gamma=\delta=0}$ is a test for the existence of habit formation with a null hypothesis H_0: $\gamma=\delta=0$. The corresponding *p*-value is included in square brackets.

Hansen's *J–test* evaluates the extent to which the residuals are effectively orthogonal to the instrument set. It is clear that Hansen's *J–test* does not reject the null hypothesis at the 1% level for all models, supporting the specification defined in equation (7-5). Simultaneously, the $Wald_{\gamma=\delta=0}$ statistics rejects the null hypothesis, H_0: $\gamma=\delta=0$, proving the significance of habit formation in most cases. This also shows the limitation of the framework introduced by Ceglowski (1991), where $\gamma=\delta=0$, and adds encouragement to our model.

The estimated parameters γ and δ from different cases are statistically significant with expected signs. The estimated coefficients are little different from each other between the two cases. In Table 7.4, γ is estimated to be 0.610 to 0.643 and δ − 0.143 to − 0.131 for China, indicating that imported goods for China present some durability as defined by Ferson and Constantinides (1991). Whereas γ is estimated to be 0.595 to 0.633 and δ 0.397 to 0.401 for Japan, and γ is estimated to be 0.623 to 0.626 and δ 0.378 to 0.405 for Korea. The estimated coefficients imply that in Japan and Korea, previous domestic consumption has a greater impact on current utility than previous import consumption. In addition, China has the greatest habit formation of domestic consumption among the three countries. All the parameters of habit formation would be used to estimate the modified IES in equation (7-10).

Table 7.5 presents the Ljung-Box and ARCH-LM tests for the residuals from GMM estimation. Ljung-Box *(p)* is for *p*th-order serial correlation in the residuals of an MA model. Ljung and Box (1978)'s modified Q^* *(m)* statistic is introduced by Box and Pierce (1970) to increase the power of the test. Ljung-Box statistics is given by $Q^*(m) = T(T+2) \sum_{l=1}^{m} [\hat{\rho}_l^2/(T-l)] \sim \chi_\alpha^2(m)$. Simulation studies suggest that $m = \ln(T)$ provides better power performance and m is equal to five for all tests. The decision rule is to reject H_0 of absence of serial correlation if $Q(m) > \chi_\alpha^2$. ARCH(p) LM is a standard Largrangian multiplier introduced by Engle (1982) to test whether there is *p*th-order ARCH effects in the estimated residuals.

Table 7.4 Generalized method of moments (GMM) results of equation (7-5)

	IES values based on table 3	γ	δ	$J-test$	$Wald_{\gamma=\delta=0}$
China	$1/\hat{\rho} = 1.891$, $1/\hat{\upsilon} = 1.999$	0.643***	−0.143*	0.118	3116
		(0.012)	(0.078)	[0.999]	[0.000]
	$1/\hat{\rho} = 1.983$, $1/\hat{\upsilon} = 2.132$	0.610***	−0.131*	0.122	24798
		(0.005)	(0.075)	[0.999]	[0.000]
Japan	$1/\hat{\rho} = 0.291$, $1/\hat{\upsilon} = 0.331$	0.633***	0.401***	0.110	102169
		(0.002)	(0.004)	[0.999]	[0.000]
	$1/\hat{\rho} = 0.252$, $1/\hat{\upsilon} = 0.321$	0.595***	0.397***	0.121	35148
		(0.004)	(0.002)	[0.999]	[0.000]
Korea	$1/\hat{\rho} = 0.343$, $1/\hat{\upsilon} = 0.635$	0.626***	0.405***	0.080	215111
		(0.001)	(0.003)	[0.999]	[0.000]
	$1/\hat{\rho} = 0.370$, $1/\hat{\upsilon} = 0.606$	0.623***	0.378***	0.067	137980
		(0.002)	(0.008)	[0.999]	[0.000]

Note: Numbers in parentheses are standard errors. Numbers in square brackets stand for *p*-value. *: significant at 10%, ***: significant at 1%.

Table 7.5 Misspecification tests of gmm estimation[/CAP]

	Equation System	Ljung-Box (2)	Ljung-Box (5)	ARCH(2) LM	ARCH(4) LM
China	Equation (1)	0.410	0.580	0.048	0.198
		[0.815]	[0.989]	[0.976]	[0.995]
	Equation (2)	5.772	34.353	34.766	40.289
		[0.056]	[0.000]	[0.000]	[0.000]
	Equation (1)	0.156	0.211	0.079	0.198
		[0.925]	[0.999]	[0.961]	[0.995]
	Equation (2)	4.808	32.314	33.840	38.873
		[0.090]	[0.000]	[0.000]	[0.000]
Japan	Equation (1)	1.841	0.530	0.039	0.072
		[0.398]	[0.767]	[0.981]	[0.999]
	Equation (2)	1.978	4.783	0.579	1.422
		[0.852]	[0.443]	[0.749]	[0.840]
	Equation (1)	1.820	4.327	0.164	0.343
		[0.403]	[0.503]	[0.921]	[0.987]
	Equation (2)	1.076	3.291	0.452	0.671
		[0.584]	[0.655]	[0.800]	[0.955]
Korea	Equation (1)	2.068	2.507	0.152	0.387
		[0.356]	[0.775]	[0.927]	[0.984]
	Equation (2)	0.708	0.749	0.018	0.029
		[0.871]	[0.980]	[0.991]	[0.999]
	Equation (1)	0.085	1.605	0.188	0.336
		[0.959]	[0.901]	[0.910]	[0.987]
	Equation (2)	0.424	1.453	0.037	0.058
		[0.809]	[0.918]	[0.982]	[0.999]

Note: Numbers in square brackets stand for *p*-values.

These test results suggest that there is no serial correlation and ARCH effects in the estimated residuals for Japan and Korea, and it is also true when we come to test the first equation for China. Whereas, there are serial correlation and ARCH effects in the second equation for China. In short, according to the two tests, serial correlation and ARCH effects do not affect our GMM estimation seriously. Therefore, the estimated results of GMM are credible and reliable.

In order to derive the relationship between import consumption and domestic consumption, we have to analyze the substitution effect between the two types of goods. Since the share of spending on domestic goods (s) is time-varying, the Marshallian price elasticity of imported goods calculated by equation (7-8) is in the range of -2.037 to -1.887 for China, -0.392 to -0.347 for Japan and -0.748 to -0.676 for Korea. The price elasticity is also time-varying with the change of s.

As presented in Table 7.6, the average price elasticity of imported goods is -1.976, -0.357 and -0.708 respectively for China, Japan and Korea. The estimated average price elasticity are different from those in Kee, Nicita and Olarreaga (2008), whose estimated import demand price elasticity is -2.54 based on HS six digit and -1.12 based on ISIC three digit for China, -4.05 based on HS six digit and -1.23 based on ISIC three digit for Japan and -2.08 based on HS six digit and -1.10 based on ISIC three digit for Korea. However, all the results suggest

Table 7.6 Price and expenditure elasticity for domestic and imported goods

	Type of goods	Average price elasticity	Average expenditure elasticity	Nature of goods
China	Imports	−1.976	1.061	Luxury
	Domestic	—	0.995	Necessity
Japan	Imports	−0.357	1.189	Luxury
	Domestic	—	0.992	Necessity
Korea	Imports	−0.708	1.571	Luxury
	Domestic	—	0.903	Necessity

that a decline in the relative price between imported and domestically produced goods would tend to raise the demand for imported goods in all the three countries, especially in China.

We then analyze different consumer behaviors of pursuing import and domestic goods. By doing so, the expenditure elasticity of import and domestic goods from equations (7-8) and (7-9) are derived. As reported in Table 7.6, the average expenditure elasticity of imported goods are 1.061, 1.189 and 1.571 respectively for China, Japan and Korea, and the corresponding average expenditure elasticity of domestically produced goods are 0.995, 0.992 and 0.903. These results mean that imported goods are on average luxurious, but domestically produced goods are necessities.

Next, we continue to analyze the characters of consumer behavior. China has the largest IES and modified IES of both import and domestic consumptions, partly because Chinese consumers are more vulnerable to liquidity constraints than their Japanese or Korean counterparts (Table 7.7). As seen in Figure 7.4, the average per-capita disposable income in China is significantly less than that in Korea and Japan. Therefore, the optimal inter-temporal consumption pattern for Chinese consumers is easily disrupted by liquidity constraints.

Furthermore, the IES of import consumption is larger than that of domestic consumption, because domestic goods act as a necessity, while imported goods as

Table 7.7 Comparisons of consumer behavior in different countries

Type of consumption	China	Japan	Korea
IES of imports	2.066	0.326	0.621
IES of domestic goods	1.937	0.272	0.357
AES between import and domestic goods	0.938	0.832	0.575
Modified IES of imports	2.617	0.105	0.203
Modified IES of domestic goods	0.202	0.032	0.039
Modified AES	0.077	0.307	0.193
Habit formation of imports	−0.137	0.399	0.392
Habit formation of domestic goods	0.627	0.614	0.625
Relationship Import/domestic goods	complement	substitute	substitute

Notes: IES = inter-temporal elasticity of substitution, AES = intra-temporal (or intra-period) elasticity of substitution between imports and domestic goods.

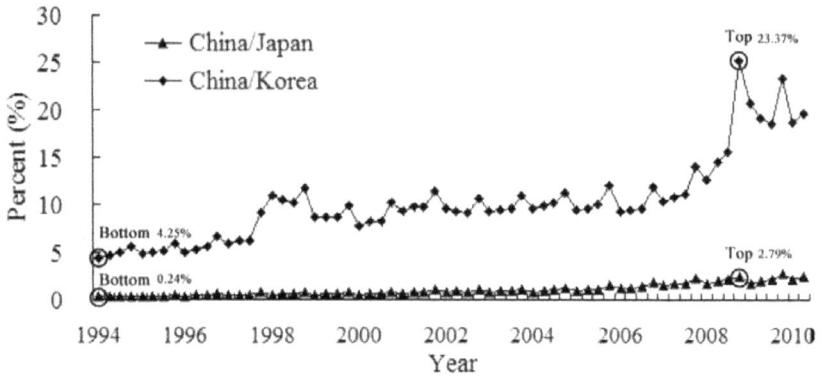

Figure 4. The Ratio of Average Per-capita Disposable Income

Figure 7.4 Average per-capita disposable income ratio for China/Japan and China/Korea

a luxury. However, habit formation of domestic consumption is larger than import consumption, and imported goods for China even present some durability.

Constantinides (1990) argues that habit formation introduces a gap between IES and modified IES, and the latter is about one fourth of the size of the former. However, Naik and Moore (1996) find the gap between the two to be about one half. Moreover, Ferson and Constantinides (1991) and Ogaki and Park (1997) point out that a relatively low modified IES is compatible with a relatively high IES when habit formation is allowed. Croix and Urbain (1998) show that IES of domestic consumption is five times larger than the modified IES, and IES of import consumption is nearly three times larger than the modified IES for the USA. Our estimated results prove that IES of domestic consumption is nearly nine times as large as the modified IES, while the two elasticities of import consumption are almost the same for China. But for Japan and Korea, IES of import consumption is about twice larger than the modified IES. The results reveal that habit formation plays an essential role in affecting consumer behavior.

Finally, whether import consumption crowds out domestic consumption needs to be addressed. The modified IES of domestic consumption ($1/\tilde{\rho}$) is 0.202 and the AES ($\tilde{\upsilon}/\tilde{\rho}$) is 0.077 for China (Table 7.7). IES is greater than AES ($1/\tilde{\rho} > \tilde{\upsilon}/\tilde{\rho}$). The results support the argument that imports and domestically produced goods are complements rather than substitutes in China. This has a critical policy implication as far as currency appreciation is concerned, as it implies that imported goods may have little crowding out effect on domestically produced goods caused by a decline in the relative price between these two types of goods.

However, due to the high IES of domestic consumption and the existence of habit formation, inter-temporal consumption optimization implies that a decline in intra-temporal consumption would increase the implied per-capita income, which would increase the demand for imported goods as well as domestic goods in the current period through an income effect. The bigger IES, the more will be consumed in the current period at the expense of future consumption. This income effect is opposite to the intra-temporal substitution effect. Since IES is bigger than AES, there is no crowding out effect on current domestic demand.

In addition, imported goods present some durability and substitute little for domestic goods in China. That is also why the modified AES is only 0.077 as compared to 0.307 for Japan and 0.193 for Korea. Thus domestic consumption is little influenced by intra-temporal optimality choice when the relative price of imports and domestically-produced goods declines. This is why imports and domestic consumptions act as complements to each other.

In contrast, IES is smaller than AES in Japan and Korea, implying that import and domestic consumptions are substitutes in both countries. This may be explained as follows. Firstly, as Japan and Korea have a good medical and insurance system, unlike their Chinese counterparts, Japanese and Korean consumers are less vulnerable to liquidity constraints. As a result, IES and modified IES in Japan and Korea are smaller than those in China. Therefore, the inter-temporal substitution effect in Japan and Korea is not as strong as in China. Secondly, Table 7.7 shows that the average expenditure elasticity of import consumption in Japan and Korea are greater than that in China, indicating that Japanese and Korean consumers would spend more on imported goods than their Chinese counterparts as a result of rising per capita incomes. Thirdly, the ratio of average per-capita disposable incomes between China and Japan was only about 2.8% and that between China and Korea 20% in 2009 (Figure 7.4). This means that a decline in the relative price between imported and domestically produced goods would sharply raise import consumption in Japan and Korea due to an income effect, strongly crowding out domestic consumption because of an intra-temporal optimality choice. That is also why the modified AES in Japan and Korea are much greater than in China.

Conclusion

In this chapter, we employ a two-good permanent-income model to investigate whether imports crowd out domestic consumption in China, Japan and Korea. We take full advantage of the well-developed theory of co-integration to investigate IES of both import and domestic consumptions, pursue GMM approach to estimate the habit formation parameters, and calculate the modified IES and modified AES on habit formation. The modified IES of domestic consumption are estimated to be 0.202, 0.032 and 0.039 for China, Japan and Korea, respectively, and the corresponding modified IES of import consumption 2.617, 0.105 and 0.203. The estimated AES are 0.077, 0.307 and 0.193 respectively for China, Japan and Korea.

As the IES between import and domestic consumptions is greater than the AES in China, it suggests that import and domestic consumptions are complements. In Japan and Korea, the IES is smaller than the AES, suggesting that import and domestic consumptions are substitutes. These results imply that the crowding out effect of imports on domestic consumption is limited in China but strong in Japan and Korea.

Three possible explanations are offered for the different results between China and the other two countries. First, China's per capita income is significantly lower than that in Japan or Korea. This implies that Chinese consumers must have been more vulnerable to liquidity constraints than their Japanese or Korean counterparts. Therefore, the Chinese pay more attention to current consumption than their Japanese and Korean counterparts. Consequently, a decline in the relative price between imported and domestically produced goods leads to a rise in implied per-capita income, which would increase the demand for imported goods as well as domestic goods in the current period through an income effect. However, as AES is very small in China, the substitution effect of imports on domestic consumption is critically diluted by the income effect.

Second, since the average expenditure elasticity of import consumption in Japan and Korea are greater than that in China, compared to their Chinese counterparts, Japanese and Korean consumers tend to spend more on imported goods as a result of rising per capita disposable incomes.

Third, China has the highest IES of domestic consumption among the three countries. Compared to their Japanese and Korean counterparts, Chinese consumers tend to consume more domestically produced goods in the current period relative to such future consumption. In addition, imported goods present some durability, which makes the modified AES as small as 0.077, compared to 0.307 in Japan and 0.193 in Korea. Thus domestic consumption is little impacted by intra-temporal optimality choice when the relative price between imported and domestically produced goods declines.

Our results have striking policy implications for China relating to currency appreciation. As habit formation is an important element in consumer behavior, it reduces IES in a big scale. This suggests that the modified IES is important for investigating consumer behavior of inter-temporal substitution choice. It also reveals the limitations in the framework introduced by Ceglowski (1991), Clarida (1994), Amano and Wirjanto (1996) and Xu (2002), where all parameters of habit formation are set to zero. Compared with China, domestic consumption in Japan and Korea is more sensitive to the relative price between imported and domestically produced goods. In addition, our empirical results imply that import and domestic consumptions are complements for China. Therefore, China should continue to speed up the pace of opening-up and develop international trade. However, one should not be over optimistic, as the consumption capability of Chinese consumers would depend on a steady increase of their average disposable incomes. If import consumption contained less luxurious goods compared to domestic consumption, there would be no difference between imported and domestically produced goods in China. Consequently, intra-temporal substitution effects would increase, reducing the degree of complementarities between import and domestic consumptions.

Appreciation of the Chinese currency would have this anticipated effect, as it will reduce the relative price between imported and domestically produced goods. In the short run, the crowding out effect of imports on domestically produced goods may be limited due to a low intra-temporal substitution effect. In the long term, however, the situation may change, especially when per capita income in China rises. In that case, China's consumption habit may approach that of Japan's or Korea's, meaning that the crowding effect of imports on domestically produced goods will increase over time.

Notes

1 This research is supported by Humanities and Social Sciences Youth Project, Chinese Ministry of Education (12YJC790006),Guangdong Planning Youth Project of Philosophy and Social Sciences (GD11YYJ01), and South China Normal University Youth Teachers' Research Fund.

2 In Section 2, we can see that the IES and AES have to be modified based on habit formation. When habit formation is encompassed, we define them as modified IES and modified AES.

3 In this chapter, data for China, Japan and Korea seem to support this assumption.

4 The advantages of using a co-integrating approach to estimate the preference parameters of the utility function is pointed out and discussed by Ogaki (1992) and Ogaki and Park (1997).

5 Proofs for equations (7–8) and (7–9) are available on request, or see Clarida (1994), Croix and Urbain (1998), Ogaki (1992) and Nishiyama (2005).

6 United Nations Statistics Division website provides the detail of correspondence between SITC and BEC, BEC and SNA. Website: http://unstats.un.org/unsd/cr/registry/regdnld.asp?Lg=1

7 As China has not yet published the Import Price Index of consumer goods and the Producer Price Index of manufactured products monthly fixed base index, this chapter uses China's Import Price Index of consumer goods and Producer Price Index of manufactured products monthly year-on-year index and seasonally adjusted index to construct China's Import Price Index of consumer goods and Producer Price Index of manufactured products monthly fixed base ratio index (with 2005 as the base year).

8 We use the Import Price Index for Japan and Korea, and the Import Price Index of consumer goods for China; the Producer Price Index for Japan and Korea, and the Producer Price Index of manufactured products for China.

9 Where S is standard error when using *OLS* to regress equation (7–7). A consistent estimate of $\hat{\lambda}$ is obtained as follows: $\hat{\varepsilon}_t$ is residuals of *OLS* regression on equation (7–7), fitting an $AR(p)$ process to the residuals, from $\hat{\varepsilon}_t = \rho_1 \hat{\varepsilon}_{t-1} + \rho_2 \hat{\varepsilon}_{t-2} + \ldots + \rho_p \hat{\varepsilon}_{t-p} + e_t$, where $t = p + 1, \ldots, T$, and then use *AIC* to pick the lag length. Given $\sigma^2 = \dfrac{1}{T-p} \sum_{t=p+1}^{T} e_t^2$, then we can derive $\lambda^2 = \dfrac{\sigma^2}{(1-\rho_1 - \ldots - \rho_p)^2}$.

10 See Hansen (1992, 2002) for further detail.

Bibliography

Amano, R. A., Wirjanto, T. S., (1996), 'Intertemporal substitution, imports and permanent income model', *Journal of International Economics,* 40: 439–457.

Amano, R. A., Ho, W. M., and Wirjanto, T. S., (1998), 'Intraperiod and intertemporal substitution in import demand', *Cahiers de recherche CREFE Working Paper.*

Boldrin, M., Christiano, L., Fisher, J., (1995), 'Asset pricing lessons for modeling business cycles', *NBER Working Paper* No. 5262.

Box, G. E. P., Pierce, D. A., (1970), 'Distribution of residual autocorrelations in autoregressive-integrated moving average time series models', *Journal of the American Statistical Association,* 65: 1509–1526.

Ceglowski, J., (1991), 'Inter-temporal substitution in import demand', *Journal of International Money and Finance,* 10: 118–130.

Clarida, R. H., (1994), 'Co-integration, aggregate consumption, and the demand for imports: a structural econometric investigation', *The American Economic Review,* 84: 298–308.

Constantinides, G. M., (1990), 'Habit formation: a resolution of the equity premium puzzle', *Journal of Political Economy,* 98: 519–543.

Cooley, T. F., Ogaki, M., (1991), 'A time series analysis of real wages, consumption, and asset returns under optimal labor contracting: a cointegration-Euler equation approach', *Rochester Center for Economic Research Working Paper* No. 285, Rochester, New York: University of Rochester.

Croix, D. L., Urbain, J. P., (1998), 'Inter-temporal substitution in import demand and habit formation', *Journal of Applied Econometrics,* 13: 589–612.

Duesenberry, J. S., (1949), *Income, Saving and the Theory of Consumer Behavior,* Cambridge, MA: Harvard University Press.

Eichenbaum, M. S., Hansen, L. P., Singleton, K. L., (1988), 'A time series analysis of representative agent models of consumption and leisure choice under uncertainty', *Quarterly Journal of Economics,* 103: 51–78.

Engle, R., (1982), 'Autoregressive conditional heteroskedasticity with estimates of the cariance of U. K. inflation,' *Econmetrica,* 50: 987–836.

Engle, R., Granger, C., (1987), 'Cointegration and error correction: representation, estimation and testing', *Econmetrica,* 55: 251–276.

Ferson, W. E., Constantinides, G. M., (1991), 'Habit persistence and durability in aggregate consumption', *Journal of Financial Economics,* 29: 199–240.

Hansen, B. E., (1992), 'Tests for parameter instability in regressions with I(1) processes', *Journal of Business and Economic Statistics,* 10: 321–335, Reprinted in Twentieth Anniversary Commemorative Issue, *Journal of Business and Economic Statistics* (2002) 20: 45–59.

Hansen, L., (1982), 'Large sample properties of generalized method of moments estimators', *Econometrica,* 50: 1029–1054.

Kee, H. L., Nicita, A., Olarreaga, M., (2008), 'Import demand elasticities and trade distortions', *The Review of Economics and Statistics,* 90: 666–682.

Ljung, G. M., Box, G. E. P., (1978), 'On a measure of lack of fit in time series models', *Biometrika,* 65: 297–303.

MacKinnon, J. G., (1996), 'Numerical distribution functions for unit root and cointegration tests', *Journal of Applied Econometrics,* 11: 601–618.

Muellbauer, J., (1988), 'Habits, rationality and myopia in the life cycle consumption function', *Annales d'Economie et de Statistique,* 9: 47–70.

Naik, N.Y., Moore, M. J., (1996), 'Habit formation and intertemporal substitution in individual food consumption', *The Review of Economics and Statistics,* 78: 321–328.

Newey, W. K. and West, K. D., (1987), 'A simple, positive semi-denite, heteroskedasticity and autocorrelation consistent covariance matrix', *Econometrica,* 55: 703–708.

Newey, W. K. and West, K. D., (1994), 'Automatic lag selection in covariance matrix estimation', *Review of Economic Studies,* 61: 631–653.

Nieh, C. C., Ho, T. W., (2006), 'Does the expansionary government spending crowd out the private consumption? Cointegration analysis in panel data', *Quarterly Review of Economics and Finance,* 46: 133–148.

Nishiyama, S. I., (2005), 'The cross-Euler equation approach to inter-temporal substitution in import demand', *Journal of Applied Econometrics,* 20: 841–872.

Ogaki, M., (1992), 'Engel's law and cointegration', *Journal of Political Economy* 100: 1027–1046.

Ogaki, M., Park, J. Y., (1997), 'A cointegrating approach to estimating preference parameters', *Journal of Econometrics,* 82: 107–134.

Phillips, P., Hansen, B. E., (1990), 'Statistics inference in instrumental variables with I(1) processes', *Review of Economic Studies,* 57: 99–124.

Stock, J. H., Watson, M. W., (1993), 'A simple estimator of co-integrating vectors in higher order integrated systems', *Econometrica* 61: 783–820.

Xu, X., (2002), 'The dynamic-optimization approach to import demand: a structural model', *Economic Letters,* 74: 265–270.

8 Land sales as a public financing tool in China and India

Kala Seetharam Sridhar, Shuzhong Gu,
Shujie Yao[1]

Introduction

The main objective of this chapter is to assess the role of public land leasing and sales as a municipal financing tool in India and China. The motivation for this research stems from the fact that a poor financial situation exists in Indian cities and land sales have become an increasingly important source of finance in Chinese cities. Most Indian cities have now abolished the highly buoyant source of revenue, the octroi, which is now generally accepted to have been distortionary in its effects. Further, the property tax base is at best subjective and has not yet become a resilient source of revenue.

The sphere of municipal taxation in India was enlarged to include land tax sometime ago. However, with a few exceptions, little progress has been reported regarding the levy/enhancement of land taxes by local bodies. A high tax rate on land encourages improvements on land and provides a disincentive for large speculative landholdings. A high land value tax would decrease the market value of land and provide a stimulus to develop all land to its full potential.[2] However, local governments frequently have more flexibility in *managing* their assets than they do in adjusting tax rates, or introducing new taxes which require higher-level governmental approval, as in China, or are prohibited entirely by the fiscal framework.

One of the means by which local governments increase revenues in the absence of an effective taxation system is through public land leasing (Ding, 2005). An option that has been given much less attention in municipal finances is their land assets. In fact, many cities and municipal governments have access to substantial land assets such as public buildings, housing, and municipally owned enterprises.

In many instances, asset sales are attractive as a way to mobilize investment resources. This is not an example without precedent. In fact, the city of Bratislava, Slovakia, financed about 15% of its annual capital budget from privatization proceeds (Peterson, 2007).

While such examples can only be a temporary arrangement, there is no doubt that land is the most valuable asset on municipal balance sheets. This is easy to understand since local governments make infrastructure investments on their land such as water supply networks, roads, and schools, which are likely to be capitalized in the land value. Further, urbanization and economic growth drive up land prices. In fact, Sridhar (2004) summarizes the disparity in real estate prices between the central business district and the suburbs of some of India's metropolitan areas. Hence, municipal governments have rights enabling them to capture the outcome of economic growth which manifests itself in increased land prices, and also their own investment through sales (Peterson, 2007).[3] Land in urban areas is a scarce resource which needs to be optimally utilised if the objective of affordable housing is to be attained.

In this chapter, we attempt to understand the role of land leasing or sales as a revenue source in some selected Indian and Chinese cities. We will also discuss the policy implications of land leasing/sales on regional economic growth and the wellbeing of the urban populations in both countries.

The key objective of this research is to compare evidence regarding the actual potential of municipal land as a revenue source in India and China. In India, a large amount of urban land is held by urban development authorities (UDAs) and it is possible to use the revenues from their sales as an infrastructure financing strategy. However, there is very little systematic research thus far that throws light on the important role played by land held by the UDAs, in municipal financing. In China as well, there is little systematic evidence on the use of land as a financing tool by cities, while property prices are soaring.

Hence an attempt is made to answer the following questions.

a. What is the potential of land as a revenue-generating source in India's cities, when we compare it to the total revenues, own source revenues and property tax revenues being generated? We compare the importance of revenues from land leasing in China's cities to that which we find in India's cities.
b. How are the proceeds from land leasing and sales realized, given that land is held by agencies different from the municipal authorities in many cases? Answers to this question are quite important since it means that infrastructure financing can become a much simpler process once the value of land is realized.

UDAs in India's cities hold substantial amounts of land as part of urban development projects (Peterson, 2007). In new areas, these UDAs acquire land under public purpose regulation, which has come under a lot of public scrutiny recently because of special economic zones, develop it with infrastructure networks, and then sell to developers and end-users. Once the capital costs of the projects are recovered, UDAs typically hand over the developed parcels to the municipal government for their operation and maintenance. This is notwithstanding the several institutional overlaps that exist with respect to land use in India's cities (Sridhar, 2006; Sridhar and Reddy, 2010).

Considering the huge amount of land the governments own and accumulate in various ways in India and China, and the expected speculation and capitalization that have been taking place, the state and local governments in these countries must be using land as an effective financing tool.

This chapter is organized as follows. Section 2 highlights the importance of urban, public land as a source of revenue in India and China. Section 3 provides the evidence from other countries with respect to the potential of public land leasing and sales. Section 4 outlines the research methodology. Section 5 focuses on the potential of land leasing and sales as a revenue source for selected cities in India and China. The final section summarizes the findings and draws policy implications.

Importance of land as a source of revenue: India and China

While there is substantial variability in the revenue capacity of India's cities, we explore the potential of land as a revenue-raising tool for municipalities and compare this with the evidence from China's cities.

There is plenty of anecdotal evidence that big ticket land sales have been taking place across India. For instance, the government of Karnataka acquired land for the new international airport (at *Devanahalli*) from farmers and village/town inhabitants. It handed over 1,600 acres to the Bangalore International Airport Ltd. and retained 408 acres. In March 2007, the government announced it would auction off the retained land in parcels of 25 acres, for an estimated INR 20 billion. However, in late June 2007 the chief minister announced that this decision was being reconsidered and that the land might be leased instead.

There is another example of the land phenomenon from Bangalore. Bangalore has a Prevention of Unauthorised Construct Cell within the Bangalore Urban Deputy Commissioner's Office. It is clearing land of unauthorized construction, and either selling the cleared land at auction or allocating it to the Bangalore Development Authority (BDA) for low-income housing. There was some indication that some land may be allocated to Karnataka Housing Board and Karnataka Slum Clearance Board as well. In all, authorities found that 18,447 acres had been illegally encroached upon in the outskirts of Bangalore. As of mid-July 2007, 8,000 acres had been recovered. Of this, 4,000 acres were to be auctioned off and 4,000 to be allocated, mostly for low-income housing. The auctioned land was sold for up to INR 10–20 million per acre. On June 27, 2007, 18 acres in various parcels were auctioned for INR 95.5 million. On June 28, 2007, 28.18 acres were auctioned for INR 191.2 million, based on news items from the Hindu and Deccan Herald, June and July 2007. Thus the auctioned land was sold respectively for INR 5.3 million and INR 6.8 million per acre.

Similarly, the Hyderabad Urban Development Authority auctioned off 69 acres in 15 plots at *Kopatet*, 20 km from the city. This is land next to the outer ring road that is being built. Land was acquired for road construction. The 69 acres were auctioned on July 20, 2006, for INR 7.03 billion. The minimum price per acre for auction was set at INR 45 million per acre. However, the average actual price exceeded INR 100 million. The highest priced parcel was sold for INR 144.5 million per acre.

Several such examples abound from other cities in India. Between December 2006 and March 2007, the Haryana Urban Development Authority auctioned off land for INR 7.4 billion, including one 2,700 square meter site for INR 734 million. Some of this land was proposed for public private partnership (PPP) models of development. A 5-acre site was auctioned on February 4, 2007 in Gurgaon for INR 2.552 billion, which turned out to be more than INR 500 million per acre, or US$12 million per acre, targeted for 5-star hotel development. The NOIDA Authority auctioned land in November, 2006 for INR 83.1 million, at a price of INR 611,000 per square meter. There are significant variations in the price of land across cities based on the above examples.

China has a central government budget and each local government has its own local budget. In China, land leasing has been a key element of China's fiscal decentralization. The central government retains all tax policy authority over local governments. Similar to what we find in India, municipalities in China cannot change tax rates, introduce new taxes or scrap dysfunctional local taxes. They also need higher government approval for adjustments in user charges. Thus land leasing was an attempt by municipalities to gain control over a revenue source genuinely within their control (Peterson, 2007). Land leasing in China involves the up-front sale of long-term occupancy and development rights. This practice was introduced on an experimental basis in 1987 in Shenzhen and other coastal cities. The land leasing reforms were intended to stimulate locally led economic development by allowing cities to attract foreign investment by providing stable land occupancy rights to investors. Land leasing provided a potentially large source of income for China's municipalities, whose revenues were to be invested primarily in infrastructure and enhancing cities' competitive position for economic growth.

In China, urban land is owned by the state through municipal governments (Choui, Leman and Rufei, 2009). Since 1988, land use rights can be leased from municipal governments for up to 70 years, depending on the use of land. Land leasing income is essentially retained by local governments (90–95%) and, until 2007, was lodged as off-budget revenue. Since 2007, the central government has required all land leasing revenues to be shown in on-budget accounts. The State Council also ordered that, starting in 2007, all municipalities must retain land leasing revenues in a declining reserve for a period of three years; honor the revenue-sharing arrangement whereby 5–10% of land leasing revenue is sent to the central government, a practice largely ignored for many years; allocate a portion of their land leasing revenues to land reclamation and protection; and lease all land, including industrial land, through public auction or open tenders. However, municipalities have always defied the revenue sharing arrangement proposed by the central government.[4]

Revenues from leasing of land use rights accounts for 30–50% of annual fiscal revenues for most cities, and up to 80% in some cities (Huang, 2005). Municipalities in China try to acquire as much as land as possible, as cheaply as possible, then either sell it at market rates, or use it as collateral for infrastructure loans, or provide it at below market rates to strategic (mostly foreign) investors for industrial development.

Thus in China as well as India, there are significant variations in the price of land across cities based on the above examples. It is not quite clear if these variations are due to the quality of the disposal process or the nature of land contracts.

Evidence from other countries

Land leasing and sales have been time tested in other similar countries. This has been documented in the literature. In fact in the aftermath of Proposition 13, which froze property tax assessments in the state of California, USA, California's localities turned to land assets as a means of financing infrastructure. Such a phenomenon is not restricted to developed countries alone.

In China, it was only in 1988 that the Constitution was amended and in 1990 was the ground lease system formally approved by the central government, and nation-wide adoption of public land leasing started in 1992 (Deng, 2005). The chapter finds that without public land leasing, local public goods are completely capitalized in wages. Deng finds that public land leasing is Pareto improving because it eliminates free riding on the consumption of local public goods and establishes the link of rent capitalization. It also helps to shift local government's role from a production manager to public goods provider.

Peterson (2007) presents evidence that many cities in China have financed more than half of their urban infrastructure investment from land leasing, while borrowing against the value of land on their balance sheets to finance much of the remainder. Most land leasing revenues were assigned to municipal governments in the ratio 5:95, i.e., 5% to central government and 95% to local government, as part of the 1994 fiscal reforms (Chan, 1997). Several municipalities studied in the World Bank's City Development Strategies had freed up land for resale in the urban centres by moving their city halls and other related municipal buildings to a new location outside the urban centres and auctioned the vacated land to developers (Chroed, 2005). Hong (1996) found that the Hong Kong Government captured about 39% of the land-value increments occurring between 1970 and 1991 from land leased in the 1970s. More importantly, the captured value financed 55% of the average annual infrastructure investment during 1970–91.

The evidence regarding Ethiopia, which recently introduced land leasing as a financing device for cities, is from Peterson (2007). Except for water tariffs, which some regions allow municipalities to adjust in light of service costs, land leasing is the only source of revenue over which municipalities have policy control. Ethiopian policy, by specifying that a municipality shall earmark 90% of all land-leasing proceeds for infrastructure investment, ties revenues from land leasing directly to municipal infrastructure investment.

Peterson (2007) also presents evidence from India, focusing on land sales and auctions by the Mumbai Metropolitan Regional Development Authority (MMRDA). The startling finding is that sales from MMRDA land auctions in just one complex, Bandra-Kurla complex, in January 2006 was a staggering INR 23.0 billion, which was twice more than the total infrastructure investment made by the Mumbai Municipal Corporation during 2004–05 (INR 10.4 billion) and four times more than MMRDA's own infrastructure investment in 2004–05 (INR 5.4 billion). Indeed, *Vision Mumbai* by Bombay First and McKinsey (2003) identifies land sales as one of the most important components in the public sector's contribution to infrastructure financing.

In China, the potential for revenue mobilization is indicated by two individual land-auction transactions consummated in Shanghai, one at the end of 2005, the other in January 2006 (Peterson, 2007). Sale of lease rights to two land plots in downtown Shanghai generated more than RMB 6.5 billion (US$810 million), with leasing rights selling at US$9,300 per square meter in one transaction and US$7,500 in the other. As an indication of the volume of land leasing, Shanghai, in the third quarter of 2003, leased at auction 805 hectares (8.05 million square meters) of land, mostly in the new development area of Pudong. Chengdu, capital of Sichuan province, sold a single mixed commercial-residential site outside the central zone for the equivalent of US$97 million, or roughly $1,350 per square meter.

One may also ask how land can be made a part of overall financing. Table 8.1 presents several such examples from around the world where land leases are a significant mode of financing urban infrastructure. The startling evidence presented in Table 8.1 indeed shows that land is not an asset in any country that can be overlooked or ignored for its role as a financing tool.

What is missing in the above discussion indeed is the fact that no systematic studies have been conducted to evaluate the collective potential of land in India or China's cities. Specifically, no studies have looked at the potential of land as a revenue-generating source in India's municipalities, let alone compare this with evidence from China. No attention has been paid to the importance of land assets

Table 8.1 Selected cases of land-based financing in developing countries

Location and activity	Amount and use
Cairo, Egypt, 2007 Auction of desert land for new cities, 2,100 hectares	$3.12 billion, to cover costs of infrastructure and highway connecting Cairo Ring Road
Cairo, Egypt, from 2005 Private installation of public infrastructure for developable land	$1.45 billion of private infrastructure investment, and to government for moderate-income housing
Mumbai, India, 2006–07 Auction of financial centre land, 13 hectares by Mumbai Development Authority (MMRDA)	$1.2 billion, to finance projects in Mumbai's metropolitan transportation plan
Bangalore, India: Planned sale of land to finance access highway to new airport	$500+ million. On hold; land will be used instead for ministry buildings and government-built industrial space
Istanbul, Turkey, 2007 Sale of old municipal bus station and former administrative site	$1.5 billion in auction proceeds, to be dedicated to capital investment budgets
Cape Town, South Africa, 2006. Sale of Victoria and Albert Waterfront property	$1.0 billion, to recapitalize Transnet and support nationwide investment in transport infrastructure
Bogotá, Colombia: Betterment levy	$1.0 billion collected in 1997–2007, and $1.1 billion planned for 2008–15, for financing city street and bridge improvement

Source: Peterson (2009).

in municipal balance sheets or the revenue stream from land, and how they could contribute to financing municipal infrastructure. In this chapter, we study the revenue stream from land in a sample of four large Indian cities over a ten-year period to assess its contribution to municipal finances and compare this with the evidence from China's cities.

In any case, it is clear that big ticket land transactions are taking place in cities across India and China. However, there has been no collective attempt to assess the quantitative relevance of such land deals on the fiscal health of urban local bodies in these two countries.

Methodology

Since comprehensive municipal budgets are not released to the public in most countries, it is difficult to put together reliable data on the magnitude of land leasing except through case studies. Given the sparse research in this emerging area, we gather data from field visits to a selected million-plus cities in India regarding the revenues UDAs and municipal corporations in India have realized from land leasing and sales. Once these data are gathered, we compare them with revenues from the property tax, their total revenues, own source revenues and actual expenditures on various infrastructure projects. For China's cities we did not have detailed information on the expenditure by the cities financed by revenues from land lease and/or sales.

For India's cities, we start from Urban Local Bodies' (ULBs') revenues that could result from land sales and leases by UDAs as an addition to existing municipal revenues.

Currently, in Indian cities, some land is held by municipal corporations. Revenues from the sale or lease of land are classified under their non-tax revenues. However, as described earlier, a substantial amount of land is held by UDAs in cities and their revenues do not accrue to the ULBs, and hence is not accounted for in the ULB revenues reported by the various finance commissions. Thus this work has implications for merging functions of the UDAs and the ULBs in India's cities. It is useful to note that since India's Jawaharlal Nehru National Urban Renewal Mission (JnNURM) specifies municipalities to prepare a City Development Plan and other statutory plans, a review of the role of UDAs vis-a-vis municipalities will be required to be done by all cities. But we do not observe such fragmented institutional arrangements for land use in China's cities, where land is owned by the state through municipal governments. For purposes of this work, we chose four million-plus cities in India-Bangalore, Jaipur, Ahmedabad and Kolkata – that are representative of a variety of characteristics.

The Chinese cities from which data are available on revenues from public land leasing and sales are Beijing, Shanghai, Dalian, Tianjin, Wuhan, Hangzhou, Nanjing, Chengdu, Chongqing and Wuxi. There is also some other systematic data on land leasing and sale/auctions and their revenues from *China Land and Resources Statistical Yearbook* (2002–2009) for Beijing, Shanghai, Tianjin, Chongqing, Shenyang and Xi'an.

The sample of Chinese cities is geographically representative of the country, since they represent the north (Beijing and Tianjin), east (Dalian, Shanghai, Nanjing, Wuxi and Hangzhou), northeast (Shenyang) and west/central (Xi'an, Wuhan, Chongqing and Chengdu) parts of China.

The sample of Indian cities is geographically far flung enough to be representative of several regions in the country. They are also from a variety of states experiencing different stages of economic growth. Bangalore and Ahmedabad are located in fast-growing states, whereas Jaipur and Kolkata are in the relatively slower growing regions of the country.

The size of these cities is also diverse enough to be representative of a wide variety across the country. Among the sample Chinese cities, Shanghai has the largest population of 23 million people, followed by Beijing at 19 million, and Wuxi has the smallest population of 4.8 million residents.

In India, while Bangalore and Kolkata are metropolitan, with their population being greater than five million, where big ticket land transactions have been taking place, Ahmedabad and Jaipur are million-plus cities which are medium-sized cities with moderate public land transactions, when compared with the others. Moreover, Jaipur is in Rajasthan where municipalities, particularly the smaller ones, derive a large proportion of their revenues from land leasing and sales. The sample of Indian cities also represents a variety of fiscal arrangements in cities used by them for financing their expenditures. Ahmedabad in Gujarat continues to have the octroi, whereas the other cities are in states that have long since abolished the octroi.

The next section focuses on the importance of revenues from land leasing and sales in Indian and Chinese cities. We make hypothetical computations of how much land, which is currently with UDAs, can contribute to revenues of the municipal corporations in each of the Indian cities. While we provide a hypothetical profile of municipal expenditures financed by revenues from land leasing and sales for India's cities, we summarize the revenues from land leasing and sales in China's cities (and/or provinces), given we did not have detailed information on the expenditure financed out of land lease and sales in China's cities.

Land as a source of local revenue in Indian and Chinese cities

For Indian cities, we focus on finances of the UDAs primarily from the viewpoint of land. We concentrate on revenue sources for UDAs and municipal corporations in the selected Indian cities. In each of these Indian cities, we highlight the potential of land as a proportion of its total revenues, own source revenues and revenues from property tax. Such a presentation enables us to make a realistic assessment of the potential of land in the context of the existing revenue structures in place in these cities.

Table 8.2 summarises the role of land as a revenue option (as a proportion of own source revenues) for all the selected Indian cities, putting together the various hypothetical computations that were performed for India's cities. On average, Ahmedabad and Kolkata Municipal Corporations can realize only about 6% and

Table 8.2 Revenues from UDAs' land leasing and/or sales as a proportion of selected indian municipal corporations' own source revenues*

Year	Average (%)
2000–01	80.47
2001–02	70.98
2002–03	63.46
2003–04	98.25
2004–05	71.32
2005–06	105.27
2006–07	141.97
2007–08	108.37
Average	89.46
Std. Deviation	33.67
Maximum	147.44
Minimum	51.26

Source: Sridhar and Reddy (2010).

* The selected municipal corporations are Bangalore, Kolkata, Jaipur and Ahmedabad.

12% respectively of their total own source revenues from their respective UDAs' sale and lease of land. In other cities, this is much higher, being nearly 39% of BBMP's own source revenues in Bangalore and nearly 10 times more, i.e., being 390% of own source revenues in Jaipur.

On average, taking all cities into account, revenue from land lease and/or sales by UDAs accounts for nearly 90% of existing own source revenues of municipal corporations (Table 8.2), 33% of their total revenues, but more than nine times the property tax revenues (Sridhar and Reddy, 2010). Jaipur is an outlier. Even when Jaipur is removed, UDAs' land leasing and sale revenues contributed to nearly 50% of property tax revenues on average, in Indian cities.

Our findings based on municipality revenues and UDA revenues both from land leasing and sales, suggest two groups of cities in India: one set is able to capitalize on land for raising revenues (Jaipur and Bangalore) and the other unable to do so (Kolkata and Ahmedabad). These city types are representative of many we find in India.

We investigate causes of these discrepancies between Indian cities in terms of the potential of land as a revenue-generating source. The causes of these discrepancies could be embedded in the institutional arrangements for land use in the cities. For instance, in the case of Kolkata, we found that the funds transferred by developers into the KMDA's escrow account are not taken into account in the KMDA revenues from land leasing and sales. This could be one reason why Kolkata comes a distant third in terms of KMDA's contribution to the municipality's (KMC) revenues. In Ahmedabad (AUDA), its inability to make money out of land leasing and sales seems to arise due to constraints imposed on it by the Gujarat Town Planning Act. The Gujarat Town Planning and Urban Development Act specifies reservation to the extent of 10% of land for providing housing to the socially and economically weaker sections, 15% for roads, 5% for parks, playgrounds and open space, 5% for social infrastructure such as schools, dispensaries, fire brigade, and only 15% for sale by the authority for residential, commercial or industrial use depending on the nature of development.

In Jaipur, it is worthy to note that the sale of land is an important source of non–tax income for municipalities in Rajasthan, particularly for the smaller municipalities. In Rajasthan, the poor financial position of ULBs, and the lack of an adequate tax base (due to the abolition of octroi in 1998) have led to attempts on the part of municipalities to improve their other sources of income. We surmise that land lease and sales are the most important of these.

Another reason why the impact is huge in Jaipur is because JMC's own source revenues are low, average of INR 605 million during 2000–01 to 2006–07 or average of INR 224 per capita, compared with the JDA's revenues from land leasing and sale, average of INR 2.3 billion or INR 829 per capita over the same period. However, in contrast, the revenues of Ahmedabad and Kolkata are huge, average of INR 7.7 billion and INR 7.3 billion respectively over the same period, compared to that from their UDAs' revenues from land leasing and sales, INR 821 million and INR 973 million respectively for AUDA and KMDA. Hence the impact of additional revenues from UDAs in Ahmedabad and Kolkata are muted.

In Jaipur, while the revenues from JDA have been fairly stable, there is substantial variability in the revenues of the JMC, hence there is variability in the proportion JDA revenues account for out of JMC's revenues.

In Bangalore, corner sites are sold off by the BDA through auction which yield a revenue of nearly INR 130 million per plot (which is possibly much higher than the per plot price of up to INR 10 million, based on secondary data), compared with a mere INR 5.2 million per plot sold in Ahmedabad by AUDA. This explains Bangalore's relatively higher revenues from land lease compared with that in Ahmedabad. In Bangalore, the city corporation, the Bruhat Bengaluru Mahanagara Palika (BBMP) thus far has not used land as a revenue-generating source, but only for charitable purposes. But the BDA has been relatively more prolific in its use of land for revenue generation. This explains these findings here.

Summarizing the reasons for the discrepancies we have found across the Indian cities in terms of the ability of land lease and sales as a revenue-generating mechanism, one answer could lie in the institutional arrangements for land use and the escrow mechanisms used to transfer revenues from private parties to UDAs. Another reason could be the relative financial strength of the municipality vis-à-vis that of the UDA. Yet another reason could be the land disposal process itself – usually auctioned-off plots or sites are sold at a higher premium than are other sites.

Hence transfer of funds and functions from the UDAs to the municipal corporations is recommended for orderly growth of cities, doing away with the multiplicity of agencies with respect to land use, and respecting the financial autonomy and decentralization spirit of the 74th CAA.

We are, however, unable to say anything certain regarding the impact of lease or sale on revenues. While in Ahmedabad and in Kolkata leasing of land is more remunerative from a revenue point of view, in Bangalore and Jaipur, outright sale of land by the UDA is more conducive for higher revenue potential. In general, we may surmise that outright sale would be more conducive for revenue potential, given that there are a number of terms and conditions associated with leasing.

Further, in all the cities, most of the revenues of the UDAs are spent on capital projects. We may be reasonably sure that resources from land leasing and sales are being used for developing infrastructure of some sort. Our discussions also confirm that there is enough local autonomy at least on paper for spending limited resources (i.e., funds up to a ceiling) as seen by the existence of local representatives on committees appointed to approve spending decisions.

Table 8.3 summarizes what proportion of the capital expenditure in each of the Indian cities, revenues from land leasing and sales in each of the cities' UDAs can be expected to finance. Even on average, if UDA revenues from land leasing and sales were to be transferred to cities, they can expect to finance more than 100% (in some cases more than 200%) of the cities' capital expenditures. So it is clear that UDA revenues from land leasing and sales are a very promising way of financing much needed city capital expenditures in Indian cities.

Land sales have been used exclusively by China's local governments, which use land sales and other local revenues for local developments, including developments in the urban areas. In the past, land sales were a small proportion of total local revenues. Since 1998, when housing commercialisation was widely promoted, land sales have become an increasingly important part of local revenues.

Land leasing revenues in selected China's cities are presented in Table 8.4, which summarizes information from various case studies regarding land leasing revenues and their size, relative to total local spending or the local capital budget. Although land leasing is viewed as an infrastructure financing tool by Chinese municipalities, there is no legal requirement to dedicate revenues to the capital budget. These data suggest that direct revenues from land leasing can generate a

Table 8.3 Proportion of selected Indian cities' capital expenditures financed by UDA revenues from land leasing and sales*

Year	Average (%)
1998–99	28.58
1999–00	26.49
2000–01	67.60
2001–02	157.40
2002–03	124.30
2003–04	113.35
2004–05	90.02
2005–06	148.97
2006–07	244.88
2007–08	136.51
Average	113.81
Maximum	244.88
Minimum	26.49
Std. Deviation	65.43

Source: Sridhar and Reddy (2010).

* The selected cities are Bangalore, Kolkata, Jaipur and Ahmedabad.

Table 8.4 Revenue from land leasing in selected cities of China

City	Period	Revenue raised (in billion RMB)
Shanghai	1992–2004	>100
Beijing	1995–96	6.9
Chengdu	2002–03	4.7
Hangzhou	2002	6
Guangdong province	1992	9.4

Source: Peterson (2007).

substantial part of the municipal capital budget for a period of 10–15 years, even when investment levels are as high as they have been in China, given that urban land values in China have risen at a frantic pace.

In China, local governments buy pieces of land from farmers at low prices and then lease (sell) them to property developers and other investors at much higher prices through auction. The price differential becomes net revenue accruing to the local governments. In addition, land ownership permanently belongs to the state. Local governments act as state agents to lease (sell) land to investors. A typical lease is for 70 years.

Table 8.4 shows that in Shanghai, more than 100 billion RMB (US $12 billion) was generated during 1992–04 from up-front payments for land leasing rights, all of which was injected into urban infrastructure networks or infrastructure support for improvement of the city's housing condition (Gao, 2007). By leasing land at market values, the government has not only obtained a large amount of capital needed for upgrading urban infrastructure, but has also helped rationalize the spatial layout of the central city. Industrial sites have been moved out of the city centre and vacated land has been leased to higher value users who can take better advantage of the central location. Thus, at least in China, it has been proven that land resources can be translated into capital in a market economy in which urban infrastructure is no longer treated as a 'charity' and payment is required for the use of scarce land resources and infrastructure access. This is a major change from what we find in India's cities, which continue to be obligated to use their land for public projects such as hospitals, schools, parks and roads.

Table 8.5 shows the top 10 cities in China in terms of land sales and the rapid increase in terms of the percentage change in land sales revenues in all the 10 cities covered, from 2009 to 2010. Land sales revenues accounted for 70% of total local revenue for Beijing and 60% for Shanghai in 2010.

Table 8.6 shows that total land sales revenues as a proportion of total local government revenues was increasing rapidly for one decade, especially during the last 5 years. In 2010, for example, over 60% of local revenues came from land sales, rising from 16.7% in 2001.

Figures 8.1 and 8.2 summarize the average revenues from land leasing and sales and the respective land areas leased or sold, in six important cities in China – Beijing, Shanghai, Tianjin, Shenyang, Chong Qing and Xi'an over a 6-year period, 2003–08. Figure 8.1 shows that on average, the transaction price and net income, i.e. the balance of the transaction price value after making an allowance for the

Table 8.5 Top 10 cities by land sales in China, 2009–2010 (billion yuan)

City	2010	2009	Change %
Beijing	162.8	92.8	43.0
Shanghai	151.3	102.5	32.3
Dalian	115.8	27.5	76.3
Tianjin	90.1	73.8	18.1
Wuhan	81.3	36.1	55.6
Hangzhou	73.8	109.5	−48.4
Nanjing	57.2	22.4	60.8
Chengdu	51.1	35.6	30.3
Chongqing	50.7	44.8	11.6
Wuxi	41.2	22.1	46.4

Source: http://news.dichan.sina.com.cn每日经济新闻作者：杨羚强2011/1/6.

Table 8.6 Local revenues and land sales in China, 2001–2010 (trillion yuan)

Year	Local revenue	Land sales	Land sales as % of revenue
2001	0.78	0.13	16.7
2002	0.85	0.24	28.2
2003	0.98	0.54	55.1
2004	1.19	0.64	53.8
2005	1.51	0.59	39.1
2006	1.83	0.77	42.1
2007	2.36	1.19	50.4
2008	2.66	0.96	36.1
2009	3.26	1.59	48.8
2010	4.46	2.71	60.8

Source: http://blog.soufun.com/29013141/11227929/articledetail.htm

Notes: (1) Data are from media reports and Ministry of Land and Resources of China.
(2) Non-land sale revenue in 2010 is estimated by authors based on a 5% rise from the non-land revenue of 2009.

cost paid by the government for land acquisition, including the cost of dismantlement and removal due to land requisition, and cost of land development, has been on a steady upward trend since the beginning of the decade, more so since 2005, although there was a spike in 2004.

Liu and Jiang (2005) find that land financing became an important source of local revenue and funds for urbanization. It is interesting to note that on average, the net income from land sold is always higher than that leased, which has actually been declining in importance, on average, taking all the above cities into account.

Figure 8.2 summarizes the average land area which has been sold/auctioned or leased during 2002–08 in the six cities of China. The figure shows that the land area sold/auctioned is much higher on average, taking the six cities into account, when compared to leased land which peaked in 2006. This was primarily because

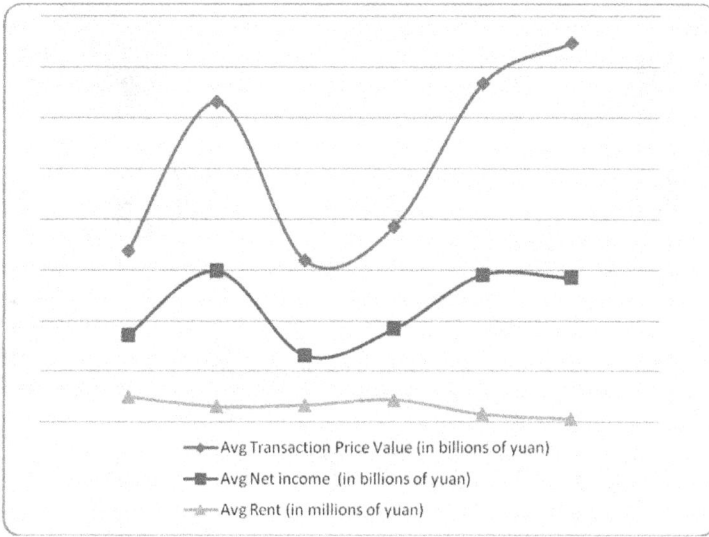

Figure 8.1 Average transaction price, net income and rent from land sales and leasing, China's cities, 2002–2008

Source: China Land and Resources Statistical Yearbook (2002–2009).

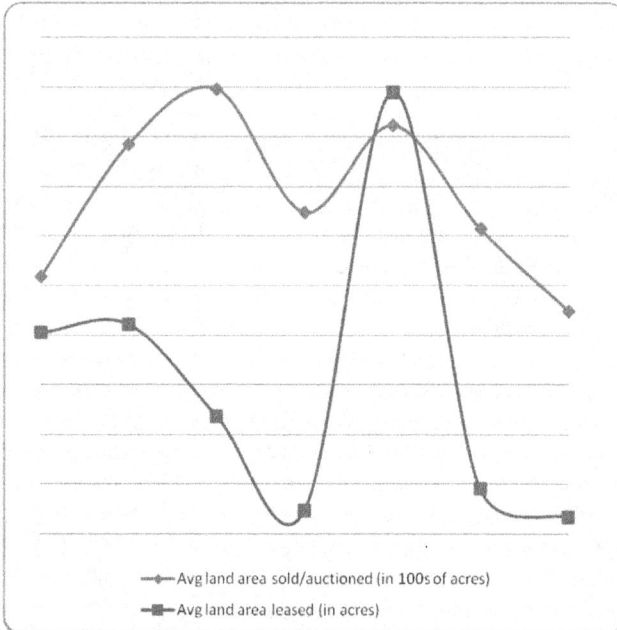

Figure 8.2 Land area sold and leased, China's cities, 2002–2008

Source: China Land and Resources Statistical Yearbook (2002–2009).

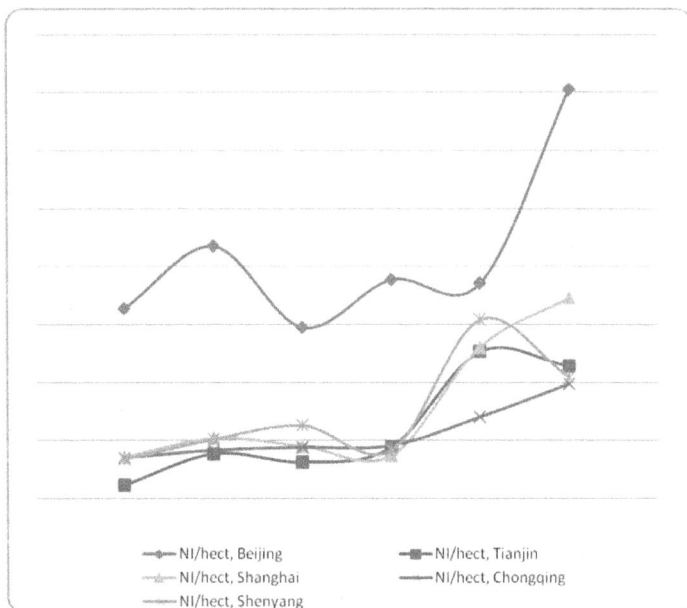

Figure 8.3 Net income per hectare of land sold (RMB million), China's cities, 2003–2008

Source: China Land and Resources Statistical Yearbook (2002–2009).

of Shanghai which leased nearly 265 hectares of land in 2006 at a total of 10.69 million yuan or a price of 40,400 yuan per hectare.

Figure 8.3 compares net income per hectare of land sold in the six cities of China over 2003–09. This figure shows that the net income per hectare of land sold in Beijing has always been well above that in other cities, and is continually increasing. All other cities are in a lower level equilibrium with a rising trend, nonetheless, as far as net income per hectare of land sold is concerned. However, there are a few cities (Tianjin, Shenyang and Xian) which have witnessed a declining net income per hectare of land sold.

It should be noted nonetheless that the emphasis on revenues from land leasing and sales has promoted speculation in China's land and real estate market.

The China Land Surveying and Planning Institute, under China's Ministry of Land and Resources (MLR), noted that average land prices reached 2,882 yuan ($437.13) per square meter in the final quarter of 2010 in some key cities it monitored, up 2.53% compared to the previous quarter (China Daily, 2011). Rising land prices have pushed up property prices in China's cities. China's national property-price index rose 11.7% in March 2010 from a year earlier, accelerating from February's 10.7% rise, according to China's National Bureau of Statistics. The increase was the largest since July 2005, when the bureau switched to an index based on data in 70 cities rather than 35 (Wall Street Journal, 2011). Thus the steep rise in housing prices since 2005 has given an opportunity for local governments to sell lands at high prices. Peng and Thibodeau (2011) find that the market for residential land became less efficient after municipal governments gained direct control of land supply.[5]

Land sales revenues rocketed in 2009 and 2010 as a result of strong demand for commercial housing and rising house prices in China. It is intuitive that any factor which increases the supply of serviced land will also increase the supply of housing capital and will impact house prices. However, there is some evidence that in the context of Hong Kong, there is no relationship between land supply and housing prices (Tse, 1998).

Policy implications and concluding remarks

This chapter has shown that the institutional arrangements for land use are frag-mented between the UDAs and town planning departments of municipal cor-porations in India's cities. There are overlaps among various agencies as far as planning and development of schemes for town planning are concerned. Given municipal corporations have limited control over land assets especially for com-mercial purposes (leasing and selling), they cannot leverage their land resources for raising revenues.

In China, land is owned by the state, there is no fragmentation in the institutional arrangement for land use and land resources can be translated into capital in a market economy in which urban infrastructure is no longer treated as a 'charity' and pay-ment is required for the use of scarce land resources and infrastructure access. This is a major change from what we find in India's cities, which continue to be obligated to use their land for public projects such as hospitals, schools, parks and roads.

However, in Indian cities, given UDAs have control over huge land resources and are entitled by law to dispose them, they are in a position to raise substantial revenues from leasing and selling. We find that if UDA revenues from land leas-ing and/or sales alone were to be added to Indian municipal corporations' rev-enues, they would contribute to municipal finances in a substantial way. Because of this, this chapter suggests that in Indian cities, UDAs have to be merged with the town planning departments of the municipal corporations of cities. This merg-ing has the following advantages:

1.   Cities would have enough resources to finance their urban infrastructure pro-grams, which would be in line with the provisions of the 74th CAA.
2.   The multiplicity of institutions with respect to land use would be done away with, enabling a more orderly growth of cities.

Having said this, we should recognize that land acquisition, land development, land sales and leasing, and preparation of master plans including long-range urban planning and determination of land uses are specialized functions. Such required expertise might not be available in most Indian ULBs. As Mathur and Peterson (2006) point out, the scale and complexity of urban planning could overwhelm the ULBs' primary function of service provision and maintenance if such functions were transferred to the ULBs. Hence they suggest that it is unrealistic to simply transfer these functions to ULBs by a stroke of the pen.

We also need to recognize that despite the many advantages the development authorities have with regard to land-related activity, in practice, the functioning of development authorities and other similar agencies has been found to be far from satisfactory. They have not been able to control haphazard development on the periphery and on lands that are either notified for acquisition or acquired for development. Nor have they been able to effectively put in place cost-recovery principles for charging for the services that they provide. Thus it is fundamental to decentralization for ULBs to participate in the planning decisions that affect their future development and future service responsibilities.

Hence, taking the above discussion into account, we think that there is a need for revisiting the institutional roles of the UDAs versus the municipal corporations in India, and seriously considering transfer of institutional autonomy and requisite resources to municipal authorities in matters relating to land, given it can constitute a substantial addition to municipal revenues in India's cities.

In China's context, there is a need for the State Council of China to revisit its mandate regarding the revenue-sharing arrangement from land leasing and sales. This is to ensure vertical fiscal balance, given that China's cities have access to fewer sources of revenues, when compared with the central government, as described earlier. A fairer revenue-sharing system between central and regional governments will reduce the dependency on land sales as a major source of local finance. The purpose of this is to restrain rapid growth in land and house prices, as high and rising house prices have become a major factor of unhappiness among the urban population, especially the migrant workers and their families.

While this research has shown that land can be quite attractive as a financing tool for India's cities, it has implications for the institutional arrangements pertaining to land between UDAs and municipal corporations. We looked at a sample of only four, but diverse, Indian cities and compared this with the evidence from China where cities have been capitalizing on revenues from land leasing and sales. While there is no fragmentation with respect to land use in China's cities, we nonetheless find significant vertical fiscal imbalances in China's cities, since land sales proceeds have almost exclusively accrued to local government budgets. This has encouraged local authorities to push up land prices which have been widely blamed for the high and rising house prices across the Chinese cities.

Cities in both India and China have experienced rising property prices because of speculation and a monopolized land market. The end user to be hurt in this process is the home buyer. This is not to say that land leasing and sales should not be done at all, but there should be some kind of regulation of the process, so that real estate transactions and speculation may be tracked. Further, the revenues so gained from land leasing and sales should be pumped back into providing better public infrastructure such as water supply, sewerage, roads, sanitation and solid waste management.

Apart from the questions examined here, there are several other questions which would be worth examining in the context of India and China's cities: Are the cities efficient in their use of proceeds from land lease/sales? How can the land market be best regulated so that rising house prices can be controlled and public services better provided? These questions are important but they are beyond the scope of this chapter and require future research.

Notes

1 The authors are grateful for comments made by conference participants at the University of Nottingham and the time allowed by UNU-WIDER and Public Affairs Centre. Financial support from the Thirteenth Finance Commission, Government of India is gratefully acknowledged for the work on Indian cities. We thank Venugopal Reddy for his assistance on the India part of this chapter and city government officials and urban development authorities of Ahmedabad, Jaipur, Kolkata and Bengaluru, India for providing valuable information and data.
2 Japan and New Zealand are countries where property tax is levied on land only (OECD, 1983). Jamaica and the state of Hawaii of the United States are examples of entities where there are many landowners with large landholdings and where they have shifted their tax bases and increased the tax on land. www.unescap.org/huset/m_land/chapter9. htm. *Municipal Land Management in Asia: A Comparative Study*, UNESCAP: Bangkok, 1995.
3 In India, a number of state government agencies such as the Karnataka Industrial Areas Development Board (KIADB) acquire and dispose land. For instance, as of July 2008 (Times of India, July 24, 2008), the KIADB had acquired 869 acres of farmland for a proposed hardware park, in addition to the over 50,000 acres of surplus land waiting to be disposed through a specially formed realty corporation. There have been reports that over 1000,000 acres of land was lying with the state government of Karnataka in 2007 of which some 28,000 acres were encroached upon by politicians, builders, government servants, and many landless poor (some of them being former owners who lost their land during acquisition). A committee (Venkatswamy Committee) was set up to investigate these encroachment cases, but little was known of its report or recommendations (Times of India, July 24, 2008).
4 Similarly, a total of 49 Chinese cities recently defied a central government order by failing to announce their property price control measures for 2011. http://english.peopledaily.com.cn/90001/90778/90862/7338351.html, retrieved April 6, 2011.
5 The distribution of benefits from land conversion also produces impacts on the fairness and efficiency of land allocation between agricultural and non-agricultural sectors. Zhu and Qu (2006), based on a case study in the northern city of Jiang Su Province, found that farmers got little compensation from land acquisitions, which could hardly maintain their living standards in the long term and brought a negative influence on the fairness and the farmers' enthusiasm for farmland protection. On the other hand, the city governments' larger share of land benefit provided incentives for them to convert farmland for purposes of capital accumulation and provide land resources to developers at relative lower prices. This chapter found that as a result, farmland was converted to non-agricultural sectors excessively.

Bibliography

Bombay First and McKinsey & Company, (2003), *Vision Mumbai: Transforming Mumbai into a World Class City.* Mumbai: Bombay First.

Chan, Kam W., (1997), 'Urbanization and urban infrastructure services in the PRC,' in *Financing local government in the People's Republic of China,* Wong, Christine P.W. (ed.), Hong Kong: Asian Development Bank and Oxford University Press.

China Daily (2011), accessed online: April 6, 2011, from www.chinadaily.com.cn/business/2011-01/18/content_11871549.htm

Chreod Ltd (2005), *Report to World Bank on City Development Strategies II,* Ottawa: Chreod Ltd.

Deng, Frederic, (2005), 'Public land leasing and the changing roles of local government in Urban China', *Annals of Regional Science,* 39, 2: 353–73

Ding, Chengri, (2005), *Property Tax Developments in China, Land Lines, 17, 3* Cambridge, Massachusetts: Lincoln Institute of Land Policy

Gao, Guofu, (2007), 'Urban infrastructure investment and financing in Shanghai,' in *Financing Cities,* Peterson, George, Annez, Patricia Clarke (eds.), Washington, DC: Sage Publications and the World Bank.

Hong, Yu-Hung, (1996), 'Can leasing public land be an alternative source of local public finance?', *Lincoln Institute of Land Policy Working Paper* WP96YH2. Accessed online: April 30, 2008, from http://66.223.94.76/pubs/dl/145_hong96web.pdf

Huang, Xiajin, (2005), 'The relationship of housing price and land price in China: Observation and policies', *in Chinese,* accessed online: from *www.nj-tudi.com/html/special-news-details.php?news_id=90* (the website of Nanjing Municipal Land Reservation Center)

Kamal-Chaoui, L., Leman, E., Rufei, Z., (2009), 'Urban trends and policy in China', *OECD Regional Development Working Papers,* 2009/1, OECD Publishing, doi: 10.1787/225205036417

Liu, Shou-ying, Jiang, Xing-san, (2005), 'Financial risks of land financing by local governments – a case study of a developed area in east China', *China Land Science,* 5: 3–9

Mathur, O.P., Peterson, George, (2006), *State Finance Commissions and Urban Fiscal Decentralization in India: India Urban Initiatives,* Washington, DC: The Urban Institute The Ministry of Land and Resources of China, Beijing <query?>

National Bureau of Statistics of China, (2002–09), *China Land and Resources Statistical Yearbook, various issues.*

National Institute of Public Finance and Policy, (2007), 'Improving the fiscal health of Indian cities: A pilot study of Kolkata', Draft report submitted to the World Bank, Washington, D.C., June

OECD, (1983), *Taxes on Immovable Property,* Paris: Organization for Economic Co-operation and Development

Peng, Liang, Thibodeau, Thomas G., (2011), 'Government interference and the efficiency of the land market in China', *Journal of Real Estate Finance and Economics,* doi: 10.1007/s11146-011-9300-9

Peterson, George E., (2007), 'Land leasing and land sale as an infrastructure financing option,' in *Financing Cities,* Peterson, George E., Annez, Patricia (eds.), Washington, DC: Sage Publications and the World Bank

Peterson, George E., (2009), *Unlocking Land Values to Finance Urban Infrastructure,* Trends and policy options series, Washington, DC: World Bank

Rajaraman, Indira, Mathur, O.P., Majumdar, Debdatta, (2005), *Restructuring State and Local Finances for Rajasthan,* New Delhi: NIPFP, December

Sridhar, Kala S., (2004), 'Cities with suburbs: Evidence from India', *National Institute of Public Finance and Policy Working Paper No.23/2004*

Sridhar, Kala S., (2006), 'Institutional arrangements for land use in Ludhiana, Punjab,' in

India Infrastructure Report 2006: Urban Infrastructure, 3i Network, New Delhi: Oxford University Press

Sridhar, Kala S., A.Venugopala, Reddy, (2010), *State of Urban Services in India's Cities: Spending and Financing*, New Delhi: Oxford University Press

Tse, Raymond Y.C., (1998), 'Housing price, land supply and revenue from land sales', *Urban Studies,* 35, 8: 1377–1392

Wall Street Journal (2011), http://online.wsj.com/article/SB10001424052702303695604575183143413892542.html

Zhu, Pei-xin, Qu, Futian, (2006), 'Distribution of land benefit and land allocation between agricultural and non-agricultural uses – a case study of N City of Jiangsu Province', *Journal of Nanjing Agricultural University (Social Sciences Edition),* 6: 1–6

9 Stochastic convergence of the Greater China economies: a panel unit root approach

Chun Kwok Lei[1] and Pui Sun Tam

Introduction

As the most populous country in the world, with the second largest total output level[2] and the third largest land area in the world, the economic reforms of Mainland China and the incurred development in spatial inequality among its provinces and municipalities have caught the interest of economists worldwide. Following the availability of more reliable statistics in the 1980s, a group of studies have been conducted to address the issue of income disparities in Mainland China. The hypothesis of converging income level among Mainland Chinese provinces in the pre- and post-reform period has been thoughtfully examined in Chen and Fleisher (1996), Jian, Sachs and Warner (1996), Gundlach (1997), Raiser (1998) and Zhang and Yao (2001), amongst others. It is generally believed that income distribution among Mainland Chinese provinces was rather unequal in the pre-reform period with little tendency toward convergence at the provincial level. Since the start of economic reforms in 1978, the spatial income disparity among provinces has started to decline and the initially poorer provinces have been able to grow faster than the initially richer ones, achieving the so-called β-convergence. Growth determinants such as capital investment, human capital and openness level were found to have contributed to the convergence process. Nevertheless, a tendency toward deterioration in income equality has been found after the 1990s. Researchers have attributed this to the divergence in trade exposure, endowments and attractiveness to incoming foreign direct investment, amongst other factors. The hypothesis of 'club divergence' has also been proposed, which suggested that Mainland Chinese provinces have formed different 'growth clubs,' consisting of the coastal, central and inner regions. While income convergence was found within each club, an enlarged income gap was observed across different clubs.

Although the issue of spatial income disparity across Mainland Chinese provinces and municipalities has been widely assessed, discussions have been largely limited to provincial disparities without considering the Special Administrative Regions (SARs) of Hong Kong and Macau, which have become important, and indivisible parts of China after their handovers in 1997 and 1999 respectively. The only exceptions were studies recently conducted by Lei and Yao (2008) and

Lei and Tam (2010). Pooling up Mainland China, Hong Kong and Macau, income convergence was observed among this group of Chinese economies in the post-reform period, and openness was found to play a significant role in accelerating the pace of convergence of the poorer Mainland Chinese provinces with the richer Hong Kong and Macau economies by Lei and Yao (2008). Lei and Tam (2010) adopted the recently advanced panel unit root tests and provided evidence for stochastic convergence among Mainland China at the provincial level, Hong Kong and Macau in the post-reform period. Nevertheless, there was no evidence to support convergence between fast-growing and highly open Mainland Chinese provinces such as Guangdong province, and the two SARs in the long-run, given the diversified growth paths followed by these economies.

In spite of the presence of multi-dimensional studies on the convergence issue of Mainland China, it is surprising that another important Chinese economy, Taiwan, has been left out completely in this line of research. In fact, the two sides of the Straits have already formed a well-established indirect civil connection through Hong Kong and Macau since the 1990s. In Wang and Schuh (2000), it was reported that Mainland China, Hong Kong and Taiwan could enjoy a 1.7 to 4.3 per cent growth in real gross domestic product (GDP) from the formation of a free trade area (FTA). Following the bilateral agreement signed by the two sides of the Straits in 2008 on 'direct communications', and the Economic Cooperation Framework Agreement (ECFA) signed in 2010, cooperation between Mainland China and Taiwan has entered into a new era toward the formation of an FTA with deepened economic integration. Together with the Closer Economic Partnership Arrangement (CEPA) between Mainland China and the two SARs of Hong Kong and Macau, the legal settings for the construction of an FTA across the Greater China economies are ready. Consequently, economic linkages among these economies will be tightened, and this will potentially contribute to the strengthening of growth prospects in the Greater China economies. The expected integration-led growth may alter the order of income distribution across these economies, which deserves special attention and investigation. This chapter aims to fill the gap in the existing empirical literature by pooling up Mainland China at the provincial level, Hong Kong, Macau and Taiwan for the first time to evaluate the income convergence issue of 'Greater China.' The role played by external trade as indicated by the openness ratio in the process of the Greater China income convergence is also addressed.

The remainder of this chapter is organized as follows. Section 2 contains the literature review which highlights the major findings of relevant empirical studies, and the methodology which describes the model framework and panel unit root techniques employed for the study of stochastic convergence among the Greater China economies. Section 3 reports the descriptive statistics of the Greater China economies and empirical results from the stochastic convergence analysis. The last section concludes the chapter and discusses the implications drawn from the empirical results.

Literature review and methodology

Literature review

Different approaches have been applied to address the issue of income convergence in Mainland China. The cross-sectional approach typically utilizes the ordinary least squares estimation method to regress the growth rates of per capita income on the initial income levels of different economies, with or without the other growth determinants as added regressors. If the estimated coefficient of the initial income variable is negative, β-convergence is said to hold, that is, the initially poorer economies grow faster than the initially richer ones, which reduces their overall income gap. This method was adopted by Chen and Fleisher (1996), Jian, Sachs, and Warner (1996), Gundlach (1997), Raiser (1998) and Démurger (2001), and their estimation results were supportive of income convergence among Mainland Chinese provinces in the early post-reform period. Since the 1990s, however, the process of income convergence discontinued with an enlarged income gap among the coastal, central and inner provinces of Mainland China. These studies also showed that investment ratio, human capital, infrastructure, and more importantly openness ratio, have contributed to the convergence process of Mainland China. In fact, the significance of openness, or external trade, has been emphasized not only in the literature on income convergence, but also in the export-led growth studies. As documented in Shan and Sun (1998), Lin (1999) and Ljungwall (2006), there was uni- or bi-directional causality between the growth of exports and economic growth. For Mainland China as a whole, Shan and Sun (1998) found bi-directional causality between exports and real industrial output. At the provincial level, Lin (1999) revealed that provinces with faster growth of exports had a tendency to grow faster and vice-versa for the period of 1978 to 1995 and investment in private enterprises has contributed to economic growth as well. Similar findings were also observed by Ljungwall (2006) for the extended period of 1978 to 2001. Given that export growth tends to bring about economic growth and therefore higher per capita income, it is likely that Mainland Chinese provinces with higher amount of exports or trade exposure may grow faster to catch up with Hong Kong, Macau and Taiwan in terms of per capita income.

Aside from the cross-sectional approach, some studies have also adopted the time-series approach to investigate the income convergence issue of Mainland China. In Yao and Zhang (2001), Mainland Chinese provinces were divided into coastal, central and western regions and the stationarity of relative incomes was tested using univariate unit root testing techniques. The unit root null was rejected for the coastal and western regions but not for the central region, which implied that Mainland Chinese provinces had been divided into different growth clubs with convergence within each of these clubs and divergence across them. In Zhang, Liu and Yao (2001), similar investigation was conducted and stochastic convergence within the coastal and western regions was evidenced as in Yao and Zhang (2001). Employing the panel unit root techniques instead of the univariate ones, which have their shortcomings in the near unit root and small sample cases, Pedroni and Yao (2006) found convergence among Mainland Chinese provinces in the pre-reform period but divergence in the post-reform period. Their test results also indicated divergence among coastal provinces but convergence among the inner and western provinces.

Investigating the Mainland Chinese provinces in conjunction with Hong Kong and Macau, Lei and Yao (2008) observed β-convergence among them in the post-reform period of 1978 to 2002, based on the cross-sectional regression approach. Trade openness was found to play a significant role in the income convergence process. Nevertheless, mixed results on income convergence were obtained when adopting the time series approach in analyzing these economies. However, given that Lei and Yao (2008) have considered a short time period and employed the univariate unit root testing method, the reliability of their findings is in question. Lei and Tam (2010) therefore extended the work of Lei and Yao (2008) by applying the more advanced panel unit root testing techniques, and provided evidence to support income convergence among Mainland Chinese provinces, Hong Kong and Macau in the post-reform period. At the disaggregated level, however, stochastic convergence between fast-growing and highly open Mainland Chinese provinces such as the Guangdong province and the two SARs was not observed due to their diversified growth paths.

Stochastic convergence hypothesis

We employ the notion of stochastic convergence suggested by Carlino and Mills (1993) and investigate the income convergence issue among Mainland China, Hong Kong, Macau and Taiwan using a time-series approach. This approach has also been used to study income convergence among the US regions by Carlino and Mills (1993) and Lowey and Papell (1996), OECD countries by Li and Papell (1999) and Romero-Ávila (2009), Latin American countries by Galvão Jr. and Reis Gomes (2007), and Mexican states by Carrion-i-Silvestre and German-Soto (2007). In the multi-economy context, stochastic convergence is said to occur among a group of economies if the logarithm of the per capita income of one economy relative to the average per capita income of the group is stationary. This means that external shocks to relative incomes are temporary, so that there is a tendency for individual per capita incomes to stochastically converge toward the average.

For a group of N economies indexed by i, $i = 1, ..., N$, denote the per capita income of each i at time t, $t = 1, ..., T$, by x_{it}, and the average per capita income of then at time t by $\bar{x}_t$. Under the stochastic convergence framework of Carlino and Mills (1993), y_{it}, the logarithm of x_{it} relative to $\bar{x}_t$, is made up of the time-invariant equilibrium differential, y_i^e, and the deviations from this equilibrium, v_{it}:

$$y_{it} = y_i^e + v_{it}, \tag{9-1}$$

where v_{it} follows:

$$v_{it} = v_{i0} + \beta_i t + u_{it}, \tag{9-2}$$

with u_{it} being a stochastic process. Combining (9-1) and (9-2) and letting $\mu_i = y_i^e + v_{i0}$ give:

$$y_{it} = \mu_i + \beta_i t + u_{it}. \tag{9-3}$$

The stochastic process u_{it} is modeled as a general autoregressive-moving average (ARMA) process represented by $A_i(L)u_{it} = B_i(L)\varepsilon_{it}$, where $A_i(L)$ and $B_i(L)$ are polynomials in the lag operator L of order p_i and q_i respectively, and ε_{it} is a sequence of independent and identically distributed innovations.[3] If all the roots of $A_i(L)$ are strictly outside the unit circle, u_{it} and therefore y_{it} are stationary processes. They are nonstationary if $A_i(L)$ has one unit autoregressive root and all other roots are outside the unit circle. The ARMA representation can be approximated by an AR(k_i) one, so that testing for stochastic convergence among the group of economies is in effect testing for the stationarity of y_{it} based on the augmented Dickey-Fuller (ADF) test equations:

$$\Delta y_{it} = \alpha_i + \gamma_i t + \phi_i y_{i,t-1} + \sum_{j=1}^{k_i} c_{ij} \Delta y_{i,t-1} + \varepsilon_{it}. \tag{9-4}$$

Panel unit root testing methodology

In hypothesis testing, we employ the panel unit root tests developed by Levin, Lin and Chu (2002, hereafter LLC), Im, Pesaran and Shin (2003, hereafter IPS), and Maddala and Wu (1999, hereafter MW), which are all based on the univariate ADF test. By increasing the sample size through pooling time series observations across various cross-sections, these panel unit root tests possess higher power than the ADF test. Under the null of a unit root, $\phi_i = 0$ for all i in (9-4). Under the alternative of stationarity, LLC assumes a common AR coefficient for all i, that is, $\phi_1 = \phi_2 = \ldots = \phi_N = \phi < 0$, whereas IPS and MW allow for heterogeneous AR coefficients, that is, $\phi_i < 0$ for some i. As such, in panel unit root testing, while LLC uses a pooled estimator, IPS and MW employ a combination of test evidence across i.

LLC suggests a three-step procedure for unit root testing. In the first step, the lag order k_i in each ADF test equation is determined. This can be done by the general-to-specific t-sig method, which is based on the t-statistic on the coefficient associated with the last lag in the estimated autoregression. Starting with an upper bound $k_{max} = 4$ for k_i, if the last included lag is significant at the 10 per cent level, choose $k_i = k_{max}$. If not, reduce k_i by 1 until the last lag becomes significant. If no lags are significant, set $k_i = 0$. Two auxiliary regressions are then run to get the orthogonalized residuals

$\hat{e}_{it} = \Delta y_{it} - \hat{\alpha}_i - \hat{\gamma}_i t - \sum_{j=1}^{k_i} \hat{c}_{ij} \Delta y_{i,t-j}$ and $\hat{v}_{i,t-1} = y_{i,t-1} - \tilde{\alpha}_i - \tilde{\gamma}_i t - \sum_{j=1}^{k_i} \tilde{c}_{ij} \Delta y_{i,t-j}$. The residuals are normalized as $\tilde{e}_{it} = \hat{e}_{it}/\hat{\sigma}_{ei}$ and $\tilde{v}_{it} = \hat{v}_{it}/\hat{\sigma}_{ei}$, with $\hat{\sigma}_{ei}$ being the regression standard error from each ADF regression. In the second step, the ratio of the long-run standard deviation to the innovation standard deviation is estimated as $\hat{s}_i = \hat{\sigma}_{yi}/\hat{\sigma}_{ei}$. Notice that the long-run variance can be estimated by

$$\hat{\sigma}_{yi}^2 = \frac{1}{T}\sum_{t=2}^{T}\Delta y_{it}^2 + 2\sum_{L=1}^{\bar{K}} w_{\bar{K}L}\left[\frac{1}{T-1}\sum_{t=2+L}^{T}\Delta\tilde{y}_{it}\Delta\tilde{y}_{it-L}\right],$$ where $\Delta\tilde{y}_{it}$ is the

detrended Δy_{it}, and $w_{\bar{K}L} = 1 - \left[\dfrac{L}{\bar{K}+1}\right]$ is a Barlett kernel, in which $\bar{K}$ can be

selected according to the rule of $\bar{K} = 3.21T^{1/3}$. The average standard deviation

ratio across i is then computed as $\hat{S}_N = \dfrac{1}{N}\sum_{i=1}^{N}\hat{s}_i$. In the third step, the

pooled regression $\tilde{e}_{it} = \delta\, v_{i,t-1} + \tilde{\varepsilon}_{it}$ is run. The t-statistic for testing $\delta = 0$ is

$$t_\delta = \frac{\hat{\delta}}{STD(\hat{\delta})}, \text{ where } \hat{\delta} = \frac{\sum_{i=1}^{N}\sum_{t=2+k_i}^{T}\tilde{v}_{i,t-1}\tilde{e}_{it}}{\sum_{i=1}^{N}\sum_{t=2+k_i}^{T}\tilde{v}_{i,t-1}}, STD(\hat{\delta}) = \hat{\sigma}_{\tilde{\varepsilon}}\left[\sum_{i=1}^{N}\sum_{t=2+k_i}^{T}v_{i,t-1}^2\right]^{-2},$$

with $\sigma_{\tilde{\varepsilon}}^2\left[\dfrac{1}{N\tilde{T}}\sum_{i=1}^{N}\sum_{t=2+k_i}^{T}\left(\tilde{e}_{it}-\delta\tilde{v}_{i,t-1}\right)^2\right]\tilde{T}= T-\bar{k}-1$, and $\bar{k}=\dfrac{1}{N}\sum_{i=1}^{N}k_i$. Panel

unit root testing is conducted using the adjusted t-statistic:

$$t_\delta^* = \frac{t_\delta - N\tilde{T}\hat{S}_N\sigma_{\tilde{\varepsilon}}^{-2}STD(\hat{\delta})\mu_{m\tilde{T}}^*}{\sigma_{m\tilde{T}}^*}, \tag{9-5}$$

where the mean adjustment $\mu_{m\tilde{T}}^*$ and standard deviation adjustment $\sigma_{m\tilde{T}}^*$ are tabulated in LLC for different $\tilde{T}$ combined with the corresponding $\bar{K}$. This panel test statistic follows the standard normal distribution asymptotically under the assumption of cross-sectional independence.

For each i, denote the individual ADF test statistic for testing $\phi_i = 0$ in (9-5) by t_i. The IPS test uses the average of all the individual ADF statistics, $\bar{t} = \dfrac{1}{N}\sum_{i=1}^{N}t_i$, and conduct panel unit root testing based on:

$$W_{\bar{t}} = \frac{\sqrt{N}\left[\bar{t} - \dfrac{1}{N}\sum_{i=1}^{N}E(t_i \mid \phi_i = 0)\right]}{\sqrt{\dfrac{1}{N}\sum_{i=1}^{N}Var(t_i \mid \phi_i = 0)}}, \tag{9-6}$$

where $E(t_i \mid \phi_i = 0)$ and $Var(t_i \mid \phi_i = 0)$ are the mean and variance adjustment terms respectively. Under the assumption of cross-sectional independence, the panel test statistic converges to a standard normal distribution. It can be noted that the adjustment terms depend on the time span and lag order used in each individual ADF regression, which are simulated using 500,000 replications as in IPS.

The MW test makes use of the p-values for the individual ADF test statistics, each of which is denoted by π_i. It is a Fisher-type test that combines the p-values as:

$$\lambda = -2\sum\nolimits_{i=1}^{N} \ln \pi_i, \tag{9-7}$$

which has a χ^2 distribution with $2N$ degrees of freedom under the no cross-sectional dependency assumption. We follow MW and obtain the p-values from simulated distributions out of 500,000 replications.

Data and empirical results

Data

The per capita gross domestic product (GDP) for each of the Mainland Chinese provinces, Hong Kong, Macau and Taiwan is in real terms denominated in US dollar (USD) with 2001 as the base year. The openness ratio is defined as the percentage of total exports and imports in total GDP, where all monetary values are in nominal terms and denominated in local currency units. Data are extracted from the National Bureau of Statistics China's Statistical Yearbook, Census and Statistics Department of the Hong Kong SAR Government, Statistics and Census Service of the Macau SAR Government and National Statistics of Republic of China. Subject to the availability of data, only 30 Mainland Chinese provinces and municipalities are included in this study. Furthermore, due to the limitation of the GDP statistics of Macau, the sampling period of 1982 to 2007 is considered.

Preliminary analysis

China was separated into four individual entities after the Civil War, namely Mainland China, Hong Kong, Macau and Taiwan. The Communist Party took control over Mainland China and established the People's Republic of China with socialist central planning as the governing philosophy in 1949. A 'closed-door' policy was adopted in Mainland China until the economic reforms in 1978. The Kuomintang, which was defeated by the Communist Party in the Civil War, had retreated to Taiwan to exercise its governance over the Island. Taiwan has been exercising capitalism based on the market mechanism, and maintaining its economic linkages with major western countries in the decades that followed. The territories of Hong Kong and Macau remained under the administration of the UK and Portugal respectively until the handovers in the late 1990s. With highly liberalized economic policies, they have been playing important roles as entrepôts in the Greater China region and the 'windows' of Mainland China. Given their widely diversified historical background, as well as huge differences in endowments, economic ideologies and variations in exogenous shocks, it is not surprising to observe huge income gaps among these Greater China economies before the economic reforms of Mainland China.

As shown in Table 9.1, in 1982, the per capita GDP of Mainland China was recorded at USD 211, which implied shocking income gaps with Hong Kong, Macau and Taiwan at just 1.77, 2.09 and 4.7 per cent of their income levels respectively. With the adoption of open door policies, the encouragement of external trade and incoming foreign direct investment, the launching of various responsibility systems and the implementation of structural adjustments on ownership, the productivity and output level of Mainland China have been strengthened to a large extent. Since the economic reforms, the per capita income level of Mainland China has been increasing rapidly with a higher growth pace than Hong Kong, Macau and Taiwan, leading to a continuous contraction of income gaps with these Greater China economies. As indicated in Table 9.1, Mainland China has been catching up with Hong Kong, Macau and Taiwan in terms of per capita income.

Open door policies and the liberalization and promotion of international trade are core evolutions of Mainland China in the process of economic reforms. Table 9.2 suggests that Mainland China's external trade transactions as indicated by the openness ratio have experienced speedy expansion from less than 15 per cent in 1982 to over 66 per cent in 2007. Being a large economy with abundant supplies of resources and raw materials, the extent of openness for Mainland China is high,[4] despite the presence of huge gaps in the openness ratio between this economy and the resource-lacking tiny or small-scaled economies of Hong Kong, Macau and Taiwan. The total trade turnover of Mainland China has increased from the nominal amount of USD 22.32 billion in 1982 to USD 1217.78 billion in 2007, implying an expansion by 54.6 times. With reference to Shan and Sun (1998), Lin (1999) and Ljungwall (2006), exports have a positive impact on the economic growth of Mainland China at the national level, and either uni- or bi-directional causality with output growth have been found in some provinces. Consequently, the increased degree of openness has helped to accelerate the economic growth of Mainland China, thereby reducing income gaps between Mainland China and the other Greater China economies of Hong Kong, Macau and Taiwan. Nevertheless, the observed ongoing catching-up process of Mainland China may not be sufficient to support income convergence among the Greater China economies,

Table 9.1 Per capita GDP of Mainland China, Hong Kong, Macau and Taiwan and their ratios for selected years

Year	[a] Mainland China (USD)	[b] Hong Kong (USD)	[c] Macau (USD)	[d] Taiwan (USD)	[a]/[b] (%)	[a]/[c] (%)	[a]/[d] (%)
1982	211	11,937	10,094	4,426	1.77	2.09	4.77
1985	294	13,918	10,681	5,330	2.11	2.75	5.52
1990	397	19,866	13,765	7,843	2.00	2.88	5.06
1995	668	26,585	14,986	10,608	2.51	4.46	6.30
2000	965	25,471	13,916	13,477	3.79	6.93	7.16
2001	1,038	24,769	14,140	13,093	4.19	7.34	7.93
2002	1,125	23,867	15,398	13,628	4.71	7.31	8.25
2003	1,230	22,357	17,385	14,044	5.50	7.07	8.76
2004	1,347	21,444	21,551	14,854	6.28	6.25	9.07
2005	1,478	21,313	22,003	15,419	6.93	6.72	9.59
2006	1,641	21,113	24,290	16,111	7.77	6.76	10.19
2007	1,827	21,508	29,505	16,854	8.49	6.19	10.84

Table 9.2 Openness ratio of Mainland China, Hong Kong, Macau and Taiwan for selected years (%)

Year	Mainland China	Hong Kong	Macau	Taiwan
1982	14.79	171.47	238.31	93.12
1985	22.67	204.93	223.71	93.04
1990	29.58	252.61	193.94	86.54
1995	38.58	290.85	137.91	92.80
2000	39.57	282.08	165.05	105.32
2001	38.47	272.87	167.82	95.39
2002	42.70	290.76	168.01	98.69
2003	51.86	332.77	164.58	106.72
2004	59.77	371.44	161.71	122.74
2005	63.57	384.96	152.90	124.24
2006	66.22	399.68	147.14	133.72
2007	66.24	405.11	142.96	139.46

as income gaps between Mainland China and the rest of the economies are still persistently large, with the per capita income level of Mainland China at less than 11 per cent of those of Hong Kong, Macau and Taiwan in 2007.

Figure 9.1 presents a scatter plot of the average per capita GDP growth rate between 1982 and 2007 against the logarithm of per capita GDP in 1982 for all Mainland Chinese provinces, Hong Kong, Macau and Taiwan. We can observe

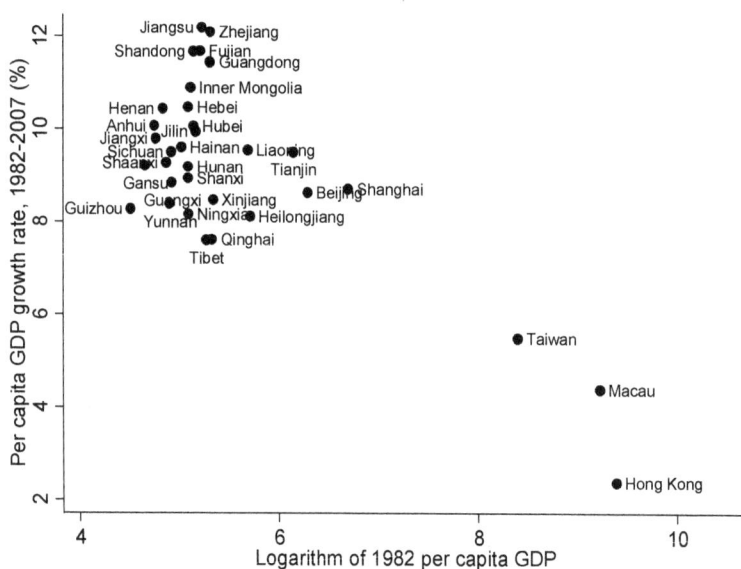

Figure 9.1 Per capita GDP growth rate, 1982–2007 versus logarithm of 1982 per capita GDP

that all Mainland Chinese provinces have higher growth rate and lower initial GDP than the other Greater China economies. It can also be noted that the fastest growing provinces and provinces with the highest levels of initial GDP are those provinces with high trade openness, defined as those with total trade (exports plus imports) that is 20 per cent or more of total GDP. These include 10 provinces, namely Guangdong, Shanghai, Tianjin, Hainan, Jiangsu, Beijing, Liaoning, Zhejiang, Fujian and Shandong in descending order of trade openness. The annual growth rate of per capita GDP in real terms for this group of high openness provinces is 10.61 per cent on average between 1983 and 2007, which is 1.37 per cent higher than that of the low openness provinces. This has motivated us to explore income convergence in the context of trade openness of Mainland Chinese provinces. Specifically, we are interested in exploring whether Mainland China as a whole, or at the disaggregated level with reference to the degree of openness, has achieved income convergence with Hong Kong, Macau and Taiwan.

Stochastic convergence analysis

We begin with a graphical inspection of the logarithm of relative per capita GDP between 1982 and 2007. Figure 9.2 depicts the time series of all Mainland Chinese provinces, Hong Kong, Macau and Taiwan. The tendency for the series to close in on each other provides evidence to support income convergence among the Greater China economies.

In our formal analysis for stochastic convergence, aside from studying all economies together, we also investigate the possibility of club convergence.

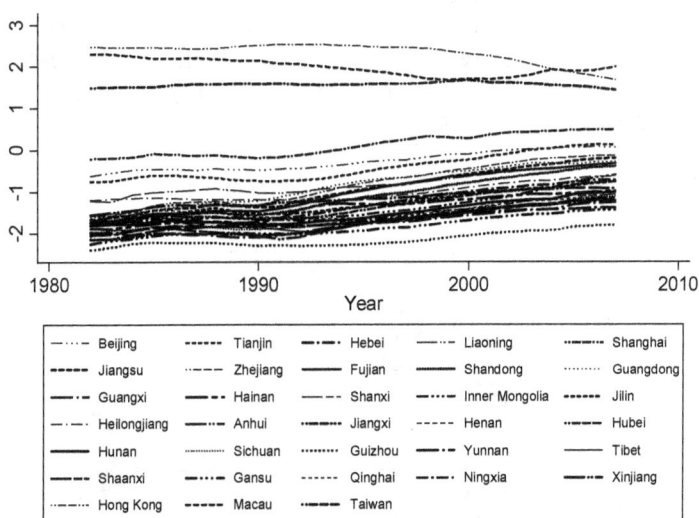

Figure 9.2 Logarithm of relative per capita GDP, 1982–2007

Specifically, we consider three broad scenarios, all of which include the Mainland Chinese provinces, which are sub-divided into provinces with high openness and provinces with low openness. In the first scenario, all the other three Greater China economies are considered. In the second scenario, Taiwan is excluded from the study, whereas focus is put on Taiwan only in the third scenario.

Since the panel unit root tests employed are rested on the assumption of cross-sectional dependence, it is important that we test for its validity. To do so, we make use of the CD test advanced by Pesaran (2004). The CD test statistic is given by

$$CD = \sqrt{\frac{2T}{N(N-1)}} \left(\sum_{i=1}^{N-1} \sum_{j=i+1}^{N} \hat{\rho}_{ij} \right), \tag{9-8}$$

where $\tilde{\rho}_{ij}$ is the estimate of the pair-wise correlation coefficient of the income residuals from the ADF regressions. It follows the standard normal distribution asymptotically. Table 9.3 shows the CD statistics for all club cases. The null hypothesis that the income residuals are cross-sectionally independent can be rejected at conventional levels in every case. It is noteworthy that the test statistics are the smallest when considering Mainland China and Taiwan only, reflecting the lack of direct communications across the Straits for decades, leading to relatively weak economic linkages among them. It can also be noted that the statistics are much larger when studying the low openness provinces than when investigating the high openness provinces for all clubs. In other words, stronger co-movements can be found among low openness provinces than among high openness provinces, along with the other Greater China economies.

Since the assumption of cross-sectional independence is violated, the distributions of the employed panel test statistics depend on nuisance parameters and are unknown. Thus, we simulate empirical distributions of the test statistics using the bootstrap method for hypothesis testing.[5] The bootstrap approach has the advantages of capturing general forms of cross-sectional dependence and correcting for finite-sample bias.

The panel unit root test results are presented in Table 9.4. For all Greater China economies together, the null of nonstationarity can be rejected at the 5 per cent level by all tests, which provide evidence to support the presence of stochastic

Table 9.3 Cross-sectional dependence test results for ADF regression residuals

Plus	Mainland Chinese provinces					
	All		*High openness*		*Low openness*	
	Statistic	p-value	Statistic	p-value	Statistic	p-value
HK + M + T	32.941	0.000	10.993	0.000	27.214	0.000
HK + M	34.876	0.000	11.213	0.000	29.538	0.000
T	7.739	0.000	3.467	0.000	12.931	0.000

Note: HK, M and T stand for Hong Kong, Macau and Taiwan respectively.

Table 9.4 Convergence test results for Mainland Chinese provinces, Hong Kong, Macau and Taiwan

Club	LLC		IPS		MW	
	Statistic	p-value	Statistic	p-value	Statistic	p-value
C + HK + M + T	−8.285	0.010	−4.154	0.040	142.393	0.023
C + HK + M	−8.317	0.012	−5.090	0.027	146.372	0.019
C + T	−1.694	0.693	1.322	0.845	63.768	0.827

Note: C, HK, M and T stand for Mainland China, Hong Kong, Macau and Taiwan respectively.

convergence among them. The notion of club convergence among Mainland China, Hong Kong and Macau is also supported at the 5 per cent level by all tests, a result that is consistent with that of Lei and Tam (2010). However, we find no evidence for stochastic convergence between Mainland China and Taiwan at conventional significance levels using the three tests.

Tables 9.5 and 9.6 contain the panel unit root test results for Mainland Chinese provinces with high openness and low openness respectively, along with the other Greater China economies. With such breakdown of Mainland Chinese provinces according to the degree of openness, we find that stochastic convergence among the Greater China economies derived in Table 9.4 is mainly driven by stochastic convergence among Mainland Chinese provinces with low openness, Hong Kong, Macau and Taiwan. While the null of nonstationarity can be rejected by only one test at the 10 per cent level for the club containing provinces with high openness, the unit root null can be rejected at the 5 per cent level or less by all tests for the

Table 9.5 Convergence test results for high openness Mainland Chinese provinces, Hong Kong, Macau and Taiwan

Club	LLC		IPS		MW	
	Statistic	p-value	Statistic	p-value	Statistic	p-value
C + HK + M + T	−2.967	0.139	−1.917	0.090	44.470	0.140
C + HK + M	−2.045	0.437	−1.569	0.237	42.036	0.182
C + T	−2.788	0.189	−0.634	0.446	33.911	0.293

Note: C, HK, M and T stand for Mainland China, Hong Kong, Macau and Taiwan respectively.

Table 9.6 Income convergence test results for low openness Mainland Chinese provinces, Hong Kong, Macau and Taiwan

Club	LLC		IPS		MW	
	Statistic	p-value	Statistic	p-value	Statistic	p-value
C + HK + M + T	−9.709	0.000	−5.343	0.015	121.738	0.012
C + HK + M	−10.218	0.000	−6.364	0.007	125.970	0.010
C + T	−1.732	0.551	1.721	0.850	49.204	0.584

Note: C, HK, M and T stand for Mainland China, Hong Kong, Macau and Taiwan respectively.

club including provinces with low openness. Qualitatively similar conclusion can also be drawn regarding the stochastic convergence among Mainland China, Hong Kong and Macau. As for the club containing Mainland China and Taiwan only, no evidence for stochastic convergence can be found even at the disaggregated level with reference to the differentiating degrees of openness of the Mainland Chinese provinces.

Conclusion and implications

Conclusion

This study pools up Mainland Chinese provinces, Hong Kong, Macau and Taiwan for the first time in the literature to conduct an integrated analysis on income convergence. The objective is to examine whether the rapid economic growth of Mainland Chinese provinces in the post-reform period may help to reduce their income gaps with Hong Kong, Macau and Taiwan, thereby bringing about income convergence among them. In the descriptive analysis, a catching up process for Mainland China is observed and the gaps between the per capita income of Mainland China at the national level and those of Hong Kong, Macau and Taiwan have been declining. Simultaneously, there is also a continuous increase in the degree of trade openness of Mainland China in line with the economic reforms that have been taking place.

Adopting the notion of stochastic convergence and employing panel unit root techniques, there is evidence to support convergence among Mainland China at the provincial level, Hong Kong, Macau and Taiwan. Stochastic convergence is also observed, at the disaggregated level, among low trade openness, rather than high trade openness, Mainland Chinese provinces, Hong Kong, Macau and Taiwan. The finding of no convergence among high openness Mainland Chinese provinces, Hong Kong, Macau and Taiwan corroborates the result of Lei and Tam (2010) that no tendency of stochastic convergence was observed among the highly open Guangdong province, Hong Kong and Macau. As regards the club of Mainland China and Taiwan, results are not supportive of the existence of stochastic convergence at both the aggregate and disaggregate levels.

Implications

The income divergence among high trade openness Mainland Chinese provinces, Hong Kong, Macau and Taiwan may be explained by the diversified growth potentials between the highly open Mainland Chinese provinces and the other Greater Chinese economies. Despite the presence of a high degree of openness for Hong Kong, Macau and Taiwan, the high trade exposure of these economies is driven by transshipment businesses, exportation of gaming services and exportation of intermediate products respectively. The production structures of these economies are very different from those of the highly open Mainland Chinese provinces, which have specialized in foreign direct investment (FDI) driven by trade and/or inward processing trade with developed economies such as the US and the EU as their major markets. It is believed that the highly open provinces are able to gain access to the state-of-the-art foreign technologies, to acquire internationally recognized production skills and experiences and to upgrade their productivity through the learning by doing process.[6] This group of highly open Mainland Chinese provinces may then be equipped with stronger growth potential than Hong Kong, Macau and Taiwan, and are therefore likely to out-perform these economies over time, leading to income divergence among them. As indicated in Ghose (2004), trade liberalization and the resulting improvement in growth progress tends to reduce the inequality between trade partners. As such, there is the possibility that income convergence is taking place among the highly open Mainland Chinese provinces and their trade partners, such as the US and the EU. This scenario, however, remains uncertain and requires further investigation in future research work.

Another source of divergence is the disparity across different Mainland Chinese provinces that have high trade openness which has been explained in Pedroni and Yao (2006). Such deviation may be attributed to product specific international demand shocks. It is believed that the various Mainland Chinese provinces which are highly open would exercise their comparative advantages and devote more efforts to the production of certain goods. In the case of a product specific international demand shock, such as a change in consumer preferences, the highly open provinces which specialize in the production of the relevant goods may suffer from stronger adverse impacts. Provinces which specialize in the production of other goods may not be seriously affected, given such a product specific shock. As a result, it may bring about divergence to the group.

In contrast, the low trade openness Mainland Chinese provinces are mostly central and inner provinces with poorer endowments and no advantage in geographical location. They are less attractive from the point of view of foreign investors and have fewer opportunities to be exposed to foreign advanced technologies and experience, and are not subject to significant product specific international demand shocks. Consequently, this group of less open central and inner provinces may be more 'inward' looking and may experience similar problems inherited from their initial endowments and geographical location which was called 'geographically-isolated' according to Pedroni and Yao (2006). Their income levels thus have stronger tendency to converge. Furthermore, as stated in the Solow (1956) growth model and the implied diminishing return assumption, this group of less open provinces may enjoy higher rates of return to capital compared with Hong Kong, Macau and Taiwan, given their initial backwardness. This allows the income levels of the less open Mainland Chinese provinces to converge with those of Hong Kong, Macau and Taiwan over the long-run. In addition, the tendency of income convergence among the less open provinces is so strong that it has dominated the divergence force present among the highly open provinces to bring about stochastic convergence among the Greater China economies.

The findings of stochastic convergence among all the Greater China economies but stochastic divergence between Mainland China and Taiwan suggest that in the absence of direct and barriers-free economic connections between the two sides of the Straits, the two SARs of Hong Kong and Macau have been playing a significant role in enhancing the income convergence process between Mainland China and Taiwan. With the implementation of the recently concluded ECFA, economic cooperation between Mainland China and Taiwan is expected to deepen and widen. Given the liberalization on trade and investment transactions, direct economic activities between Mainland China and Taiwan should develop rapidly and a quasi-free trade area could be formed among the Greater China economies of Mainland China, Hong Kong, Macau and Taiwan over time. The integration-led efficiency improvement and economies of scale could bring about better growth prospects to all the entities in the region. Intensified integration may contribute to further reduce their income gaps and the possibility of sustained convergence among these economies in the long-run. Nevertheless, uneven development with regard to economic integration remains a critical issue as FDI from Hong Kong, Macau and Taiwan are currently concentrated in the coastal region of Mainland China. This may turn out to be a risk to the future growth prospects for the Greater China region as a whole. Taking advantage of the enforcement of ECFA, new policy measurements could be launched to enhance the economic cooperation between the central and inner parts of Mainland China, Hong Kong, Macau and Taiwan or full scale integration would be hard to achieve.

Notes

1 Corresponding author: Department of Finance and Business Economics, Faculty of Business Administration, University of Macau; email: henrylei@umac.mo
2 The ranking is based on output measured in terms of purchasing power parity in 2007 according to the World Bank.
3 This generalizes the ARMA (2,0) process used in Carlino and Mills (1993).
4 The openness ratios of Japan and the US were 35 and 29 per cent respectively in 2007.
5 To conserve space, the bootstrap procedure is not detailed here, but is available upon request.
6 Similar argument has also been put forth by Zhang (2001), Zhang (2006) and Jayanthakumaran and Verma (2008) in analyzing the relationship between trade and income convergence.

Bibliography

Carlino, G.A., Mills, L.O., (1993), 'Are U.S. regional incomes converging?', *Journal of Monetary Economics*, 32: 335–346
Carrion-i-Silvestre, J.L., German-Soto, V., (2007), 'Stochastic convergence amongst Mexican states', *Regional Studies*, 41: 531–541
Chen J. and Fleisher, B.M., (1996), 'Regional income inequality and economic growth in China', *Journal of Comparative Economics*, 22: 141–164
Démurger, S., (2001), 'Infrastructure development and economic growth: An explanation for regional disparities in China?', *Journal of Comparative Economics*, 29: 95–117
Galvão A.F. Jr., Reis Gomes, F.A., (2007), 'Convergence or divergence in Latin America? A time series analysis', *Applied Economics*, 39:1353–1360

Ghose, A.K., (2004), 'Global inequality and international trade', *Cambridge Journal of Economics*, 28: 229–52

Gundlach, E., (1997), 'Regional convergence of output per worker in China: A neoclassical interpretation', *Asian Economic Journal*, 11: 423–442

Hong Kong SAR Government (1982–2007), *Hong Kong Monthly Digest of Statistics*, various Issues, Census and Statistics Department, the Hong Kong SAR Government, accessed online: on 15 June, 2009 from www.info.gov.hk/censtatd/eng/hkstat/index.html

Im, K.S., Pesaran, M.H., Shin, Y., (2003), 'Testing for unit roots in heterogeneous panels', *Journal of Econometrics*, 115: 53–74

Jayanthakumaran, K., Verma, R., (2008), 'International trade and regional income convergence: The ASEAN-5 evidence', *ASEAN Economic Bulletin*, 25: 179–94

Jian, T., Sachs, J.D., Warner, A.M., (1996) 'Trends in regional inequality in China', *China Economic Review*, 7: 1–21

Lei, C.K., Tam, P.S., (2010), 'A panel data approach to the income convergence among Mainland China, Hong Kong and Macao', *Journal of the Asia-Pacfiic Economy*, 15, 42–435.

Lei, C.K., Yao, S., (2008), 'On income convergence among China, Hong Kong and Macau', *The World Economy*, 31: 345–366

Levin, A., Lin, C.-F., Chu, C.-S. J., (2002), 'Unit root tests in panel data: Asymptotic and finite-sample properties', *Journal of Econometrics*, 108: 1–24

Li, Q., Papell, D., (1999), 'Convergence of international output: Time series evidence for 16 OECD countries', *International Review of Economics and Finance*, 8: 267–280

Lin, S., (1999), 'Export expansion and economic growth: Evidence from Chinese provinces', *Pacific Economic Review*, 4: 65–77

Ljungwall, C., (2006), 'Export-led growth: Application to China's provinces, 1978–2001', *Journal of Chinese Economic and Business Studies*, 4: 109–126

Lowey, M.B., and Papell, D.H., (1996), 'Are U.S. regional incomes converging? Some further evidence', *Journal of Monetary Economics*, 38: 587–598

Macau SAR Government, (1982–2008), *Yearbook of Statistics of Macau*, various issues, Statistics and Census Services, the Macau SAR Government, accessed online: on 15 June, 2009 from www.dsec.gov.mo

Maddala, G.S., Wu, S., (1999), 'A comparative study of unit root tests with panel data and a new simple test', *Oxford Bulletin of Economics and Statistics*, 61: 631–652

National Bureau of Statistics of China (NBS), (1982–2008), *China Statistical Yearbook*, various issues, Beijing: China Statistics Press

National Statistics (1982–2008), Republic of China, accessed online on 15 June 2009 from http://www.stat.gov.tw

Pedroni, P., Yao, J.Y., (2006), 'Regional income divergence in China', *Journal of Asian Economics*, 17: 294–315

Pesaran, M.H., (2004), 'General Diagnostic Tests for Cross Section Dependence in Panels', *Cambridge Working Paper in Economics 0435*, University of Cambridge

Raiser, M., (1998), 'Subsidizing inequality: Economic reforms, fiscal transfers and convergence across Chinese provinces', *Journal of Development Studies*, 34: 1–26

Romero-Ávila, D., (2009), 'The convergence hypothesis for OECD countries reconsidered: Panel data evidence with multiple breaks, 1870–2003', *The Manchester School*, 77: 552–574

Shan, J., Sun, F., (1998), 'On the export-led growth hypothesis: The econometric evidence from China', *Applied Economics*, 30: 1055–1065

Solow, R., (1956), 'A contribution to the theory of economic growth', *Quarterly Journal of Economics*, 70: 65–94

Wang, Z., Schuh, G., (2000) 'Economic integration among Taiwan, Hong Kong and China: A computable general equilibrium analysis', *Pacific Economic Review*, 5: 229–262

Yao, S., Zhang, Z., (2001), 'On regional inequality and diverging clubs: A case study of contemporary China', *Journal of Comparative Economics*, 29: 466–484

Zhang, J., (2006), 'International Trade, Convergence and Integration', *Conference Paper Presented at 8th Meeting of the European Trade Study Group, September 7–9 2006*

Zhang, Z., (2001), 'Trade liberalization, economic Growth and convergence: Evidence from East Asian economies', *Journal of Economic Integration*, 16: 147–164

Zhang, Z., Liu, A., Yao, S., (2001), 'Convergence of China's regional incomes 1952–1997', *China Economic Review*, 12: 243–258

Zhang Z. and Yao S. (2001), 'Regional Inequalities in Contemporary China Measured by GDP and Consumption', *Economic Issues*, 6: 13–29.

10 Does Chinese financial reform improve bank performance? Evidence from individual commercial banks

Puyang Sun, Yi Jin, Shujing Jin[1]

Introduction

China's financial system has been governed by the central government and granted monopolistic power until the 1980s. However, following the 'open door' policy implemented in 1979, the typical central planning banking system has not been consistent with the rapid development of the economy. The Chinese government has thus proposed a series of banking reforms to improve the banking system and support the macro-economy. Although aggressive progress has been observed, the Chinese banking system has still experienced low efficiency and large amounts of non-performing loans, particularly after accession to the World Trade Organization (WTO). In this chapter, we aim to estimate whether Chinese bank performance has improved in the presence of financial reforms in a post-WTO period.

The banking industry has had to face challenges that are similar to other emerging countries: the fundamental problem of the Chinese banking system is state ownership, which has dominated the Chinese banking industry (Chen and Wu, 2010; Yin, et al., 2010; Tobin and Singh, 2008; Yao, et al., 2008, Goodhart and Zeng, 2006). The main shortcoming of a centralized banking system is the lack of autonomy of individual banks, which are limited to effectively allocating their assets. Bank loans are often offered on a geographical and sectional basis, which exclusively depends on the need of the development of the macro-economy. As a consequence, the amount of non-performing loans (NPL) increases, which is expected to have a significant impact on bank performance, even though the Chinese government has changed the fundamental structure of the banking system. In addition, government interventions restrict competitive and free markets, where banks can enhance their efficiency levels. The final protection provided by the Chinese government generates the moral hazard problem. They are not willing to concentrate on bank management but would rather expand bank assets. Therefore, this study constructs a comparison between joint-equity banks and state-owned banks to explore the effect of government intervention on bank performance. Compared with banks from developed countries, liquidity risk seems to be less significant in the Chinese banking system in the presence of the huge base of deposits.[2] However, such a large amount of liquidity assets may increase operational costs and reduce bank profitability; thus, we attempt to investigate two paradoxes between liquidity asset holding and either bank profitability and management efficiency. Although the mono-banking system has been broken during the past three decades, state-owned banks (SOBs) still dominate the banking market (their market share was 63% of consumer deposits and 70% of corporate loans in 2005[3]). Furthermore, the capital adequacy of Chinese-listed banks is no more than 10%, which is significantly lower than that of Hong Kong-listed banks (18%)[4] In this case, valid protection to Chinese banks is provided by the government instead of the sufficient capital ratio. Therefore, the measurement of bank capitalization should be also considered in this study.

Since China joined the WTO in 2001, Chinese banks have had to face challenges from foreign banks in the absence of protection from the Chinese government. How banks survive in this competitive market is a substantial concern for both academic researchers and policymakers. Our departure point of this chapter is to test the effect of traditional bank specific characteristics on bank performance. The study extended the sample period of eight years from 2003 to 2010 to capture Chinese bank performance in the post-WTO period, and also employed 68 banks that have different ownership to address the specific effect of state ownership on the Chinese banking industry. The results suggest that non-performing loans still have a significant impact on bank performance. This negative effect cannot be eliminated through a series of Chinese banking reforms. Two paradoxes between liquidity asset holding and either bank profitability and bank management efficiency have been identified, which demonstrates that a large amount of liquidity asset in Chinese banks does not yield a positive effect on bank performance, but it would rather increase operational costs and reduce bank profitability. Therefore, our results suggest that Chinese financial markets have to seek new liquidity management tools in order to take advantage of this large number of liquidity assets. Moreover, good capitalization has a negative effect on bank profitability, particularly it is robust to the alternative measure of bank profitability (return on equity), which suggests that the protection from equity (shareholders) forces banks to employ prudent businesses associated with a lower level of profits; this in turn, reduces the level of bank profitability. In addition, we examined the differences in bank performance between state-owned banks and joint-equity banks. The equity-jointed banks have more advantages in improving bank efficiency than state-owned banks, as expected. The empirical results also suggest implications for policymakers, who have to consider the specific characteristics of Chinese banks associated with different ownership in formulating policy.

The structure of this chapter is organized as follows. The next part shows the key steps in the Chinese banking system reforms since 1979. This is followed by a section introducing the current structure of the Chinese banking system. Two further sections show the variables and the data of the empirical study, while the penultimate part concentrates on the empirical results and analyses. Conclusions are drawn in the last section.

Chinese banking system reforms

Yin, et al. (2010), Lin and Zhang (2009), Fu and Heffernan (2007), Chen, et al. (2005) and Li, et al. (2001) have all shed light on the stages of Chinese banking reforms. In this section, we summarize the main steps in chronological order, which contributes to the implications of the subsequent empirical analysis.

Prior to 1978, the Chinese banking system employed the mono-bank model. The People's Bank of China (PBOC) combined the functions of a central bank with those of a commercial bank. All other credit corporations as local institutions were subordinate to the PBOC.

The separation of the central bank and commercial banks was implemented between 1979 and 1993. The functions of the central bank and commercial banks were separated from the PBOC. The PBOC, as a central bank, remained in charge of monetary policy and supervision. The various commercial banking functions were gradually allocated to four SOBs: the Bank of China (BOC), the Agriculture Bank of China (ABC), the Construction Bank of China (CBC) and the Industrial and Commercial Bank of China (ICBC). Regardless of profitability, the main objective of these four SOBs was to assist SOEs to complete their planned outputs, which resulted in the significant problem of non-performing loans because of the poor performances of SOEs. In addition, these four SOBs did not have any incentive to compete with each other in the presence of the bail-out provided by the Chinese government, which in turn reduced the efficiency of SOBs.

Commercialisation emerged in response to an increase in the amount of non-performing loans in SOBs (1994–2001). In 1994, three policy banks were established to take over policy-based lending, which had originally been allocated to SOBs. These were the State Development Bank of China, the Export and Import Bank of China and the Agriculture Development Bank of China. However, these three policy banks were not consistent with the needs of policy-based lending. The main policy-based loans were still provided by SOBs. In 1995, the Central Bank Law and Commercial Bank Law became effective, which in turn promoted the emergence of city-based commercial banks and rural credit corporations. Given the development of city-based commercial banks and rural credit corporations, competition within China's banking sector became increasingly fierce. In 1998, the Ministry of Finance issued 30-year special government bonds at RMB 270 billion to recapitalize SOBs and cope with non-performing loans. In 2001, China became a member of the WTO, which indicated that Chinese banks were already on their way to internationalisation.

In the past 10 years, the transformation and internationalisation of the Chinese banking system has deepened in the context of the rapid development of the macro-economy. Since joining the WTO in 2001, the Chinese banking industry has had to face unprecedented challenges from foreign banks. In response to this serious issue, the Chinese government provided USD 45 billion for the reform of the four big SOBs in order to support the shareholding transformation. The principle of this reform is a 'principal–agent' theory (Yin, et al., 2010; Yao, et al., 2004). The government (principal) as the ultimate protector always rescues banks (agents) in trouble, which allows banks to unlimitedly increase non-performing loans. The reform of shareholding banks removes the responsibility of the Chinese government and forces banks to engage in the competitive market. The Chinese government injects capital to eliminate non-performing loans, which enables Chinese banks to operate on a level playing field with foreign banks in the short-term. Banks have to rely on an equity base provided by the financial markets instead of government capital injections in the long-term. In 2005, 2006 and 2010, the BOC, CBC, ICBC and ABC were listed on the Hong Kong stock market, which indicated that the big four SOBs had already successfully transformed from state ownership to partial private ownership. A description of main stages of the Chinese banking reform from 1979 to 2010 is shown in Annex 10.1.

The current Chinese banking structure

At the end of 2010, the Chinese financial system consisted of depository institutions and non-depository institutions. Depository institutions are structured by 3 policy banks, 4 state-owned commercial banks and 13 joint-equity commercial banks (Bank of Communications (BOCS), CITIC Industrial Bank (CITICIB), China Everbright Bank (CEB), Hua Industrial Xia Bank (HXB), China Bank (CIB), China Minsheng Banking Corporation (CMBC), China Guangfa Bank (CGB), Shenzhen Development Bank (SDB), Shanghai Pudong Development Bank (SPDB), China Merchants Bank (CMB), China Bohai Bank (CBB), China Evergrowing Bank (CEB), and China Zhenshang Bank (CZB)) as well as city-level commercial banks and rural-level commercial banks. Table 10.1 shows the current structure of the Chinese banking system. There are 250 banks in China's banking system, including the central bank, three policy banks, four SOBs, 13 joint-equity commercial banks, 149 city commercial banks, 43 rural credit corporations and 37 foreign banks. Total assets amount to RMB 72,647.65 billion and total net profit is RMB 620.44 billion. It is clear that SOBs still dominate market share with 55% of total assets and 65% of total net profits.

Table 10.1 The structure of the Chinese banking system in 2010

	Total assets (RMB billion)	Market share (%)	Total net profit (RMB billion)	Market share (%)
Policy banks (3)	6945.61	9.56	35.25	5.68
State-owned Commercial banks (4)	40089.02	55.18	400.12	64.49
Joint-equity commercial banks(13)	11784.98	16.22	92.5	14.91
City commercial banks (149)	5680.01	7.82	49.65	8
Rural credit corporations (43)	6771.62	9.32	36.28	5.85
Foreign banks (37)	1349.23	1.86	6.45	1.04
Total	72647.65	100	620.44	100

Source: China Banking Regulatory Commission www.cbrc.gov.cn/chinese/info/xglj/index_jrjg.jsp

Empirical variables

This chapter concentrates on bank ownership and the micro-problems associated with bank management in order to investigate Chinese bank performance. In a market-based financial system, the objective of bank management is to maximize the value of banks and their interests on behalf of shareholders. Bank management is made up of asset quality management, liquidity management and capital management as a whole, while the level of bank management is reflected by the effect of three kinds of management on bank profitability and efficiency.

According to the objective of this chapter, the ratio of costs to operating income (COI) is used as a proxy of bank efficiency, which is consistent with the empirical studies of Chen and Wu (2010) and Kwan (2003). Return on assets (ROA) and return on equity (ROE), as measure of bank performance, have also been employed in numerous previous banking studies (Stiroh, 2006; Stiroh and Rumble, 2006; DeYoung and Rice, 2004; Demirgüç-Kunt and Detragiache, 1998). The ratio of non-performing loans to gross loans (NPLGL) represents the quality of bank assets. An increase in NPLGL leads to a reduction in the profit and efficiency of banks, which in turn decreases ROA and ROE and raises COI.

For historical reasons, NPLs are still a big issue for Chinese banks, especially for SOBs, even though the government allocates policy-based loans to three policy banks and the Ministry of Finance has issued 30-year special government bonds at RMB 270 billion to recapitalize four SOBs. According to the Almanac of China's Finance and Banking (2010), at the end of 2010 the amount of NPL was RMB 497.33 billion. SOBs held RMB 362.73 billion (72.94% of total NPL), while joint-equity banks held RMB 63.72 billion (12.81% of total NPL), city-based commercial banks held RMB 37.69 billion (7.58% of total NPL), rural-level commercial banks held RMB 27.01 billion (5.43% of total NPL) and foreign banks held only RMB 6.18 billion (1.24% of total NPL). It is obvious that SOBs still held the majority of NPL. Compared with foreign banks, NPL significantly reduce the competitiveness of Chinese SOBs.

The ratio of liquid assets to total assets (LATA) is a measure of liquidity assets. Liquidity management has been emphasised in recent years. However, liquidity management seems to be treated as a 'Cinderella' in the banking sector, as it was thought to be unnecessary because of financial innovation. Basel I was not able to achieve agreement on this topic, which also contributes to the ignorance of liquidity management. However, the early stage of the global financial crisis of 2007–08 can be seen as a liquidity crisis, as observed either by an individual bank run, or by a liquidity crisis in financial markets.

In addition, liquidity management relies on public confidence. Depositors prefer depositing in a bank, which is protected by the government. Once public confidence bursts, a bank run will occur. The mechanism is shown as follows: either a bank run or a finance problem of banks in capital markets takes place in the case of a bank associated with illiquidity but solvency. The bank has to sell its assets at a fire-sale price, which is extremely lower than the value on the books. Thus, this contributes to the ultimate bank failure.

Chen and Wu (2010) emphasised the paradox between liquidity and profitability. Specifically, liquidity assets are associated with less profitability; however, this can act as a buffer against potential liquidity risk. In other words, banks tend to reduce liquidity assets in order to make more profits, which in turn have a negative impact on the bank's safety. Hence, bank management should balance profitability and liquidity. In this chapter, the LATA ratio measures bank liquidity, which is expected to be negatively related to ROA and ROE. In regards to bank efficiency, an increase in liquid assets implies less efficiency because it sacrifices profits and raises operational costs. Thus, LATA is expected to be positively related to COI.

The ratio of equity to total assets (ETA) is a measure of the capitalisation of banks. Owing to asymmetric information, the problem of moral hazard and adverse selection is a serious concern for Chinese banks. Based on Gu and Yu (2010), the capital requirement reduces the incentives of banks to perform activities associated with higher risk levels and, at the same time, provides protection for depositors, which explicitly reflects the effects of bank regulation and supervision on bank behaviours. Hence, the minimum capital adequacy requirement is emphasised by Basel II. Compared with Basel I, Basel II offers a specific requirement for pillar one. The supplements or modifications in Basel II concentrate on the distinctions between risk level, namely how the risk level of a bank's assets can be estimated properly. The new approach of Basel II improves risk assessment and highlights the capital minimum requirement.

In addition, the market discipline of pillar one of Basel II has an impact on another pillar capital adequacy requirement. Depositors can withdraw their deposits or demand a higher interest rate in response to a lower capital holding. Hence, under effective market discipline, banks have to maintain sufficient capital holdings in order to support their reputations and avoid a bank run. However, there is another paradox between capital holding and profitability, as the costs of capital requirement reduce the profit and efficiency of banks. Therefore, ETA is expected to be negatively related to ROA and ROE and positively related to COI.

To capture the specific effect of Chinese banks that have different types of ownership, dummy variables were employed in this chapter. D_state-owned equals 1 for SOBs and 0 otherwise; and D_joint-equity equals 1 for joint-equity banks and 0 otherwise.[5] Table 10.2 describes the variables.

Table 10.2 Variables in this study

Symbol	Definition
Dependent variables	
ROA	Return on assets
ROE	Return on equity
COI	Costs to operating income
Independent variables	
NPLGL	Non-performing loans to gross loans
LATA	Liquid assets to total assets
ETA	Equity to total assets
D_state-owned	Equal to 1 for SOBs, 0 otherwise
D_joint-equity	Equal to 1 for joint-equity banks, 0 otherwise

Data

Data selection

Owing to the limitation of using Chinese banks' data, the data sources are inconsistent. The data are chosen from the database of Bankscope, the Almanac of China's Finance and Banking, the annual financial reports posted on the websites of individual banks and the listed banks' financial reports, which follow various accounting standards. The reports of the Almanac of China's Finance and Banking and the individual bank websites follow the Chinese Accounting Standards and International Accounting Standards. The reports of Bankscope follow the Generally Accepted Accounting Principles and the International Financial Reporting Standards. In addition, the reports in terms of different years of a bank might follow various accounting standards.

The Chinese Accounting Standards have been improved frequently in the past 10 years, which allows bank reports to change data disclosure over time. Thus, data information might not be able to provide a consistent database. In addition, the data of most rural-level commercial banks and city-level commercial banks are not available since they are not forced to release their financial reports by the China Banking Regulatory Commission.

Despite the shortcomings in Chinese banks' data, 68 banks were picked from Bureau Van Dijk Bankscope, the Almanac of China's Finance and Banking and the websites of individual banks from 2003 to 2010. The sample included all SOBs and all joint-equity banks, 30% of city-level commercial banks and 16% of rural-level commercial banks. Table 10.3 shows that the sample includes four SOBs (5.88% of the total sample), 13 joint-equity banks (19.12%), 44 city-level commercial banks (64.71%) and seven rural-level commercial banks (10.29%). This is an unbalanced panel data, which indicates that some observations have been lost in different years for individual banks.

Data statistics

Table 10.4 shows the statistics on the sample data of ROA, ROE and COI from 2003 to 2010. In light of profitability, the sample means of ROA and ROE increased

Table 10.3 Summary of numbers of individual banks

Year	SOBs	Joint-equity banks	City-level commercial banks	Rural-level commercial banks	Total
2003	4	13	44	7	68
2004	4	13	44	7	68
2005	4	13	44	7	68
2006	4	13	44	7	68
2007	4	13	44	7	68
2008	4	13	44	7	68
2009	4	13	44	7	68
2010	4	13	44	7	68
Total	32	104	352	56	544

Table 10.4 Summary statistics of the dependent variables during 2003–2010

	2003	2004	2005	2006	2007	2008	2009	2010
ROA								
Sample mean	0.004	0.004	0.006	0.007	0.010	0.011	0.010	0.011
Mean of SOBs	0.005	0.007	0.006	0.007	0.010	0.011	0.010	0.010
Mean of joint-equity banks	0.004	0.003	0.006	0.006	0.011	0.012	0.011	0.012
Mean of city-level commercial banks	0.004	0.005	0.006	0.007	0.010	0.012	0.010	0.011
Mean of rural-level commercial banks	0.008	0.005	0.006	0.008	0.009	0.012	0.011	0.014
ROE								
Sample mean	0.126	0.134	0.111	0.107	0.188	0.196	0.167	0.193
Mean of SOBs	0.140	0.085	0.015	0.124	0.088	0.077	0.158	0.186
Mean of joint-equity banks	0.133	0.128	0.049	0.024	0.212	0.192	0.177	0.195
Mean of city-level commercial banks	0.097	0.125	0.137	0.140	0.194	0.209	0.195	0.207
Mean of rural-level commercial banks	0.365	0.261	0.142	0.153	0.164	0.197	0.185	0.197
COI								
Sample mean	0.562	0.536	0.451	0.416	0.366	0.360	0.402	0.370
Mean of SOBs	0.537	0.531	0.451	0.536	0.408	0.389	0.433	0.385
Mean of joint-equity banks	0.500	0.478	0.483	0.423	0.353	0.353	0.372	0.347
Mean of city-level commercial banks	0.582	0.521	0.429	0.377	0.356	0.348	0.394	0.371
Mean of rural-level commercial banks	0.521	0.763	0.558	0.410	0.355	0.382	0.404	0.348

from 2003 to 2008, reaching a peak at approximately 1.15% for ROA and 19.6% for ROE. After a reduction in 2009, the sample means of ROA and ROE recovered in 2010 to 1.1% and 19.3%, respectively. The profitability of China's banks seems to be improved from 2003, as the reduction in bank profitability in 2009 can be explained by the global financial crisis. It is worth noting that the lowest profitability of SOBs appeared at the end of 2010 with 1.0% ROA and 18.6% ROE. Regarding bank efficiency, the mean of COI generally reduced over time as the efficiency of China's domestic banks has significantly improved; however, the exception in 2009 can be explained by the recent financial crisis. Furthermore, the efficiency of SOBs was lower than that of Chinese banks with other forms of ownership, which offers an insight into implementing banking reforms, particularly considering SOBs.

Table 10.5 shows the statistics of the non-performing loan ratio, liquidity ratio and equity ratio. NPLGL generally reduced over time, based on the mean value of the overall sample. However, the large amount of NPLGL dominates SOBs and rural-level commercial banks. To cope with the issue of non-performing loans over the past two decades, three policy banks have been established to take over

Table 10.5 Summary statistics of the independent variables during 2003–2010

	2003	2004	2005	2006	2007	2008	2009	2010
NPLGL								
Sample mean	0.154	0.103	0.089	0.073	0.063	0.021	0.016	0.015
Mean of SOBs	0.189	0.142	0.108	0.097	0.080	0.029	0.019	0.017
Mean of joint-equity banks	0.076	0.042	0.041	0.030	0.022	0.013	0.009	0.009
Mean of city-level commercial banks	0.130	0.117	0.074	0.050	0.039	0.021	0.014	0.012
Mean of rural-level commercial banks	0.173	0.123	0.061	0.052	0.049	0.024	0.006	0.005
LATA								
Sample mean	0.166	0.166	0.174	0.178	0.220	0.235	0.233	0.287
Mean of SOBs	0.155	0.135	0.162	0.148	0.167	0.195	0.190	0.231
Mean of joint-equity banks	0.161	0.174	0.185	0.206	0.247	0.248	0.258	0.298
Mean of city-level commercial banks	0.151	0.161	0.169	0.174	0.217	0.232	0.230	0.273
Mean of rural-level commercial banks	0.419	0.201	0.234	0.168	0.219	0.249	0.226	0.255
ETA								
Sample mean	0.047	0.040	0.045	0.055	0.056	0.061	0.062	0.058
Mean of SOBs	0.007	0.004	0.043	0.054	0.056	0.059	0.054	0.061
Mean of joint-equity banks	0.029	0.036	0.032	0.056	0.051	0.049	0.046	0.051
Mean of city-level commercial banks	0.061	0.049	0.050	0.056	0.056	0.066	0.069	0.059
Mean of rural-level commercial banks	0.021	0.023	0.046	0.049	0.056	0.056	0.058	0.057

policy-based loans. Furthermore, the Ministry of Finance issued 30-year government bonds to recapitalise SOBs, four asset management companies were established to deal with non-performing loans and the CAMELS (capital adequacy, asset quality, management quality, earnings, liquidity management, and sensitivity to market risk) rating standard has been employed to control non-performing loans. All measures seem to be successful, as the amount of non-performing loans has reduced in the past decade. However, based on Goodhart and Zeng (2006), we should be concerned about 'Special Mention Loans', which have increased by RMB 190 billion from 2003 for the big four. In particular, in the recent years Chinese banks have suffered a new crop of problem loans, although the amount of non-performing loans has dropped, as Beijing has begun to tighten market liquidity and restrict the Chinese housing market.

Liquidity management has been emphasised through Basel II, particularly in developed financial markets that have complex financial instruments. We may argue that the liquidity assets in Chinese banks are sufficient because of the large amounts of deposits, which can be reflected by the mean value of the overall sample. This increased from 16.7% in 2003 to 28.7% in 2010. However, as various investment ways are gradually highlighted over time, bank deposits will no longer be a single way for Chinese householders to invest, which in turn reduces the sources of bank deposits. In addition, liquidity management tools are rare compared with developed financial markets, and thus the liquidity problem might become a concern for banking operations.

Generally, the equity ratio does not show a significant change over time based on the mean value of the overall sample. Since 1998, the Chinese government has been implementing measures to increase the capital ratio of SOBs, for instance it has injected capital into SOBs using fiscal expenditure; the remaining earnings were then transferred to capital; and SOBs were allowed to issue subordinated debt. The Commercial Bank Capital Adequacy Regulations issued in 2004 required the capital adequate ratios of commercial banks to be 8% by the end of 2006. Table 10.6 shows the capital adequacy rates for the main commercial banks. In short, the amount of capital held by SOBs was mandatory for all banks excluding the ABC. From 2007, the majority of joint-equity banks achieved the minimum capital requirement except the China Guangfa Bank (7.14), China Evergrowing Bank (7.02) and Shenzhen Development Bank (5.77). In this chapter, we employ the equity ratio as a measure of capitalisation.

Results and analyses of empirical models

Model specification

$$OP_{it} = \gamma_i + \beta_{nplgl}NPLGL_{it} + \beta_{lata}LATA_{it} + \beta_{eta}ETA_{it} + \beta_{d\_state}D\_state_{it}$$
$$+ \beta_{d\_joint}D\_joint_{it} + \varepsilon_{it} \tag{10-1}$$

Table 10.6 Capital ratios for the main commercial banks

Year	2005	2006	2007	2008	2009	2010
SOBs						
BOC	10.42	13.59	13.34	13.43	11.14	12.58
ICBC	9.89	14.05	13.09	13.06	12.36	12.27
ABC	—	—	—	9.41	10.07	11.59
CBC	13.59	12.11	12.58	12.16	11.7	12.68
Joint-equity banks						
Bank of Communications	11.2	10.83	14.44	13.47	12	12.36
Bank of Communications	8.04	9.27	9.15	9.06	10.34	12.02
China Industrial Bank	8.13	8.71	11.73	11.24	10.75	11.22
China Merchants Bank	9.01	11.39	10.4	11.34	10.45	11.47
Hua Xia Bank	8.27	8.28	8.27	11.4	10.2	10.58
China Guangfa Bank	—	6.7	7.14	11.63	8.98	11.02
CITIC Industrial Bank	8.11	9.41	15.27	14.32	10.72	11.31
China Evergrowing Bank	10.07	9.42	7.02	8.91	12.08	11.08
China Minsheng Banking Corporation	8.59	8.26	8.2	10.73	9.22	10.83
Shenzhen Development Bank	3.7	3.71	5.77	8.58	8.9	10.2
China Zhenshang Bank	—	11.84	11.87	8.55	10.01	11.06

where, OP_{it} is a general dependent variable, representing bank performance for the i th bank in year t. The indicators of bank performance employed in this model are ROA, ROE and COI. Hence, the general model can be specified as follows.

$$
\begin{aligned}
ROA_{it} = \gamma_i &+ \beta_{nplgl}NPLGL_{it} + \beta_{lata}LATA_{it} + \beta_{eta}ETA_{it} \\
&+ \beta_{d\_state}D\_state_{it} + \beta_{d\_joint}D\_joint_{it} + \varepsilon_{it}
\end{aligned}
\tag{10-2}
$$

$$
\begin{aligned}
ROE_{it} = \gamma_i &+ \beta_{nplgl}NPLGL_{it} + \beta_{lata}LATA_{it} + \beta_{eta}ETA_{it} \\
&+ \beta_{d\_state}D\_state_{it} + \beta_{d\_joint}D\_joint_{it} + \varepsilon_{it}
\end{aligned}
\tag{10-3}
$$

$$
\begin{aligned}
COI_{it} = \gamma_i &+ \beta_{nplgl}NPLGL_{it} + \beta_{lata}LATA_{it} + \beta_{eta}ETA_{it} \\
&+ \beta_{d\_state}D\_state_{it} + \beta_{d\_joint}D\_joint_{it} + \varepsilon_{it}
\end{aligned}
\tag{10-4}
$$

where, ROA_{it} represents the ROA for the i th bank in year t. ROE_{it} represents the ROE for the i th bank in year t. COI_{it} is the ratio of COI for the i th bank in year t. $NPLGL_{it}$ represents the ratio of NPLGL for the i th bank in year t. $LATA_{it}$ represents the ratio of LATA for the i th bank in year t. ETA_{it} is the ratio of ETA for the i th bank in year t. $D\_state_{it} = 1$ if the i th bank is a SOB, 0 otherwise; $D\_joint_{it} = 1$ if the i th bank is a joint-equity bank, 0 otherwise; γ is a constant; $\beta_{\nu\pi\lambda}, \beta_{\lambda\alpha\tau\alpha}, \beta_{\epsilon\tau\alpha}, \beta_{\delta\_\sigma\tau\alpha\tau\epsilon}, \beta_{\delta\_\varphi\omicron\iota\nu\tau}$ are the vectors of coefficients; ε_{it} is a disturbance term.

Results and analyses of the empirical model

The fixed effects and random effects models for each regression were employed in this chapter, and the year dummy variables were also used in order to capture the time-specific effect during the sample period. In addition, the performances of SOBs and joint-equity banks were compared.

ROA

The results of the fixed effects and random effects models are shown in Table 10.7, where the adjusted R-squares are 39.4% and 38.62%, respectively. For both models, the coefficients of the three main independent variables are negative and significant as expected, other than the result of the equity ratio in the fixed effects model.

As concerns the non-performing loan ratio, the negative result implies that the effect of non-performing loans on bank performance is still a big issue in the post-WTO period. For historical reasons, SOBs are associated with a large amount of non-performing loans. To cope with this serious problem, the Chinese government has implemented a series of banking reforms to eliminate the amount of non-performing loans in order to maintain a stable financial system, which can be used to support the rapid development of the macro-economy. In addition, a capital injection and the establishment of asset management companies have enabled

Table 10.7 The results of the empirical model in terms of ROA

Independent variables	Fixed effects		Random effects	
	Coefficient	t-statistics	Coefficient	t-statistics
Constant	−5.40303***	−8.46	−4.67664***	−8.74
NPLGL	−0.25442***	−3.60	−0.20451***	−3.96
LATA	−0.27388*	−1.89	−0.27805**	−2.19
ETA	−0.03567	−1.29	−0.02870*	−1.68
2004	−0.01507	−0.09	0.06530	0.39
2005	0.00172**	2.01	0.03156**	2.19
2006	0.09676	1.56	0.13880*	1.83
2007	0.33776*	1.78	0.34352*	1.94
2008	0.50200**	2.53	0.47944**	2.58
2009	0.32297	1.51	0.32333*	1.67
2010	0.29008	1.17	0.29480	1.31
SOBs	−0.33005**	−2.13	−0.32338**	−2.19
Joint-equity banks	0.05056	1.17	0.06267	1.47

Note: *, ** and *** denote significance at the 10%, 5% and 1% levels, respectively. Adjusted R-squared is 39.4% for the fixed effects (within) regression and 38.62% for the random effects GLS regression.

Chinese banks to operate on a level playing field with foreign banks, particularly after joining the WTO. However, this result may suggest that the problem of non-performing loans still dominates the Chinese banking industry, which might put heavy pressure on the recent banking reform. As mentioned above, Chinese banks are suffering a new crop of bad loans as Beijing has begun to shrink market liquidity and restrict the housing market. Our result is consistent with the arguments of Chen and Wu (2010), Yin, et al. (2010) and Goodhart and Zeng (2006).

Regarding the liquidity ratio, the significant and negative results suggest that a paradox between the liquidity and profitability of banks exists. An increase in liquidity assets leads to a reduction in bank profitability, while it can be applied as a buffer against potential liquidity risk. This result is consistent with the findings of Yin, et al. (2010) and Yao, et al. (2004). However, considering the Chinese investment market and the financial market, bank deposits can be thought of as the safest way to invest, since the government provides final protection to banks, which is seen as a form of explicit deposit insurance. Moreover, as China is a socialist country, although some private banks have become involved in the financial markets, most Chinese banks are seriously controlled by the government. Thus, Chinese householders have much stronger confidence in Chinese banks than they do in those of developed countries, particularly in the context of the lack of investment diversification in China. Thus, we may suggest that liquidity risk is less significant in determining Chinese bank performance than are other factors, such as non-performing loans.

The negative and significant coefficient of the equity ratio implies another paradox between the capitalisation and profitability of banks, although the result in the fixed effects model is not significant. Goodhart and Zeng (2006) indicate that the capital holdings of Chinese-listed banks are significantly lower than are those of Hong Kong banks. This result suggests that the profitability of Chinese banks may stem from a lower level of capitalisation instead of efficient bank management. However, insufficient capital holding leads to a higher level of potential risk-taking by banks, as suggested by Gu and Yu (2010), since the minimum capital requirement can be used as a buffer against risk-taking, which in turn maintains a stable financial market in the long-term. As China is a member of the WTO and follows the Basel Agreement, we may believe that sufficient capital holding will be a crucial concern in Chinese banking reforms.

The results of the ownership dummy variables are consistent with expectations and the data, which suggests that SOBs are less profitable than are other banks because of inefficient bank management and historical reasons. In addition, the year dummy variables suggest that bank profitability went up from 2004 to 2008, but reduced from 2008 onwards, which can be interpreted as the lag effect of the global financial crisis in 2007–08.

ROE

Table 10.8 shows the results of both the fixed effects model and the random effects model in terms of ROE. Their adjusted R-squared values are 42.2% and 39.64%, respectively. For both models, the coefficients of independent variables follow expectations, which is also consistent with the results of the first empirical model on ROA. As concerns the equity ratio, both coefficients are negative and significant, which indicates that equity is more sensitive to changes in bank-specific variables than are assets. In addition, the negative effect of non-performing loans, the liquidity ratio and the equity ratio on bank performance has been proven in this study. The year dummy variables are insignificant other than in 2008, which suggests that the year-specific effect cannot be found based on this empirical model.

Table 10.8 The results of the empirical model in terms of ROE

	Fixed effects		Random effects	
Independent variables	*Coefficient*	*t-statistics*	*Coefficient*	*t-statistics*
Constant	−4.07189***	−6.13	−3.75019***	−6.80
NPLGL	−0.22138***	−3.02	−0.17591***	−3.30
LATA	−0.38348**	−2.54	−0.33648**	−2.57
ETA	−0.64736***	−5.15	−0.53325***	−4.96
2004	−0.12286	−0.70	−0.06999	−0.40
2005	−0.09174	−1.52	−0.06570	−1.38
2006	−0.02603	−1.15	0.02268	1.13
2007	0.14568*	1.74	0.18113**	1.99
2008	0.26763**	2.30	0.29284**	2.53
2009	0.08498	1.38	0.12607	1.63
2010	0.08074	1.31	0.13081	1.57
SOBs	−0.22939**	−2.47	−0.21604**	−2.41
Joint-equity banks	0.03391	1.08	0.03758	1.39

Note: *, ** and *** denote significance at the 10%, 5% and 1% levels, respectively. Adjusted R-squared is 42.2% for the fixed effects (within) regression and 39.64% for the random effects GLS regression.

COI

Table 10.9 shows the results of both the fixed effects and random effects model in terms of COI. The adjusted R-squared values are 40.05% and 39.51%, respectively. The coefficients of the independent variables are positive and significant other than the results of the equity ratio. An increase in non-performing loans leads to a rise in bank operation costs, as this is a serious burden for bank operations. As suggested by Goodhart and Zeng (2006), Chinese banks seek every possible opportunity to expand bank assets, since non-performing loans can be diluted by a large base of loans. However, they claim that if new loans also generate the same proportion of problem loans or even larger numbers of loans, this strategy seems to be useless. Furthermore, the growth of problem loans increases the probability of bank failure, and in China all debts of banks are paid by the government, in other words by taxpayers. Therefore, we believe that a reduction in non-performing loans has a positive effect not only on banks, but also on all Chinese householders.

A higher level of liquidity is also associated with high operational costs, although this can be used as a buffer against potential liquidity risk. This result suggests the paradox mentioned above. A large amount of liquidity assets is closely related to the huge base of deposits, which indicates that banks dominate the investment market. However, a higher level of market concentration prevents the banking sector from improving operational efficiency based on the findings of Sathye (2001) and Chen and Shih (2004). Thus, we suggest that bank management should balance liquidity and efficiency, particularly in the case of a large base of liquidity assets. New liquidity management tools are also welcomed to manage the liquidity assets of Chinese banks.

Table 10.9 The results of the empirical model in terms of COI

Independent variables	Fixed effects		Random effects	
	Coefficient	t-statistics	Coefficient	t-statistics
Constant	−0.54935***	−3.01	−0.75649***	−2.98
Non-performing loans ratio	0.30801**	2.56	0.28084**	2.03
LATA	0.12047**	2.32	0.11785**	1.98
ETA	0.06597	0.96	0.02147	0.68
2004	−0.00127	−0.03	−0.02076	−0.42
2005	−0.15392***	−3.16	−0.16786***	−3.46
2006	−0.22739***	−4.56	−0.24446***	−4.98
2007	−0.34038***	−6.32	−0.24446***	−6.96
2008	−0.36015***	−6.41	−0.37999***	−6.97
2009	−0.24097***	−4.01	−0.26920***	−4.70
2010	−0.30137***	−4.32	−0.33883***	−5.11
SOBs	−0.00147	−1.02	−0.00900	−1.14
Joint-equity banks	−0.05645**	−2.09	−0.10127**	−1.96

Note: *, ** and *** denote significance at the 10%, 5% and 1% levels, respectively. Adjusted R-squared is 40.05% for the fixed effects (within) regression and 39.51% for the random effects GLS regression.

The insignificant coefficients of the equity ratio do not suggest another paradox between capitalisation and efficiency. As mentioned by Goodhart and Zeng (2006), Chinese banks do not hold sufficient capital compared with those in developed countries, which has no significant effect on bank operational efficiency. Our results are consistent with the argument of Goodhart and Zeng (2006).

Regarding the year dummy variables, operational costs reduced during the sample period, particularly in 2007–08. As suggested by Chen and Wu (2010), because of the Asian financial crisis in 1997, the Chinese banking system is on the way to achieving stability and efficiency. Since 2001, China has been a member of the WTO, which has hastened Chinese banking reforms; therefore, it has made impressive progress. Moreover, numerous foreign banks are now involved in the Chinese banking market, which forces Chinese banks to accelerate bank reforms. Our results are consistent with the actual scenario of the Chinese banking system in recent years. As concerns ownership, joint-equity banks are associated with higher levels of operational efficiency, as shown by the previous analysis. SOBs are still subject to the government, which prevents them from improving bank efficiency. An intervention from the Chinese government also imposes a huge burden on SOBs, such as political lending, which in turn decreases bank efficiency. In addition, banks that have large numbers of employees and branches might have lower efficiency.[6]

A comparison between SOBs and joint-equity banks

We now compare the bank performances of SOBs with those of joint-equity banks as they dominate the Chinese banking market. Table 10.10 shows the results of three empirical models in terms of banks that have different forms of ownership.

The significant coefficients of all these empirical models in terms of SOBs and joint-equity banks follow the previous regressions as expected. Generally, a higher value of constant[7] in the empirical model based on joint-equity banks indicates that SOBs are associated with higher levels of profitability but lower levels of operational efficiency than are joint-equity banks. The negative effect of non-performing loans is more significant in SOBs based on the higher absolute value of the coefficients of NPLGL. However, the negative effect of the liquidity ratio is more significant in joint-equity banks. In addition, the equity ratio only matters for ROE according to the empirical models of both SOBs and joint-equity banks. The significant differences between SOBs and joint-equity banks can be interpreted as follows. First, for historical reasons, SOBs have long been associated with large amounts of non-performing loans. The performances of SOEs have a significant impact on SOBs because of plan-oriented bank operations in the early stages of the Chinese reforms. Although three policy banks have been founded to support political lending and alleviate the burden of SOBs, SOBs are still dominated by numerous non-performing loans. In addition, the rapid development of the macroeconomy in China (8–10%) in the past two decades has also contributed to the growth of non-performing loans. Thus, we believe that the banking reform cannot be successful without SOE reform. By contrast, joint-equity banks are associated with lower levels of non-performing loans than are SOBs.

Second, government intervention reduces the incentives of SOBs to improve bank efficiency. The lack of autonomy of SOBs in determining bank assets and liabilities aggravates inefficient bank management, which in turn increases operational costs. However, we have to acknowledge that some interventions by the Chinese government are necessary, in particular for the big four, as they provide substantial support to the recapitalisation of SOBs and enable them to operate on a level playing field with foreign banks. Most Chinese householders also prefer the big four because of their lower number of investment options and thus have strong confidence in SOBs. Therefore, we may argue that government protection supports Chinese householders rather than the banks in this case. As concerns joint-equity banks, they sacrifice profitability in order to increase the efficiency of bank management, which also proves the paradox between the liquidity and profitability of banks.

Third, a lack of competition contributes to inefficient bank management, as SOBs have dominated the Chinese banking market for three decades, which allows them to have less incentive to improve bank management. However, since joining the WTO, all Chinese banks have had to compete with foreign banks. Therefore, it is important for them to hasten banking reforms for them to be free from government influence. Although huge progress has been made by Chinese banks, our analyses still point out that Chinese banks have a long way to go in the process of banking reforms.

Table 10.10 A comparison between SOBs and joint-equity banks

SOBs	ROA		ROE		COI	
	Coefficient	*t-statistics*	*Coefficient*	*t-statistics*	*Coefficient*	*t-statistics*
Constant	−3.27085***	−4.25	−4.08375***	−4.30	−0.26306**	−2.50
NPLGL	−0.38070**	−2.26	−0.42587**	−2.77	0.39275***	3.20
LATA	−0.15988*	−1.66	−0.22839*	−1.93	0.11515	1.40
ETA	−0.09814	−0.97	−0.64795***	−3.51	0.07813	1.02
Fixed effect	included	—	included	—	included	—

Joint-equity banks	ROA		ROE		COI	
	Coefficient	*t-statistics*	*Coefficient*	*t-statistics*	*Coefficient*	*t-statistics*
Constant	−4.96098***	−4.15	−4.24899***	−3.34	−0.88402**	−2.06
NPLGL	−0.15591*	−1.87	−0.09331**	−2.05	0.20342***	2.94
LATA	−0.40017***	−2.83	−0.39667**	−2.71	0.14801*	1.74
ETA	−0.02378	−1.32	−0.56784**	−2.24	0.04129	0.56
Fixed effect	included	—	included	—	included	—

Note: *, ** and *** indicates significant at the 10%, 5% and 1% significant levels, respectively.

Conclusion

Given the significance of the Chinese banking system in determining the development of the macro-economy, the Chinese government has implemented substantial reforms in the banking sector, particularly for SOBs. Therefore, the aim of this chapter was to investigate the effects of bank-specific variables and ownership on bank performance in the post-WTO period. Despite imperfect Chinese banking data, an empirical analysis was employed in this study.

Overall, the empirical results are consistent with expectations; nevertheless, they also show the shortcomings of the banking system, even though it has undergone a series of reforms over the past three decades. The problem of non-performing loans still has a negative effect on bank performance, particularly for SOBs, in which the efficiency of bank management is also lower. The big four take every possible opportunity to increase returns to scale, which may not be able to improve bank efficiency but does increase the amount of non-performing loans because of a lower level of screening. The effect of government intervention is also significant in Chinese banks, which prevents them from improving bank efficiency. Although the liquidity ratio affects bank performance, we believe that the liquidity problem is less significant than are other factors, such as non-performing loans. In addition, the equity ratio plays an important role in determining Chinese bank performance, as the government now encourages the big four to finance through the public channel, such as the stock markets, which enhances bank efficiency and competition. Since our results have proven the paradox between liquidity and profitability, how banks balance them will be a concern for the banking reforms, and this is left as a future research issue. We cannot deny the impressive progress made by the Chinese banking system reforms; however, considering the special characteristics of China, Chinese banks still have a long way to go.

Notes

1 Corresponding author: Puyang Sun, School of Economics, Nankai University, China and University of Birmingham, UK (puyangsun@nankai.edu.cn);Yi Jin, Department of Economics, University of Birmingham, UK (YXJ700@bham.ac.uk); Shujing Jin, School of Economics, Nankai University, China (jshujing@163.com). We thank for advice from some seminar participants at CES Annual Conference (Beijing, 2011). Financial support for this paper from National Education Funds from the Ministry of Education in China is acknowledged.
2 According to Yin, et al. (2010), this large amount of deposits arises from the rapid economic growth of China (8–10%) and the traditional culture of Chinese households. In addition, expenses for education, housing and health care force Chinese households to deposit in banks, which are thought to be the safest place by Chinese people.
3 Source: the Almanac of China's Finance and Banking.
4 Source: Goodhart and Zeng (2006).
5 We do not employ dummy variables for city-level and rural-level commercial banks because of the small numbers of them, which might generate a misleading result.
6 There were 144,000 branches and 1.67 million employees in the big four banks at the end of 1998. Although 34,000 branches have since been closed and 127, 200 employees laid off, a huge number of branches and employees remain.
7 We consider the absolute value of constant here.

Bibliography

Benink, H., Danielsson, J., Goodhart, C. (2009), *The Future of Banking Regulation: The Basel II Accord*, Blackwell

Berger, A., Clarke, G. R. G., Cull, R., Klapper, L. and Udell, G. F. (2005). 'Corporate governance and bank performance: A joint analysis of the static, selection, and dynamic effects of domestic, foreign, and state ownership'. *Journal of Banking and Finance*, 29: 2179–2221.

Berger, A. N. and DeYoung, R. (1977), 'Problem loans and cost efficiency in commercial banks'. *Journal of Banking and Finance*, 21: 849–870.

Berger, A. N. and Mester L. J. (1977), 'Inside the block box: What explains differences in the efficiencies of financial institutions?' *Journal of Banking and Finance*, 21: 895–947.

Bowles, P. and White, G. (1989), 'Contradictions in China's financial reforms: The relationship between banks and enterprises'. *Cambridge Journal of Economics*, 13: 482–495.

Chen, C. H. and Shih, H. T. (2004), *Banking and Insurance in the New China*, Cheltenham: Edward Elgar.

Chen, C. H. and Wu, H. L. (2010), 'Operational performance of commercial banks in the Chinese transitional economy'. *Journal of Developing Areas*, 44(1): 383–396.

Chen, X. G., Skully, M. and Brown, K. (2005), 'Banking efficiency in China: application of DEA to pre- and post- deregulation eras: 1993–2000'. *China Economic Review*, 16: 229–245.

China Society for Finance and Banking (2011), *Almanac of China's Finance and Banking 2010* (English Edition). China Financial Publisher, Beijing, China.

Demirgüç-Kunt A., Detragiache E. (1998), 'The determinants of banking crisis in developing and developed countries'. IMF Staff Paper 45(1): 81–109.

DeYoung R. and Rice, T. (2004), 'Non-interest income and financial performance at U.S. commercial banks'. *Finance Rev 39*(1): 101–127.

Fu, X. and Heffernan, S. (2007). 'Cost X-efficiency in China's banking sector'. *China Economic Review*, 18: 35–53.

Goodhart, C. and Zeng, X. S. (2006). 'China's banking reform: Problems and potential solutions'. *Journal of Chinese Economic and Business Studies*, 4(3): 185–198.

Gu, X. M. and Yu, X. (2010), 'Capital requirement and banking performance'. *Chinese Market*, 48: 102–105.

Hope, N. and Hu, F. (2006). 'Reforming Chinese banking: How much can foreign entry help?' Centre for international Development, Stanford University, Working Paper, 276.

Kwan, S. H. (2003), 'Operating performance of banks among Asian economies: An international and times series comparison'. *Journal of Banking and Finance*, 27: 471–489.

Li, S. L., Liu, F., Liu, S. G. and Whitmore, G. A. (2001), 'Comparative performance of Chinese commercial banks: Analysis, findings and policy implications'. *Review of Quantitative Finance and Accounting*, 16: 149–170.

Lin, X. C. and Zhang, Y. (2009), 'Bank ownership reform and bank performance in China'. *Journal of Banking and Finance*, 33: 20–29.

Sathye, M. (2001). 'X-efficiency in Australian banking: An empirical investigation'. *Journal of Banking and Finance*, 25: 613–630.

Stiroh K. J. (2006), 'A portfolio view of banking with interest and noninterest activities'. *J Money, Credit and Banking,* 38(5): 1351–1361.

Stiroh K. J. and Rumble, A. (2006), 'The dark side of diversification: the case of U.S. financial holding companies'. *J Bank Finance* 30(8): 2131–2161.

Tobin, D. and Singh, S. (2008), 'International best practices, domestic constraints and international listing: Evidence from China's state banking sector'. *Journal of Chinese Economic and Business Studies,* 6(4): 341–361.

Yao, S. J., Feng, G. F. and Jiang, C.X. (2004), 'Chinese banking efficiency: An empirical analysis'. *Economic Research*, 8.

Yao, S. J., Han, Z. W. and Feng, G. F. (2008), 'Ownership reform, foreign competition and efficiency of Chinese commercial banks: A non-parametric approach'. *The World Economy*, 31(10): 1310–1326.

Yin, Y. P., Broadbent, M. and Shang, J. (2010), 'Decomposition of the efficiency of the Chinese state-owned commercial banks at the provincial level'. *Journal of Chinese Economic and Business Studies*, 8(1): 45–65.

Zhou, X. and Zhu, L. (1987), 'China's banking system: current status, perspective on reform'. *Journal of Comparative Economics*, 11: 399–409.

Annex 10.1 Main stages of Chinese banking reforms from 1979–2010

Year	Political activities	Expected effect
Until 1978	Mono-bank model	—
1979	'Open door'	1 Develop the macro-economy.
1979–1984	Establishment of state-owned specialized banks (ICBC, CBC, BOC and ABC or the 'big four')	1 Serve the needs generated from the Chinese government's economic plans.
1994	Three policy banks (China Development Bank, the Expert-Import Bank of China and Agriculture Development Bank of China) were formed	1 Remove the political pressure from commercial banks. 2 Serve the special needs of the government's economic plans.
1995	Central bank law and commercial bank law were founded	1 Enable city-based commercial banks and rural credit corporations to be formed. 2 Enhance competition intensity.
1998	Issued special government bonds worth RMB 270 billion	1 Recapitalize SOBs. 2 Reduce the amount of non-performing loans associated with SOBs.
2001	Joined the WTO	1 Internalisation. 2 Enhance competition. 3 Take advantage of foreign investments. 4 Operate on a level playing field with banks from developed countries.
2002–2009	Capital injection to the big four	1 Eliminate the amount of non-performing loans. 2 Recapitalisation.
2005, 2006 and 2010	Big four were listed	1 Remove the final protection from the government. 2 Enhance competition. 3 Finance to rely on the equity base from stock markets. 4 Improve operational efficiency. 5 Abide by international financial rules.

Part III
Sustainable development and good governance

11 E-government in China: Opportunities and challenges for the transformation of governance in the information age

Sabrina Ching Yuen Luk

Introduction

Electronic government (e-government) is the use by state authorities of information and communication technology (ICT), in particular the Internet, to deliver information and public services and to encourage civic participation. Since the early 1990s, local, regional, and national governments worldwide have established or expanded a presence on the World Wide Web (Jaeger, 2003: 323–4). E-government is regarded as an innovative force and an important tool to reform the public sector and foster good governance. Within the administrative perspective, e-government creates a new paradigm of service delivery that enhances efficiencies and achieves cost savings by providing integrated, seamless and one-stop online public services. Within a governance perspective, e-government provides a new channel for the government to interact and communicate with citizens that can improve government accountability, political stability, government effectiveness, regulatory quality, rule of law and control of corruption.[1] Hence, e-government has the vast potential of transforming the model of public service delivery, organizational settings and the state-society relationship that stimulates political, economic and social progress of the society in the long run (Yong and Koon, 2003: 12–3). It is crucially important for the government to utilize the power of e-government so that it can adapt to an ever-changing environment in the information age. The rest of this study is organized into six primary sections: (1) literature review and research questions; (2) conceptual and theoretical framework of e-government; (3) methodology and data collection; (4) e-government development in China; (5) the extent e-government has transformed governance in China; and (6) the opportunities and challenges for transforming governance in China. A brief conclusion then follows.

Literature review on e-government and research gaps

Since the 1990s, there has been a surge of scholarly interest in e-government. However, many studies are western-centric, with a focus on the United Sates (U.S.). The author conducted the survey of 11 academic journals published from

2002 to 2006 in the field of public administration, information systems and communication in order to examine the prominence of e-government studies in Asia.[2] It shows that there are only 18 out of 104 journal articles (about 17 percent) on Asian e-government. The author conducted another survey of books on e-government. It shows that only two out of 41 books (about 5 percent) have the main focus on e-government in Asia. Both surveys show that research on e-government in Asia is lacking.[3]

According to the *Annual Global E-government Survey* of Brown University, Asian countries which included Taiwan, Singapore and Hong Kong had been internationally recognized as leading e-government countries that ranked among the top 25 e-government countries out of 198 nations for seven consecutive years (2002–2008).[4] In 2006, the *Annual Global E-government Survey* showed that South Korea, Taiwan, and Singapore were the top three e-government countries, followed by the U.S., Canada, and Britain. China ranked among the top 25 e-government countries out of 198 nations for four consecutive years (2002–2005). It ranked 7th, 12th, 6th and 5th in 2002, 2003, 2004 and 2005 respectively. In 2005, China was chosen as having one of the best set of practices for top government websites. It shows that e-government performances in some of the Asian countries, in fact, are comparable to and have even surpassed those of Western countries. The study of leading e-government countries in Asia can be a valuable reference for other countries. Since e-government in Asia does not receive as much discussion as it merits, this chapter fills the research gap by examining e-government in China. It attempts to answer the following five questions: (1) Why does China implement e-government? (2) What is the development trajectory of e-government in China? (3) What is/are the development stage and role(s) of e-government in China? (4) To what extent has e-government transformed governance in China? (5) What are the opportunities and challenges for the transformation of governance in China in the information age?

Conceptual and theoretical frameworks

In order to answer these research questions, this study respectively adopts the conceptual model of Five Stages of Development for E-government to analyse which stage the government websites of China belongs to and Three Models of Interaction to examine the role(s) of e-government in China. The five-stage development model developed by the United Nation-American Society for Public Administration (UN-ASPA) (2002) describes discrete stages of e-government development based primarily on the content and deliverable services available online and analyses structural transformations. The five stages are (1) emerging – web presence with basic, static, and limited organizational information; (2) enhanced – providing more updated web sites, and more dynamic and specialized information with greater regularity; (3) interactive – access to a wide range of government institutions and services, contact officials, make appointments and requests; (4) transactional – providing complete and secure financial transactions online; and (5) seamless/connected – access any service in a 'unified package' with the removal of departmental lines of demarcation (See Table 11.1 in Annex 11.1). The five-stage development model helps evaluate the government's maturity and sophistication in its use of e-government and depicts growth and evolution of e-government in different stages. However, the stage-based model does not mean that all government websites go through every stage or proceed in a linear order (Holden, et al., 2003: 328; West, 2005:9) because stage adoption is subject to the influence of political, economic, and social contexts.

Three Models of Interaction which are constructed based on the existing litera-ture on the relationship of ICTs, politics and democratic theory include the mana-gerial model, the consultative model, and the participatory model (Chadwick and May, 2003:278–281). The managerial model is a 'push' model focusing on faster delivery of public services online and provision of a simple and unilinear flow of information that ignores democratic communications. The consultative model is a 'pull' model which facilitates the communication between the government and citizens and greater democratic participation through e-voting and online opinion poll. But communication is limited to direct question-asking activities by the government to generate quantifiable and comparative responses to particular policy issues. The participatory model involves a complex and multidirectional interactivity that constitutes democracy by utilizing online discussion forum, bul-letin boards, chat rooms and file sharing that creates a new cyber civil society. Unlike the five-stage development model which focuses on how e-government transforms the administrative functions and organizational structure of the gov-ernment, Three Models of Interaction focuses on how e-government transforms governance and the state-society relation. Therefore, the adoption of these two models can provide a more comprehensive perspective on evaluating the role of e-government in China.

Methodology and data collection

This study is based on a secondary analysis of data obtained from the international and local benchmarking studies of e-government. Firstly, it obtains data from the flagship series of *The United Nations E-Government Survey*,[5] which uses a com-posite index to measure the overall performance in e-government readiness in approximately 190 countries.[6] For the research purpose, this study only focuses on the web measure index and e-participation index. The web measure index is based upon the five-stage development model to measure the sophistication of government websites. The web measure assessments are based on a questionnaire which allocates 'a binary value to the indicator based on the presence/absence of specific electronic facilities or services available' (The United Nations, 2008: 15). Countries which proceed to upper stages of e-government are ranked higher in the web measure index. As to the e-participation index, it measures the quality and usefulness of online information and services provided by a country to engage citizens in public policy making. Secondly, this study obtains data from *the 2008 Chinese Government Web Site Performance Assessment Report* (Chinese version) conducted by China Software Testing Center, which uses a composite score to measure and rank government websites at ministries, provincial city, district and county levels in China. The composite score comprises information disclosure index, dealing with business online index, public engagement index, website usability and design index, and daily protection index. This study focuses on the performance of government websites at the level of ministries and provincial city. Thirdly, this study obtains data from the study of Xia (2006), which has detailed analysis of 29 government websites at the provincial/metropolitan level in China in terms of information available, services provided, transparency and responsiveness. Since these international and local benchmarking studies collected data at different points of time and using different survey instrument, they may include inaccuracies and gaps. Nevertheless, they provide high-quality datasets gathered from well-established and rigorous procedures for the researcher to ask new questions, draw new interpretations and produce new knowledge.

E-government development in China: an overview

China's enthusiasm in applying ICT can be traced back to the 1980s. The emphasis on informatization (*Xinxihua*), which connotes the meaning of ICT promotion, was first enunciated in 1984 by Deng Xiaoping for modernization and economic growth (Seifert and Chung, 2009: 12; Yong, 2003: 70). During the 1980s, government agencies used computer technology to operate an office automation (OA) system for documentation inputting and data storage in order to improve work efficiency (Li, 2009: 126). In December 1993, China launched its first national ICT programme known as the Golden Projects (*Jinzi Gongcheng*) to create an infrastructure backbone for data networks, information exchange and financial transactions through the application of Internet technology. In January 1999, China launched its first official e-government project known as the Government Online Project (GOP) to interconnect government agencies, make government documents and databases available online and allow the public to transact with the government online. In December 2001, China issued *Guiding Suggestions on Constructing China's E-government* to improve the administration, standards, security levels and service quality of e-government (Seifert and Chung, 2009: 15) (See Table 11.2 in Annex 11.1).[7] In 2006, China announced that popularizing e-government was one of the key strategies to carry out informatization for the following 15 years (Seifert and Chung, 2009: 14). In brief, China intended to use e-government to enhance its administrative capacity in terms of efficiency, effectiveness and transparency and facilitate economic development (Ma, et al., 2005: 24).

Development stage and the role(s) of e-government in China

International benchmarking studies

Since the early 1990s, the implementation of e-government has become a global phenomenon. Many benchmarking studies of e-government have been undertaken to measure the performance of e-government among countries. The international benchmarking surveys conducted by the UN show that China admirably improved its overall performance in e-government readiness from 2003 to 2008. It improved its ranking from 74th to 65th within five years. It proceeded to the upper stages of e-government with an increased web measure index from 0.332 in 2003 to 0.5084 in 2008. It belonged to middle-scoring countries, with the total utilization percentage of the five stages of service delivery increasing from 29 percent in 2003 to 45 percent in 2008.[8] Its pattern of e-services varied across all five stages (See Table 11.1 in Annex 11.1). *The UN E-government Surveys* show that China proceeded slowly in the transactional stage with a utilization percentage of only four percent. It meant that the government provided few e-services and financial transactions online. However, China performed well in other e-government stages. *The UN E-government Surveys* show that China scored 100 percent in the emerging stage. It had made vast improvement in the enhancement stage, with a score increasing from 47 percent in 2003 to 76 percent in 2008. This means that more updated, dynamic and specialized information was available online. Besides this, China showed vast improvements in the interactive stage, with a score increasing from 32 per cent in 2003 to 52 percent in 2008. This shows that the government had strengthened its communication with citizens. In fact, a strengthened interactivity could also be reflected in China's e-participation index, which dramatically increased from 0.069 in 2003 to 0.4773 in 2008. In 2008, China, together with the Republic of Korea, Singapore, Japan and Vietnam, ranked among the top 35 in e-participation index terms (Wang 2008: 3). The UN praised that China 'made significant strides' in e-participation (The United Nations 2008: 59) and that:

> The national portal of China http://www.gov.cn/ supports citizen participation and conducts online polling to obtain a snapshot of the views of the people. The site uses audio and video multimedia tools to disseminate information, policies and guidelines.
>
> (The United Nations, 2008: 33)

China also improved its performance in the connected stage with a utilization percentage of 26 per cent in 2008, although it had yet to provide an integrated portal which removed the departmental lines of demarcation. Like other countries, China has to overcome many thresholds in terms of infrastructure development, business reengineering, security and customer management before fully completing the connected stage (The United Nations, 2008: 15). Nevertheless, the rapid expansion of online infrastructure and Internet users in China make the UN optimistic about 'the expansion of e-government models in the realm of online service delivery and more transformative dimensions of the Chinese public sector' (The United Nations, 2008: 83). In brief, the international benchmarking surveys show that China has improved its overall performance in e-government readiness over the past few years.

Local benchmarking studies

While *the UN E-government Surveys* broadly measure the performance of national e-government, *the 2008 Chinese Government Web Site Performance Assessment Report* (Chinese Version) and the study of Xia (2006) are local benchmarking studies that measure government websites at ministry and provincial city levels in China. In fact, measuring the performance of websites at sub-national levels is important because it is frequently sub-central agencies that are information hubs, service providers and contact points for citizens (Holliday and Yep, 2005: 240).

The 2008 Chinese Government Web Site Performance Assessment Report, which examined a total of 75 government websites at ministry level and 32 government websites at provincial city level, found that the top 10 government websites at ministry level were the website of (1) the Ministry of Commerce, (2) the Ministry of Agriculture, (3) the General Administration of Quality Supervision, Inspection and Quarantine, (4) the National Development and Reform Commission, (5) the Ministry of Transport, (6) the State Administration of Taxation, (7) the Ministry of Science and Technology, (8) the Ministry of Finance, (9) the Ministry of Water Resources, and (10) the General Administration of Customs (See Table 11.4 in Annex 11.1). Moreover, it found that the top 10 government websites at provincial city level were (1) Beijing, (2) Shanghai, (3) Zhejiang, (4) Hainan, (5) Shaanxi, (6) Guangdong, (7) Anhui, (8) Sichuan, (9) Fujian, and (10) Hunan (See Table 11.5 in Annex 11.5). *The Assessment Report* shows that some ministries and provincial cities have a better e-government performance in terms of website usability, design and security, information disclosure, service delivery, financial transaction and public engagement.

The study of Xia (2006) also showed that some provincial and metropolitan websites were more sophisticated and had better e-government performance in terms of service provision, transparency, openness and responsiveness. Of all the government websites reviewed, the study found that 96 per cent of the government websites provided government documents, 93 per cent provided access to government laws and regulations, 41 per cent provided bidding information, 34 per cent provided international, national and local news and current events while only 27 per cent provided officially approved price information (e.g. drug prices, school fees) and 10 per cent provided civil service employment information (Xia, 2006: 33–6). This means that some government websites were more open and transparent than others by providing more information. The study also found that 72 per cent of the government sites provided Governor's or Mayor's mail boxes, 45 per cent provided online public opinion surveys, 44 per cent provided an accusation box for citizens to anonymously report corrupt government officials, 37 per cent provided government agency hotlines while only 27 per cent provided chat rooms and 20 per cent provided a grievance box for citizens to report government officials who abused their power (Xia, 2006: 36–7). It meant that some government websites were more responsive than others by providing more online channels for citizens to contact government officials and express their views on policy issues.

For example, the Fujian government website conducted an online opinion poll on citizens' expectation of the government. It found that of 9,978 respondents, 48 per cent wanted an improvement in the morality of government officials, 31 per cent wanted an increase in government transparency, and 18 per cent mentioned either an increase in government efficiency, or easier access to government officials (Xia, 2006: 39). However, the study of Xia (2006) found that only five government websites (i.e. Beijing, Shanghai, Tianjin, Guangdong and Hebei) provided fully executable public services online, while the majority of government websites provided service guidelines which informed citizens how to obtain the service. Guangdong took the lead in providing seven executable services online, while Beijing and Shanghai came in second with five executable services online (Xia, 2005: 35). The common executable services available online included e-taxation, the renewal of business licences and applications for student loans and home-owner certificates (Xia, 2005: 35).

The extent to which e-government has transformed governance

Based on secondary analysis of data obtained from the international and local benchmarking studies of e-government, this study finds that e-government has improved the overall governance performance of the Chinese government in terms of efficiency, transparency, openness, accountability and responsiveness. Traditionally, the Chinese government practised a system of information and censure that certain government documents were only available to members of the Communist Party or government officials at a certain level (Xia, 2006: 39–40). The implementation of e-government provides citizens with easier and open access to government information and databases, thereby making the Chinese government more open and transparent. Traditionally, the Chinese government's intensive control over distribution and concentration of power in its own hand eroded public trust in government and weakened social cohesion (Xia, 2006: 40). The implementation of e-government provides different channels to engage citizens in policy making and foster inclusiveness. Besides, it provides citizens with different channels to make enquiries, express their opinions on policy issues and government performance, and voice out their concerns and grievances. E-government becomes a platform that strengthens the government's connection, communication and interactivity with ordinary citizens, thereby making the government more accountable and responsive. Traditionally, the Chinese government delivered public services by the Weberian model of bureaucracy that was often criticized for being inefficient, ineffective, rigid, and time-consuming. The implementation of e-government is conducive to delivery of public services in a faster, more convenient and more efficient way. At present, however, e-government in China provides citizens limited public services online.

Having looked at e-government through Three Models of Interaction, this study finds that e-government in China does not belong to a pure model of interaction. Instead, it belongs to a mixed model, which simultaneously plays the managerial and consultative roles. E-government in China plays a managerial role in the sense that it makes government documents, regulations and databases and some public services available online. At the same time, it plays a consultative role in the sense that it provides citizens with different online channels to make enquiries, express opinions, exchange ideas and lodge a complaint. The sophistication and performance of government websites vary at ministry and provincial/metropolitan levels. One interpretation is that the capital investment and the attitudes of government officials affect the pace of e-government development and the sophistication of websites at different levels. Under the leadership of Deng Xiaoping, both the administrative and fiscal powers were decentralized to local governments in order to stimulate the local governments' responsiveness to market forces in China. Local governments were granted autonomy to decide how to implement e-government within its own jurisdiction. Indeed, the political consideration can affect the sophistication of government websites. It is because e-government can hurt the interests and authority of the government by making government information and databases online. It means that the government has to give up at least part of its monopoly on information. Local governments which are conservative may not disclose too much information on their websites. Besides, financial adequacy can affect the sophistication of government websites. Although e-government has the potential to achieve cost savings, it is an expensive capital investment. Only local governments which enjoy a faster pace of economic development have sufficient funding to establish, maintain and upgrade their websites. For example, the major cities such as Beijing and Shanghai and the more developed provinces such as Guangdong and Fujian are more affluent places to implement e-government with multiple features. Local governments which are less affluent can only develop e-government in a modest way.

Opportunities and challenges for transforming governance in China in the information age

The implementation of e-government has undoubtedly made the Chinese government more efficient, transparent, open, accountable and responsive. Indeed, the Internet is 'more than a technological breakthrough in service delivery' (Ho, 2002: 434) but a powerful tool that stimulates 'a transformation in the philosophy and organization of government' (Ho, 2002: 434). It shifts the focus of governance from an inward-looking approach which emphasizes managerial concerns to an outward-looking approach which emphasizes the concerns and needs of ordinary citizens (Ho 2002: 435). Nevertheless, achievements are accompanied with problems in the process of developing e-government (Wang 2008:4). The Chinese government faces several barriers which affect its progressiveness of e-government development.

Firstly, there is insufficient support, coordination and collaboration from governments at different levels to pursue the e-government paradigm that can transform the government in a better way. This can be due to the conservative attitude of government officials toward e-government or their lack of ICT skills and awareness. The Chinese government can provide IT training courses to government officials so that they can embrace the benefits of e-government and welcome the development of e-government.

Secondly, there is the lack of financial resources to develop e-government at the local level, leading to variations in the pace of e-government development and sophistication of government websites. Under decentralization, local governments are responsible for establishing, maintaining and upgrading their own government websites. Without sufficient funding, they can hardly advance the development of e-government. The central government can provide financial assistance to local governments in order to achieve a more consistent pace of e-government development among local governments.

Thirdly, there is limited provision of fully executable public services online. This can be due to the lack of technical levels, the lack of departmental support and coordination and the lack of online security measures. In fact, online transaction in the private sphere is popular among ordinary citizens in China. *The Statistical Survey Report on the Internet Development in China* showed that online shopping became one of the top ten net applications and that there were about 63 million online shoppers who favored online payment and online banking (CNNIC 2008b: 25). If the government can utilize the Internet to provide more public services online, it can help promote economic development and enhance administrative efficiency and effectiveness. The government can utilize the online opinion poll to ask citizens about the types of e-government services they favor. It can provide authentication measures which are easy for citizens to use in order to ensure online security.

Fourthly, there is the lack of e-government users in China. This can be due to the lack of promotion or online public services being not user-friendly enough. For example, *the Statistics Survey Report on the Internet Development in China* showed that only 2.5 per cent of the netizens used e-taxation (CNNIC 2008a: 50). The government can use financial or non-financial incentives to boost the e-government usage rate. Overseas experience shows that financial incentives like coupons and price cut or non-financial incentives such as providing value-added services through e-channels is effective to attract more e-government users. (Information Technology and Broadcasting Bureau 2002: 5).

Finally, the problem of digital divide limits the influence and benefits of e-government in China. Digital divide – the division between those who have access to new ICT and those who have not – is influenced by socioeconomic backgrounds (Ho, 2002; Thomas and Streib, 2003). By December 2007, the CNNIC survey found that 53.34 million people that amount to 25. 4 per cent of netizens had visited government websites (CNNIC, 2008a: 48). These netizens were younger people aged 25 to 30 (35.4 per cent), in professions such as government officials or enterprise executives (55.4 per cent), clerks (41.6 per cent), and experts/technical staff (40.1 per cent) (CNNIC, 2008a: 48–9). The digital have-nots are those who lived in the inner parts of China and those who lack computer and IT literacy. In order to diffuse e-government to more people, the government can consider building more IT infrastructure, running digital inclusion programmes and providing IT education for the citizens.

Conclusion

To conclude, e-government is an innovative force and an important tool to reform the public sector and foster good governance. It is a new paradigm and a powerful tool to transform the philosophy and organization of government. It shifts the focus of governance from an inward-looking approach to an outward-looking approach which strengthens the government-citizen relationship, fosters inclusiveness and citizen engagement in policy making. E-government in China has improved the overall governance performance in terms of efficiency, transparency, openness, accountability and responsiveness. However, the pace at which governance has been transforming in China varies among ministries, provincial city, district and county levels due to the varying pace of e-government development and varying degrees of website sophistication that are affected by capital investment and the attitudes of government officials. This study suggests that the Chinese government can utilize the power of the Internet to further strengthen its quality of governance by increasing support, coordination and collaboration from governments at different levels, providing financial assistance to local governments in order to achieve a more consistent pace of e-government development, providing more executable and customer-oriented public services online, ensuring online security and privacy, boosting e-government usage rate by using both financial and non-financial incentives, and solving the problem of digital divide. This study is based on a secondary analysis of data obtained from the international and local benchmarking studies of e-government. Since these international and local benchmarking studies collected data at different points of time and using different survey instruments, they may include inaccuracies and gaps. Future studies can use different methodologies such as conducting interviews and distributing questionnaires to examine the impact of e-government on governance in China. Future studies can also adopt a demand-side approach by examining how ordinary citizens view e-government in China.

Notes

1 According to Kaufmann, et al. from the World Bank (2003), good governance can be measured by six dimensions: (1) voice and accountability which measures civil liberties and political rights; (2) political stability which measures the stability of the government in power; (3) government effectiveness which measures the qualities of public service provision and bureaucracy; (4) regulatory quality which measures the incidence of market-unfriendly policies; (5) rule of law which measures the effectiveness and predictability of the legal system, and (6) control of corruption which measures the perception of corruption.

2 Five of the journals selected rank among top 20 world's leading journals in public administration by Journal Citation Reports ®, which is the recognized authority for evaluating journals (Thomson Scientific, 2007). They are *Journal of Public Administration Research and Theory (J-PART)*, *Public Administration Review*, *Administration & Society*, *American Review of Public Administration*, and *Public Administration and Development*. Other journals in public administration selected include *International Journal of Public Administration*, *Public Performance & Management Review*, and *Review of Public Personnel Administration*. As to journals in information systems and

communication, they include *Government Information Quarterly (GIQ)*, *Journal of Global Information Management*, and *New Media & Society*.

3 These two books are: (1) Karim, Muhammad Rais Abdul, and Khalid, Nazariah Mohd (2003). *E-government in Malaysia: improving responsiveness and capacity to serve* (Subang Jaya, Selangor Darul Ehsan, Malaysia: Pelanduk Publications); (2) Yong, James SL (2003). Enabling Public Service Innovation in the 21st Century E-government in Asia (Singapore: Times Editions).

4 Global E-government Survey (2002–2008) can be found at www.InsidePolitics.org.

5 *The United Nations E-government Survey* has four volumes, namely *UN Global E-government Survey 2003*, *UN Global E-government Survey 2004: Towards Access for Opportunity*, *UN Global E-government Readiness Report 2005: From E-government to E-inclusion*, and *The United Nations E-government Survey 2008: From E-government to Connected Governance*.

6 The composite index includes the web measure index, infrastructure index, human capital index and e-participation index.

7 *Guiding Suggestions on Constructing China's E-government* was promulgated by the State Council as Decree No.17 in 2002.

8 According to the *UN E-government Survey 2008*, countries belong to top scoring countries if their total utilization percentage of the five stages of service delivery is 67 per cent or higher. Countries belong to middle-scoring countries if their total utilization percentage ranges from 34 to 66 per cent. Countries belong to low scoring countries if their total utilization percentage is 1 to 33 per cent.

Bibliography

Chadwick, Andrew, May, Christopher, (2003), 'Interaction between states and citizens in the age of the Internet: e-Government in the United States, Britain, and European Union', *Governance: An International Journal of Policy, Administration, and Institutions*, 16, 2: 271–300

China Internet Network Information Center (CNICC), (2008a), 'Statistical Survey Report on the Internet Development in China (January 2008)', accessed online: on 15 July, 2009, from www.cnnic.cn/uploadfiles/pdf/2008/2/29/104126.pdf

China Internet Network Information Center (CNICC), (2008b), 'Statistical Survey Report on the Internet Development in China Abridged Edition (July 2008)', accessed online: on 15 July, 2009, from www.cnnic.cn/download/2008/CNNIC22threport-en.pdf

China Internet Network Information Center (CNICC), (2009), 'Statistical Survey Report on the Internet Development in China (January 2009)', accessed online: on 15 July, 2009, from www.cnnic.cn/uploadfiles/pdf/2009/3/23/153540.pdf

Ho, Alfred Tat-Kei, (2002), 'Reinventing Local Governments and the E-Government Initiatives', *Public Administration Review*, 62, 4: 434–444

Holden, Stephen H., Norris, Donald F., Fletcher, Patricia D., (2003), 'Electronic Government At the Local Level: Progress to Date and Future Issues', *Public Performance & Management Review*, 26, 4: 325–244

Holliday, Ian, Yep, Ray, (2005), 'E-government in China', *Public Administration and Development*, 25: 239–249

Information Technology and Broadcasting Bureau, (2002), 'Progress Update on the E-government Programme for 2002', accessed online: on 15 July, 2009, from www.legco.gov.hk/yr01-02/english/panels/itb/papers/itb0708cb1-2172-3e.pdf

Jaeger, P.T., (2003), 'The endless wire: E-government as global phenomenon', *Government Information Quarterly*, 20: 323–331

Kaufmann, Daniel, Kraay, Aart, Mastruzzi, Massimo, (2003), 'Governance Matters III: Governance Indicators for 1996–2002', accessed online: on 12 September, 2011, from http://siteresources.worldbank.org/INTWBIGOVANTCOR/Resources/govmatters3.pdf

Li, Zelin, (2009). 'How E-government Affects the Organizational Structure of Chinese Government', *AI & Society*, 23, 1: 123–130

Ma, Lianjie, Chung, Jongpil, Thorson, Stuart, (2005), 'E-government in China: Bringing Economic Development Through Administrative Reform', *Government Information Quarterly*, 22: 20–37

Seifert, Jeffrey W., Chung, Jongpil, (2009), 'Using E-government to Reinforce Government Citizen Relationships: Comparing Government Reform in the United States and China', *Social Science Computer Review*, 27: 3–23

Thomas, Georgia, Streib, Gregory, (2003), 'The New Face of Government: Citizen-Initiated Contacts in the era of E-Government', *Journal of Public Administration Research and Theory*, 13, 1: 83–102

The United Nations and American Society for Public Administration (UN-ASPA), (2002), 'Benchmarking E-government: A Global Perspective', accessed online: on 6 July, 2004, from http://unpan1.un.org/intradoc/groups/public/documents/UN/UNPAN021547.pdf

The United Nations, (2003), 'UN Global E-government Survey, 2003', accessed online: on 11 September, 2009 from http://unpan1.un.org/intradoc/groups/public/documents/un/unpan016066.pdf

The United Nations, (2004), 'UN Global E-government Survey 2004: Towards Access for Opportunity', accessed online: on 12 September, 2011 from http://unpan1.un.org/intradoc/groups/public/documents/UN/UNPAN019207.pdf

The United Nations, (2005), 'UN Global E-Government Readiness Report 2005: From E-government to E-inclusion', accessed online: on 11 July, 2009 from http://unpan1.un.org/intradoc/groups/public/documents/un/unpan021888.pdf

The United Nations, (2008), 'The United Nations E-Government Survey 2008: From E-Government to Connected Governance', accessed online: on 11 July, 2009, from http://unpan1.un.org/intradoc/groups/public/documents/UN/UNPAN028607.pdf

Wang, Jianhua, (2008), 'E-government of China: Performance, Problems and Prospects', accessed online: on 12 July, 2009, from http://unpan1.un.org/intradoc/groups/public/documents/UN/UNPAN031352.pdf

West, Darrell M., (2004), 'Global Perspectives on E-Government', accessed online: on 24 March, 2009, from www.ksg.harvard.edu/digitalcenter/event/West_2004.pdf

West, Darrell M., (2005), *Digital Government: Technology and Public Sector Performance*, Princeton: Princeton University Press

West, Darrell M., (2005), Global E-government, accessed online: on 12 September, 2011 from www.insidepolitics.org/egovt05int.pdf

Xia, Li Lollar, (2006), 'Assessing China's E-Government: Information, Service, Transparency and Citizen Outreach of Government Websites', Journal of Contemporary China, 15, 46: 31–41

Yong, James S.L., (2003), 'Enter the Dragon: Informatization in China', in Yong, James (ed.), *Enabling Public Service Innovation in the 21st Century E-government in Asia*, Singapore: Times Editions: 65–96

Yong, James S.L., Koon, Lim Hiap, (2003), 'E-government: Enabling Public Sector Reform', in Yong, James (ed.), *Enabling Public Service Innovation in the 21st Century E-government in Asia*, Singapore: Times Editions: 3–21

Annex 11.1

Table 11.1 UN-ASPA five stages of e-government

Stage	UN-ASPA stage description	Specific characteristics/features to look for
Stage one	**Emerging web presence** • Sites serve as a public information source • Static information on the government is provided • FAQs may be found • Contact information is provided	☐ Telephone numbers ☐ Postal address ☐ Email address ☐ Services offered ☐ Mandate, organizational structure, FAQs, related RAs
Stage two	**Enhanced web presence** • Access to specific information that is regularly updated • A central government hpmepage may act as a portal to other department sites • Useful documents may be downloaded or ordered online • Search features, e-mail and areas for comments are accessible	☐ Updated in the past 15 months ☐ Forms are available (html, word, sometimes zip, pdf) ☐ Search function/site map ☐ Message board/feedback form ☐ Newsletters or publications/purchase information
Stage three	**Interactive web presence** • A national government website frequently acts as a portal • Users can search specialized databases • Forms can be downloaded and/or submitted online • Secure sites and passwords begin to emerge	☐ Downloadable forms (pdf, zip) ☐ Specialized databases ☐ On-line forms submission ☐ Interactive elements e.g. chatroom/forum/discussion board ☐ User log-in and password (internal use or public)
Stage four	**Transactional web presence** • Users will be able to conduct complete and secure transactions online • The government website will allow users to customize a portal in order to directly access services based on specific needs and priorities • Sites will be ultimately secure	☐ Public use log-in and password (NOT exclusive for internal use) ☐ Secure[1] ☐ On-line payment ☐ Confirmation of request (e-mail confirmation/acknowledgement receipt) ☐ Display of security and privacy policy
Stage five	**Fully integrated web presence** • Country provides all services and links through a single portal • No defined demarcation between various agencies and departments • All transactional services offered by government will be available online	☐ All department information and services may be accessed through the department portal ☐ Cohesive interface covering all attached agencies, concerned agencies and all services ☐ Frontline services are fully-transactional online ☐ User may customize his department portal page ☐ Search engine encompasses attached websites

1 Secure = padlock or solid key security icon appears at the bottom of browser; URL starts with https instead of http

Reference: Secure sockets layer – http://www.webopedia.com/TERM/S/SSL.html

Adapted from: www.ncc.gov.ph/files/un-aspa5stagesegovt.pdf

Table 11.2 Guiding suggestions on constructing China's e-government guiding suggestions on constructing China's e-government

1.	Establish and integrate a unified e-government network. To accelerate the pace of constructing a unified network platform, we should unify standards, use a unified network platform, and promote the sharing of resources and communication between every key project.
2.	Build and improve key operational systems. To improve supervision and service abilities, we must accelerate the establishment of 12 main task projects and continue to improve on the four projects that have already begun to show initial success – namely, the Public Operations Resource System, Golden Customs, Golden Taxation, and Golden Finance Supervision Projects. We should also launch and accelerate the establishment of eight task projects – namely, the Macroeconomic Administration, Golden Finance, Golden Shield, Golden Audit, Social Security, Golden Agriculture, Golden Quality, and Golden Water projects. These key projects must be established using a unified plan.
3.	Plan and develop important government information resources. To satisfy society's cry for administrative information, we should design an information resource directory system and construct basic information databases for population, corporation units, natural resources, macroeconomic indicators, etc.
4.	Promote services to enterprises and citizens. The government departments at all levels should accelerate the pace of making administrative information known to the public. We should require every level of government to create its own web site and promote services such as "Openness of Government Affairs (*Zhengwu Gongkai*)," online "Administrative Examination and Approval System (*Xingzheng Shenpi Zhidu*)," social security, education, etc.
5.	Build an information security system. We should improve the security management system and put more energy in developing key security products.
6.	Improve standards and criteria for constructing e-government. Full e-government standards, measures, and mechanisms should be built more quickly.
7.	Improve the training program for government officials. We should develop more diverse and intensive training programs to provide better knowledge and skills of information technology to officials. Examination standards and systems should be formulated.
8.	Establish a legal system for e-government administration. Regulations and policies for electronic signatures, "Openness of Government Affairs," network information security, and e-government administration should be enacted more quickly.

Adapted from: Seifert and Chung (2009), Using E-government to Reinforce Government Citizen Relationships: Comparing Government Reform in the United States and China, p.15.

Table 11.3 Per cent utilization of e-government in different stages in China

	Emerging	Enhanced	Interactive	Transactional	Connected	Total	Rank (I-V)
Stage	I	II	III	IV	V	I–V	—
2003	100	47	32	0	0	29	48
2004	75	66	46	0	6	38	55
2005	100	75	71	5	24	54	35
2008	100	76	52	4	26	45	47

Source: The United Nations E-government Survey (2003, 2004, 2005, 2008) www.unpan.org/egovernment.asp

Table 11.4 Top 10 government websites at ministry level in China

Ranking	Ministry	Total score	Information disclosure index	Dealing with business online index	Public engagement index	Website usability and design index	Daily protection index
1	Ministry of commerce www.mofcom.gov.cn	79.15	0.83	0.84	0.87	0.96	0.61
2	Ministry of agriculture www. agri.gov.cn	75.30	0.86	0.79	0.85	0.97	0.48
3	General administration of quality supervision, inspection and quarantine www.aqsiq.gov.cn	74.98	0.88	0.91	0.71	0.76	0.55
4	National development and reform commission www.sdpc.gov.cn	74.27	0.89	0.73	0.75	0.87	0.55
5	Ministry of transport www.moc.gov.cn	73.77	0.83	0.78	0.80	0.84	0.53
6	State administration of taxation www.chinatax.gov.cn	71.41	0.83	0.86	0.71	0.96	0.47
7	The ministry of science and technology www.most.gov.cn	68.78	0.86	0.59	0.72	0.65	0.52
8	Ministry of finance www.mof.gov.cn	66.64	0.75	0.81	0.63	0.65	0.48
9	The ministry of Water Resources www.mwr.gov.cn	65.65	0.75	0.81	0.63	0.65	0.48
10	General Administration of Customs www.customs.gov.cn	65.58	0.73	0.74	0.73	0.66	0.43

Source: The 2008 Chinese Government Web Site Performance Assessment Report (Chinese Version).

Table 11.5 Top 10 government websites at provincial city level in China

Ranking	Provincial city	Total score	Information disclosure index	Dealing with business online index	Public engagement index	Daily protection index	Users' survey index	Website usability and design index
1	Beijing	78.12	0.82	0.95	0.90	0.67	0.13	0.88
2	Shanghai	72.6	0.84	0.83	0.76	0.62	0.12	0.85
3	Zhejiang	65.07	0.78	0.54	0.85	0.58	0.10	0.76
4	Hainan	64.96	0.79	0.57	0.85	0.55	0.10	0.72
5	Shaanxi	62.9	0.72	0.61	0.80	0.55	0.09	0.68
6	Guangdong	59.39	0.69	0.60	0.60	0.57	0.10	0.88
7	Anhui	56.72	0.65	0.49	0.65	0.57	0.09	0.78
8	Sichuan	55.25	0.58	0.56	0.66	0.53	0.08	0.70
9	Fujian	54.78	0.66	0.52	0.57	0.52	0.07	0.77
10	Hunan	53.62	0.65	0.53	0.57	0.50	0.08	0.65

Source: The 2008 Chinese Government Web Site Performance Assessment Report (Chinese Version).

12 The role of corporate social responsibility in China's sustainable development

Claire Seung-eun Lee

> This is the true meaning of corporate social responsibility: to operate in a manner that promotes broad social objectives, including nonmarket goals, in a manner consistent with core business principles, values, and practices. It constitutes much more than corporate philanthropy. It demands creativity.
>
> Jeffrey D. Sachs (2008)

Introduction

The purpose of this chapter is to analyse the topic of Corporate Social Responsibility (CSR) in China with special reference to environment-related issues, based on the understanding that it is imperative that companies accept responsibility regarding energy conservation practices as part of the development of an eco-friendly harmonized society. It will consider the 2008 'Green Olympics' (*Lvse Aoyun*) with reference to sustainable development. The CSR policies in three multinational companies (MNCs), namely Samsung, Sony and Panasonic, during the Olympics will be examined to understand why MNCs should take the initiative and set a positive example for Chinese companies to follow in the future.

Theoretical approaches to CSR

A concern for social responsibility can be traced back to the 1930s in western countries. Chester Barnard's 1938 publication *The Functions of the Executive* and Theodore Krep's *Measurement of the Social Performance of Business*, published in 1940, were two early references that dealt with the social responsibilities of executives and business in the United States. The 1950s saw the start of the modern era of CSR when it was more commonly known as social responsibility or SR.[1] In 1953 Howard Bowen published his book *Social Responsibilities of the Businessman* and he is largely credited with coining the phrase 'corporate social responsibility'. Bowen asked: 'What responsibilities to society can business people be reasonably expected to assume?' Bowen also provided a preliminary definition of CSR: 'It refers to the obligations of businessmen to pursue those policies, to make those decisions, or to follow those lines of action which are desirable in terms of the objectives and values of our society' (Bowen, 1953).

The CSR doctrine holds to the view that businesses are more than profit-seeking entities and have an obligation to benefit society, sometimes at the cost of earnings. Several CSR principles and practices date from early last century, but a major resurgence began in the United States during the 1960s (Philips and Lim, 2007: 65–84). The notion of voluntarism was first seen in Clarence C. Walton's *Corporate Social Responsibilities (1967)*, when he linked CSR with the idea that companies need to voluntarily acknowledge and accept they have relationships of responsibility beyond the corporate fortress.

Archie Carroll used the organizational hierarchy as a conceptual tool to assess socially responsible organizational performance (Carroll, 1991; Carroll, 1999). According to Carroll, a corporation has four responsibilities: economic profit making, abiding by the law, ethical responsibility, and philanthropic obligation. First, 'economic responsibility' is the foremost responsibility of CSR. Corporations, as the basic economic units of society, take responsibility for producing goods and services. Second, 'legal responsibility' stands for the fact that a corporation is required to perform its economic activities within the structure of the appropriate legal requirement framework. Third, 'ethical responsibility' signifies a set of activities expected of a corporation as a constituent of the society. Lastly, 'charitable responsibility' involves a business's judgment or choice to make voluntary social contributions, to a drug abuse prevention program or to childcare management. Thus, a corporation that has social responsibility is an ethical and devoted 'corporate citizen,' which strives to follow its economic interest as well as abide by the law (Shin, 2003). Carroll points out that, whereas corporations voluntarily carry out their economic responsibility for their survival, the other three responsibilities are ones that corporations do for others.

The pertinent literature of the 1990s into the new century has not so much expanded the definition of CSR, but rather used the concept as the base point, building block, or point-of-departure for the development of other related concepts and

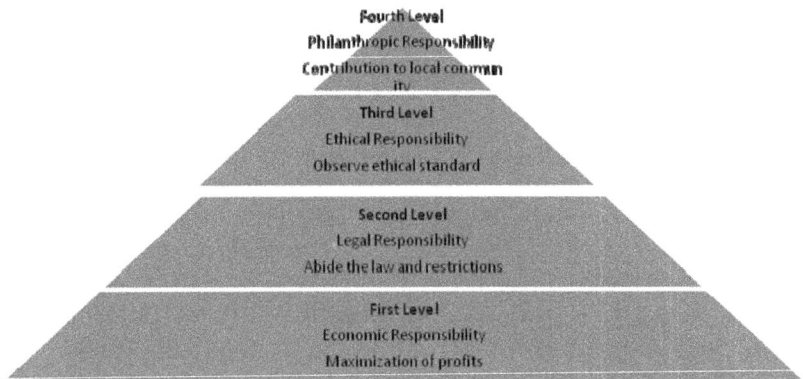

Figure 12.1 Carroll's classification of corporate social responsibility
Source: (Carroll, 1991: 32–33).

themes, many of which have embraced CSR-thinking. Among these, stakeholder-theory, business ethics theory, and corporate citizenship were the major developments that took centre stage in the 1990s (Thomas and Nowak, 2006). All these approaches accept that enterprises contribute to a society by improving efficiencies and cutting costs so as to help maximize their profits. Alternatively, Friedman has argued that a corporation's given role is limited to profit-making, and its 'social' responsibility is sufficiently fulfilled by its taxation and employment creation. He also points up that donation activities tend in general to be against the interests of the shareholders and so are subject to possible prohibition (Friedman, 1970; 1983). CSR then, is only closely related to social contribution as long as it does not conflict with the pecuniary interest of shareholders. But in the case of a progressive business, 'economic achievements' and 'social achievements' cannot be separated insofar as its interests and that of a local community ultimately merge into one. In the long run, then, a socially responsible corporation reaps more benefit for its shareholders but is oriented towards social action (Chung and Han, 2008).

CSR has become increasingly popular to give corporations a caring human face. With the collapse of Enron in 2001, the claims of an organization against the reality of its conduct entered the bright spotlight of public scrutiny. Undoubtedly, the call for greater accountability and transparency in the wake of the Enron debacle has led to the current climate in which it is *de rigeur* for a company to engage in CSR. Corporations perceive that their active socially responsible role enhances their image and so they undertake to deliberately integrate this into their growth strategy.

Corporations acknowledge that CSR activities are critical to enhancing corporate competitiveness and so they duly incorporate social responsibility into their corporate growth strategies with the grand aim of expanding corporate influence on the global scale. This especially applies to MNCs whose corporate influence impacts within and beyond the boundaries of individual national economies. In reality, issues on human rights and environmental encroachment by multinational corporations are being seriously treated, while in some developing countries such activities are being sponsored by their governments. This has led to stricter regulations in the code of conduct of MNCs that deal with CSR. Guidelines require MNCs to abide by certain rules, and international organizations such as the OECD contribute leading ideas to the programmatic practices of CSR.

MNCs are especially facing new challenges posed by civil groups oriented against neo-liberalism. Civil groups such as labor unions or consumer organizations actively engage in and counteract the exploitation of labor and the degradation of the environment caused by MNCs. They also protest against the infringement of human rights, and a few states that are precautionary towards the overt expansion of MNCs tacitly approve the activities of such civil groups (Ibid.). The normative starting point of oppositional groups is that a company should not only be an economic organization that pursues profit. Faced with the protest of anti-globalization groups, MNCs realize that CSR can mollify and even be an antidote to negative branding and can contribute to guaranteeing ethical and transparent business practices.

Background in China: *The 11th Five-Year Plan* and the Beijing Olympics

The recent policy framework for understanding CSR in China is embodied in the ten main principles of the policy document *Explanation of the Outline of the Eleventh Five-Year Plan for National Economic and Social Development (2006–2010) in China* (Zheng, 2005). The plan includes the two main targets of the Central Committee and the State Council of China: 'The scientific outlook on development' (*Kexue fazhan guan*) and creating a 'harmonised society' (*Hexie shehui*), which give direction to China's future. 'The scientific outlook on development' was introduced by President Hu Jintao in the report he delivered to the 17th National Congress of the Communist Party of China (CPC) on 15 October 2007. This principle emphasizes the quality of sustainable economic growth suitable for the creation of a developmental model relevant to the Chinese situation. The second principle, with the stress on constructing a 'harmonized society', is intended as the path that will lead to the construction of a secure and stable social order in China that has suffered gross imbalances in its dual social and economic structures.

Up to the publication of this policy document the term 'CSR' (*Qiye shehui zeren*) had not been used much in China. However, it was among the topics of *The 11th Five-Year Plan* approved by the Fifth Plenum of the Chinese Communist Party in October 2005. The report clearly links sustainable development with economic growth and sets the direction for future debate on this issue-area.

The 11th Five-Year Plan (2006–2010) includes strong stipulations regarding the control of pollution. This did not figure in *The 10th Five-Year Plan* (2001–2005), which showed that emissions of the main pollutants decreased by 10 percent. However, a substantial amount of sulphur dioxide emissions increased by 27% and CO_2 emissions were only up by 2% – effectively a reduction below the target started in 2000. *The 11th Five-Year Plan* still maintains a 10% reduction target and the emissions of major pollutants have eased since 2006.

The three main concepts informing the Beijing Olympics were the 'Green Olympics' (*Lvse Aoyun*), Humanity (*Renwen*) and Science (*Keji*). Here I will focus on the Green Olympics, which was thematized as follows: (1) Environmental improvement, resource and ecosystem conservation to realize sustainable development; (2) Improvement of environmental quality for the whole city; (3) Enhancing public environmental awareness; and (4) Avoiding negative impact on the environment in the process of preparing and staging of the Olympics Games.

CSR with special reference to environmental and scientific innovation

China's economic growth has led to other countries and international society putting pressure on China to play a constructive role as an environmental participant. *The 11th Five-Year Plan* (11.5 plan) as well as the Beijing Olympics has had a great influence on China's policy orientation. MNCs will be discussed with reference to the 'sustainable environment' during the Beijing Olympics according to their CSR activities and their background programs. The reason why Samsung, Sony, and Panasonic were chosen as case studies of CSR in China is that they have issued CSR Reports on an annual basis. Also Samsung and Panasonic were well-known worldwide as official Olympics partners. The examples of the CSR policies of Samsung, Sony, and Panasonic during the Olympics will be considered, given the imperative that MNCs should take the initiative and set a positive example for Chinese companies to follow in the future.

Samsung

Samsung is the overseas company respected and liked the most in China. Every year the *Guangming Daily* details the twenty companies that it estimates have contributed the most to Chinese society and awards a public welfare prize – *Guangming Gongyishang*. In 2007 Samsung China – and for a second successive year, too – was chosen as the company that had made the most outstanding contribution to Chinese society and was duly honoured with an enterprise reward. Samsung's core business philosophy is about devoting its talented people and technologies to offering the best products and services to contribute to global society.

Before the start of the Beijing Olympics on 27 July 2008, thirty-two volunteers from Tianjin Samsung Electronics Co. Ltd cleaned the streets gathering garbage, in so doing striving to show Samsung's contribution to the 'Green Olympics.'[2] In 2008 Samsung Electronics was selected as the *greenest* company from eighteen major electronics companies operating in China. As part of environmental initiatives for the company to maximize the value, Samsung developed a 'green business plan' as part of the company's sustainable development strategy.[3] This initiative was an expression of Samsung's commitment to developing new technologies to improve people's lives as an integral component of its concept of sustainable development through the full range of the product life cycle from beginning to end.

Samsung's site activity centre during the Olympic Games in Beijing was its promotional Center (*OR@S*) that offered wireless communications, entertainment, and a green environmental education centre. Specifically for the Beijing 2008 Olympics Samsung built a 'green' promotional hall as the expression of its core design concept. This hall was intended as a unique 'embryonic' type, representing nature, hopes, and dreams all in one. The building is fully recyclable, using natural materials according to an architectural concept of sustainable development, incorporating energy-saving building systems and an environmentally friendly building design approach.[4]

Sony

The business philosophy Sony stresses is 'Rooted in China, enduring development' and the CSR philosophy of Sony is encapsulated in the idea of 'for the next generation'. The core of Sony's CSR is to enhance its corporate value through innovation and sound business operations. Recognizing fully that its business activities impact both society and the environment directly and indirectly in a variety of ways, Sony pursues CSR activities with an emphasis on realizing a sustainable society, as expressed in the key phrase 'For the Next Generation'. Therefore, business decision-making in the company takes full account of stakeholders – shareholders, customers, employees, suppliers, business partners, local communities, and other relevant organizations. Sony endeavours to comply with this aim in carrying out its CSR.[5]

Sony aims to help maintain a healthy global environment, including biological diversity, for subsequent generations and to work in partnership with its diverse stakeholders to address global issues through innovative and effective approaches. Sony's enduring contribution resides in the creativity of its employees devising of new ways to meet challenges. As part of Sony's corporate governance, it has established management systems that serve as a strong foundation for the CSR activities noted above. It also conducts a wide range of initiatives to continually raise employee awareness of environmental and social issues.

Sony undertakes a wide range of activities with the aim of promoting CSR initiatives overall. Most recently, in 2006 Sony launched Green Management 2010 – new mid-term targets outlining the challenges facing the Sony Group between now and fiscal 2010. The targets will guide the Sony Group in its efforts to help prevent global warming, recycle resources, ensure appropriate management of chemical substances, and address a broad range of other complex environmental issues. When setting targets for Green Management 2010, Sony gave full consideration to the conclusions drawn from its review of Green Management 2005, as well as to legislative trends that could affect the Sony Group in the medium to long term. Consideration was also given to the concerns of investors, to environmental nongovernmental organizations (NGOs) and other stakeholders regarding Sony, and to the direction of its business over the next five years. As a part of these activities, Sony exchanged opinions with several environmental NGOs, regarding specific themes such as the prevention of global warming and natural environmental conservation.

Panasonic Corporation of China

Panasonic's main orientation, activities, and achievements in the fiscal year of 2008 were: (1) creation and expansion of businesses for a recycling-oriented society; (2) strengthening the relationship of trust with stakeholders; (3) rollout of social contribution activities; and (4) reducing CO_2 by promoting energy-saving design in lighting equipment (Panasonic Electric Works, *CSR Report 2008*: 16).

In recognition of it being an environmentally-conscious company in China, Panasonic received an award at the Second Annual China Green Company Conference in Beijing, which was hosted by *China Entrepreneurs Magazine*, the Daonong Center for Enterprise, and the Guanghua School of Management at Peking University from 22–23 April 2009. The China Green Company Award accredits companies with development potentiality and sustainable competitiveness in the fields of the environment, society, business, culture, and innovation. In the fiscal year 2008, just the second year of the award, ten foreign-affiliated companies as well as ten from China garnered praise. Panasonic China won the Award for its original environmental technologies and active environment-contributing activities in China. The company has been promoting a group-wide China Eco Project since 2007 and announced its Declaration of Becoming An Environmentally-Contributing Company in China in September 2007 (28 April 2009).

Panasonic has three 'eco ideas' initiatives – for products, manufacturing, and ideas for everybody, everywhere, for its operations in China. It is important to specify the details of these ideas: first, 'Eco ideas' for products involves successively launching top-level energy-saving products. Panasonic will continue its pursuit of top-level energy-saving performance across all of its products and aim to develop top-level energy-saving products in all categories to which the Chinese government's Energy Efficiency Label is applied. Initiatives will extend not only to energy saving in products, but also to energy generation, storage, and management, as Panasonic sets out its brand identity for several years into the future.

Second, 'Eco ideas' for manufacturing centres on offering the know-how of environmentally-conscious manufacturing to society. Panasonic aims to utilize factory environmental management know-how and the human resources it has cultivated over many years to train factory engineers in other Chinese companies. Specialist engineers will be dispatched to the Chinese government's programs for training human resources in order to share basic environmental management information, know-how, and specific case studies, with the aim of training engineers in Chinese factories.

Third, 'Eco ideas' for everybody, everywhere, focuses on spreading employees' eco activities into local society. On this front, Panasonic aims to provide environmental education to one million children in the regions where its various sites are based over the next ten years, with a view to enhancing environmental awareness.

Table 12.1 The transformation of panasonic into 'clean factories'

	China's 11th Five-Year Plan (2010 target vs 2005)	Matsushita Group's Chinese environmental target (FY'10[6] target vs. FY' 06[7])
Energy	Reduce energy consumption per GDP unit by 20%	Reduce CO_2 emissions per basic unit of production output by 20%
Waste	Achieve a 60% or higher total solid industrial waste utilization rate	Achieve a 90% or higher recycling rate
Chemical substances	Reduce the total release of key pollutants by 10%	Reduce the total release and transfer of Key Reduction-target substances (368 types) by 10%
Water consumption	Reduce water consumption per unit of industrial production by 30%	Reduce water consumption per basic unit of production output by 30%

a FY' (Fiscal Year) 10: From April 2009 to March 2010.
b FY' (Fiscal Year) 06: From April 2005 to March 2006.

A total of one million trees will also be planted over the next ten years to absorb CO_2 and improve the natural environments of these regions. In this regard, the Panasonic Center in Beijing is intended to serve as a base for environmental communicators, allowing as many people as possible to learn about the importance of environmental affairs.

Panasonic aims to achieve the key environmental targets set in its 11th Five-Year National Economic and Social Development Plan (2006–2010) one year ahead of schedule. As part of its initiatives, all of its manufacturing business units aim to pass its clean production audit[8] to ensure that each of its twelve Chinese companies becomes a National Environment-friendly Enterprise[9] at the municipal, provincial/autonomous municipal and national levels in China.

Concluding remarks

Generally speaking, CSR is a significant trend within the world of international business. However, since the advent of globalization, the relationship between companies and societies has changed. Nowadays the expectations of businesses include far greater consideration of the natural environment and society as a whole, while at the same time driven to increase profits. The civic imperative companies *qua* corporate citizen's face are to act responsibly and to participate constructively in social development and public affairs. The positive offshoot of doing so for companies is that they can expect to garner higher profits because of their enhanced corporate image and the added consumer value that adheres to their products and/or services. Generally, then, the civic consciousness of companies in our internationalizing world is a new strategic current to be noted.

Without a doubt the social contribution of companies can improve corporate recognition, national image, and of course profits. Regarding the latter, some companies will consider price, product design, or preferences regarding name recognition; other people will emphasize cheaper prices for products and/or services. As there is the trend for Chinese companies to develop by adopting or copying the products of foreign companies, these are responding by aiming for product differentiation and further technological innovation.

Compared to other countries, CSR in China is at an early stage of development and the relevant law on the social contribution activities of companies and taxation newly passed has not yet yielded benefits for Chinese or foreign companies. But remarkably, within just a few years more Chinese companies have become focused on CSR activities then before. The State Council of the People's Republic of China announced 'Guidelines and Opinions on the Corporate Social Responsibility of State-Owned Enterprises' (*Guanyu zhongyangqiye lvxing shehui zeren de zhidao yijian*) in January 2008 for State-Owned Enterprises (SOEs) to participate in CSR. SOEs laid the groundwork for a planned Chinese economy from 1949 to 1978 and today both state and private Chinese companies endeavour to play an important role in engaging in CSR activities upon the request of the Chinese government. More recently, the 'Responsible Company, Harmonised Society' Olympics CSR Conference was held in Beijing on 28 January 2008, in the wake of the Beijing Olympics that concentrated on the social role of Chinese companies (30 January 2008).

On the basis of the brief survey carried out in this chapter and a consideration of the policy implications for companies vis-à-vis CSR, two main findings can now be stated. First, MNCs usually emphasize environmental protection, recovery from disasters, and educational issues, but they also manage their competences to society focusing on R&D and technological development and the job market. Overall, engaging in CSR certainly improves the image of a company.

Second, no matter how or to what extent a foreign company expands its CSR programs in China, the key factor to success remains sustained support from the top. Especially, companies keen on the Chinese government's policy set their plans to include CSR. Although the development of non-governmental organization in China falls behind, due to Chinese characteristics, organizations affiliated with the Communist Party of China such as Project Hope,[10] Greenpeace, and other organizations have fared well. MNCs that gain favor with local people then can surely expect a good outlook in the long run to the extent that they cultivate globalized business practices with beneficial social effects.

Generally, the interim conclusion proffered at the end of this chapter is to emphasize Jeffrey Sach's point that, globally speaking, 'the real meaning of corporate social responsibility (is) to operate in a manner that promotes broad social objectives, including nonmarket goals, in a way consistent with core business principles, values, and practices' (Sachs 2008: 288). Specifically, the role of corporate social responsibility in China's sustainable development will have to mean much more than 'corporate philanthropy', meritorious though this will surely be. The contribution of CSR to the making of a harmonized society will require creativity; let us say 'CSR with Chinese characteristics'.

Notes

1 There are many terms: 'corporate citizenship' (CC), 'triple bottom line', 'corporate sustainability' (CS), 'corporate ethics', 'corporate sustainability management' (CSM), 'corporate responsibility' or 'responsible business sustainable entrepreneurship' etc.
2 'Samsung Electronics Company Set a Model for the "Green Olympics,"' July 27, 2008, http:// china.samsung.com.cn/news/news_detail.asp?newsid=4020&type=2
3 'Samsung: Olympics, China, Environment,' June 10, 2007, http://china.samsung.com. cn
4 'Samsung Runs a "Green Olympics" Promotion Center (OR@S) during the Beijing Olympics,' August 5, 2008, http://china.samsung.com.cn/news/news_detail.asp?newsid= 4096&type=1
5 www.sony.com.cn/csr/html/a/a_a/content_84.html
6 FY' (Fiscal Year) 10: From April 2009 to March 2010.
7 FY' (Fiscal Year) 06: From April 2005 to March 2006.
8 Clean production audit: Factory audit system established by the Chinese government to reduce the environmental impacts of factories.
9 National Environment-friendly Enterprise: System to commend companies at the industry's leading level in total environmental conservation activities implemented by the Chinese government. The levels include municipal, provincial/autonomous municipal and national levels.

10 Project Hope (*Xiwang gongcheng*), launched by the China Youth Development Foundation in October 1989, under the immediate supervision of the Chinese Youth Party, is a nationwide project to promote education in the most impoverished areas in China.

Bibliography

Barnard, Chester I., (1938), *The Functions of the Executive*, 30th Anniversary Edition (2007), Cambridge, MA: Harvard University Press

Bowen, Howard, (1953), *Social Responsibilities of the Businessman*, New York: Harper

Carroll, Archie B., (1991), 'The pyramid of corporate social responsibility: Toward the moral management of organizational stakeholders', *Business Horizons* 34: 39–48

Carroll, Archie B., (1999), 'Corporate social responsibility: Evolution of a definitional construct', *Business and Society* 38, 3: 268–295

Chung, Sang-eun, Han, Suk-hee, (2008), 'Analysis of corporate social responsibility (CSR) of multinational corporations (MNC) in China', (in Korean) *The Korean Journal of Area Studies*, 26, 2: 141–170

Cui, Xinjian, (2007), '*Kuaguogongsi shehui zeren de gainian kuangjia- Kuaguogongsi yu guoji touzi*' (The Conceptual Frame of Transnational Corporation's Social Responsibility), *World Economy Research* 4: 64–68

Friedman, Milton, (1970), 'The social responsibility of business is to increase its profits', *The New York Magazine*, September 13

Friedman, Milton, (1983), 'The Social Responsibility of Business is to Increase its Profits,' in Snoeyenbos, Milton, Almender, Robert F. and Humber, James F. (Eds.), *Business Ethics and Corporate Values and Society*, New York: Prometheus Books, 73-79

Krep, Theodore, (1962), 'Measurement of the social performance of business', *American Academy of Political and Social Science*, 343,1: 20–31

Ministry of Finance of the People's Republic of China and the State Administration of Taxation, (2006), *The Law of the People's Republic of China on Foreign-Capital Enterprises*, Ministry of Commerce, Published on 20 July

Panasonic, (2009), 'Panasonic China wins the China Green Company Award', Published on 28 April, http://panasonic.cn/about/news/contents/568

Panasonic Electric Works, (2008), *CSR Report*, CSRM Community Relations Office and Corporate Advertising Department of Panasonic, 16

Philips, Joe, Lim, Suk-jun, (2007), 'Finding an international footing: Enhancing Korea's power through corporate social responsibility', *The Korean Journal of Area Studies*, 25, 2: 65–84

Sachs, Jeffrey D., (2008), *Common Wealth: Economics for a Crowded Planet*, New York: Penguin

Samsung Community Relations, (2007), 'Samsung People in the World', *Magazine Samsung Community Relations*

Shen, Genrong, (2005), '*Qiye shehui zeren yu woguo qiye guanli chuangxin*' (Corporate Social Responsibility and Business Management Innovation in China), *Shanghai Dianjixueyuan Xuebao*. August 4, 8

Shin, Gang Gyun, (2003) 'The effectiveness of CSR (Corporate Social Responsibility) campaign: A case study of 20 years activities of Keep Korea Green Campaign', *The Korean Journal of Advertising* 14, 5: 205–21

Thomas, Gail, Nowak, Margaret, (2006), 'Corporate Social Responsibility: A definition', Graduate School of Business, Commerce, Management, Tourism and Services, Curtin University of Technology, *GSB Working Paper Series* 62: 1–20

Walton, Clarence, (1967), *Corporate Social Responsibilities*, Belmont, CA: Wadsworth Publishing

Xi, Guoming, (2000), *1999 Shijie touzi baogao* (1999 World Investment Report), Trans (in Chinese), Beijing: Zhongguo caizheng jingji chubanshe

Zheng, Yongnian, (2005), 'The new policy initiatives in China's 11th 5-year plan', *University of Nottingham China Policy Institute Briefing Series*, 1: 1–12

Zhongguowang, (2008), 'Zeren Qiye, Hexie Shijie: Aoyun shehui zeren dahui zai Beijing juxing (Responsible Companies, Harmonious World: Beijing held the Conference on Social Responsibility of the Olympics)', (in Chinese), 30 January, www.china.com.cn

Websites

China Youth Development Foundation (CYDF) www.cydf.org.cn/index.asp
Greenpeace China www.greenpeace.org/china/en/about/how-we-work
Ministry of Environmental Protection of the People's Republic of China www.zhb.gov.cn
Panasonic http://panasonic.cn
People's Daily www.people.com.cn
Samsung Community Relations www.samsunglove.co.kr
Samsung http://china.samsung.com.cn/index.asp
Sony www.sony.com.cn
The Beijing News www.thebeijingnews.com
World Business Council for Sustainable Development (WBCSD) www.wbcsd.org
Zhongguowang www.china.com.cn

13 Access to resources for farmer professional cooperatives in China: An empirical study of two cases in Shicun Village, Tengzhou City, Shandong

Gubo Qi, Benjian Wu and Bin Wu[1]

Introduction

A dilemma facing millions of small household farmers in China since its rural reform and adaptation of the Household Responsibility System in the early 1980s has been that it is difficult for individual farmers to access relevant resources and market information. Farmer Professional Cooperatives (FPCs) were considered an alternative organization for the industrialization of agricultural production, facilitating the standardization and sustainability of agricultural production (Gulati, et al., 2007; Guo, et al., 2001; Yuan, 2001; Huang, 2008). Smallholders also faced benefits-sharing problems in the market, where farmers were at the lowest part of the commodity chain for agricultural products. In order to reduce transaction costs and get more benefits, cooperation between farmers could play a role through organizing the scattered farmers and enhancing their negotiation capacity particularly on price (Hellin, et al., 2009; Huang, 2008).

Two strengths pushed forward the appearance and development of farmers' cooperative organizations in the context of such a unique economic background. One came from farmers themselves by way of production process cooperation, which enhanced their competitiveness in the market. Another came from government, which made space for farmers' cooperation, for example the No. 1 document of the Central Communist Party[2] in 1984, which pointed out clearly that farmers could organize various formats and sizes of cooperative professional economic organizations. Under government support, the demonstration and fiscal funding support for these initiatives have been institutionalized since 2003, for example the 0.515 billion RMB Special Fund for FPC from the Central Government during 2003–2007, the 0.46 billion RMB Special Fund from the Provincial Government during 2004–2007, and 'the Demonstration Program for Farmer Professional Cooperative Organizations' implemented by the Ministry of Agricultural from 2004 onwards.

Approaching the mid-2000s, an increase in cooperatives was very apparent. Up to 2006, there were 150,000 various Farmer Professional Cooperatives with 38.7 million household members amongst them, accounting for 13.8% of total farmer households in China, 7.2 times of that in 2002.[3] With respect to the distribution of specialty in the areas of agricultural production, 40% of the total FPCs were focused on relevant services and production of farming, and 20% on animal husbandry and 23% on agricultural machinery and other activities. Regarding the initiative agents, 69% were farmers' elites and farmers with a bigger scale of production and 13% were local extension departments. By June of 2011, the total numbers of FPC in China had increased to 446,000.

Besides the growth in number, there have also been many new institutional formats in collaborative practices generated by farmers and institutions. These include contracted linkage between companies and farmer households (called *gongsi* + *nonghu* in Chinese), the combination of middle-man organization and farmer households (*zhongjiezuzhi* + *nonghu* in Chinese), the combination of professional association and farmer households (*zhuanyexiehui* + *nonghu*) and the combination of cooperatives and farmers households (*hezuoshe* + *nonghu*). Cooperatives and associations have taken a different role when compared with other leading institutions in the collaborations with farmers, since farmers are components of cooperatives and associations rather than only being the partner or client in collaborations involving companies or middle-men.

The rapid growth of farmer cooperatives since the mid-2000s cannot be separated from the favorable policy environment. Farmer Professional Cooperative (FPC) Law has been effective since 2007 (Deng, et al., 2010). Whilst governmental support is important for the initial phase or establishment of FPCs (Yuan, 2001), a dilemma facing FPCs is sustainability, which cannot rely on external resources only because most FPCs face serious market competition and have commonly lacked a capacity for self-reliance.

In theory, an FPC should be initiated by farmers themselves, as they have their own interests and needs to pursue collective actions. In reality, few if not none are initiated by farmers because many key agricultural resources, such as land, water, seeds, finance and banking are actually controlled by governments. It is also largely due to the imbalance among actors, for example, market information and public resources do not reach farmers at grassroots if the individual farmer's efforts are relied on solely. As a result, it is quite often the case that interests between farmers and governments are inconsistent, a salient characteristic in China (Jia, et al., 2010). The scale of the cooperatives is on average less than 50 household members and focus on cropping and animal husbandry though do cover almost each industry in agricultural industry.[4]

Of the many constraints affecting the development of cooperatives, capital scarcity is perhaps the most serious one, due to the small scale of its internal funding and difficulty to get loans under the name of the cooperative. In addition, lack of management talent is also a serious constraint affecting the development of the cooperatives. A common challenge faces a large number of cooperatives in China, which is the transformation required from relying on government or external support to self-mobilization and self-development.

From the perspective of capacity building and sustainability of FPCs in China, this chapter intends to examine resource constraints and coping strategies adopted by farmers. In particular, it intends to address the following questions: What are the resource constraints affecting the maintenance and development of FPCs? What channels and mechanisms are used by farmers to obtain relevant resources? What are the key factors which influence the access and security of key resource supply? What are the implications for China if it enhances the capacity for building, and maintaining sustainable development for farmer cooperative organizations in China? The above questions will be addressed via four parts which follow this introduction. The next section reviews relevant literature on organizational resources for cooperative development in China and beyond. It is followed by a description of observation indicators and case selection. Major findings are displayed in Section Four. This chapter ends with a discussion and conclusion.

Literature review: organizational resources for cooperative development

Although nobody can deny the importance of resources for the establishment and development of farmer cooperative organizations, different people may have different understandings or emphases on organizational resources. Bakke, et al. (1960), for instance, argue that the basic resources for organizations include human resources, physical resources, financial resources, natural resources, ideological resources, and the business field of the organization. Shi (1998) pointed out that the resources an enterprise requires access to are administrative resources and law, production and operational resources, management resources and cultural resources. Hite, et al. (2006) categorized resources into physical resources, human resources, governance resources, social/emotional resources, political resources and social capital resources. A common idea on resources concentrates on physical ones and ideological ones, and both are dynamic and changed and mobilized on the basis of the organizational capacities.

Whilst the use of resources is the concern of most of scholars, according to Pfeffer and Sutton (2006), a more important issue is how to get access to resources, the key for an organization's survival. For a powerful governmental organization, the access to resources is more enforced, stable, certain, sustained and consistent, compared with a private sector or NGO. For Farmer Professional Cooperatives, which have the features of both NGOs and private sector organizations, we cannot ignore their internal resources, channels and means which may be crucial to mobilising external resources, opportunities and capacity for their organizational development.

Some research on the private sector's access to resources has been inclined to explore the social network and characteristics of the leaders of an organization. For instance, Lai and Ding (2009) argued that some business owners are in general unwilling to share their resources with others due to lack of confidence and understanding of the nature of business development during the early stage of entrepreneurship. To deal with this issue, they proposed a model for mobilizing resources at this specific phase. Yu (2009) argued that the integration of internal and external strengths through networking could be helpful for getting more resources to improve enterprises' internal capacity. Wang and Bao (2007) pointed out that the broader the social relationships of a small scale enterprise, the more possibility that this enterprise will be able to obtain external resources and then the more secure the enterprise's growth and performance. Hite, et al. (2006) analysed the approaches to resources of schools in Sub-Saharan Africa and found that exchange of resources through building network platforms was a key way to get resources; furthermore, principals of the schools played an important role through the application of their social relationship network. Li (2007) focused on taskforce organizations or temporary organizations and found they had different characteristic ways of obtaining resources when compared to ordinary organizations.

With respect to resources and cooperative development, the overwhelming attention has so far been paid in addressing the government's role in providing resources in FPC development (Hellin, et al., 2009; Berdegué, 2001; Yuan, 2001; Zhang, 1991; Zhang, 2004; Xu, et al., 2005; Feng, 2003; Liao, 2001). By contrast, little has been done regarding the initiatives FPCs have taken in their approach to resources. Nonetheless, a number of researches (Kong, et al., 2010, Hellin, et al., 2009; Huang, 2008) have discussed the farmers' needs for human resources and other scarce resources to consolidate the base of a cooperative.

It seems clear that how farmers access and secure relevant resources is an under-researched but a crucial one for the development of cooperatives in China. It is unclear, however, how farmers use and develop social networks, the most important resource they can mobilize and use, to get access to other scarce resources for FPC development. The importance of access to the resources can be seen from some researches on the role of stock-sharing cooperatives for mobilizing financial capital which has been recognized as a trend in the development of China's cooperatives (Luo, et al. 2004, Ying, et al. 2002). By way of case studies on FPC development, this chapter will fill knowledge gaps relating to the above.

Fieldwork in Shicun Village: framework and profiles of two cases

To get a better understanding about resource constraints and coping strategies adopted by farmers to maintain and develop their FPCs in China, an empirical study has been undertaken in Shicun Village of Longyang Township where two Farmer Professional Cooperatives are very famous in Tengzhou City, Shandong Province.

Tengzhou Farmer Cooperative on Animal Husbandry (Animal Husbandry Cooperative thereafter), was initiated by village communist party secretary general Xu in 2007. This cooperative had 156 members, with 20 mu (1.4 ha) of farmland and 36 chicken sheds for producing chickens and eggs obtaining an income of 15.6 million yuan, with profits of 1.36 million yuan in 2009. Raising chickens increased from 1000 chickens per household to 5000 chickens per household in terms of scale during the period. Like many village leaders in China, interestingly, Mr. Xu had not lived in the village long as his family had moved into an urban town a few years prior. This, however, did not impede villagers' trust in him as village leader and head of the Animal Husbandry Cooperative. Rather, his village mates acknowledged benefits from his dual roles across rural and urban boundaries.

Tengzhou Yinong Vegetable Production and Marketing Professional Cooperative (Vegetable Production Cooperative thereafter) was previously called

Tengzhou Yinong Vegetable Production and Marketing Association but was also legally allowed to do marketing. It registered under its current name after July 2007 when the implementation of FPC law took place. There were only 5 persons when it was set up and it now has 140 members with 3000 mu (200 ha) farmland for producing potatoes, radishes and green Chinese onions and it managed 1.2 million yuan in sales income in 2009. It already achieved commercial branding that was issued by the State Bureau of Industrial and Commercial Administrative and its products made from potatoes went directly into Carrefour Supermarket, along with its having obtained a contract with Dongyi Food Production Limited Corporation to whom it sold 300 tonnes of produce in autumn 2009. It also applied for and got approval to export its products abroad.

In order to understand the key factors behind the development and success of the two cases above, a conceptual framework has been established as a guideline for information collection and analysis. It consists of five resources (or factors/ dimensions) associated with a number of indicators, measures and questions for information collection (Table 13.1).

These categories merge interior and exterior resources. As for physical resources, house/factory, land, greenhouses and other fixed assets owned by members are examples. Funding, loans, external projects and other assets are external resources under the same category. Social capital includes trust building, internal sustainable development and trust relationships formed between the cooperative and the outside world. Technology resources cover not only the production process but also prediction, monitoring, organizational management and marketing manage-

Table 13.1 Categories of resources, key indicators and measurements

Category/ Dimension	Indicators, measures and questions
Physical	Construction of the cooperative
	Funding support, how to get funding support
	Situation of collaborated enterprises
	How to make connections with collaborated enterprises
	Supported projects
	How to get those projects
Social	Internal trust
	How social networks were set up
	Relationship among members and between members and managers of cooperative
	How the relationships contributed to the development of the cooperative
	Construction of social networks between the cooperative and the outside world
	Relationship with government departments,
	enterprises & other cooperatives
Technology	Technologies, agencies and personnels
	Access to key technological resources (knowledge, information, seeds)
Policy and regulation	Familiarity (understanding) of relevant laws, regulations and policies at various levels
	Access to the above information or learning process
Image and reputation	Perception of members, public image/support, clients/official participation
	Public relationship strategies, barriers and constraints in this regard

ment. Image and reputation resources include recognition, trust and attention of various people involved in the cooperative. Though the above framework may be helpful for research and analysis purposes, it may be difficult to distinguish them from one another as they are often interwoven and jointly used in reality.

Main findings from the fieldwork

Based upon the framework described in the previous section, major findings from the two cooperatives in the Shicun Village can be summarized and discussed from the perspective of the access to and security of five key resources listed as follows.

Access to physical resources

Mobilization inside the cooperative and outside the cooperative is the main approach the cooperative uses to get access to physical resources. The two cooperatives get access to the production house, farm and greenhouses through mobilizing resources within the cooperative, which means the accumulation of member households' contributions. When the two cooperatives were first set up, they were all small scale and had limited members. Most villagers were waiting to observe more concrete results. Incentives such as free consultancy services and marketing services reduced costs in the commodity chain and increased the additional value of products. Those profits were allocated to households that provided more land and greenhouses for enlarging the scale of the production base.

For the vegetable production cooperative, the process of fixed assets accumulation can be illustrated as in Box 13.1.

Box 13.1 Accumulation of fixed assets through the internal mobilization approach

Seeking a stable purchasing price is the main incentive for farmers to not only join and maintain their involvement in cooperatives, but also take positive steps and make an effort towards production and quality control. The vegetable production cooperative, for instance, had made an agreement with Carrefour Supermarket in May 2009 to provide vegetables, but the quality of the potatoes in the first process of selling did not achieve the requirements of Carrefour due to their surpassing the required soil weight. As a result, they had to sell their potatoes at a much lower price to Carrefour, netting them a big loss equivalent to 10000 yuan in total. This loss was deducted from the profit but the cooperative did not reduce the purchasing price. So this cooperative attracted more and more farmers to join in and contribute to physical resource accumulation, which combined with efforts to improve vegetable quality simultaneously, resulted in a stable supply and price of vegetable products with Carrefour.

(Source: interview with villagers on April 2, 2010.)

Box 13.1 suggests that to obtain external sources, the cooperatives relied mainly on their social network, particularly the social network of the leader. Normally, exchanges with outsiders at the beginning were in the name of individuals but not cooperatives. Exchange among cooperatives is quite rare, though there is a United Association for the Tengzhou Rural Cooperative Economy.

Access to social capital

Compared with other resources, social capital is perhaps the most important one and involves the establishment, maintenance and enhancement of trust among members of the cooperatives. At the initial stage of cooperative formation, trust-building normally relied on mutual consensus between individuals. In this stage, the chairperson of the board was a very important influence as regards building the villagers' trust about cooperatives. The capacity, background, physical base and even personality of the leaders were key in the process of villagers making the decision to join the cooperatives and their contributions.

Social networks between the cooperatives and the outside world were externally formed through cooperation, individual relationships and accumulated trust. In the Animal Husbandry Cooperative, the cooperative set up a collaborative relationship with Yi'an Biological Corporation Ltd and Lunan Agro-industrial Corporation, by which they were able to gain consultations and receive comments and suggestions once they faced production problems which they needed to sort out. The Vegetable Production Cooperative, which cooperated with Carrefour supermarket, Yinzuo Supermarket, Dongyi Food Production Corporation Ltd did this also and as a result they could contact more clients and were able to negotiate to their advantage. Box 13.2 outlines the process of social capital accumulation for business links.

In general, institutional cooperation is much more important than interpersonal relationships in the establishment of cooperatives. The Vegetable Production Cooperative, for instance, has received more and more attention from the directors of Tengzhou Municipal Agricultural Bureau after they set-up formal cooperation with the Carrefour supermarket, which then brought in some clients from Malaysia.

Box 13.2 Accumulation of social capital in the Vegetable Production Cooperative

Initiated by Shandong provincial government, Tengzhou municipal government organized discussions with cooperatives and defined 10 cooperatives as demonstration of 'combination of cooperatives and supermarkets', the Vegetable Production Cooperative was luckily one of them. The leader of the cooperative went to talk with the director of Tengzhou Municipal Agricultural Bureau who gave his support through official and also personal channels with the Carrefour supermarket. However, the Cooperative got Carrefour's trust only after it provided its first qualified production.

Source: interview with Mr. Miao of this cooperative on April 3, 2010.

Access to technological resources

Any FPC, by definition, must concentrate on or be specialized in one specific mode of agricultural production. In this sense, relevant technological resources cover the areas of production, management and marketing. In our cases, key technologies are summarized in Table 13.2.

Table 13.2 Key Technologies and access in two cooperatives

Case Item	*Animal Husbandry Cooperative*	*Vegetable Production Cooperative*
Production technology	Early stage of disinfection to overall animal husbandry area which came from an individual called Xu Bin who had been raising chickens for 14 years and received training from researchers. Ventilation and insulation: keeping temperature as 32 degrees centigrade for chicks and reducing by 2 degrees every week to normal temperature. Biological medicine as alternatives for antibiotics.	Potato Production package technology: 2 sheds and 3 plastic covers to save watering and make maturing take place early for marketing and better price; Stalk for composting: increase temperature of land by 1–2 degrees centigrade for reducing the application of fertilizer and chemical medicine.
Vaccination	Vaccinations for preventing chicken new castle disease: eye/nose drops on the 7th day and injection on the 15th day for preventing infectious bronchitis in chickens; Drinking clone vaccine melted in water after chicken had been without drink for 4-5 hours on the 30th day	Set up pre-warning mechanism for potato diseases: a specific group monitored the field situation and corresponding measures once problems found
Monitoring	Observe appearance of chicken concerning their behaviour, colour of cockscomb, color and shape of manure etc. Listen to clucking sounds at night after turning off the lights Dissection: deep checking after chick got diseases, 'three look': look at trachea, look at intestine, and stomach	Pesticide residue detection and facilities. Specific pre-warning group. Learning about potato and reen radish disease prevention and gdetection technology
Leadership	Chairperson has plentiful experience because he had been general manager in Tengzhou Haibing Animal Husbandry Corporation Ltd. He had participated in training on cooperatives organized by country economy and management bureau. Chairperson's social contacts and collaboration with outside experts.	Chairperson went to Cooperative College in Qingdao Agricultural University for studying cooperative management methods. He also took part in training on cooperatives organized by country economy and management bureau, and training in financial management; He took part in specific training on cooperatives in Taian and training on technology

Table 13.2 shows that major technological resources including production technologies, vaccination and detection were mostly from members' own accumulative experience. In addition, the chairperson in each cooperative and his social network played important roles in the establishment and development of the cooperatives. Nonetheless, cooperatives provide a sound platform for all members to learn and share relevant knowledge, experience and information more effectively with a significant decline of risks in production and selling.

In terms of leadership in technological learning and accumulation, the chairperson of the Animal husbandry Cooperative started chicken raising in 1995 and he stayed in chicken sheds day and night for the first several years. He wrote diaries while observing and accumulated many key technologies, which helped a lot for the cooperative's technology improvement at the start-up phase. The chairperson of the Vegetable Production Cooperative had worked on agricultural products marketing and agricultural production materials services for ten years. He summarized lessons and experiences in planting potatoes and researched organic production technology, so it was helpful for the cooperative to set up pesticides residue detection stations, which formed a basis for cooperation with Carrefour supermarket, which had standard requirements on pesticide residue.

It is worth noting that a government program, 'Science and technology going to the countryside' advocated by the Ministry of Agriculture, had positive impacts on technology learning and development in our cases, which can be seen from Box 13.3.

Access to governmental support for favorable policies

Since the 1980s, Chinese governments at various levels have made and issued a lot of favorable regulations and policies to foster and support cooperative development. In practice, however, most cooperatives have not been able to get the

---

Box 13.3 Impact of the 'science and technology going to countryside' program in the Animal Husbandry Cooperative

Of various channels for technology learning, the 'science and technology going to countryside' program is an important one. Based upon relevant books and journals donated by this program, a small library has been established which is very helpful for all members who can read relevant information. In addition, the cooperatives input 10000 yuan to connect to the Shandong Remote Education System website allowing members to consult with experts. It also built up a good relationship with experts and officials from the Tengzhou Animal Husbandry Bureau, and the experts came to cooperatives sooner or later whilst members also went to the said bureau to ask questions.

Source: interview with villagers on April 1, 2010.

access to those resources promised by regulations or policies because they were only at the status of having been 'heard about' or 'known and understood' but not 'applied'. And in many cases, although not like the cases described in this chapter, the cooperatives even had not even heard about the relevant supportive policies. For example, 55% of the total cooperatives in Longyang Town of Tengzhou did not know the policy concerning subsidies for cooperatives desiring to take part in exhibitions, because there was no meeting or public announcement informing the cooperatives. Those cooperatives that got the information actually went to the local government or the United Association of Rural Cooperative Economy on a regular basis. So in the process of this kind of top-down announcement, policy makers at top levels had the full power to disseminate, guide the direction and even control the resources to implement the policies. During the time of this study, there were no clear institutions to regulate the behaviour of those at higher levels. The understanding of the cooperatives had to be based on daily communication and personal linkages, which required the cooperatives to show themselves off more in front of higher level officialdom. Cooperatives at a lower level were in the passive position of acceptance and application of those policies; if they did not have the capacity to carry out 'information searching' and 'rent seeking', those existing policies were meaningless.

Taking the Animal Husbandry Cooperative as an example, although there was an announcement from the Ministry of Finance to encourage the financial system to support cooperatives' funds, banks were not willing to provide loans to this cooperative due to a low internal rate of return. The chairperson went to the director of the Tengzhou Economy and Management Bureau through a personal relationship. Learning the situation and policies, the director went to the Mayor of Tengzhou, who was very keen to support cooperatives. The Mayor replied very positively and provided a lower interest rate through a subsidy from the fiscal budget. On the basis of this case, the Mayor issued a 'Tenure Model of Utilizing Rural Land.'[5] Rural Credit Cooperatives gave a loan to Animal Husbandry Cooperative at a 100000 yuan per 1000 chickens standard. (Source: interview on March 31, 2010)

Reputation and image of cooperatives

It is not less important for the development of FPC to gain a good reputation and public image, which in turn could enhance royalties and cohesion for all members. Table 13.3 summarizes the achievements and 'soft power' of two cooperatives in this regard.

As shown in Table 13.3, some members of the cooperative did not even know that they were members, but after the cooperative got benefits from its collaboration with Carrefour and other enterprises, the attention and trust from the members increased a lot. For those potential participants, more and more attention and trust would attract them to join in. Positive recognition and trust from the clients may enlarge the business areas.

Information dissemination about the effectiveness and performances of the cooperatives is one approach for trust building and then getting access to public

Table 13.3 Attractiveness, royalty and public image

	Animal Husbandry Cooperative	Vegetable Production Cooperative
Members	55.6% of members think the cooperative deserves trust; 33.3% of members think it does not matter; 22.1% think the cooperative did not play and only played the role of getting policy benefits for minorities[6] Only one member did not think he was a member Notice: market price fluctuation influenced the members' attitude to animal husbandry activity	85% of members think the cooperative deserves trust; 50% think they got benefit from cooperative by reducing risks Notice: at the beginning, members were enforced to take part in but nowadays this has changed
Clients/ partners	As companies and corporations, we all need to look for a production base, which could be provided by cooperatives. And the cooperative, as an organization, had a better public reputation than individuals. The stability of product supply, integrated purchase and dissemination secure the products' quality.	Transaction costs are lower when doing business with the cooperative, and the quality is more secure, as expressed by Carrefour staff. It deserves trust and the making of a contract.
Officials	The Vice-Mayor of Zaozhuang Municipality, leaders of Tengzhou Agricultural Bureau and Economy and Management Bureau, the Minister of Shandong Province all came to the cooperative for a visit. But the economy and management station and agricultural technology station in the town did not pay much attention to it.	It was built up based on its own capacity, but it was also built up with some government officials. The Vice-Director of the Tengzhou Agricultural Bureau took good care of this cooperative and helped it to proceed to having a foreign trade certificate.

opinions. The dissemination platform included internal daily exchange among members, between the management team and normal members, between the management team and clients and officials; marketing channels such as exhibitions and the internet. Tengzhou Potato Festival, Zaozhuang Agricultural Products Exhibition, Shouguang World Vegetable Exhibition, Beijing Agricultural Products Exhibition, China Agricultural Information Website and the Alibaba website had all played roles in disseminating cooperative information and marketing services information.

There are also some minor channels that helped the cooperatives to get public opinions, such as personal exchange and communication, based on indigenous connections in the village and previous personal relationships between the cooperative leaders and outside officials.

Though two cooperatives interviewed got public opinions through daily business exchange and information dissemination for trust building, it was not intentionally implemented, or it was not institutionalized. Actually, getting public opinions on the operation and effectiveness of the cooperatives could be integrated into the monitoring system of the cooperatives and putting public opinions into use, but the cooperatives did not thus far consider public opinions as a resource.

Discussion and conclusion

The cooperatives had their own ways to access various resources that were needed for the cooperatives' development. In general, economic exchange, social relationship utilization, trust building, and information dissemination are key approaches. In applying these approaches, the cooperatives have to be concerned about obtaining the largest benefits from production and business activities, mobilizing previous social connections, enlarging the number of marketing partners, making best use of their leaders or member capacities and investing into innovative marketing methods.

The cooperatives themselves act as a resource or base to attract more resources. Whether they are operating in a systematic/institutionalized way or free-style, the formal legal identity lends them exposure to opportunities to obtain further resources, particularly resources related to those laws and policies. The members' realization of this process would facilitate their ownership of the cooperatives since they form part of this resource and received benefits from this resource but not individually in terms of those supportive policies targeting only cooperatives. However, the elites of the cooperatives were always the key direct persons initiating the organization of and obtaining access to more sources, due to their advantage of capacity. The more the leaders input, the more responsibility they will have; on the contrary, the less normal members input, the less responsibility they will have. So the ownership of the members in the cooperatives is not only a matter of getting benefits but also a matter of contribution. Sustaining a base for approaching for more resources, involving members and stimulating their participation would be as important as enhancing the capacities of those leaders.

Therefore, involvements of the members in various exchange and training activities or other public sharing events, which are now provided by the government in many ways, are critical for improving their responsibilities and ownership and increasing the benefits they can get from the cooperatives. The recipients of benefits from such activities or events are not necessarily the leaders of the cooperatives only.

The approaches for gaining access to resources for cooperatives are still very informal and are not institutionalized, as mentioned above. On most occasions, they rely on the enthusiasm of one or two elites and their personal attraction. Therefore, a change of macro-environment and individuals may bring unexpected disasters to the organization. Nevertheless, existing access and methods do present a perspective on cooperatives' adaptation to the whole institutional, economic and social environment and local cultures. Xiong (2009) argued that '*Mingshi Fenli*' (absorbing nominal institutions by market organizations) is one prevalent strategy absorbed by more and more Farmer Professional Cooperatives to adapt to the institutionalizing environment. Our findings provide support to the debates on how much those actions in reality still rely on the nominal names to a greater extent.

On one hand, informal approaches helped initiatives of FPCs in their start-up phase; on the other hand, some individuals might take advantage of this opportunity to make more private benefits rather than benefits for members. It is difficult to differentiate the motivation and behaviour of different types of cooperatives, based on the current system without a sound monitoring and evaluation mechanism. Apart from enabling a transparent policy environment to make information sharing as equal as possible, it is also important for the government at various levels to build up a monitoring system accompanied by a commercial system to supervise the nature of the cooperatives.

Notes

1 Authors are grateful for funding support from the International Development Research Center, Canada (the project number 102005), and UK's ESPA (Ecosystem Services and Poverty Alleviation in the Developing Countries) jointly funded by Research Councils (NERC/ESRC) and Department of International Development. This chapter is based on the field work conducted by research team of COHD, China Agricultural University.
2 'No. 1 document of CPC' is the first document issued by the Central Communist Party of P. R. China every year. This document is a guideline for state tasks in development in the whole year. The problems raised in 'No. 1 document of CPC' are always the problems to be solved urgently.
3 Data is from Division of Professional Cooperation, Department of Economy and Management, Ministry of Agriculture of P.R. China, 'New characters of Farmers Professional Cooperatives Development' at website of China Farmer Professional Cooperatives. 2007-12-05, www.cfc.agri.gov.cn/cfc/html/78/2008/2008072713210746 8942269/20080727132107468942269_.html
4 News Office, Ministry of Agriculture of P.R. China. The improvement of quality and quantity of Farmer Professional Cooperatives in China, at website of Ministry of Agriculture of P.R. China, December 9, 2010, www.moa.gov.cn/ztzl/zyncgzhy/201012/t20101222_1795797.htm
5 This concept of Tenure of Rural Land Utilization is to use land use right as a mortgage for getting a three-year loan. If the cooperative could not repay, the three years' outputs from the land could be enough for repayment; at the same time, the farmers won't lose their land after three years' duration. It was implemented in Tengzhou and had 20 demonstration cooperatives in 2010. (Source: interview with Director Cao of Longyang Town Agricultural Technology Station, and Director Du of Economy and Management Station on April 4, 2010).
6 Source: group discussion on April 1 and April 3, 2010.

Bibliography

Alchian, A. A., Demsetz, H., (1972), 'Production, information costs, and economic organization', *American Economic Review*, 62: 778–795

Bakke, E., Wight, Kerr, Clark, Anrod, Charles W., (1960), *Unions, Management, and the Public*, 2nd edition, New York: Harcourt, Brace

Berdegué, J., (2001), *Cooperating to Compete – Associative Peasant Business Firms in Chile [D]*, Ph.D.Thesis, Wageningen University. (Secondary source from: Hellin, Jon,

Lundy, Mark, Meijer, Madelon, (2009), 'Farmer organization, collective action and market access in Meso-America', *Food Policy* 34: 16–22)

Central China Communist Party and State Council, (1995), 'Suggestions on how to proceed agriculture and rural work in 1995', *Zhongfa* number 6, published 31 March

Deng, Hengshan, Huang, Jikun, Xu, Zhigang, Rozelle, Scott., (2010), 'Policy support and emerging Farmer Professional Cooperatives in rural China', *China economic review*, 2010, doi:10.1016/j.chieco.2010.04.009

Feng, Kaiwen, (2003), 'Collaborative evolution of village autonomy, cooperatives and agro-industrialization. *Chinese Rural Economy*. (2): 45–50

Gulati, A., Minot, N., Delgado, C., Bora, S., (2007), 'Growth in high-value agriculture in Asia and the emergence of vertical links with farmers', in Hellin, Jon, Lundy, Mark, Meijer, Madelon, (2009), 'Farmer organization, collective action and market access in Meso-America', *Food Policy* 34: 16–22

Guo, Hongdong, Xu, Keqing, (2001), 'Facilitating agricultural economic development through agricultural cooperative organizations, roles and practices in Zhejiang's Cixi', (in Chinese), *Academic Journal of Northwest Agro-forestry Science and Technology University* (Social Science version), 11: 15–17

Hellin, Jon, Lundy, Mark, Meijer, Madelon, (2009), 'Farmer organization, collective action and market access in Meso-America', *Food Policy* 34:16–22

Hite, Julie M., Hitea, Steven J., Jacobb, W. James, Rewa, W. Joshua, Mugimua, Christopher B., Nsubugac, Yusuf K., (2006), 'Building bridges for resource acquisition: Network relationships among head teachers in Ugandan private secondary schools', *International Journal of Educational Development*, 26, Issue 5, 26: 495–512

Huang, Zuhui, (2008), Issues of theories and practices of the development of China's cooperative organizations, *Chinese Rural Economy*, (11): 4–7

Jia, Xiangping, Huang, Jikun, Xu Zhigang, (2010), 'Marketing of Farmer Professional Cooperatives in the wave of transformed agrofood market in China', *China Economic Review*, doi:10.1016/j.chieco.2010.07.001

Kong, Xiangzhi, Jiang, Chenchen, (2010), 'Impacts of heterogeneous of members on governance system of cooperatives – example of United Fruit Cooperatives in Jingjing County of Sichuan Province', (in Chinese), *Rural Economy*, 9: 8–11

Lai, Xiao, Ding, Ninging, (2009), 'Research model of access to resources in a new phase of an enterprise', *Inquiry into Economic Issues*, 5: 90–94

Li, Dong, (2007), *Study on Access to Resources of a Taskforce Organization*, Ph.D. Dissertation, China Renmin University, May 2007

Liao, Yunfeng, (2001), *Cooperative Economy Beijing*, (in Chinese), Beijing: China Commercial Press

Luo, Biliang and Pan, Guanghui, (2004), Share cooperation in Egongling village: From close to open, *Chinese Rural Economy*. (5): 17–23

O'Brien, Kevin J., (1994), 'Chinese people's congresses and legislative embeddedness: Understanding early organizational development', *Comparative Political Studies*, 27, 1: 80–107

Pfeffer, Jeffrey, Sutton, Robert I., (2006), *Hard Facts: Dangerous Half-truth and Total Nonsense*, Harvard Business School Press, (translated version in Chinese (2008), China Renmin University Press)

Poter, P. K, Scully, G. W., (1987), 'Economic efficiency in cooperatives', *Journal of Law and Economics*, 30, 2: 489–512

Saich, Tony, (2000), 'Negotiating the State: The development of social organizations in China', *The China Quarterly*, 161: 124–141

Shi, Xiuyin, (1998), 'Social network base for the success of entrepreneurs in China', (in Chinese), *Management World*, 6: 187–196

Wang, Qingxi, Bao, Gongmin, (2007), 'Social network, access to resources and small enterprises development', (in Chinese), *Journal of Industrial Engineering and Engineering Management*, 21, 4: 57–60

Xiong, Wansheng, (2009), 'China's cooperative: As unintended consequences of institutionalizing processes', *Chinese, Sociological Studies*, 5: 83–109

Xu, Wei, Zeng, Xuhui, (2005), 'Rationale thinking on development of farm cooperative organization in China', *in Chinese, Economic System Reform*, 3: 76–79

Ying, Ruiyao and He, Jun, (2002), 'Discussion on the theoretical issues of China's agricultural cooperatives, *Issues in Agricultural Economy.* (7): 2–7

Yu, Hongjian, (2009), 'Research on strategic selection of internal capacity development in a new phase of an enterprise with the perspectives of access to resources and organizational learning', (in Chinese), *Scientific Management Research*, 3: 86–90

Yuan, Peng, (2001), 'Research on farmers cooperative economic organization in marketing process in rural China', *Social Sciences in China*, 6: 63–73 (in Chinese)

Zhang, Xiaoshan, (2004), 'Facilitate the development of cooperatives with main members of agricultural production – example of Farmer Professional Cooperatives in Zhejiang Province', *China Rural Economy*, 11: 4–10

Zhang, Xiaoshan, Yuan, Peng, (1991), *Practices and Theories of Cooperative Economy*, Beijing: China Urban Press, 44

Annex 13.1 Summary of physical resources in two cooperatives

Physical resources ╲ Case	Animal Husbandry Cooperative	Vegetable Production Cooperative
Farm for production	36 sheds for chicken raising; modern chicken farm with standard of accommodating 30,0000 chickens covering 106 mu land	3000 mu farm and exploring two modern experiments' field with each 200 mu
Fund	Fixed assets 3.6 million yuan and flow fund 2 million yuan	Registered fund 0.5 million yuan, selling income 1.2 million yuan
Loan	10,000 yuan loan for 1000 chickens	None
Project	Biological medicine in animal husbandry for preventing use of antibiotics on chickens, from Shandong Yian Biological Company	Applying project of 'exporting base construction' to municipal fiscal bureau and the total amount is 200,000 yuan

14 Farmer innovation in ecologically fragile areas of China: Profiles and characteristics of innovative farmers in Yanchi, Ningxia[1]

Li Chen, Ting Zuo, Tianlai Gou,
Haofang Chai, Fengyang Li, Ronnie Vernooy

Introduction

Innovation is a series of activities aimed at improving the efficiency of resource allocation (Schumpeter, 1934). Extensive research has been conducted about the proposition that it has an important role in the tremendous progress of social development. Business is the domain area of application (Klomp, 2004; Hambrecht, 2008). When speaking on the subject of innovation, society tends to pay more attention to business innovation that has been conducted by the elite who are rich in resources, but few care about the innovation made by common people. In the field of rural development, farmer innovation is such a neglected area and is usually viewed as a product of rich groups, having nothing to do with the petty farmers and resource-poor households. It has never drawn headlines in newspapers (Egziabher, 2001).

However, this kind of leading social discourse cannot hide the existence of farmer innovation. After long-term field experience, anthropologists began to recognize farmers' own experience and innovation (Johnson, 1972) and in the 1980s, Robert Chambers and his colleagues drew wider attention to this. In agricultural development, 'innovation' was first used in literature and practice with regards to farmers' adoption of technologies which had been introduced, in line with Rogers' (1962) theory on diffusion of innovations. More recently, the term 'local innovation' was invented to describe the new technology, management practices and institutions that local people have developed themselves (Waters-Bayer, et al., 2009). The 'Endogenous Agricultural Innovation System' became more important than the 'Exogenous Agricultural Innovation System' (Assefa, et al., 2006). The concept of 'innovation' refers to the search for, development, adaptation, imitation and adoption of technologies that are new to the specific context (Opondo, et al., 2009). The process of local innovation leads to technical, socio-economic and institutional innovations and the farmer and his nature constitute the first actor in rural technological and social change (Wu, 2003).

In ecologically fragile areas, this kind of innovation is more important and necessary. For resource-rich communities, the local farmers can achieve development either by way of Township Enterprise development or by the industrialization of local rich resources, while resource-poor areas must be more reliant upon traditional agricultural development having Complex, Diverse and Risk-prone characteristics (CDR) (Chambers, et al., 1989). Besides this, the ecologically fragile areas are usually marginalized and the packages of standardized extension systems are poorly suited to the diverse and variable conditions of smallholders. With growing population pressures and a growing awareness of environmental degradation, farmers are seeking more productive ways to use their available resources without depleting them (Reij, et al., 2001). Local innovation has become a way of life for resource-poor farmers who are challenged by constant changes in policy, market and the environment and they must innovate to survive (Fenta, et al., 2009). Innovation has become an important way for the farmers to lead themselves out of poverty and gain the opportunity to develop.

In China, farmer innovation has entered into the political arena and become a mainstream discourse, such as the Household Contract Responsibility System and Construction of Small Towns, but overall, grassroots' innovations tend to be pulled out only when they can provide scaled service to politics and the economy. However, theoretical research on Chinese farmer innovation is still a blank slate (Li, 2007) and there are few research papers on the generation, development approach and influential factors of individual farmers' innovation (Zhang, 2008). Under such circumstances, resource-poor farmers' innovation in ecologically fragile areas is even less attractive and greatly underestimated. In the last 30 years, China has made great improvements and a state-led development model has contributed a lot to the progress, but the efforts of common farmers and innovations in their development cannot be ignored, especially in the process of understanding China's rural development in ecologically fragile areas.

Based on the points above, this chapter sheds light on China's ecologically fragile rural development from the perspective of farmer innovation. What are the profiles and characteristics of farmer innovators? What kinds of context enlighten local farmers? How do the innovations happen? Which roles do different development assets play in the process of innovations? And which kind of results and influences do the innovations lead to? Answers to all of these questions are shown in Section three. The research approach and conclusions are given in Sections two and four.

Research approach and methodology

Research design

To explore farmer-level innovations, two main research actions have been taken: the first being the recognition of farmer innovators and the identification of their innovations, and the second being individual interviews with the innovator using a semi-structured questionnaire.

For the first one mentioned, the authors adopted action research. Action research is a kind of research paradigm in which research is aimed at understanding the social reality and the key characteristics include: research and action informing each other, participatory learning, human emancipation and a degree of cyclic iteration (List, 2006). It emphasizes that multiple stakeholders with a variety of knowledge and practical experience should cooperate widely and participate in real-life situations. They should gain knowledge of social development from the process of learning by doing (Vernooy, et al., 2004; Li, et al., 2008). Networking has become a key component in action research (Levy, 2003).

To identify typical innovative farmers and their innovations, different stakeholders were interviewed such as agricultural officers, non-governmental organizations and different types of farmers involved in the action research network organized by the project at the county and township level. All members respectively gathered to discuss the concept of farmer innovation, and identify the key factors concerning the farmers and the innovations. As linked to innovation theory, farmer innovation can be identified as follows: based on their own development need and under a certain external condition, the farmer implements a series of activities to reallocate a variety of livelihood resources with some social, economic and environmental benefits. In the process of networked action research, innovative farmers and their innovations have been confirmed.

After the identification of farmer innovators and their innovations, the second step was to individually and respectively carry out the in-depth interviews. Innovative farmers' basic demography information was collected and the process of innovation behaviours was traced in detail. The demography information contained the age, gender, education background and the former or on-going social status. The key questions for the innovating behaviours included: which factors enlighten your thoughts on the innovations? How do you think about the ideas? What kind of measures do you take to test the idea? What kind of assets have you used to implement the innovations? What are the outputs and influences of your innovations? Moreover, the surrounding natural environment was observed and common villagers' comments on the farmer innovators and their innovations were recorded by way of interviews. When all the cases had been collected, the related research materials were documented in reports and database entries.

Research area

The research project was implemented in Yanchi County, Ningxia Hui Autonomous Region (Figure 14.1) in 2007 and 2008 by the College of Humanities and Development in China Agricultural University and Ningxia Center for Environment and Poverty Alleviation. Financial support was received from Oxfam Hong Kong.

Yanchi is an ecologically fragile area located in the typical agro-pastoral ecotone of Northwest China. It has some of the advantages of cropping and grazing. Historically, it used to be a place with lush pastures. Along with a social stable development, the local population has doubled. Between the 1950s and 1970s, the national food-oriented development strategy and an unclear development direction caused lots of grassland to be changed into agricultural land and the

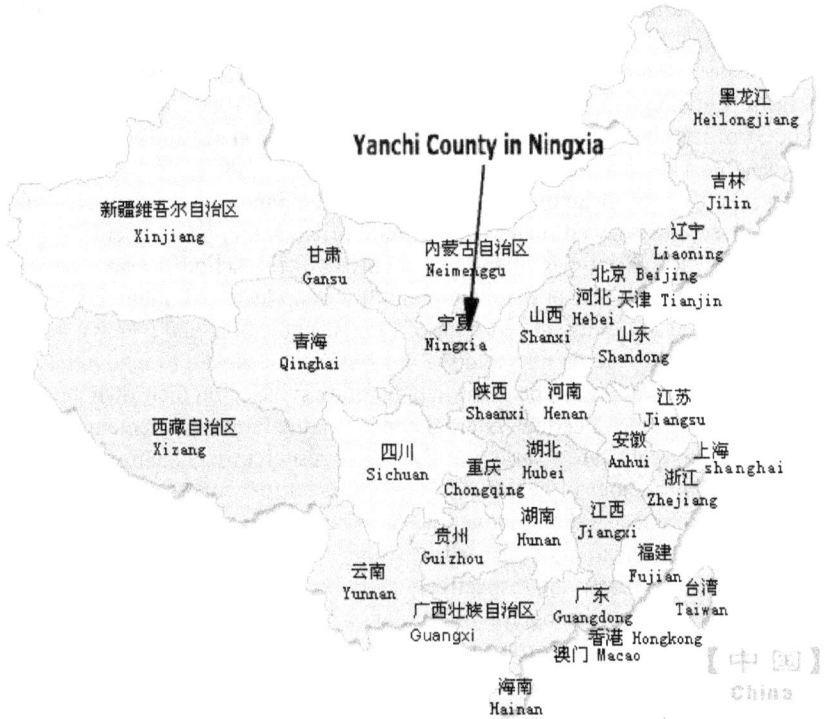

Figure 14.1 Map showing the location of the research county

population of breeding livestock greatly increased. All the development made local land a subject of great dissertation (Fu, et al., 1987; Fan, et al., 2005). Meanwhile with global climate change, local precipitation decreased and became more unstable and extreme weather became more usual. Under such complex, diverse and risk-prone circumstances, local agriculture has been facing the challenge of ecological frangibility.

After the Household Contract Responsibility System, local farmers have had more freedom to arrange their agricultural activities and household labor distribution. However, marginality, local diversity and a lack of non-agricultural resource endowment has made it impossible to develop Township Enterprises and the industrialization of agriculture. Under such conditions, local labor mobility has happened much later than in other rural areas of China and in lower volume. Therefore, local farmers have to make full use of the resources around them to innovate and this is an important part of local development. In 2008, Yanchi County had 19.3 persons per square kilometre, 266.7 mm of rainfall per year and 323 sandstorms per year at speeds of more than 5 meters per second. In the thirty years between 1979 and 2008, local farmers' net income per capita had increased from 185 RMB to 3002 RMB (1 Dollar = 6.94 RMB in 2008) annually (Statistical Bureau in Yanchi County, 2009). The great improvement could not have been achieved without farmer innovation.

Data collection and analysis

Yanchi County has an agricultural population of 130 thousand distributed over eight townships, 98 administrative villages and 675 natural villages, which make selection and collection of candidates for research fraught with challenges. During the two-year selection procedures, the project participants carried out a variety of collection methods, including: sending regular mail-shots to all administrative villages; getting recommendations from different relevant stakeholders, such as the functional departments at the county level (containing the Bureau of Agricultural Economy, Group of Agricultural Investigation, Bureau of Animal Husbandry, Grassland Station, Forestry Bureau, Science and Technology Bureau, Agriculture Bureau, Communist Youth League, Service Centre of Farm Machinery in Yanchi County), the township government, loan officers[1] of Yanchi micro-finance service centre and the award-winning farmers in the 2007 session; publicizing the information in related newspapers and disseminating the information through related web sites. The Project Selection Committee firstly made telephone communications and having found out the basic conditions of those farmers recommended through a variety of channels, carried out a preliminary screening of the recommended farmers and determined the list of names for field visits during which in-depth interviews would be conducted. After that, they implemented the field visit, collected and processed the case information of innovative farmers.

Having put together all of the collected cases at the starting point of the research, case samples for this study were finalized. Some selection and exclusion according to the characteristics of each case took place for the purposes of this chapter. There are three domains referred to in innovative farmer selection, including technical or management innovation in the production and life of individual farmers, organizational innovation of the group farmers in public affairs and innovation in the heritage of traditional knowledge and protection of local culture. Based on the feasibility and pertinence of the research, this study chose to concentrate on the individual farmers and their innovative behaviours, so all relevant cases belonged to the first domain. Besides the above, considering the completeness of the information and typification of the farmers' innovation, the researchers filtered cases, numbering 28 with 11 farmers in 2007 and 17 farmers in 2008, covering eight towns in Yanchi County, 18 administrative villages and 22 natural villages.

When the data collection process had been completed, key indicators were chosen through research group discussion, based on the knowledge garnered about the cases. Then all the cases were documented, and sorted by the indicators. Finally, a database was established and analysed through word tables using the Cross-Case Synthesis method.

Research findings

Individual characteristics

Age

Putting ten-years as an interval, the respondents' age distribution is listed in Table 14.1. The proportion of all interval ages is relatively balanced and the number of people aged 30–39 is slightly less than the normal number; meanwhile, 50% of the respondents were between the ages of 30–39 when they began innovation, and more farmers started innovation between the ages of 40–49 than those between the ages of 27–29. So it can be seen that there is no obvious relationship between innovative capacity and age, and farmers really need quite a long time to get to the final successful innovation stage.

This shows that young farmers are more likely to try new things in the innovation field, and the government policy support has a strong guiding function in the young farmers' innovation, while older farmers are more likely to find a combination of new elements from their original livelihood approach in order to get a better socio-economic benefit for the innovation.

Gender

Gender is an important research perspective in the field of development study, which always provides a new understanding of the problem. In the question of whether gender can become an innovation factor, many traditional views consider that 'women have long hair but short insight,' and women's role and capacity for innovation are often underestimated. Out of the total of 28 respondents, a total of 6 respondents were women as the main innovator, accounting for 21.43%. Five were involved in livestock breeding and one in planting of fields. Two innovative women had taken on totally different areas from their original livelihood approach, and five of the women's income from innovation had become the family's main cash source. So it can be seen that women's ability to innovate is really not worse than men's.

From the point of view of family structure, it was found that one female respondent was divorced and another female's husband was disabled, and their occupations were found to be different. For the 26 other households, harmonious relationships existed between husband and wife, in terms of division of labor and

Table 14.1 Age distribution of the respondents (N = 28)

	Age in 2009			Age at the beginning of the innovation			
Age	33–39	40–49	50–57	27–29	30–39	40–49	50
Respondents	8	10	10	5	14	8	1
Per cent	28.58%	35.71%	35.71%	17.86%	50.00%	28.57%	3.57%

Source: analytical result of field interviews in 2007 and 2008.

mutual support between spouses, which proves that the complement of gender relationship and ways of thinking can influence and promote innovation. Therefore, women farmers' role in innovation depends on the family structure and their functional role played in the family (Mendras, 1970).

Educational background

It is generally believed that people's innovation capacity is closely related to their former education level, but this research data does not support the same conclusion. The distribution of formal education is relatively uniform among the respondents and the proportion of people with primary and high school education are equal. Innovation experiences and lessons from Indian farmers also served to support the idea that although the farmers received little or no formal education, they really have the ability to innovate, which mainly comes from their practical experience, sensitive observation and the confidence in success (James, 2005). Therefore, the farmers' innovation capacities also depend upon the knowledge gained not only through formal education, but also through informal education. Informal education involves the farmers' own practice, their interaction with the outside world, participation in some policy-related projects and self-organized visits. To some considerable extent, practical experience can replace the experience of formal education, and this is an especially prominent observation in older farmers whose prolonged inputs and experience in agriculture help them form correct judgments on local agricultural resources and production.

The main forms of interaction with the outside world includes working outside, doing business and military service and 32.14% (N = 9) had had such experiences. In this way, innovative farmers acquired communication skills, gained courage, understood the importance of knowledge and being hard working, and had more economical aspects to their livelihood and access to market information. Learning through the interaction phenomenon provided innovative farmers with the opportunity to widely improve their level of awareness and way of thinking in their lives.

Some innovative farmers had been apprentices in order to learn techniques related to their work; for example, farmer WQ started learning carpentry after graduation. Outside visits and study can also enhance innovative work; for instance, farmer ZSB initiated pig farming and visited different counties in order to exchange experiences and learn from other pig farmers and build his career on a long-term basis in this field. However, his experience of informal education cannot be presented by way of conventional statistical indicators of human capital. It is important to note though, that such experience indeed has played a vital role in farmer innovation.

Innovative farmers, who have had a relatively moderate formal education, have the capacity to learn more quickly. This advantage provides them with more incentives to innovate. Having said that, there is no absolute borderline between formal and informal education; the most important thing is that both types of education accumulation can facilitate innovative farmers to understand what information is useful, generate appropriate knowledge and apply new technology.

Social status

Among the 28 cases, there were 12 farmers (accounting for 42.86 %) who had worked or were serving in a social functional department, showing a certain degree of social and political status. The farmers involved in gaining a position possessed positive personal qualities, extensive networks and social relationships, which are extremely important elements in a modern market economy.

With the improvement of village selection in China, electors often have a high expectation of the new electee to lead the whole village in becoming richer, which objectively promotes the leader to demonstrate innovative behaviour. On the other hand, social duties always involve the leader dealing with some public affairs, which helps them to understand government policy better than common villagers. All these elements have promoted innovation. The other 57.14% (N = 16) farmers do not have experience of service in functional departments, but the facts have nonetheless shown their great innovation potential and capacity. Therefore, farmers' innovation is not strictly related to social position.

Consequently, it can be concluded that each type of farmer has a strong potential for innovation, and farmers' innovation has no obvious correlation with their age, gender, formal education and social position. The capacity for innovation exists in farmers across the board, in opposition to the theory which says that farmers are risk-averse due to small-size production and weak capacity, withstanding the risk (Ellis, 1998). Social stereotyping has limited the understanding of farmer-initiated innovation and what we need to do is to encourage right thinking and rethink farmer innovation from a new perspective.

Social contextual factors

Innovation is often linked with environment; the environment can shape the human experience, but can also change the human being. The environmental characteristics before and after farmer innovations, include the farmers' own economic environment and the physical environment of the community. The market and policy environment is analysed as follows.

Household economic situation

Innovative behaviours require strong inner incentives for farmers and the innovation often has a strong correlation with the demands of their own livelihood. Among research respondents, before innovation, around 78.57% (N = 22) of the farmers' main source of income was from agriculture and animal husbandry, which are determined by the geographical environment. Their cash income mainly relied upon livestock, the lesser part relying on agricultural farming. Besides this, there were about 32.14% (N = 9) of farmers who had experience of working or doing outside business, which might help them to acquire certain social capital, or accumulate a certain amount of financial and human capital. All the experience gained from the outside world changes their way of thinking and improves their sense for innovation.

From the review of the innovative family's condition, it has been demonstrated that when the innovation occurs, 28.57% (N = 8) of families have the pressure of their children's education and 28.57% (N = 8) of families face vulnerability in terms of their livelihood, living under conditions of poverty and striving for survival. These pressures force farmers to seek innovation and can be regarded as the farmers' natural reaction and a kind of self-adjustment. The remaining 42.86% (N = 12) of families were more wealthy, while they were able to maintain a normal life and still have some leftover funds. Among the 12 innovative farmers, 6 started farming after finishing school, and had been engaged in agriculture for 28 years on average, with the longest time being 44 years and the shortest15 years. All of the six farmers have their own level of patience, care and kinds of intention in their life and in agriculture these characteristics have caused innovation to happen naturally. Out of the other six innovative farmers, four had been involved in business ventures for several years, two experienced working outside for 6 to 7 years and showed variability in the ways of living their life outside the village. They are also sensitive to market-related information, which is commonly linked with business ventures and setting up of innovation.

Community physical environment

The land available for agricultural production and livestock feed are important production elements for Yanchi farmers. On the basis of analysis from 2009, 39.29% (N = 11) of farming land in a farmers' village consists of dry land and crop harvests entirely rely on the weather. This type of climate leads to an inadequate supply of plant raw materials ultimately, which will increase the cost of feed to animals and have an effect on the sustainability of the farmers' livelihood. The harsh natural environment has forced the farmers to take innovative steps to sustain their family's survival. The remaining 60.71% (N = 17) of villages have relatively good irrigable land resources. The development of the Yanghuang project[2] and motor-pump contributed well to the increase in crop yield and to profit-making from livestock breeding at a low cost to the farmers. The Yanghuang project has been implemented by the government and provides a good physical capital, ultimately to promote the innovation more widely.

External connected environment

On average, farm households began to innovate around the year 2000, the earliest being in 1982, and the most recent in 2007. The innovative farmers began innovations mainly after 1995, and the ratio can be seen to have been as high as 92.86%.

A farmer's decision to start innovation has a close relationship to the external market environment and government policy, according to the semi-structured interviews with the local officials. Firstly, the interviews showed that all the starting times for innovation were after the implementation of the Household Contract Responsibility System which has provided a wide vacuum for rural development.

Secondly, to cope with the influence on agriculture of raging sandstorms and decreasing rainfall, the Yanghuang Project was planned in the 1970s, implemented in 1995 and came to its peak around 2000. Meanwhile, in 2001, to protect the environment, the local government started to implement a comprehensive and strict grazing ban policy, which significantly limited access to grassland resources for traditional breeding. The introduction of water and reduction of pasture resources disrupted the local farmers' livelihood system and broke the balance of the traditional livelihood approach of the farmers, which eventually forced them to recombine production elements and to search for a new livelihood approach.

As a farming-pastoral zone for Yanchi County, the special geographical environment is rich in Chinese herbal resources. There are more than 130 kinds of wild Chinese herbal medicines distributed within the country, with a majority containing liquorice and 'bitter beans grass' which cover an area of 200 million mu or more. In 1995, the county was named as the 'Hometown of Liquorice' by the State Council, and in 2003 it was named 'the Township of China's Tan Sheep.' And behind this name-giving, changes have accompanied the government's advocacy, attention and support having been given to the relevant industry.

From the three policies above, it can be seen that the institutional change factor has had a prominent impact on farmer innovation. Big institutional changes have brought tremendous challenges to the way of life for the farmers, and they have had to struggle to find new activities to promote their own development. On the other hand, accompanying the changes, new resources, information and markets will help to stimulate farmers' innovation. In addition to policy changes, the market is also a kind of external related factor for the innovative farmers. After 1995, the local mutton price began to steadily rise and sustained a high price for the following five years. At the same time, the supply of liquorice in the domestic market tightened and the price began to rise dramatically. Market factors create significant incentives for farmers to innovate.

Another important change factor in the market is the formation of township fair markets. During the research, the market times in 8 towns of Yanchi County were unified already, and farmers could participate in every market at a set market time. This kind of market system can be seen as an informal system for farmers' to communicate, gain market information and form their own basic judgments on the market demand. The above factors have provided a basic guarantee for farmer's innovation and to some extent, have reduced the risk of innovation.

Summarizing the three aspects of the farmer's innovative environment it can be concluded that survival pressure caused by poor environmental conditions is an important incentive factor for innovation, and farmers' innovation behaviours are affected by both their internal needs and external environmental changes; the poverty of the family, the pressures from children's education needs and seeking a stable life are the important internal factors for farmer's innovation; intense policy and market changes are the external factors, while the improvement of livelihood and physical capital and betterment of the understanding and application of the production elements are the substantial guarantee of the success of innovation. Considering the trend of improvement of China's rural development and farmers' innovative work, opportunities and modes of freedom to act have been provided by the farmers themselves through their own efforts to gain a degree of social mobility.

Key steps in the innovation process

Innovation can be a positive process which involves the reconstruction of a variety of factors. In order to get a more detailed understanding of the farmer's innovation process, the following part will explore the origination of innovative ideas, the consideration and implementation of innovative ideas, and the result of the innovation.

Enlightenment

The non-linear innovation development has proved that science, technology and the economy gradually interact with each other throughout the whole process of innovation (Wu, 1999) and knowledge is becoming the core of innovation (Zhu, 1998). In the area of innovation, knowledge is often divided into two areas, traditional knowledge and modern scientific and technological knowledge. Traditional knowledge is generated from long-term historical experience, while modern scientific and technological knowledge evolves from a complete scientific system.

The research cases show that all the farmers encountered a certain stimulation by some information at the time they initiated innovative ideas, and those pieces of external information played a dominant role with 71.43% (N = 20) of households, while the remaining innovation came from an internal process. The cases have shown that the discovery of related information has a strong relationship to farmers' sense of confidence and their experience.

The origin of external information resources can be several channels including social networks, reading books and watching television, participating in a government project and observing the work of other people.

Among the 8 respondents who described a social network, 3 relied on a strong network of relationships, which mainly reflected in the 'relative' level, and 5 rely on the strength or weakness of ties in a network, mainly presented in the occasional social network, which shows increased diversity of the farmers' social networks brought by the high degree of mobility in modern society. If there were not any implementations of government projects, there would be no single household inspired by the government-led extension system. The relevant information obtained by the innovative farmers often related to their experiences and knowledge, forming opinions and trying to apply it to generate new techniques and innovative ideas. Therefore, innovative farmers may not have well-defined knowledge, but they do have a huge capacity to generate and apply knowledge.

Various considerations

Innovation is often seen as a contradictory and uncertain process (Robin Williams, et. al., 1996). Therefore, opportunities and risks often coexist within the innovation; 46.43% of the farmers conducted accounting and profit calculations of market values, which shows farmers' consideration of cost/benefit analysis after receiving innovative ideas.

> Farmer CZ, 40 years old, passed primary school in 1986 and engaged in farming and breeding work. The family planted corn and alfalfa to feed the 300 sheep which was the main cash income of the household. After the implementation of a grazing ban policy in 2001, he had to feed the sheep in the sheepfold and get the feed from the market. During this practice and given his lengthy experience, he found that the market feed had a negative effect on breeding the sheep. In the end, he decided to compound the sheep's variable food by himself referring to the market feed label's list of ingredients in 2007. His traditional experience told him that agricultural grains are the main food for sheep, bone-meal can act as a gustatory stimulus, encouraging the sheep to eat and soybeans contain a lot of nutrition. In his experiment on ten sheep, he decreased the proportion of traditional grains and increased the proportion of bone-meal and the soybeans. During the experiment, he found the bone-meal ratio was a little too high, so he reduced the amount of bone-meal and added more soybeans. In order to aid the sheep's digestion, he added some yeast powder; and to make the food more preferable to the sheep's taste, he added some salt. At the end, he found that the ten sheep eating the experimental feed had grown much faster than the others. He then extended the self-made feed to the whole sheep group.
>
> (Source: field interview in 2008)

Turning now to the uncertainty of risk, 17.86% (N = 5) of farmers study and exchange relevant technology through their own social networks, and implement accordingly, of which 3 households communicated within a close village network, while the other two visited outside places, producing related goods at their own expense; 14.29% (N = 4) of farmers tried small-scale experiments after knowledge exchanges with others, which ultimately reduces risk and sustains livelihood security as a best outcome; 35.71% (N = 10) of farmers directly carried out a few small-scale experiments, based on their understanding of innovation and experiences; the remaining 32.41% (N = 9) of farmers implemented their innovative ideas directly.

In sum, 50% of farmers tried specific small-scale experiments prior to implementation, 32.14% communicated and learned ideas with persons around them, and the remaining 32.14% used direct implementation. During the interviews, 100% of the farmers admitted that the adoption of innovation indeed takes some risk, and believe risk is necessary for any development tasks. For the farmer who has set up the business, the risk is usually huge, while for the normal farmer, existing present poverty requires them to take some risks to dig themselves out of poverty. Therefore, all innovative farmers have taken innovation costs and risks into account and most of them have taken some real actions (like communicating with others, going outside for visits and study, doing small-scale experiments etc.) to reduce the risk and try to gain high benefits. Besides these points, innovative farmers' personality traits like go-aheadism and preference on risk can also influence the consideration of innovation, as Mendras (1970) mentioned in an evaluation of French farmers: though agricultural workers were in difficult conditions and with no means to determine the direction, all of them showed a spirit of enterprise, a sense of economy, a kind of imagination and a remarkable and admirable courage.

Reallocation of available resources

After making the decision, the innovative farmers would transfer all related resources to carry out the innovation, those being mainly physical, financial and human resources. As for physical resources, 100% of household respondents have used local resources in the areas surrounding the villages conveniently and at low cost. Taking sheep breeding as an example, the innovative farmers with an abundance of dry-land for planting have used local abundant grass and small grains as the main sheep feed, while the farmers abundant in Yanghuang paddy fields have chosen to plant special corn to feed the sheep.

In terms of financial resources, 100% of farmers have used their economic savings including cash savings and livestock savings which was mainly in sheep; 25% (N = 7) of farmers called on some other external funds to promulgate innovation, five farmers' external financial capital was from their own social network while the other two used the support of a government project. Two externally funded farmers have ticked off some materials to alleviate financial difficulties and obtain a certain amount of time to reach the required turnover.

As for the cost of innovation,[3] common farmers always obtain a low input with 24,078.57 Yuan on average and the proportion of the cost which is less than 10 thousand has reached 71.43%. For the relatively high cost, farmers have an obvious inclination to set up the business and systematically implement innovation.

Despite the innovation cost being relatively low from an outside view, it is really a big amount of money for innovative farmers. So, having a certain amount of start-up funds is an important parameter for local farmers, which will be shown as follows. Thus, for the government and rural development agencies, how to find the seeds of the farmer's innovation and to make early intervention to provide support to reduce the variety of restriction conditions is a matter of concern.

> Farmer WDY is 47-years old and graduated from junior high school. In 2005, while reading books he occasionally found out about the popularity of plastering. He decided to study plastering craft in Jiangsu province. He took a 7 month course at his own expense with 20,000 Yuan. After returning, he decided to do this as a business and calculated that he required 60,000 Yuan to set up, which he could not raise in a short timeframe. Thus, he needed to plant more crops and raise more sheep. Up to the beginning of 2007, he sold out the family assets to start the innovation.
>
> Farmer YHJ is 41-years-old with two children studying at primary school. In 2001, the grazing ban policy was implemented and during that period, he planned to do sheep farming through a stall feeding system. In the year of 2007, he started this innovative business and has been up to the date of

interview. The reason for not implementing his innovative business before 2007 was due to the priority of being considerate for his children's need for education and the concept of livelihood security.

(Source: field interview in 2008)

Concerning human resource, knowledge is the key element. Our survey shows, current innovative knowledge sources are diversified with multiple phases. While 25% of innovative farmers (N = 28) mainly rely on traditional knowledge, 17.86% have begun relying on modern scientific and technological knowledge.

Specifically looking at the source of knowledge, different innovative farmers use different knowledge resources (See Table 14.2). Traditional knowledge is acquired from farmers' own long-term experience and modern knowledge gained from government technicians and communication media, on the whole television, books and web-sites (9 in 11 farmers' knowledge was gained from books). All innovative farmers have taken their own initiative in the process of innovation no matter the knowledge source.

Broadly, the knowledge sources promoting farmers' innovation are relatively lacking in diversity. The scope of interaction and frequency of traditional knowledge and modern science and technology knowledge is really very low. Moreover, in the whole process of the innovation's implementation, it can be seen that all farmers' innovative knowledge is formed and practiced on the basis of drawing from surrounding knowledge with a trial and error approach as to the success and as a process of learning by doing. Therefore, it can be concluded that the construction and implementation of farmer's innovative knowledge are the result of the agency interaction with the multiple resources around them.

Distinguishing features of the innovations

Diversity

The innovative areas of farmer innovations are diverse, as shown in Table 14.3. All the innovations are in accordance with the geographical distribution and

Table 14.2 Resource of traditional and modern knowledge of innovative farmers

	Traditional knowledge (N = 23)		*Modern science and technology (N = 21)*		
	Consult a experienced old person	*Own long-term experience*	*TV/book/ website*	*government technician*	*Learn outside by himself/herself*
Respondents	2	22	11	13	3
Per cent	8.70%	95.65%	52.38%	61.90%	14.29%
Two Resource Channels	1		5		
Per cent	4.35%		23.81%		

Source: analytical result of field interviews in 2007 and 2008.

Table 14.3 The innovation area distribution of the cases (N = 28)

Innovation area	Innovation type	Respondents	Per cent	Summing up per cent
	Inter-planting cultivation of a variety of economic crops	1	3.57%	
	Liquorice planting	3	10.71%	
Planting	Mushroom planting	1	3.57%	35.71%
	Warm canopy planting	3	10.71%	
	Corn planting	1	3.57%	
	Seedling production	1	3.57%	
	Sheep breeding	8	28.57%	
Breeding	Pig breeding	4	14.29%	50.00%
	Special poultry breeding	1	3.57%	
	Diverse breeding	1	3.57%	
	Planting and breeding integrated	2	7.14%	
Others	Improvement of agricultural machinery	1	3.57%	14.29%
	Plaster craft	1	3.57%	

Source: analytical result of field interviews in 2007 and 2008.

farmers' own livelihood system. Results also show that 92.86% (N = 26) of households have amalgamated planting and breeding as an integrated livelihood approach and the tendency for innovative farmers' to specialize concurrently with industry development.

Systematical entity

From the perspective of innovation itself, innovation is a series of affairs, but for the individual farmer, innovation is an aggregation of multiple and continual innovative activities. In the process of innovative development, broadly, there are four phases: introduction of new knowledge and related technology, access to market information, re-allocation of dependent factors such as infrastructure, human capital, and systematic development in large areas. Meanwhile, farmer innovation has begun to show itself as highly important regarding the combined tendency of agricultural production and its operation.

As for rural development and community development, many candidates' innovations in the project are not exactly innovations in the strict scientific definition, but their behaviors have changed their own life and brought new elements (such as technology, concepts and an operational model) to the local community, whose influence cannot be underestimated. As regards social acceptance, the successful farmer's innovation is often recognized by the economic benefits it brings, while the higher level of income translates as attractive power and a demonstrated effect on the surrounding population. With innovative farmers, the county has come forth with a number of specialized villages with feeding of sheep and liquorice planting, and some farmer cooperatives have also emerged.

Multiple knowledge integration

From the original resource of the innovation data, 75% of farmers' innovations belong to secondary innovation, that is, absorbing new technology and operational methods from outside, localizing and recreating them, while 25% of farmers rely on traditional knowledge and their innovations belong to the original innovation category, which always shows a transcendent originality and scientific values. However, until now, formal social institutions to guarantee the innovative farmers' benefits do not exist. In the process of survey data collection, the interviewee farmers have shown a strong awareness of property rights. In fact, most of the innovative farmers have been the local experts, but many of their innovations exist in the form of knowledge that is deemed unimportant by others, skill and experience which still has some distance between concept and application. Therefore, while emphasizing the demonstration effect of innovative farmers, the government should take the intellectual property rights of the local farmer's innovation into consideration.

In summary, at present, local innovative farmers are in a period of time where traditional and modern types of knowledge are mixed together. Their differences were embodied in their innovative sources of knowledge and information, in the understanding and application of knowledge, and in the decision-making considerations and implementation of innovative resources. Generally speaking, most traditional farmers are relatively conservative and their innovations are based on their own experience, technical innovation being the main type; they are more likely to innovate when having the pressure of children's schooling and relatives' illnesses. But as for the modern innovative farmers, they are more likely to be enlightened by multiple knowledge holders in the modern knowledge system of science and technology, while they pay much more attention to the building and possession of social capital, and place emphasis on the initiative and awareness of the market. Modern farmers don't have much subsistence pressure, and most of their innovations are in the category of setting up businesses and their innovation area covers each link of the market chain. However, in general, no matter what kind of innovative farmers, they all have the same care and patience, have positive initiative in their heart and are going back and forth to change their lives with hard work and diligent hands. They are accumulating innovative thinking through learning by doing to improve their livelihood and pursue development.

Discussion and conclusion

Innovation is an important driving force for national development and a crucial way for farmers to bring themselves out of poverty and to pursue development.

Firstly, each kind of farmer has a strong innovation potential and capacity no matter what their age, gender, education and social status. Society should get rid of the leading discourse's stereotyping effect on farmer innovation and lend farmer innovation its proper position by way of public advocacy. The education and social position of farmers may be a sufficient condition in terms of individual characteristics but not the necessary condition for innovation development.

Secondly, the initiative factors in farmer innovation are different depending on the seedtime of the farmer household. For traditional experienced farmers, innovation is enlightened by their own practical interaction, and for farmers under the pressure of subsistence, contact making use of the information available in their surroundings to meet their basic needs is the initiative factor, while for farmers setting-up businesses, social capital is the driving force.

Thirdly, environment is an important factor in the process of innovation, and has played a crucial role in the achievements of farmer innovation. Since China's reform and opening up, innovation awareness and the capacity of the farmers in the northwest of China has improved a lot. Many environmental factors like infrastructure, institution and market have stimulated farmers' innovative behaviours including: diversity of information channel; market enhancement of agricultural products and improvement of agricultural infrastructure. Therefore, in the practice of rural development, policy makers should create a convenient environment and moderate space for farmers' innovation, including infrastructure improvement, market foundations, support in the informal innovation network of farmers, promotion of farmers cooperatives, public advocacy on farmer innovation and promotion of building farmer innovation incentive mechanisms.

Fourthly, farmer innovation is constrained by the expectation of innovation risk. Traditional farmers and new farmers have shown different innovative behaviours when confronting risk. Concerning the uncertainty of innovation, farmers choose various ways to reduce the risk induced by innovative behaviours, such as communication with persons in surrounding areas, outside visits and study, small-scale experiments, and so on. Livelihood security is the farmer's basic principle and under that precept, farmers have begun to be inclined to burden some risk to implement innovation, taking into consideration their self-development and cognition of the market economy. Comparatively, traditional farmers' considerations concerning risk are more thoughtful and their behaviour more cautious, while the new farmers' behaviour is more audacious with greater burden of risk. Therefore, to promote farmer innovation, the government should give some policy support toward innovative risk which would constrain farmer innovation, such as property protection of farmer innovation, subsistence support and the establishment of farmer innovation venture capital, and so on.

Fifthly, if the former extension system can be viewed as a state-initiated innovation, the process that farmers use in making use of inside and outside factors in their pursuit of innovation can be called farmer-initiated innovation. Since the 1990s, China's former extension system has been dismantled, the extension worker substantially reduced and state-initiated innovation implemented in the form of development intervention projects with much more resource support and much less village coverage, which has finally created a proportionate vacuum in the expansion of modern science and technology knowledge in rural areas. For the actual model of rural development, farmer-initiated innovation has covered more areas than state-initiated innovation and is playing a complementary role in the evolution of the state-initiated development model. While the development speed of modern science and technology has overcome that of traditional development, traditional knowledge is totally ignored by development intervention programs with the national mainstream discourse condition placing more emphasis on science and technology. In fact, the integration of traditional knowledge and modern knowledge take the most frequent position when it comes to farmer innovation, showing that variable knowledge interaction can always promote the two innovation models respectively. Accordingly, society should be fully aware of the existence and importance of farmer-initiated innovation, and strengthen the interaction scope and frequency of the two kinds of models. For the former extension system, communication and sharing of farmer experience should be strengthened and the integrated innovation of multiple knowledge owners should be promoted.

Sixthly, rural development cannot become sustainable development without farmer innovation and the local variable human resource; the innovative farmers are the inner impetus of rural development. Due to that, most of the farmer's innovative human capital comes from the accumulation of learning by doing. The Government should not neglect the human capital accumulated from the practice and, on the other hand, should nurture it better and let it play its role, while increasing rural basic education and vocational education inputs. Moreover, in taking measures to expedite the transfer of rural labor forces and improving the level of urbanization, attention should be paid to the side effects impacting rural development caused by the loss of the community elite and the lack of human capital (especially innovative human capital). Lastly, in response to the phenomenon of aging innovative talents in rural areas, the government should identify, encourage and support the entrepreneurial behaviour of rural youth in setting up businesses and implement their innovative ideas, cultivate them and cause them to become the backbone of rural development.

Notes

1 This chapter is a part of an action research project called 'Action Research on Promoting Farmers' Innovation in Yanchi County' financially supported by Oxfam Hong Kong. This paper was presented at IFCCS2 conference as a part of NERC/DFID/ESRC joint funding project with title farmer innovation system in Loess Plateau.
2 The loan officer has contact with the farmer once a month and they are responsible for sending out and reclaiming the micro-finance loan, organizing client farmers to communicate the experience of production and life. During the project time, the service scope covered by the loan officer is 7 townships, 51 administrative villages and 210 natural villages.
3 Yanghuang project is a governmental project which raises the water of Huang River to the farming communities through construction of the aqueduct network.
4 Here the word of 'cost' and the following 'input' means farmers' total gross investment in the innovation process and the same hereinafter.

Bibliography

Assefa, Amanuel, Waters-Bayer, Ann, Fincham, Robert, Mudahara, Maxwell, (2006), 'Comparison of frameworks for studying grassroots innovation: Agricultural Innovation Systems (AIS) and Agricultural Knowledge and Innovation Systems (AKIS)' in Sang-

inga, Pascal, C., Waters-Bayer, Ann, Kaaria, Susan, Njuki, Jemimah, Wettasinha, Chesha, (eds.) (2009), *Innovative Africa: Enriching Farmers' Livelihoods*, UK and USA:
Earthscan

Berhan, Tewolde, Egziabher, Gebre, 'Addis Ababa, Ethiopia, forward', in Reij, Chris,
Waters-Bayer, Ann (eds.), (2001), *Farmer Innovation in Africa: a Source of Inspiration
for Agricultural Development*, London: Earthscan Publications Ltd

Chambers, Robert, Pacey, Arnold, Ann Thrupp, Lori, (1989), *Farmer First: Farmer Innovation and Agricultural Development*, London: Intermediate Technology Publications

Ellis, Frank, (1998), *Peasant Economics: Farm Households and Agrarian Development*,
Cambridge: Cambridge University Press

Fan, Shengyue, Zhou, Lihua, Ma, Yonghuan, 'Environmental protection policy effect on
households: A case study as Yanchi county', (2005), *Chinese Journal of Population,
Resources and Environment*, 3

Fenta, Tesfahun, Assefa, Amanuel, 'Harnessing local and outsiders' knowledge: experi-
ences of a multi-stakeholder partnership to promote farmer innovation in Ethiopia', in
Sanginga, Pascal, C., Waters-Bayer, Ann, Kaaria, Susan, Njuki, Jemimah, Wettasinha,
Chesha, (eds.) (2009), *Innovative Africa: Enriching Farmers' Livelihoods*, UK and
USA: Earthscan Publications Ltd.

Fu, Jinhai, Shen, Changjiang, Chen, Yie, Di, Xingmin, Wang, Kezhi, (1987), *Paper Collection on Agricultural Resource Usage in Yanchi*: Ningxia' People's Press

Hambrecht, Jürgen, (2008), *Innovation and Technology Management*, Handbook Utility
Management, Springer: Berlin, Heidelberg

James, T.J., (2005), 'Farmer innovation in Kerala', *Appropriate Technology*, 3

Johnson, Allen W., (1972), 'Individuality and experimentation in traditional agriculture',
Human Ecology, 2

Klomp, Luuk, Roelandt, Theo, (2004), 'Innovation performance and innovation policy: the
case of the Netherlands', *De Economist*, 3

Levy, Philippa, (2003), 'A methodological framework for practice-based research in networked learning', *Instructional science*, 31

Li, Xiaoyun, Qi, Gubo, Xu, Xiuli, (2008), 'Action research: a new research paradigm?'
China Rural Survey, 1

Li, Xueshu, (2007), 'Farmer innovation and poverty economics', *Inquiry into Economic
Issues*, 1

List, Dennis, (2006), 'Action research cycles for multiple futures perspectives', *Future*,
38

Liyan Zhang, (2008), *Problem Research on Farmer Innovation, Independent Innovation
and National Prosperity- Issues and Countermeasures in Building Innovation-oriented
Country with Chinese Characteristics*, Beijing: Science Press

Mendras, Henri, (1970) *The End of the Farmer, in Chinese, translated by Li Peilin*, Beijing:
Social Sciences Academic Press

Opondo, Chris, Almekinders, Conny, Mowo, Jeremias, Kanzikwera, Rogers, Birungi, Pau-
line, Alum, Winnie, Barwogeza, Margaret, 'Applying the innovation systems concept in
the field: experiences of a research team in Uganda', in Sanginga, Pascal, C., Waters-
Bayer, Ann, Kaaria, Susan, Njuki, Jemimah, Wettasinha, Chesha, (eds.) (2009), *Innovative Africa: Enriching Farmers' Livelihoods*, UK and USA: Earthscan Publications Ltd

Reij, Chris, Waters-Bayer, Ann, (2001), 'Entering research and development in land hus-
bandry through farmer innovation', in Reij, Chris, Waters-Bayer, Ann (eds.), (2001),
Farmer Innovation in Africa: a Source of Inspiration for Agricultural Development,
London: Earthscan Publications Ltd

Rogers, Everett M., (1962), Diffusion of Innovations, Glencoe: Free Press

Schumpeter, Joseph Alois, (1934), The Theory of Economic Development: An Inquiry Info Profits, Capital, Credit, Interest, and the Business Cycle, Cambridge: Harvard University Press

Scott, James C., (1976), *The Moral Economy of the Peasant: Rebellion and Subsistence in Southeast Asia*, New Haven: Yale University Press

Statistical Bureau in Yanchi County, (2009), *Yanchi Economic Situation Handbook*, Edited by Yanchi Statistical Bureau

Vernooy, Ronnie, Ykhanbai, Hijaba, Bulgan, Enkhbat, (2004), *Challenges of Participatory Natural Resource Management Research, Participatory Research and Development for Sustainable Agricultural and Natural Resource Management, A Sourcebook*, Ottawa: Cip-Upwards

Waters-Bayer, Ann, Sanginga, Pascal C., Kaaria, Susan, Njuki, Jemimah, Wettasinha, Cheasha, 'Innovation Africa: an Introduction', in Sanginga, Pascal, C., Waters-Bayer, Ann, Kaaria, Susan, Njuki, Jemimah, Wettasinha, Chesha, (eds.) (2009), *Innovative Africa: Enriching Farmers' Livelihoods*, UK and USA: Earthscan

Williams, Robin, Edge, David, (1996), 'The social shaping of technology', *Research policy*, 25

Wu, Bin, (2003), *Sustainable Development in Rural China: Farmer innovation and Self-organization in Marginal Areas*, London: Routledge

Wu, Yongzhong, (1999), 'Reconsideration on the relationship of science, technology and economy – based on the philosophy thinking of the development of innovation theory', *the Northern Forum,* 4

Yin, Robert K., (2003), *Case Study Research: Design and Methods (third edition)*, London: Sage Publications

Zhu, Lilan, (1998), 'Knowledge is becoming the core of innovation', *Global Economic Perspective of Science and Technology*, 11

Subject Index

Note: All index entries refer to China, unless otherwise indicated.

For Product Safety Concerns and Information please contact our EU
representative GPSR@taylorandfrancis.com
Taylor & Francis Verlag GmbH, Kaufingerstraße 24, 80331 München, Germany

www.ingramcontent.com/pod-product-compliance
Lightning Source LLC
Chambersburg PA
CBHW071843270326
41929CB00013B/2086